Energy Analysis for a Sustainable Future

T0293524

The vast majority of the countries of the world are facing an imminent energy crisis: the USA, China, India, Japan and EU countries in particular, but also developing countries that need to boost their economic growth precisely when more powerful economies will prevent them from using the limited supply of fossil energy.

To compound this crisis, current protocols of energy accounting have been developed for dealing with fossil energy exclusively and are therefore not useful for the analysis of alternative energy sources. The first part of this book illustrates the weakness of existing analyses of energy problems: the science of energy was born and developed neglecting the issue of scale. The authors argue that it is necessary to adopt more complex protocols of accounting and analysis in order to generate robust energy scenarios and effective assessments of the quality of alternative energy sources.

The second part of the book introduces the concept of energetic metabolism of modern societies and uses empirical results. The authors present an innovative approach – Multi-Scale Integrated Analysis of Societal and Ecosystem Metabolism (MuSIASEM) – capable of characterizing the quality of alternative energy sources in relation to both environmental constraints and socio-economic requirements. This method allows the metabolic pattern of a society to be described in relation to its feasibility, when looking at biophysical factors; and desirability, when looking at socio-economic factors.

Addressing the issue of scale in energy analysis by cutting through the confusion found in current applications of energy analysis, this book will be of interest to researchers, students and policy makers in energy within a variety of disciplines.

Mario Giampietro is an ICREA Research Professor at ICTA (Institute of Environmental Science and Technology), Department of Chemical Engineering, Universitat Autònoma de Barcelona, Spain.

Kozo Mayumi is a Professor at the University of Tokushima, Japan. He is a co-founder and organizer of the Biennial International Workshop 'Advances in Energy Studies', which started in 1998.

Alevgül H. Şorman is a Researcher in the Integrated Assessment and Societal Metabolism group at ICTA, Universitat Autònoma de Barcelona, Spain.

Energy Analysis for a Sustainable Future

Multi-scale integrated analysis of societal and ecosystem metabolism

Mario Giampietro, Kozo Mayumi and Alevgül H. Şorman

Routledge
Taylor & Francis Group

LONDON AND NEW YORK

First edition published 2013
by Routledge
2 Park Square, Milton Park, Abingdon, Oxfordshire OX14 4RN

Simultaneously published in the USA and Canada
by Routledge
711 Third Avenue, New York, NY 10017

First issued in paperback 2015

Routledge is an imprint of the Taylor & Francis Group, an informa business

British Library Cataloguing in Publication Data
A catalogue record for this book is available from the British Library

Library of Congress Cataloging-in-Publication Data
Giampietro, M. (Mario)
Energy analysis for a sustainable future : multi-scale integrated analysis of
societal and ecosystem metabolism / by Mario Giampietro, Kozo Mayumi,
and Alevgül H. Sorman. – 1st ed.
p. cm.
1. Energy consumption–Forecasting. 2. Climate change mitigation.
I. Mayumi, Kozo, 1954– II. Sorman, Alevgül H. III. Title.
TJ163.2.G525 2013
333.79–dc23
2012010257

ISBN13: 978-1-138-92806-0 (pbk)
ISBN13: 978-0-415-53966-1 (hbk)

Typeset in Times New Roman by
FiSH Books Ltd, Enfield

Contents

Illustrations

Figures

Tables

Boxes

Foreword

Much work has been done on complexity in many facets of science and society. This book represents a pressing back of an important frontier. First I will look over some of the history of studying complexity, so that what is new here is put in context. In its proper setting this book stands out. In summary, complexity as a notion was seriously addressed in the early 1960s in business administration. From 1970 on there has been a school of quantifying complexity with equations, a useful enough endeavour, but one with limited practicality.

Then through the 1970s and 1980s there was qualitative discourse, unfettered from having to prove everything. Not reliant on quantification the new effort was able to move the ideas of complexity out into realms where it has been more useful, particularly in ecology. The central difficulty in complexity is with scaling issues. Scaling may be quantitative in engineering, but in complex systems it leads to qualitative change. Engineers do not want emergent qualitative properties as they rescale, and so they struggle to avoid them. Emergence is failure in a bridge and it is avoided by studious over-building. But in biological and social systems, failure is commonplace and needs to be built into system understanding and design. Pressing hard against limits, the qualitative discourses of the 1980s ran straight into the duality of structure and process. Straightforward definitions appeared impotent, so the challenge became how to overcome those difficulties in framing issues. Then in the 1990s science looked at the political aspects of applying science to big problems. The present book moves on beyond the old quantification, beyond the qualitative discourse, and beyond the politics. But it does integrate those different facets of practical treatments of complexity. The present book is practical, but is forced into philosophical issues to get past the great difficulties at the edge of applying complexity to matters of society and energy.

When I was a student in botany, we would simply throw up our hands when complexity pertained; it was 'time to quit.' Then over the decades we developed theory and method such that we could begin to take small bites out of complexity. Early in this revolution was chaos theory and fractals. While invoking non-linear equations, chaos is in fact equilibrial, and came straight out of the equilibrium models in ecology of the 1960s. Chaos was a natural place to start, because computation gave us power to make the calculations and to move upscale as never before. All that was needed was an extension of the formal use of differ-ence equations. Those were heady days, when great things were expected soon. There was some success in the 1970s, but somehow the promise was not fully met in later quantification and algebraic treatments. That is not to underestimate the revolution that chaos and fractals did deliver, but it was not so much in the direct use of chaotic equations. It was more that abstractions, such as bounded infinity and the statistical/deterministic equivalence, found a place in biological thinking about complexity.

Chaos was of great help to the mindset of biology. With it we saw that when something shows an infinity of behavioural detail, we no longer need to surren-der. When complex patterns emerged we learned from chaos theory that it was not 'time to quit.' Chaos theory teaches us that some patterns that never repeat may still have a simple explanation in short, non-linear equations. Biological complex-ity can have simple explanations, if you look for them with sophistication.

The strange attractor of chaos is bounded, but it is a bounded infinity, and that has been a helpful realization in biology. Bounded infinity was not recognized in biology, although it was commonplace. For instance, a good field biologist would never mistake an oak tree for an elm, even at a distance. But there is an infinity of elm and oak tree forms, to the point that no two oak trees have ever been iden-tical. When you link trees upscale to their type, you are making a move across scales that requires caution. Despite the infinity of oak variation, an oak never becomes an elm. In complexity, infinity has bounds. The naturalist never makes a mistake because he is recognizing something like a strange attractor for oaks, distinguishing it from that of elms.

The idea of infinite sensitivity to initial conditions from chaos theory has become useful in addressing complexity in biology, ecology and studies of soci-eties. In complex systems there may be general manifestations that we can expect to be seen again, but a re-run of, for instance the Roman Empire, would still turn out somehow differently, and unpredictably so. Weather predictions pertain to what we can generally expect, but weather forecasters never predict a particular storm cell because that will be different every time the same general situation applies. This notion is clearly related to ideas of bounded infinity, and leads to the perennial question in any study of complexity, 'What's the same, when every-thing's different?' The general pattern that is repeated refers to 'What's the same?' The sameness of all oak trees is an example. But oak trees are only loosely predictable according to certain probabilities associated with the form of oaks in general. All this is very comforting and reassuring to those who deal with complexity in the wild. But even so, the actual use of chaotic equations has provided limited insights. The principles of complexity are what really matters, and chaos has contributed to them in important ways.

In the 1980s complexity theory began to formalize using theories of a new sort. New paradigms are resented by adherents to the old, who complain that the important questions are no longer asked. Contemporary notions of complexity do not so much reject that there is an external reality, it is just that it does not matter one way or another in complexity; anathema to modernists. Complexity is not even a material issue let alone one of ontological verity. The science of the human brain is a candidate for complexity, but if the question is evolution of the reptilian brain into the mammalian brain, then there are only three parts, and the forebrain gets bigger. Complexity depends on the question you ask, not on the material reality of what is studied.

Most work in science is only on the compression of phenomena into models. But before all of that there is a prior compression into the narrative behind the model. That first compression is taken for granted and often forgotten. In addressing complexity we need to pay particular attention to the first compression down to the narrative of the paradigm. Hierarchy theory of the 1980s and multiple scale analysis of the 2000s work on stabilizing that first compression. It gets the story straight, even as things fall apart between levels. The level at which mainstream normal science works is focal. But to expand science into arenas such as energy and society, the surrounding tacit levels must be considered. Just one level is not a rich enough description. There is no easy explicit passage from focal to tacit, but hierarchy theory struggles in that divide anyway.

In the 1990s leaders turned to look directly at the problems of application of science for practical, large issues. They pointed out that science cannot be conducted 'business as usual' in rich settings. For that situation Funtowicz and Ravetz (1992, 1993) coined the term 'post-normal science,' which applies when stakes are high, time is short, values are in conflict and uncertainty is intrinsic and great. The physician might want to get probabilities down to $p=0.05$, but the patient will be dead on Tuesday, before that can be achieved. Post-normal science says step up and decide with what you have, because you will never have models and data that are adequate by normal science standards. The present book pivots on that principle, but it raises the game on explicit data and comparison.

So all this leads us to the present work. The basic characteristics of complexity were spelled out with the quantification of the early days. In the mid-term it became clear that the solution to complexity lies not in greater quantification in normal science models, but in the first compression down to the narrative. Narratives are neither true nor otherwise, they are simply an announcement of a point of view. Modernist realism resting on the relative verity of models becomes impotent, although many still ignore that uncomfortable truth. In the1980s it was time to take responsibility for decisions that were being made anyway. Then the social context of decision-making needed explication some 20 years ago in post-normality. So how can we press the issues yet further?

This book deals with data, not just as something quantitative, but as something that requires decisions regarding level of analysis, for which responsibility must be taken. So this work is again quantitative, but in a way that is aware of the nuance in introducing quantities into narratives. Robert Rosen once said that the most abstract thing you can do is to make a measurement, because in order to get that number, one has to choose to ignore all the rest of the universe. So given those abstractions, the issue is how to turn data in a complex system into policy and remedy. All of it is in there in this volume: quantities; dualities and nuance of definition; and the political context toward which the scientific recommendation is directed. Time to quantify again, but this time right at the edge of complexity as it comes down on us. Time to quantify again, but this time in the context of a mature philosophy of science that is aware of its limits.

Timothy Allen,
Professor Emeritus of Botany,
University of Wisconsin, Madison WI.

Acknowledgements

The authors would like to thank, first of all, Sandra Bukkens for commenting, correcting, and extensively editing the material presented in the present and earlier versions of this book.

Mario Giampietro gratefully acknowledges financial support to the research presented in this book by:

(1) the Catalan Institution for Research and Advanced Studies (ICREA);
(2) the Agency for Management of University and Research Grants (AGAUR) of the Government of Catalonia (grant SGR2009-594);
(3) the EU seventh framework programme for the project, Synergies in Multi-Scale Interlinkages of Eco-Social Systems (SMILE, Contract 217213-FP7-2007-SSH-1); and
(4) the Ministry of Oil of Norway for sponsoring the special session on Energy Statistics at the VII Biennial International Workshop Advances in Energy Studies (October 2010), which inspired the writing of this book.

Mario Giampietro would further like to thank: David Pimentel, Vaclav Smil, Charlie Hall, Robert Herendeen and Sergio Ulgiati for their inspiring work; Per Arild Garnåsjordet (Statistics of Norway), Jun Elin Wik Toutain (the Oslo Group on Energy Statistics), Aldo Femia, Cesare Costantino and Giusy Vetrella (Italian National Institute of Statistics), and Lucian Albu and Raluca Iorgulescu-Polimeni (National Institute of Economic Research of Romania) for their useful insights into energy statistics. Additional thanks are due to Jesús Ramos-Martín, Louis Lemkow, and François Diaz Maurin, Joan Martinez-Alier (Universitat Autònoma de Barcelona), Andrea Saltelli and Silvio Funtowicz (European Commission JRC, Ispra), and Roger Strand (University of Bergen) for comments and feedback on earlier versions of this book.

Kozo Mayumi gratefully acknowledges the financial support of Grant-In-Aid for Scientific Research (B – 20330050) provided by the Japanese Ministry of Education, Culture, Sports, Science and Technology, which indirectly contributed to creating the contents of the present book. Mayumi also appreciates the fellowship (2010-PIV-00101) provided by the Agency for Management of University and Research Grants (AGAUR) of the Government of Catalonia supporting his stay at the Autonomous University of Barcelona (UAB) (April – October, 2011) to complete the writing of this book.

Kozo Mayumi also expresses his sincere thanks to the following people for their spiritual and moral support as well as their encouragement for the research contained in this book: Nicholas Georgescu-Roegen, Toshiharu Hasegawa, Toshihide Ibaraki, Hideo Miyahara, Takashi Negishi, Atsushi Tsuchida, Nobuo Kawamiya, Hideo Shingu, Kazuhiro Ueta, Satoshi Isaka, Ryunosuke Hamada, Takeshi Murota, Hiromi Hayashi, Toru Ishihara, Yoshio Motoki, Yasuo Oyama, Hiroki Tanikawa, Shunsuke Managi, Minoru Sasaki, Herman Daly, Joan Martinez-Alier, John Gowdy, Silvio Funtowicz, Jerry Ravetz, Sandra Bukkens, Vincent Hull, Vasile Dogaru, Giuseppe Munda, Jesús Ramos-Martín, Mark Glucina, John Polimeni, Tommaso Luzzati, Sylvie Ferrari, Heinz Schandl, Giancarlo Fiorito, Kate Farrell, Tori Mayumi, Katsuko Mayumi, Sumiyo Tashiro, Shigemi Igawa, Giichi Hirosawa, Emiko Hirosawa, Kenichirou Ohtsu, Kimiko Ohtsu, Akira Yamaguchi, Hideto Takao, Yoshie Okada, Kinzou Okada, Asami Okada and, last but not least, Yuki Okada.

Alevgül H. Şorman would like to acknowledge the FP7 – SMILE Project, Synergies in Multi-Scale Interlinkages of Eco-Social Systems, which has funded the larger part of her PhD studies. She would also like to express her deepest gratitude to her family, being physically so far away, yet so close to the heart: 'Thanks for always being there for me and supporting me endlessly throughout all my decisions in life.' Bab, Annem, Arda, Aynur, Ayda, Dayı, Bilgen, İleri Ailesi, Şensoy Ailesi, Ülkütaşır Ailesi – *her sey için çok teşekkürler*. Şorman is deeply grateful to Mario Giampietro for sharing his knowledge and insights and for his enthusiasm and encouragement, and to Jesús Ramos-Martín, Kozo Mayumi and Sergio Ulgiati for their help and endless discussions that have improved the overall quality of work. Many thanks also to Sandra Bukkens who has always managed to be there at the right time and place – her support has been one of the foundational blocks for making all of this possible. Şorman also would like to acknowledge the people at the Italian National Institute of Statistics (ISTAT), especially Luisa Picozzi, Cesare Costantino, Giusy Vetrella, Aldo Femia and Angelica Tudini, for improving the quality control of the analysis. Also, many thanks to all friends, who have been an essential part of professional and personal life during this period, especially to Arnim, Maria, Max, Tarik, Ethemcan and Ana.

Dedication

Mario Giampietro's interest in energetics was generated by the lectures on energetics given by Gino Parolini in 1978. (Yes, in the seventies the Faculties of Engineering used to have courses on energetics ...!). In his teaching, Parolini was calling for a second generation of 'energetic analysis' based on a more holistic approach.

In relation to the unavoidable second revolution within energetics the following points should be kept in mind: energetics should deal with both qualitative and quantitative aspects of both scientific and technological solutions; applications must be interdisciplinary and address simultaneously several dimensions of analysis – i.e. referring to ecological systems, demographic processes, fresh water availability, material resources, interfacing the knowledge creation with biology, cosmology, metaphysics into a holistic vision of the world.[1]

From that date Mario Giampietro has tried to develop the integrated and holistic approach to energy analysis suggested by Prof. Parolini and others of the school of Energetics at the University of La Sapienza in Rome.

Kozo Mayumi's interest in energetics was first generated by his encounter with the work of Atsushi Tsuchida, the creator of the Japanese Entropy school, and then reinforced by his interaction with Nicholas Georgescu-Roegen (his tutor in his postgraduate studies at Vanderbilt University), who once told him that it was urgent to arrive at some quantitative expression of the general flow-fund matrix in which every economic sector is divided into relevant subsectors and the corresponding flow rates are properly specified. Mayumi believes that the general scheme presented in Chapters 10 to 12 can be seen as a partial answer to Georgescu-Roegen's serious concern for the poor capacity of conventional science to represent in quantitative terms the metabolism of society.

---

1 From the lecture, *Energia: quantità e qualità*, given at the Consiglio Nazionale delle Ricerche (CNR), Roma, 11–13 April 1983. Quoted in Amendola (2005), pp. 13–14, and freely translated by M.G.

Abbreviations

AG	agricultural sector
AP	applied power
ATP	adenosine triphosphate
BEP	bio-economic pressure
BM	building and manufacturing sectors
BP	British Petroleum
DOE	US Department of Energy
EC	quantity of energy measured in joules of energy carriers
EC_i	an assessment of energy throughput in the compartment i (ET_i) measured in a quantity of joules belonging to the category of energy carriers
EIA	US Energy Information Administration
ELP	economic labour productivity
EM	energy and mining sectors
EMR	exosomatic metabolic rate
endo	endosomatic
ERDA	US Energy Research and Development Administration
ERE	energy requirement for energy
EROI	energy return on the investment
ES	energy sector
ET_{AG}	energy throughput in the agricultural sector
ET_{HH}	energy throughput in the household sector
ET_{PS}	energy throughput in the productive sectors
ET_{PW}	energy throughput in the paid work sector
ET_{SG}	energy throughput in the service and government sector
EU14	Austria, Belgium, Denmark, Finland, France, Germany, Greece, Ireland, Italy, the Netherlands, Portugal, Spain, Sweden and the United Kingdom
exo	exosomatic
FAO	Food and Agriculture Organization
GDP	gross domestic product

GER$_i$	an assessment of energy throughput in the compartment i (ET$_i$) measured in a quantity of joules belonging to the category of gross energy requirement
GHG	greenhouse gas
GSEC	gross supply of energy carriers
HA$_{AG}$	human activity in the agricultural sector
HA$_{HH}$	human activity in the household sector
HA$_{PS}$	human activity in the productive sectors
HA$_{PW}$	human activity in the paid work sector
HA$_{SG}$	human activity in the service and government sector
HH	household sector
IEA	International Energy Agency
IFIAS	International Federation of Institutes for Advanced Study
MuSIASEM	Multi-Scale Integrated Analysis of Societal and Ecological Metabolism
NSEC	net supply of energy carriers
p.c.	per capita
PES	primary energy sources
PL	public law
PS	primary and secondary production sectors or simply productive sectors
PS*	primary and secondary sectors minus energy and mining
PW	paid work sector
ROI	return on investment
SA	societal aggregate (when referring to the value of an exosomatic throughput – ET$_{SA}$ or GER$_{SA}$ or EC$_{SA}$)
SEH	strength of the exosomatic hypercycle
SG	service and government sector
SI	The International System of Units (abbreviated SI from French: Système international d'unités)
TCE	tons of coal equivalent
TET	total energy throughput
THA	total human activity
TOE	tons of oil equivalent

Units

Gh	Giga hours
GJ	Giga joules (10^9)
MJ	Mega joules (10^6)
PJ	Peta joules (10^{15})
TJ	Tera joules (10^{12})

Introduction

We are well aware that with the presentation of this book we are providing a solution to a problem that many do not yet realize they have. Indeed, whenever we claim that we have found an innovative method for carrying out energy analysis across different scales, a method capable of making robust energy scenarios and of assessing the quality of potential alternative energy sources, we witness two types of reaction. Those who are familiar with the field of energy analysis generally show excitement and are eager to know more, while those unfamiliar with the field of energetics, even if actively involved in sustainability studies, politely smile but do not seem particularly impressed, neither by our achievement nor by the chosen subject of investigation.

Alas, very few people are yet aware that the energy scenarios and assessments of alternative energy sources so far used by politicians in decision making and by the media in public discussions are not particularly robust – to put it mildly. However, we are confident that this situation will rapidly change in the near future as the consequences of peak-oil (the end of the cheap-oil era) will become increasingly evident.

Given the situation as it stands, we have organized this book into two complementing parts: the first part defines the problem, the second proposes a solution. In the first part we explain the clash of reductionism against the complexity of energy transformations and in the second part we provide a way out from the existing epistemological impasse by proposing an innovative method of energy accounting based on complex thinking. The recurrent theme of the book is that it is impossible to deal with complex phenomena by adopting simplistic analytical tools based on reductionism. If one wants to describe the behaviour of a complex system using only a single index or indicator, it is extremely likely that many if not most of the relevant aspects of the complex system will be completely overlooked. Complex systems exhibit many features that are incompatible with reductionism, such as impredicativity, multi-scale organization, and path dependence. To make things more difficult any metabolic system subject to evolution expresses an identity that is unique by definition. Metabolic systems are all special, to a certain extent. These features do not imply that we cannot study their performance, but that we have to tailor our quantitative analysis by taking into account their specific characteristics and the goals of the study.

Looking for a new approach to energy analysis that makes it possible to study the energy metabolism of modern society, the concept of how to generate a useful and pertinent accounting of energy is central to our argument. Being widespread in all sciences and being used loosely in everyday speech, the concept of energy is at the same time familiar and elusive. Probably no other scientific concept has defied so many attempts of definition and quantification as energy. The elusive nature of this concept has undoubtedly contributed to large-scale and unpunished abuse of reductionistic approaches in energy analysis.

Indeed, one can measure 'energy quantities' using different units of measurement, such as joules, kWh, kcal, Btu, or quads. However, these quantities can only be defined and measured after having selected a narrative about a well-defined and finite set of energy conversions requiring the adoption of a pertinent scale of analysis. 'Quantities of energy' can refer to the electricity consumed by a country, the kinetic energy of a molecule, the gasoline consumed by a car or the food energy required by a runner to go for five miles. Any specific quantitative assessment of 'energy' in these different settings forces us to adopt one narrative and one scale at a time. That is, in energy analysis, quantification forces us to choose and adopt a pre-analytical definition of boundaries both in space and in time for the set of energy transformations of interest.

Trouble starts when dealing with the analysis of a complex set of energy transformations, such as national accounting, which involves the aggregation of different types of energy quantities, which can only be observed and defined at different levels and scales. In this case, quantitative analysis has to deal simultaneously with distinct relevant space and time scales. Finding an effective protocol capable of integrating and aggregating non-equivalent quantities of relevant energy forms into a coherent quantitative analysis is a noble art. Furthermore, the very choice of what should be considered as a relevant energy form depends on the pre-analytical choice of relevant narratives by the analyst according to the initial goal of the quantitative analysis. For this reason, in the development of protocols of energy accounting we must avoid protocols allowing the careless merging of non-reducible assessments of quantities of energy referring to different scales, or nonsensical aggregation of energy forms defined within non-equivalent narratives about energy transformations (e.g. summing joules of mechanical work to joules of orange juice).

In this book we address, in a systemic way, the epistemological problems related to the concept of energy. Unfortunately the poor quality of energy accounting, extremely common all over the published literature, carries crucial policy implications for sustainability. Presently, many people generating quantitative analysis based on energy accounting pay lip service to the above epistemological problems, by acknowledging the existence of unspecified qualitative differences among different energy forms (e.g. a joule of electricity is loosely said to have more 'value' than a joule of coal) and by acknowledging the existence of generic problems of boundary definitions. However, it is rare to find a systemic consideration, in the pre-analytical phase, of the epistemological nature of qualitative differences among non-equivalent energy forms or the crucial implications of the issue of multiple scales for quantitative analysis. In this book, we do.

Part 1: Defining the problem

In the first part we demonstrate, in terms of both theory and practice, that, at the moment, there is a serious issue with the existing applications of energy analysis in the field of sustainability. We provide a critical overview of the knowledge and methods developed and accumulated so far to study how modern society produces and consumes energy carriers with the goal of carrying out a given set of end uses (functional tasks) in the face of a limited amount of primary energy sources (physical gradients whose existence is out of human control). In particular, we claim that:

1 The quantitative representation found in present energy statistics is based on dubious methods of aggregation at the national level and the resulting national balances (flow-charts) are not particularly useful for making informed decisions.
2 Without generating a more complex perception and representation of the metabolic pattern of societies, based on: (i) different categories of energy forms (primary energy sources, gross energy requirement, net supply of energy carriers of different kinds and end uses/functional tasks); and (ii) a multi-level analysis characterizing simultaneously the characteristics of the whole society as well as the characteristics of its various functional compartments and sub-compartments; it is impossible to generate robust scenarios.
3 At the moment, we do not have effective and comprehensive methods to assess the quality of alternative energy sources.

Our claim is clearly supported by the embarrassing policies encouraging a massive production of agro-biofuels or the high expectations held by the financial and political establishment before the Fukushima accident of the renaissance of nuclear energy.

In Chapter 1 we first provide a theoretical explanation of the inherent ambiguity to be faced when quantifying the concept of energy. Three basic conundrums can be explained using lessons from:

1 Hierarchy theory – the need for multiple scales leads to serious epistemological problems when attempting an analysis of energy transformations associated with the existence of complex self-organizing systems.
2 Classic thermodynamics – making possible a systemic quantitative assessment of the relation between different energy forms, e.g. thermal energy and mechanical energy – shows that different energy forms do have a different quality. They can only be aggregated using 'conversion factors'. The problem is that these quality factors are not substantive and do imply a change of scale in the analysis.

3   Non-equilibrium thermodynamics – metabolic systems define their own perspective on what is for them an energy input and what is waste (define on their own what is 'negative entropy' for themselves). This implies that when dealing with the analysis of these systems one must be able to tailor the protocol of accounting on the specificity of the system under analysis.

In Chapter 2 we describe the troubles experienced in the field of energy analysis. In particular after a short historical overview of the field, that experienced a peak of activity in the 1970s, we illustrate its original goals and definitions. Then we illustrate, with examples, the basic methodological problems experienced in the field that can be easily referred to the conundrums discussed in Chapter 1: (i) truncation problem; (ii) difficulties in aggregation of energy forms of different kind; (iii) joint production dilemma; (iv) the ambiguous difference between power levels and energy flows.

In Chapter 3 we provide a critical appraisal of the protocols used right now for energy accounting at the national level to compile energy statistics. In particular we focus on the controversial accounting of electricity. We show that additional confusion in the field is generated by the fact that the different entities generating energy statistics use non-equivalent protocols for the aggregation. This implies that even when starting with a common data set of the quantities of primary energy forms used by a modern society, the aggregate assessment of the amount of gross energy requirement for a given country in a given year leads to different results depending on the statistical source used.

In Chapter 4 we investigate the nature of the systemic problems of energy accounting and the need for adopting a taxonomy of semantic categories used in the accounting. We argue that at least four different categories, referring to different scales and narratives about energy conversions, are required for a useful national accounting:

1   Primary energy sources, i.e. available biophysical gradients out of human control associated with the possibility of generating energy flows under human control;
2   Gross energy requirement, i.e. the total amount of energy under human control, defined at the level of the whole country, which is required to produce and consume the energy carriers used to express the various functions;
3   Energy carriers, i.e. the local net supply of energy carriers used at the level of individual compartments or individual energy converters to express functions;
4   End uses, i.e. the practical results achieved because of the utilization of energy carriers in relation to pre-established tasks.

In this chapter we further show that the common linear representation of energy flows (flow-charts showing input/output assessments) going through the different compartments of society is inadequate because it misses the existence of an auto-catalytic loop of energy within the metabolic pattern of society.

In Chapter 5 we discuss the need to consider the requirement of power capacity and human control when assessing energy flows used in social systems. The need to do so is illustrated by discussing three theoretical aspects of the analysis of energy flows, which are all related to the issue of scale. First, in order to deal with the crucial distinction between flows of applied power (per hour) and flows of energy input (per year) we have to adopt quantitative analysis at a small-time scale (e.g. hours vs years). Second, in order to deal with an analysis of the cost of power generation, by combining together the fixed (embodied/indirect) and circulating (direct) energetic costs, we have to adopt a medium-time scale (e.g. years versus decades). Indeed, when considering the existence of these two scales (small vs medium) we can understand the crucial distinction between an assessment of the efficiency in generating power output (the ratio between power output/energy input calculated using the small scale) and an assessment including also the analysis of the energy required for making and maintaining the power capacity needed to generate the power output (discounted on the time scale of decades, when using the medium scale). Last, in order to deal with the analysis of the stability of the boundary conditions – the sustainability of the energy system – we have to make a distinction between stock-flow energy sources (non-renewable) and fund-flow energy sources (renewable). This in turn requires framing the issue of sustainability in yet a different way – stability of boundary conditions – when dealing with these two categories of primary energy sources.

In Chapter 6 we provide a critical appraisal of applications of net energy analysis. In particular, we address basic conceptual issues related to the Energy Return On the Investment (EROI) index. Using practical examples, we show the importance of a proper choice of protocols of accounting in order to avoid confusion. We conclude the first part with the 'Decalogue of the energy analyst', listing a set of crucial epistemological issues associated with energy analysis.

Part 2: Proposing a solution

The second part of the book presents an innovative and semantically open protocol of energy accounting based on the approach called Multi-Scale Integrated Analysis of Societal and Ecosystem Metabolism (MuSIASEM). Here we show that it is possible to generate a more useful quantitative representation of the metabolic pattern of society at the national level. This representation integrates, using a more complex perception of the autopoietic process of modern societies, the analysis of the desirability and feasibility of a given societal metabolic pattern. In particular, by using an integrated set of different categories of energy forms, we track across different levels of organizations the pattern of production and consumption of energy carriers in the various sectors of society. This allows us to study the set of expected relations for the characteristics of the various functional compartments, determining the viability of the dynamic energy budget of a society (production and consumption of energy carriers). In this way, it becomes possible to generate a more articulated approach to the analysis of the quality of alternative energy sources. In fact the combined use of non-equivalent character-izations makes it possible to answer questions such as:

- Given the internal characteristics of society expected to express a given set of functions, what type of supply (mix and quantity) of energy carriers is needed?
- Having assessed the resulting required consumption of energy carriers, what is the associated gross energy requirement and what types of technology are needed?
- Having defined the mix of primary energy sources available to the energy sector (the typologies of biophysical gradients needed for the gross energy requirement) what are the external limits of the resulting metabolic pattern?

In Chapter 7 we first show that by employing a more complex protocol of accounting it is possible to flush out the devil plaguing the first applications of energy analysis from the details. To this purpose we address the special features associated with the unavoidable complexity of autopoietic systems: multiple scales, impredicativity, and path dependency. Put another way, it is necessary to characterize the network of energy transformations, stabilized by the existence of autocatalytic loops of energy, across different scales. This requires the ability to combine non-equivalent quantifications of 'energy flows' in relation to different categories. This result can only be obtained by accepting the possibility of using simultaneously different boundaries and narratives about 'energy conversions'. At the local scale we can analyze the autocatalytic loop of 'energy carriers' used to exploit primary energy sources to generate a net supply of 'energy carriers' – the performance of energy technologies. At this level we can study the quality of primary energy sources in relation to technical coefficients. Then, we have to 'scale-up' the basic rationale of net energy analysis and find a rationale making possible to define the 'net energy surplus' that a society can enjoy for final consumption. This second step requires the individuation of macro-functional units within the metabolic pattern of modern societies. Using the same rationale proposed in *Theoretical Ecology* by Ulanowicz (1986) to study the metabolic pattern of ecosystems, the MuSIASEM approach splits the network of energy transformations into two parts: (i) the hypercyclic part (using energy and resources for its own operation, but providing a net surplus to the rest); and (ii) the purely dissipative parts, providing key services to the economies (transaction activities) and reproducing human activity (final consumption at the household level). The analysis of the dynamic equilibrium between the relative size and characteristics of these two parts makes it possible to study both the viability and desirability of the metabolic pattern stabilized by such a dynamic equilibrium.

Chapter 8 introduces the basic theoretical concepts related to rationale of soci-etal metabolism with practical examples. The metabolism of societies can be interpreted as a second form of metabolism of humans: an exosomatic meta-bolism – a set of energy conversions taking place outside the human body, but still under human control. This conceptualization makes it possible to develop a multi-scale analysis using an analogy with the physiological metabolism of humans: the characteristics of the metabolism of the whole are affected by and are affecting the characteristics of the metabolism of the organs (impredicative relation: top-down and bottom-up).

Chapter 9 introduces the theoretical framework based on a vectoral representation of the metabolic pattern of societies across levels making it possible to generate a multi-level matrix (data arrays) for accounting. This is the mechanism through which it is possible to scale up and down the various quantitative assessments across hierarchical levels. The protocol is based on a system of vectors or data arrays organized in matrices capable of handling the representation of energy flows based on categories referring to energy forms of different quality and to different hierarchical levels. In this way it becomes possible to:

1   assess the set of energetic transformations in different compartments defined across different hierarchical levels;
2   maintain a distinction between different energy categories (primary energy sources, gross energy requirement and energy carriers);
3   maintain a distinction between energy forms of different kind (electricity, fuels and heat); and finally
4   address the implication of the fact that different functions to be expressed by the different functional compartments of the society require different 'power levels' (a combination of the production factors 'power capacity' and 'human labour').

Exosomatic energy is used at levels of hundreds of MJ/hour in the industrial sector and at levels of a few MJ/hour in the household sector. Throughout this chapter the various concepts are introduced with practical examples based on empirical quantitative assessments. These results clearly indicate the existence of a standard pattern of structural and functional change in the metabolic pattern of modern societies, associated with economic growth.

Chapter 10 illustrates how it is possible to utilize the MuSIASEM approach to characterize the metabolic pattern 'from the inside'. The use of multi-level matrices makes it possible to define expected combinations of values characterizing the metabolic pattern of the elements defined at different hierarchical levels across rows and across columns. The constraints on the dynamic equilibrium between the requirement and supply of production factors (energy carriers, power capacity, human activity) across compartments makes it possible to check the required congruence of biophysical flows. That is, by looking at the whole multi-level matrix characterizing the metabolic pattern we can see that: (i) the characteristics of the sub-matrix combining together the service and government sector and the household sector (determining the demand/supply of production factors, a feature called bio-economic pressure); must be congruent with (ii) the characteristics of the complementing sub-matrix combining together primary and secondary sector (determining the demand/supply of production factors, a feature called strength of the exosomatic hypercycle). Therefore, the analysis of the requirement of congruence for the numerical values of the elements included in two sub-matrices within the multi-level matrix can be done by taking advantage of the 'Sudoku effect' when analyzing scenarios.

Chapter 11 illustrates how it is possible to utilize the MuSIASEM approach to characterize the metabolic pattern 'from the outside'. The energy under human control in the various compartments of the society can be measured both in terms of joules of gross energy requirement (measured in thermal equivalent) and in joules of energy carriers (of different kinds: electricity, fuels and process heat) by adopting the dual reading illustrated in Chapter 9. However, information in gross energy requirement thermal does not tell us about its compatibility with external constraints – the availability of physical gradients (both on the supply side and the sink side) required for guaranteeing the possibility of using the gross energy requirement. For this reason, this chapter illustrates how to use an additional matrix – the biophysical footprint matrix – capable of assigning to energy carriers expressed as a different kind of energy, a given profile of requirement of Primary Energy Resources – i.e. the required physical gradients on the supply side (e.g. fossil energy stock depletion, tons of uranium depletion, water requirement, land requirement), that can be associated with a corresponding environmental loading on the sink side (GHG emissions, radioactive waste accumulation, soil erosion, visual impact on the landscape, etc.). When carrying out this type of analysis it becomes extremely evident that the massive quantity of imports of energy carriers coming from stock-flow primary energy sources (oil, coal and natural gas) is the basis for the level of economic progress enjoyed by developed countries in the last decades.

Chapter 12 illustrates how to put all the pieces of the puzzle together. By adopting the MuSIASEM approach we can define what is desirable and feasible in relation to internal constraints (when studying the metabolic pattern in terms of quantities of energy measured in energy carriers 'from the inside'). This assessment can deal with technical performance (strength of the exosomatic hypercycle – bottom up analysis) and the expectations about the material standard of living (bio-economic pressure – top down analysis) in the society. Then a given metabolic pattern assessed as viable and desirable in relation to internal constraints has to be checked in relation to its compatibility with external constraints (availability of resources and disturbance to ecological processes). For this task we have to adopt the biophysical footprint matrix. The MuSIASEM approach makes it possible to establish a coherent framework to integrate these different quantitative assessments. Within this coherent framework it becomes possible to discuss the choice of a set of relevant criteria that should be considered when assessing the quality of alternative energy sources. This check is especially important when looking for metabolic patterns powered by renewable resources having a much lower quality than oil.

Appendix 1 provides a historical overview of the field of energetics and identifies the roots of the ambiguity in the definition and quantification of 'energy' still found in the field today.

Appendix 2 provides a detailed analysis of the tautological definitions of quantitative assessments in the standard 'flow chart' representing the energy flows in modern countries (the flow chart of USA in 2007 is used as a case study). In this appendix we reconstruct the heroic (and dubious) assumptions adopted by those preparing the chart assessing energy quantities referring to primary energy sources, energy carriers, losses of different types and end uses all in the same variable: quads!

MuSIASEM is a work in continuous progress. However, we believe that even in its preliminary stage, what is presented in this book clearly shows the path for a more effective way of performing energy analysis: a path based on a multi-level approach of accounting using vectors and matrices. We sincerely hope that this book may stir a discussion on how to improve our approach among those scientists interested in the building of a more complex second generation of energy analysis.

Part I
Defining the problem

1   Energy accounting

Sources of ambiguity

The roots of virtually any problem with energy accounting lead back to the inherent ambiguity of the very concept of energy itself (section 1.1, below). So to start, we analyze three epistemological sources of ambiguity that must be acknowledged by those willing to account quantities of 'energy'. First of all, we address the lessons from hierarchy theory telling us that the quantification of the generic concept of 'energy' requires us to consider and represent energy transformation one scale at a time (section 1.2, page 15). Then we get to the lessons from classic thermodynamics telling us that different energy forms – e.g. thermal energy and mechanical energy – do have different qualities, and therefore cannot be aggregated in a substantive way (section 1.3, page 18). Finally, the development of non-equilibrium thermodynamics (required when dealing with living and self-organizing systems) implies an additional semantic ambiguity associated with the fact that metabolic systems, according to their own identity, define locally for themselves what is useful (negentropy) or waste (entropy) (section 1.4, page 21).

1.1 The inherent ambiguity of the concept of energy

Consider the simple question: What is energy? It is not easy to provide a definitive, simple, and crisp answer within the traditional scientific approach of reductionism. Clicking the button 'what is energy?' of the website of the US Energy Information Administration (EIA, 2012), we find an explanation organized in three parts.

First, we find the classic 'scientific' definition typically found in textbooks:

> Energy is the ability to do work.

Second, we are presented with a list of different forms of energy:

> (i) Heat (thermal); (ii) Light (radiant); (iii) Motion (kinetic); (iv) Electrical; (v) Chemical; (vi) Nuclear; (vi) Gravitational.

And finally, we get a semantic explanation:

Energy is in everything. We use energy for everything we do, from making a jump shot to baking cookies to sending astronauts into space. There are two types of energy:

* Stored (potential) energy
* Working (kinetic) energy

For example, the food you eat contains chemical energy, and your body stores this energy until you use it when you work or play.

This elaborate explanation conveys the impression that the concept of energy can only be understood by integrating several distinct narratives and semantic referents, which are difficult to integrate into a concise and coherent formalization. Indeed, the ambiguity of the definition given by EIA is not due to a lack of expertise of those who prepared the website, but rather to the very nature of the concept of energy.

Yet, the general perception of lay people is that the concept of energy is the ultimate source of rigor and precision typical of physics, the queen of hard sciences. Nothing is farther from the truth. Energy is essentially a semantically open concept used by the human mind to study and explore the external world, and for this reason it is a concept that has successfully resisted numerous attempts of substantive definition and quantification. As Feynman, a Nobel laureate in physics, pointed out:

> ... it is important to realize that in physics today, we have no knowledge of what energy is ... it is an abstract thing in that it does not tell us the mechanism or the reasons for the various formulas
>
> (Feynman *et al.*, 1963, Chapter 4, p. 2).

One of the pioneers of energetics, Rankine, in his 'Outlines of the Science of Energetics', provides a generic definition of energy, 'the capacity to effect changes' (Rankine, 1855, p. 385). The broadness of the definition has not changed with time: 'energy is an abstraction, designed to account for the outstanding differences between the initial and final state of a system to which some change has occurred' (Crane, 2003). When providing a definition of energy, it is simply necessary to remain generic in order to avoid getting into specific context and space-time scale dependent settings. Note that the standard textbook definition of energy provided by the EIA, 'the potential to do work', in reality refers to the concept of 'free energy' or 'exergy'. This is a potential source of confusion that will be discussed further on. A drawback of the-potential-to-do-work definition is that it is an impredicative or context-dependent definition in its nature (see Box 1.1, page 14). We must first define 'work' in order to be able to identify and measure 'energy', but this solution does not solve our original problems, since the definition of 'work' is as elusive as that of energy.

Box 1.1 The distinction between predicative and impredicative definitions

In natural language it is well known that certain words such as 'right', 'left', 'before' or 'after' must rely on an external referent in order to convey meaning. Hence the meaning of these words depends on the context in which they are being used. Such words are called *deictic* and they require contextual information to be effective.

The concept of impredicativity is quite similar. We face an impredicative definition when a property is possessed by an object whose very definition depends on that property. The concept is therefore associated with the existence of a process that generates the definition of itself and its parts in a circular way.

A simple example of this concept is: how to define if one is 'tall'? A predicative definition would be: 'if a person's height is more than 183 cm (6 feet), then she/he is tall'. Having measured a person, we can define without ambiguity whether she/he is tall or not. On the other hand, an impredicative definition of being tall would be: 'if the person's height is greater than that of 75 per cent of the other persons in the group, then she/he is tall'. The outcome of this definition depends on the circumstances. For example a person of 183cm ('tall' in the predicative definition) may be defined 'short' when considered as a member of a professional basketball team.

The predicative definition is useful only if we have prior knowledge (agreement) about the associative context in which the assessment will be used. The impredicative definition, on the other hand, is not substantive but much more flexible when one has to deal with different situations and contexts.

The confusion in the use and quantification of the term 'energy' is augmented by the fact that this term is not only used in many different scientific contexts and narratives, but also in everyday language. Indeed, the everyday use of the term 'energy' and its related terms, effort and power, is extremely common and the associated semantic message is intuitive and easily grasped: 'she is an energetic teacher', 'I no longer have the energy for doing this', 'this will require a lot of effort', 'she is a very powerful person'. It is probably precisely because of this familiarity that we encounter an extreme difficulty in understanding and in properly using the various non-equivalent formalizations of these concepts when using scientific narratives.

As mentioned, in the fields of physics and engineering, use of the term energy is based on the classic impredicative definition, 'the potential to do work'. This entails shifting the problem from defining 'energy' to defining the term 'work', which is anything but easy. Certainly, work can be quantified in the ideal world of elementary mechanics using the standard definition: 'work is performed only when a force is exerted on a body while the body moves at the same time in such a way that the force has a component in the direction of the motion'. Work can also be quantified in terms of classic thermodynamics, after establishing equivalence between 'heat' and 'work': 'the work performed by a system during a cyclic transformation is equal to the heat absorbed by the system'. In this case, using a calorimetric equivalence, assessments of both work and energy are expressed in the same unit of measurement, joules (J). However, the elaborate description of work in elementary mechanics and the calorimetric equivalence derived from classic thermodynamics are of little use to characterize work in real-life situations.

In fact, in order to characterize the performance of various typologies of work we need qualitative characteristics that are very often impossible to quantify in terms of either mechanical work or heat equivalence (Giampietro and Mayumi, 2004). For example, the work of a director of an orchestra cannot be described using the above definition of elementary mechanics nor can it be measured in terms of heat. A sole accounting of the mechanical work involved would not distinguish between a famous director and an ordinary policeman regulating traffic. Similarly, measuring the joules of heat sweated by the director during the concert will not tell anything about the quality of his performance. 'Sweating' and 'quality of directing' simply do not map very well onto each other. Indeed, it is virtually impossible to provide a physical formula or general model quantifying in substantive terms the quality (or value for society) of a given work. What has been achieved after fulfilling a useful task is not directly related to a quantitative accounting of how much energy input has been consumed.

The field of economics also employs the term 'energy'. Given its relevance as a key commodity in modern economies, economists are increasingly interested in the analysis of energy flows. Energy inputs are, in fact, strategically important commodities for the successful operation of modern economies. This economic interest has led to the adoption of a new category of energy accounting, 'energy commodities', which is used, not without controversy, in the energy statistics of Eurostat and the International Energy Agency.

1.2 The lessons of hierarchy theory

Starting from the premise that energy is an elusive concept, any attempt of energy accounting cannot but be a heroic effort. Physicists and engineers have mastered how to quantify energy transformations. However, they can do so only when adopting one scale at a time. The epistemological challenge faced when trying to analyze a system using simultaneously different scales is the subject of the field of hierarchy theory (Simon, 1962; Koestler, 1968, 1969, 1978; Whyte *et al.*, 1969; Pattee, 1973; Allen and Starr, 1982; Salthe, 1985; O'Neill *et al.*, 1986; O'Neill, 1989; Allen and Hoekstra, 1992; Ahl and Allen, 1996; Giampietro, 2003). In brief, hierarchy theory can be defined as 'a theory of the observer's role in any formal study of complex systems' (Ahl and Allen, 1996, p. 29). It explicitly acknowledges the unavoidable existence of multiple, non-equivalent identities for the same system when it is observed at different scales. So the observer, deciding how to observe a complex system, defines, with the choices made in the pre-analytical phase, what will be the result of that observation. Clearly, what is observed is still the complex system, but the observer can choose, when selecting the scale and the associated descriptive domain, one particular view or aspect of it at the time. As a matter of fact, the idea of a system having multiple identities when observed at different scales provides the definition of a hierarchical system:

- 'a dissipative system is hierarchical when it operates on multiple space-time scales – that is when different process rates are found in the system' (O'Neill, 1989);
- 'systems are hierarchical when they are analyzable into successive sets of subsystems' (Simon, 1962, p. 468);
- 'a system is hierarchical when alternative methods of description exist for the same system' (Whyte *et al.*, 1969).

In the jargon of hierarchy theory, different forms of energy described on different scales can only be quantified by adopting non-equivalent descriptive domains. The concept of a non-equivalent descriptive domain was first introduced by Robert Rosen (1985, 2000) to indicate a situation in which two quantitative assessments cannot be reduced to each other within a single formal model (see also Giampietro *et al.*, 2006). In the jargon of physics this situation is described as the existence of incoherent quantitative descriptions.

A few examples of non-equivalent representations of energy forms are provided in Figure 1.1 (page 17). They specifically refer to the following non-reducible quantitative energy assessments:

- The assessment used to describe and measure quantities of energy associated with the behaviour of tiny particles, based on the electronvolt (eV), a unit of energy equal to approximately 1.602×10^{-19} J. Just to give an idea, the energy of a molecule of oxygen moving in the air we breathe is 0.03 eV.
- The assessment used to describe and measure the quantities of energy associated with cellular processes in the fields of biochemistry and physiology is based on ATP. ATP is an energy rich molecule used in biochemical processes; it is the biochemical fuel of living systems. The energy equivalent of ATP has been estimated at 58 J/g of ATP associated with 3,600 turnovers/day of 50g p.c. (http://trueorigin.org/atp.asp).
- The assessment used to describe and measure our food energy intake refers to the scale of the human body. For instance, 100g of chicken breast provides 150 kcal or 630 kJ of food energy to the human body.
- The quantitative assessment used to describe the metabolism of a social system – the different primary energy sources required to carry out a given set of societal functions – is usually expressed in tons of oil equivalent (TOE). For example, we may want to assess the energy used by New York

City and will find that this is a mix of flows of different energy forms including petroleum, natural gas, coal, wood, and electricity generated in different ways (e.g. nuclear, hydroelectric).

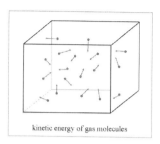

kinetic energy of gas molecules

1 Descriptive domain for electron volts

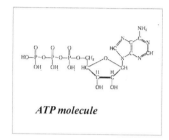

ATP molecule

2 Descriptive domain for ATP biochemistry

3 Descriptive domain for chicken breast

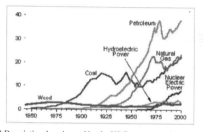

4 Descriptive domain used by the US Department of energy to handle the accounting of energy consumption of NYC

Figure 1.1 Quantitative assessments referring to energy forms observable only at different scales
Photo source: Wikicommon.

It is unrealistic to expect that a single method of accounting could exist to effectively handle the heterogeneous information space described by these four assessments covering a range of order of magnitude from 10^{-19} joules to 10^{12} joules. The fact that all of these forms of energy can be expressed in joules should not be taken as a sign that it is possible to reduce the relative quantitative assessments into a single number, by using a single comprehensive model. The information required for such accounting is based on different typologies of descriptions of networks of transformations which are in turn referring to different scales.

When trying to aggregate data referring to 'energy quantities' defined on non-equivalent descriptive domains (different scales), analysts are forced to use quantitative assessments that can only be obtained from non-equivalent measurement schemes. The problem is generated by the fact that these different measurement schemes deal with different typologies of energy transformations taking place at different scales.

In general terms we can say that data generated within non-equivalent observation processes cannot be summed even if they are expressed in the same unit. In fact, the relative measurement schemes do entail different types of error bars determined by the differences in scale. Funtowicz and Ravetz (1990) illustrated this point with the following joke. There is a skeleton of a dinosaur in a museum with the original inscription in the label reading: 'age 250,000,000 years'. However, the janitor of the museum has corrected the inscription into 'age 250,000,008 years'. When asked about the correction, the janitor replied: 'When I got this job, eight years ago, the age of this dinosaur was 250,000,000 years. So, I am just keeping the label of the age accurate.'

As noted by Funtowicz and Ravetz (1990), there are no written rules in mathematics that prevent the summing of two addends expressed in the same unit. Therefore the sum of 250,000,000 years and 8 years is admissible according to formal rules. Nevertheless, the explanation given by the janitor simply does not make sense to anybody familiar with measurements, and this is the pun of the joke. The measurement scheme used to provide an assessment of hundreds of millions of years is incompatible with that used for individual years because of the too large a difference in the associated error bars. For this reason, the 'accurate' assessment of 250,000,008 years is meaningless.

This epistemological conundrum becomes extremely relevant when dealing with analyses based on the aggregation of quantitative energy assessments at the national level. The need for adopting non-equivalent descriptive domains to describe energy forms observable only on different scales means that it is impossible to have a common measurement scheme capable of defining an overall assessment expressed in a single unit of measurement of energy. That is, a system of energy accounting and the relative measurement scheme capable of measuring the efficiency of energy conversions taking place in the appliances of a flat within Manhattan in New York City is not equivalent to the system of accounting capable of measuring the consumption of tons of oil equivalent in the USA. The fact that both assessments can be quantified using joules does not imply that these assessments can be added in a meaningful sum.

1.3 The lessons of classic thermodynamics

At the time of Galileo and Newton, when the objectives of scientific investigation were still relatively simple, the description of events in classical mechanics was and could be based on: (i) a very small set of relevant attributes (e.g. position, speed, acceleration); and (ii) the adoption of a single scale at the time. In this simple world a simple equation (e.g. $F = m \times a$) can be used to describe and predict the movements of both billiard balls and planets. The analysis of these energy exchanges could be handled with simple analytical tools only because they were using a single energy form – kinetic energy. The price to pay for this was the forced adoption of a single scale at the time. The current solution was achieved by introducing the concept of force (for more see Appendix 1).

The excess of simplification adopted in classical mechanics explains why the field of energetics – a systemic study of transformations among different energy forms – e.g. acknowledging the relevance of heat (thermal energy) as a non-equivalent form of energy when related to kinetic (mechanical) energy – required a revolution in the classic universe of science: thermodynamics was developed outside the domain of classical mechanics.

Much of the epistemological problems encountered in the field of energetics can be better understood in a historic light. The science of energetics was not developed within an established academic setting. On the contrary it started as an economic/engineering enterprise, in which theoretical discussions were following practical applications. For this reason, energetics started as a confused claim on the possibility of developing a science aimed at describing, measuring, studying, controlling and exploiting energy transformations – all types of energy transformations – as stated by Rankine in his introductory lectures.

Following the first experiments of the pioneers in this field, such as Carnot (1824) and Clapeyron (1834), it soon became clear that it was indeed possible to establish certain general relations in the process of conversions of heat energy into mechanical work (Joule, 1845). Based on this expected relation the 'science of energy' quickly experienced an extraordinary development. However, the academic interest was inspired by three distinct groups of pioneers, motivated by different interests and operating against different cultural backgrounds (Smith, 1998).

Of these groups, the most active one was based in Scotland and included no less than William Thomson (Lord Kelvin), James Joule, William Rankine, and James Maxwell. These brilliant men were not only scientists but above all engineers involved with the building and selling of engines and technology. They considered the theoretical development of this field, which Rankine baptized 'energetics', essential to gain credibility among potential buyers. To them, academic recognition meant a commercial edge on the competition, at that time, populated by practitioners without solid theoretical basis.

A second group, counting Wilhelm Ostwald and Georg Helm as leaders, was based in Germany. These scientists were looking for a new science of energy, capable of providing an alternative to the leading mechanical view of the external world (Ostwald, 1907; 1911). Ostwald, Professor of Physical Chemistry, after winning the Nobel Prize in Chemistry in 1909, became obsessed with the idea of establishing a new scientific discipline of energetics ('der energetische imperativ' or the energetic imperative) applicable to many domains of analysis, including the study of the functioning of human society.

A third group of scientists with heterogeneous backgrounds was concerned mainly with 'eliminating thermodynamics from its energetistic embellishments ... and the taking of some bold steps in the direction of axiomatization' (Smith, 1998, p. 68). This group includes names such as Ludwig Boltzmann, Max Plank and J. Willard Gibbs, who were key players in strengthening the quantitative rigour of the formulation of thermodynamic laws. So we can interpret the creation of the axiomatized body of classic thermodynamics as a formalization, within a specific definition of the field of applicability, of the original field of energetics.

The problem of how to use the abundant supply of coal (potential thermal energy) to power prime movers (actual mechanical energy) to be used within the economy was a key driver of this scientific field. As a matter of fact, Fermi (1956, p. ix) was extremely clear when expressing his opinion about thermodynamics: 'Thermodynamics is mainly concerned with the transformation of heat into mechanical work, and the opposite transformation of mechanical work into heat'.

What is relevant to our discussion on energy analysis is the methodological approach used by the pioneers of this field to axiomatize and bring rigour to the analysis of energy transformations. In relation to this point Bridgman says:

> ...the energy concept has no meaning apart from a corresponding process. One cannot speak of the equivalence of the energy of mass and radiation unless there is some process (not necessarily reversible) by which one can get from mass to radiation
>
> (Bridgman, 1961)

The quantitative analysis of the expected relations in a set of energy transformations was based on the definition of standard 'typologies' (definition of equivalence classes) of both energy forms and energy transformations. That is, typologies of energy forms and transformations (enthalpy transfer, adiabatic expansions, etc.) were imagined to take place in controlled settings: thermodynamic cycles. An example of this type of analysis is the Rankine cycle illustrated in Figure 1.2.

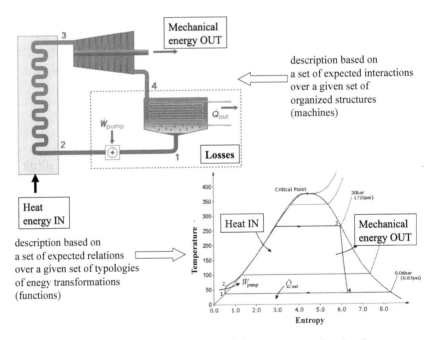

Figure 1.2 Rankine cycle: theoretical cycle and the structures performing the process
Source of the two graphs: Wikicommon, courtesy of Andrew Ainworth

Finally, having adopted this analytical framework, equivalence classes of energy transformations and typologies of energy forms could be defined because the study of thermodynamic cycles was 'substance independent'. It was aimed at defining in general terms the systemic properties of typologies of conversions of heat into mechanical power and vice versa. Later on, the analysis of the conversions of mechanical power into electricity and vice versa, obtained through electro-magnetism, was expanding the number of energy forms which could be converted and reduced to each other within combined cycles.

The possibility of generating standardized definitions of equivalence class or conversion factors among different types of energy forms – e.g. thermal energy versus mechanical energy – was an incredibly valuable result for the first pioneers of this field. These definitions made it possible to study and improve the performance of the new generation of machines developed exactly for making these conversions. So the very development and success of thermodynamics is the ultimate proof that: (i) quantities of energy referring to different energy forms – e.g. 1 joule of thermal energy and 1 joule of mechanical energy – are not equivalent when it comes to their accounting. According to the Rankine cycle, illustrated in Figure 1.2, 1J of mechanical energy requires more than 1J of thermal energy to be generated; (ii) the quality factor or the conversion factor which has to be used to aggregate different energy forms is not substantive, but it depends on the process used for the conversion. In conclusion we can say that classic thermodynamics posed the problem of how to handle the difference in quality of different energy forms and provided a series of expected relations, making it possible to establish criteria of equivalence (how many joules of an energy form A are required to get 1J of an energy form B). However, these criteria of equivalence are only valid within the specific setting of the thermodynamics cycles and at the given scale selected for the representation. For example, if we use a thermodynamic cycle to represent in an analytical way a given set of energy transformation – e.g. the Rankine cycle – then we can conclude that 1J of mechanical energy is 'more valuable' than 1J of thermal energy. But this criterion is valid only if the goal is to generate mechanical work. At the same time, using the same cycle we can say that a given quantity of heat Q is more valuable when it is transferred at 300°C than at 25°C. But this criterion is valid only if we are operating in an environment in which the room temperature is not 300°C.

1.4 The lessons of non-equilibrium thermodynamics

We saw in the previous section that classic thermodynamics (equilibrium thermodynamics) represented a first departure from mechanistic epistemology by introducing new concepts such as irreversibility, symmetry breaking and indeterminacy: when describing real world processes nothing can be the same (e.g. the same state) when it happens for the second time. A second revolution of non-equilibrium thermodynamics was initiated by the ideas of surplus entropy disposal by Schrödinger (1967, in an added note to Chapter VI of *What is Life* in 1945) and then by the work of the Prigogine school (Prigogine, 1961; Glansdorff and Prigogine, 1971; Nicolis and Prigogine, 1977; Prigogine, 1978; Prigogine and Stengers, 1984), with the introduction of the class of dissipative systems.

This second revolution required an additional change in the narratives to be used about energy conversions. These new narratives can only be adopted having abandoned one of the main ideological assumptions of reductionism (for more see Appendix 1): it is impossible to define a substantive representation of what is 'energy' and 'how useful' is an energy input which is 'the same' for different observers and agents operating in different dimensions and scales. The revolution of non-equilibrium thermodynamics implied that 'entropy' – the classic bad guy of the universe of classic thermodynamics – can be perceived as either good or bad depending on the perspective (or pre-analytical narrative) adopted for the analysis. Since dissipative systems are open systems feeding on 'negative entropy' (the expression coined by Schrödinger), an essential input they must take from their context, what is good for them (producing a lot of entropy to be exported to the environment) can be negative for the context. Clearly, the perspective from the inside (the more energy is dissipated, the more power is expressed, the better is the situation) has to be compatible with the existing boundary conditions (the context must make it possible this discharge of entropy). But still the local scale definition of what should be considered as a benign or malign set of boundary conditions (determining the survival of the death of the metabolic system) is what matters for the survival and reproduction of a dissipative system. In this way, with the introduction of the new non-equilibrium paradigm, quantitative science was confronted with the fact that when dealing with complex dissipative systems, scientists can only work with system-dependent and context-dependent definitions of entities, which, to make things more difficult, change their identity over time.

However, the inherent ambiguity of the original definition of energy made it possible to handle this additional complication in the semantic use of the term energy, by moving from a predicative definition of energy input to an impredicative definition of energy input. To explain this difference we have to go back, again, to the origin of the scientific field. The principle of energy conservation, also known as the first law of thermodynamics, played a key role in the development of the foundations of 'the science of energy' and especially in providing universal applicability of this new field. In his communication, 'On the General Law of Transformation of Energy', Rankine (1853) claimed that

> the term energy is used to comprehend every affection [state] of substances … includes ordinary motion and mechanical power, chemical action, heat, light, electricity, magnetism, and all other powers, *known or unknown*, which are convertible or commensurable with these.
>
> (quoted in Smith, 1998, p. 139, emphasis added)

Expectedly, Rankine's explicit reference to 'known and unknown forms of energy' generated a series of sceptical comments. For instance, Poincaré observed that:

In each particular case it is clearly seen what energy is and at least a provisional definition of it can be given; but it is impossible to find a general definition for it. There only remains for us one enunciation of the principle of the conservation of energy: There is something which remains constant. Under this form, it is in its turn out of the reach of experiment and reduces to a sort of tautology.

(Poincaré, 1913, p. 121)

On the other hand, it made it possible for us to use the same concept of 'energy' to describe and study in quantitative terms the movement of billiard balls, the efficiency of electricity generation in thermal power plants, and the metabolism of the human body. In fact, one can also interpret the principle of energy conservation as a powerful heuristic mechanism to study in a scientific way natural transformations, no matter whether known and unknown. If some changes cannot be explained with existing knowledge, we ought to look for hidden or new 'energy forms' capable of effectuating that change. Judging the significance of the principle of energy conservation for scientific practice, Maxwell (1877, p. 390) comments: '…in the study of any new phenomenon our first inquiry must be, How can this phenomenon be explained as a transformation of energy? What is the original form of that energy? What is its final form? What are the conditions of transformation?'

A similar view of the first law of thermodynamics is held by Ulanowicz:

Energy begins to seem less a concrete reality than an artifact of constructivist book-keeping systems necessary for estimating quantities whose roles seem far more palpable and physical relevant (Reynolds and Perkins, 1977). It has always seemed to me passing strange that the law of conservation of energy should be the only law in all science to hold without exception, everywhere, all the time. I have often speculated that perhaps things were merely defined in exactly such a way that they would always balance. Science was on a roll, what with the discoveries of conservation of momentum and caloric. Newton had declared the world to be a closed system, so why not simply define energy to be conserved? Mayer and Joule conveniently came up with the numbers that would make it so.

(Ulanowicz, 1997, p. 23)

In the same line, Smith (1998, p. 12) observes: 'Thus the "discovery" of energy conservation becomes instead a construction which has to be formulated, articulated and promoted and which might be said to constitute a simulation or representation of the external world of nature, rather than some kind of essential truth about reality'.

Thus, a semantically open definition of the concept of energy provides us with the means to discover, define and eventually measure 'new forms' of energy, any time we come upon a change for which we do not have an already-existing explanation. Indeed, with the introduction of the category potential energy as opposed to actual energy, Rankine guaranteed the integrity of the principle of energy conservation in all possible events. These two semantic categories can handle and classify any type of energy form: an unknown energy form can be considered as 'potential' before being discovered and as 'actual' after being discovered (and named) following some unexpected observation or effect. Moreover, the concept of 'energy input' can be tailored to any peculiar situation.

However, a definition of energy that includes the ambiguous category of potential energy is, by default, impredicative, for both the existence and relevance of potential energy necessarily depends on the purpose and the context. In Figure 1.3, we illustrate this impredicativity for the definition of chemical potential energy (one of the most important energy forms in the metabolism of modern societies). The quantitative assessments of hay and gasoline shown (Figure 1.3), both expressed in joules, may be meaningful or not depending on the context. For instance, hay is an energy input for a horse, but it is not an energy input for a car, the reverse is true for gasoline. More in general, as explained by Cottrell (1955), when dealing with complex systems capable of converting an energy input into a useful energy service, it is the nature of the converter that determines what should be considered an energy input, and therefore what should be considered as potential energy for that system. This is especially true for chemical potential energy. Needless to observe

Energy converter

Energy input

Hay = 11 MJ/kg

Non-equivalent energy assessments of energy inputs

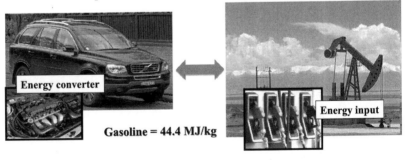

Energy converter

Energy input

Gasoline = 44.4 MJ/kg

Figure 1.3 The identity of the converter defines what should be considered potential energy
Source of the four pictures: Wikicommon, horses author 'opqr'; pasture author 'Bonus Onus'; Volvo car author 'OSX'; oil well author 'John Hill'

that these statements can be directly related to the concept of negative entropy – a specific definition of benign boundary conditions – which is different for different typologies of dissipative systems (Mayumi and Giampietro, 2004).

Even more pronounced is the situation when dealing with the concept of useful energy. For instance, wind can be a nuisance or a source of power depending on whether we find ourselves cycling against the wind or with the wind behind. Or consider the skyscrapers of New York City, which have a tremendous amount of gravitational potential energy, given their mass and the force of gravity, but are not normally included in an accounting of the relevant energy forms available to the city. Nevertheless, imagine an unexpected event would threaten the city, e.g. an invasion by large marine monsters, like in a fiction movie. In this situation the enormous gravitational potential energy of the mass of skyscrapers (an energy form that would certainly be overlooked by any energy analyst studying NYC) could be used purposefully to stop the advance of the monsters into Manhattan. In this example, it is the introduction of a new purpose that makes a hitherto unacknowledged form of energy (potential source of useful energy) relevant. Again, we find that because of the introduction and acceptance of the concept of potential energy, covering also unacknowledged or yet unknown energy forms, the energy accounting of complex adaptive systems is inevitably subject to the ambiguity typical of impredicativity.

1.5 The problems do not end here

In this chapter we have illustrated the basic epistemological problems of energy accounting. Unfortunately, the problems do not end here. Energy is ubiquitous by its very nature and throughout recent history has appealed to scientists from virtually any scientific discipline. This has led to the development of an undefined and grey interdisciplinary scientific field often referred to as 'energy analysis'. To make things even more confused, as discussed in Appendix 1 summarizing the history of energetics and thermodynamics, the issue of scale was never acknowledged as a relevant issue. Paradoxically, the issue of scale has always been at the heart of the controversies between the two approaches fighting to shape the theoretical foundations of thermodynamics: the microscopic view, developed by Boltzmann, and the statistical approach, represented by the physical chemistry of Gibbs (Smith, 1998). For all these reasons the emergence of the field of energy analysis only loosely related to thermodynamics or energetics; the conceptualized problems mentioned in this chapter were magnified to create an incredible confusion that persists till today.

In the next chapter, we take a more historical stand, and describe the development of the field of energy analysis and its related problems. In the following chapters, we approach the theme from an analytical point of view and address specific epistemological problems related to the applications of energy analysis, starting with national energy balances and relative troubles, the accounting of energy flows in processes controlled by humans, to end with the problematic application of net energy analysis.

2 Energy analysis

The troublesome birth of a new domain of knowledge

Energy analysis is a domain of knowledge that has never gained the status of established scientific discipline. The term energy analysis has been, and still is, used to refer to a fuzzy set of methodological approaches that are applied to various problems within different scientific disciplines, including chemistry, physics, agriculture, anthropology, ecology, economics, biology, and geological sciences. In this chapter we provide an overview of the events leading to the rise of energy analysis and of the problems faced by pioneer energy analysts from the very beginning.

2.1 Historic events leading to the rise of energy analysis

2.1.1 Early attempts to use energy analysis for studying the evolution and sustainability of human society

The idea that the analysis of energy transformations can be used to explain the characteristics and performance of human society is anything but new and has been explored in different disciplines since the time of the classic Greek philosophers. All the same, we can pinpoint several contributions in the fields of economics, chemistry, anthropology, and sociology that have specifically contributed to the shaping of energy analysis and that paved the way for its decade of glory in the 1970s.

Modern economists first expressed interest in the link between energy and economic development with the event of fossil energy in the nineteenth century. In particular W.S. Jevons, one of the founders of neoclassical economics, was profoundly interested in the biophysical basis of the economic process. In his famous book, *The Coal Question* (Jevons, 1865), he points at the key role that fossil energy played in the economic development of the United Kingdom and suggests several implications for policy. S.A. Podolinsky provided an energetic analysis of the performance of the agricultural sector in 1883 (Martinez-Alier, 1995, 1987). A more recent contribution was made by the Italian economist C.M. Cipolla who looked at the effect of biophysical constraints on the economic development of pre-industrial societies, specifically in relation to the ability to harness useful energy in developing empires (Cipolla, 1965). Finally,

N. Georgescu-Roegen provided a momentous contribution to the analysis of the sustainability of modern economies based on heavy consumption of fossil energy and mineral resources, by developing a comprehensive theoretical framework for bioeconomic studies (Georgescu-Roegen, 1971). All of these contributions, in one way or another, focused on the extraordinary importance of (fossil) energy in shaping events over the last two centuries and J. Grinevald has most appropriately suggested renaming the Industrial Revolution as the 'Thermo-industrial Revolution' (Grinevald, 1976, 2007).

Outside the field of economics, W. Ostwald, a Nobel Prize winner in chemistry, clearly saw the intricate link between energy and society. For him, society was a functional body coordinating its individual organs to maximize its energetic efficiency (Ostwald, 1907, 1911). F. Soddy, another Nobel Prize winner in chemistry, studied more specifically the role of energy in economic systems (Soddy, 1926). In particular, he criticized the excessive focus of economists on monetary flows to study economic changes and, with great foresight, pointed at the risk of confusing *virtual wealth* – monetary flows generated by debt (no relation to actual production of goods and services) and used to provide a temporary boost to the economy – with *real wealth* – monetary flows associated with the actual production and consumption of goods and services. A.J. Lotka provided a general principle to study the performance of biological systems: '... in the struggle for existence, the advantage must go to those organisms whose energy capturing devices are most efficient in directing available energies into channels favorable to the preservation of the species' (Lotka, 1922, p. 147). He proposed the distinction between exosomatic *energy*, indicating energy used under human control outside (exo) the human body, and *endosomatic* energy, indicating energy used under human control inside (endo) the human body (Lotka, 1956). It is a distinction instrumental to the development of the concept of exosomatic metabolism of society in which individuals behave like 'a huge multiple Siamese twin' (Lotka, 1956).

Building on Lotka's ideas, Georgescu-Roegen proposed the distinction between endosomatic instruments – part of each individual organism – and exosomatic instruments – detachable organs produced and used in the economics process (Georgescu-Roegen, 1971). Elaborating further on these concepts, Giampietro and Mayumi (1997, 2000, 2008) associate the distinction between endosomatic and exosomatic energy with different types of power capacity transforming energy under human control. Endosomatic energy is associated with applied power generated by human muscles whereas exosomatic energy is associated with applied power generated by machines and/or animals, outside the human body (Giampietro and Mayumi, 1997).

In the field of anthropology, Leslie White focused his theories on the link between energy and society. According to him (White, 1943) the primary function of culture in determining progress is enhancing the ability to harness and control energy. Later on, he proposed the basic law of cultural evolution, which states:

Culture thus confronts us as an elaborate thermodynamic, mechanical system. By means of technological instrument energy is harnessed and put to work...The functioning of culture of the whole therefore rests upon and is determined by the amount of energy harnessed and by the way in which it is put to work...culture evolves as the amount of energy harnessed per capita per year is increased, or the efficiency of the instrumental means of putting the energy to work is increased...

(White, 1949, pp. 367–9)

In the same vein, a highly creative thinker, George Kingsley Zipf, compared the organizational pattern of societies to the metabolism of 'bio-social organisms' (Zipf, 1941). He was the first to suggest that we carefully look for expected relations among internal characteristics of socio-economic complexes as their existence will dictate the expression of a predictable metabolic pattern (see Chapter 10).

In the field of sociology, W.F. Cottrell provided an extraordinary analysis of the relation between socio-economic changes and changes in the metabolic pattern associated with societal structure and function. In particular, in his seminal book *Energy and Society: The relation between Energy, Social Change, and Economic Development* (1955), Cottrell identifies and systematically expands the following ideas:

- It is the identity of the energy converter that defines the identity of the energy input.
- When assessing the quality of an energy source, it is the net surplus of energy made available to society that matters, and not the total energy theoretically available.
- The productivity of human labour in modern society heavily depends on the amount of exosomatic energy used to support an hour of work. A larger flow of exosomatic energy controlled by the worker makes its activity more effective.
- The industrial revolution is the result of massive injections of exosomatic devices (power capacity) and fossil energy (energy input) that, together, led to a major boost in the productivity of labour in the economy.

In relation to the possibility of using the analysis of energy flows to describe environmental impact and resource availability, V.I. Vernadsky (1924, 1926) developed the key concept of the biogeochemical cycle, thus proposing a systemic view of the cascade of interactions based on energy and material flows taking place in the biosphere. This big picture of the energetic process of self-organization paved the way for the energetic vision of theoretical ecology, developed not much later on.

2.1.2 The turbulent 1970s: oil embargo and sustainability

The oil embargo of 1973–1974 forced the general public to experience the effects of shortages of energy supply and unleashed a debate on sustainability both in the scientific arena and in society at large. This debate gradually evolved into a heated confrontation between the so-called cornucopians and the prophets of doom.

The label of cornucopians was given to those (mainly neoclassical economists) who claimed that whenever the price will become high enough, human ingenuity can 'produce' any required limiting resource – be it energy, water or bees for pollination – according to the needs of the moment. As a matter of fact, Robert Solow (1974, p.11), a Nobel Prize winner in economics, at the Ely Lecture to the American Economic Association literally stated: 'If it is very easy to substitute other factors for natural resources, then there is in principle no "problem". The world can, in effect, get along without natural resources...'. The most vocal of the cornucopians has undoubtedly been Julian Simon (not to be confused with Herbert Simon, one of the fathers of complexity theory). His abundant scientific production, among which *The Ultimate Resource* (Simon, 1981), and his famous public wagers with, among others, Paul Ehlrich, a prophet of doom, earned him the nickname of the Doomslayer.

On the other hand, all those who claimed that perpetual growth is impossible in a finite planet were labelled prophets of doom. The prophets of doom were unavoidably associated with the theories of the English economist, Thomas Malthus, who, in 1798, was the first to advance (in his *An Essay on the Principle of Population*) that the development of humankind was limited by the pressure that population growth exerted on the availability of food. In the 1970s, famous exponents of this view were Paul Ehrlich (author of *The Population Bomb*, 1968) and Garrett Hardin (author of *The Tragedy of the Commons*, 1968, and *Exploring New Ethics for Survival: The Voyage of the Spaceship Beagle*, 1972). Another important contribution at that time was the report of the Club of Rome (Meadows *et al.*, 1972), entitled: *The Limits to Growth*.

The confrontation between cornucopians and prophets of doom boiled down to a discussion on the methods that ought to be used to analyze and quantify the effects of economic activity on the environment and the possible consequences that technical changes can induce on the welfare of humans both in the short and long term. In this context, some cornucopian economists (e.g. Hartwick, 1977; Solow, 1974, 1986) claimed that it is possible to evaluate environmental costs using only economic narratives and monetary assessments based on prices. The other side strongly rejected this idea, arguing that the peculiar characteristics of ecological systems cannot be studied, let alone quantified, by monetary evaluations. Siding with the latter were several famous ecologists (e.g. H.T. Odum, 1973, 1977; Holling, 1973), but also important economists (e.g. Georgescu-Roegen, 1971, 1975; Daly, 1971). This debate was highly relevant for the development of energy analysis for if monetary assessments were to be judged inept for dealing with the analysis of environmental limits then energy analysis, and more in general biophysical analysis, was to play a key role in a science of sustainability.

As a matter of fact, the ideas and convictions behind this original debate of the 1970s resurfaced in the discussions among those studying sustainability within the new discipline of ecological economics established in 1989. According to the narrative adopted in ecological economics, the decision whether or not economic analysis based on prices and monetary values can effectively assess environmental limits and performance depends on the validity of the assumption that human technology can replace ecological processes and services. The unresolved discussion on the validity of that assumption has led to the development of the following two paradigms within which to develop quantitative analysis for dealing with sustainability (Common and Perrings, 1992; Brekke, 1997; Ayres *et al.*, 2001):

1   Weak sustainability paradigm: If we assume that human-made capital can replace natural resources and ecological services, then an unlimited substitution between man-made and natural capital is possible (see Pearce *et al.*, 1990, 1996). Common and Perrings (1992) called this narrative the 'Hartwick-Solow sustainability paradigm'. In this case, monetary evaluation can be obtained using the economic cost of replacing the service provided by nature for free and non-market price based evaluation (e.g. willingness to pay to preserve ecological services) to put a price tag on nature and its services;

2   Strong sustainability paradigm: If we assume that human-made capital in general cannot replace nature, then there are some types of nature capital performing functions that cannot be duplicated by manufactured capital. In this case we are talking of 'existence value', not 'exchange value', and therefore its economic price should be considered as infinite. As discussed in Giampietro *et al.* (2011), thermodynamic laws tell us that primary energy sources cannot be produced. For example, the cycle of water, which uses approximately between 35,000–44,000 TeraWatts of solar energy, simply cannot be controlled by human technology (controlling in total approximately 16 TeraWatts of exosomatic energy).

Acceptance of the strong sustainability paradigm implies that energy analysis and other biophysical analytical methods are essential to complement economic analysis.

In this regard, in the 1970s the reference to thermodynamic laws was often used to provide credibility to the quantitative results obtained by energy analysis (Gilliland, 1975). One of the favourite statements of H.T. Odum about the irrelevance of market prices to wealth was:

A tank of gasoline drives a car the same distance regardless of what people are willing to pay for it. A day of summer sunlight generates so much corn growth regardless of whether a human thinks it's free or not. A nugget of copper concentrated by geological work will make so much electric wire regardless of its price.

(Odum and Arding, 1991, p. 90)

H.T. Odum was one of the founders of systems ecology, together with his brother Eugene P. Odum and Ramon Margalef, and played a crucial role in the application of energy analysis to the study of energy and society. In fact, he proposed applying basic principles derived from ecological theory (e.g. emergy analysis) to the analysis of the metabolic pattern of socio-economic systems (H.T. Odum, 1971, 1983, 1996). In the 1970s, H.T. Odum did attempt to address, using energy analysis, several distinct problems associated with sustainability at the same time. Specifically, he worked on a systemic development of:

- a coherent quantitative approach in theoretical ecology based on the analysis of expected relations between structural and functional compartments in ecosystems;
- a theory of value based on energy transformations, which he proposed as a planning tool for choosing economic policies;
- a consistent quantitative framework to assess environmental impact and the availability of ecological services for the economy.

Needless to say that this attempt to get so many birds with a single stone translated into an injection of powerful new ideas as well as some theoretical confusion in the emerging realm of energy analysis.

The first oil embargo of 1973–1974 also set off a series of studies aimed at better understanding how and where fossil energy, and in particular oil, was used in the economy. Given this specific goal, energy analysis was interpreted by many as a promising field having the goal of studying:

- the cost of goods and services expressed in terms of fossil energy;
- the dependence of specific functional sectors of the society on fossil energy (e.g. agriculture and the food system);
- possible scenarios of alternative futures without fossil energy.

2.2 The chaotic birth of energy analysis as an independent domain of knowledge

2.2.1 The various schools of energy analysis

Given the political pressure for new analytical tools and the wide range of its possible applications, in the 1970s energy analysis came into full swing. Not surprisingly, given its long history and diverse background, a heterogeneous and rather confused set of definitions and aims came into use among energy analysts. As we will discuss in Chapter 6, this confusion accentuated the original ambiguity in the quantification of energy forms, that is, in the choice of useful narratives and pertinent protocols of accounting. At the time of maximum momentum, not even the term 'energy analysis' was universally accepted. An Editor's note of a special issue of *Energy Policy* (1974) dedicated to what was still called at that time 'energy budgets', reads:

> Forecasts of energy shortages were already stimulating analyses of patterns of energy consumption before the quadrupling of oil prices, and the interruption in supplies... This subject is so new and undeveloped that there is no universally agreed label as yet: researchers seem fairly evenly divided in their support of the terms 'energy budgets', 'energy costs', 'energy accountancy'...
>
> (*Energy Policy*, 1974, p. 91)

It is only in the International Federation of Institutes for Advanced Study (IFIAS) workshop of 1975 that the term 'energy analysis' was officially recommended for use (IFIAS, 1978).

We quote below five definitions of energy analysis, or equivalent terms, to show the incredible ambiguity prevailing at that time:

- Chapman (1974, p. 92): 'Many analyses of energy costs aim to evaluate the quantity of fossil fuel energy required to produce a consumer product such as an automobile or a loaf of bread.'
- Slesser (1977, p. 259) reporting the definition given in the first IFIAS workshop in 1974: 'Energy analysis is the determination of the energy [resource] sequestered in the process of making a good or service within the framework of an agreed set of conventions.'
- Maddox (1978, p. 136): 'Energy analysis is an accounting of the amount and kind of energy needed to support a specific activity.'
- Long (1978, p. 264): 'Energy analysis is a relatively new endeavour that is directed at the accurate assessment of both the direct energy (fuels and electricity) used in the provision of goods and services and the indirect energy incorporated in material and other non-fuel inputs to the production process.'
- Nilsson and Kristoferson (1976, p. 27) reporting on the second IFIAS workshop: 'Energy analysis is a field of science developed to study the societal use of one single aggregate resource: energy.'

Probably a reader inexperienced in energy analysis may find these five definitions quite similar and therefore redundant. However, none of them says the same thing! Chapman (1974) makes reference to 'fossil energy', which is a specific form of primary energy source. Slesser (1977) makes reference to an unspecified mix of 'energy resources', which may refer to a mix of coal, oil, or wind power used for making electricity, or to nuclear energy for making goods and service. Maddox (1978) clearly specifies that the accounting of 'energy' should be done in relation to two distinct pieces of information: which kind of energy is used and how much of each kind. Therefore, this definition of energy is only semantic and does not refer to any external referent (e.g. fossil energy or electricity). In his definition energy analysis is neither about 'fossil energy' nor 'energy resources' but about characterizing a given mix of different unspecified 'typologies' of energy flows (kind of energy) used in different quantities. Long's definition (1978) proposes yet two other new distinctions between 'kinds of energy': (i) a distinction between the consumption of different types of energy carriers (fuels and electricity) – something which is distinct from 'fossil energy' or 'energy resources'; and (ii) a distinction between the energy directly invested in the production of services and consumable goods (e.g. the circulating investment of energy input spent in production) and the energy indirectly incorporated in the making of the production factors (e.g. the fixed investment of energy spent years earlier to make the machines and infrastructures). Finally, Nilsson and Kristoferson (1976) use a very generic definition of the field: the study of the societal use of 'energy' (of an unspecified kind), which can be seen as an 'aggregate resource'. Clearly this statement clashes with the other definitions, which are making reference either to specific energy forms (of a given kind such as fossil energy or electricity) or are saying that energy analysis is about making distinctions among various categorizations (different kinds of energy), e.g. fossil energy versus non-fossil energy, energy resources versus energy carriers, fuels versus electricity, direct energy input versus indirect energy inputs. As we discuss in this book, the epistemological challenge of how to handle and aggregate different kinds of energy flows is *the* issue in energy analysis.

To avoid all these problems, it is possible to give a very generic definition of energy analysis based on a simple semantic message, such as the following one:

Bullard and Herendeen (1975, p. 268): 'The emerging art of "energy analysis" seeks to determine how much energy is required to provide goods and services'.

When using a semantic statement based on a generic reference to 'energy', we must be aware that whenever we talk of 'energy' the devil is always in the details. Indeed, the above definition is easy to give, but at the moment of crunching numbers, a sound accounting requires a wise choice of a pertinent protocol. But a wise choice of a pertinent protocol can only be done after specifying the goal of the analysis and the relevant narrative about energy transformation (scale and identity of both inputs and converters) that should be used. In energy analysis different goals and different narratives about energy transformations require the adoption of different semantic definitions and different formal protocols. In turn different protocols will generate different results, even if applied to the same set of energy transformations. This explains why Bullard and Herendeen, two well-known experts of energy analysis, carefully chose the term 'emerging art' rather than 'scientific discipline' in relation to energy analysis.

Discussing the definition of energy analysis, Jones says:

> Unfortunately, the many studies of energy use in agricultural systems have used a variety of terms such as energy accounting, energy analysis, energy budgeting, and energy costing to describe their technique, whilst each of these terms have been used to describe a variety of different methodologies.

Although some diversity of nomenclature may be expected, particularly in a rapidly developing technique, this terminology confusion has served to obscure similarities between different techniques and to complicate criticism of particular methodologies where these have shared their name with a number of different approaches.

(Jones, 1989, p. 339)

In this context, nothing is more appropriate than the famous statement of E.P. Box (1979): 'all models are wrong, some are useful'. Indeed, all protocols of energy analysis are wrong, but depending on the goal of the analysis, some are useful. However, the quote of Box also points at another problematic feature with existing applications of energy analysis, that is a systemic lack of transparency in relation to the pre-analytical decisions required for generating a quantitative assessment. Transparency means spelling out the logical criteria associated with the choice of a particular methodology: (i) scaling assumptions linked to the chosen narrative about energy transformations (goals, boundary conditions, initial conditions and time horizon); (ii) the semantic choices about the energy forms to be considered as relevant, which are required by the application of any formal protocol to special cases; (iii) the semantic choices associated with the assessment of data quality; (iv) the criteria used to evaluate the usefulness of the results; and (v) the choice of relevant indicators and the definition of their feasibility domain.

The inherent ambiguity associated with the concept of energy also generated a bifurcation in the field of physics dealing with the analysis of energy transformations. The term originally proposed by Rankine, 'energetics', was purposefully generic to include all possible types of energy transformations (see Appendix 1). For this reason, later on, those working in this field decided to adopt a different label, 'thermodynamics', in order to reduce and specify the field of applicability (see Appendix 1). The term 'energy analysis', on the other hand, has remained forever stuck in a limbo, being neither accepted as a true scientific field nor as a simple tool. Depending on its user, it may refer to either: (i) the art of generating specific protocols (methods of accounting) useful for specific purposes; or (ii) a complex realm of knowledge having as its goal the systemic study of integrated sets of energy transformations that can be associated with the stability of self-organizing dissipative systems (metabolic systems).

2.2.2 The multiple goals of energy analysis

The pioneer energy analysts of the 1970s had a clear idea of the possible, practical applications of energy analysis to study the performance of the socio-economic process and its sustainability. For example, Chapman (1974) provides the following list:

- increase the energy efficiency (of local transformations and the whole society);
- forecast energy demand and identify policies that reduce future demand;

- analyze energy consumption of functional sectors (namely agriculture or mineral extraction) for making scenarios of the effects of technical changes or resource shortages;
- generate long-term scenarios of the viability and desirability of metabolic pattern of societies based on biophysical rather than monetary flows.

A document of the statistical office of the United Nations (1982), entitled *Concepts and methods in energy statistics, with special reference to energy accounts and balances*, provides a similar list for the many uses of energy statistics:

- to study the depletion of fossil energy;
- to forecast future demand for energy;
- to study the role of nuclear generation of electricity (but this point could apply to the study of other methods of generation of electricity);
- to scope for energy saving;
- to study the direct and indirect effects of price changes for energy sources;
- to help environmental protection;
- to study combined heat and power generation (but this point could apply to the analysis of other technological improvements);
- to study the impact of renewable energy sources;
- to study the dependence on imports.

Clearly, if one would like to pursue all of these goals simultaneously, the only solution would be to develop a set of useful (goal-specific) protocols of accounting and then integrate them in some complex procedure capable of handling the different scales, the different energy forms, and the different typologies of metabolic systems (expressing special characteristics and therefore requiring a special tailoring at the moment of generating the quantitative assessment – see Chapter 1). Unfortunately, the need of simultaneously addressing and handling the three epistemological conundrums described in Chapter 1 was never explicitly incorporated in the research agenda of energy analysts. As a consequence, in its rather short history energy analysis has been struggling with systemic epistemological issues.

2.2.3 Energy analysis under attack from the inside and the outside

The impressive list of goals and possible applications of energy analysis suggests that it had all the potential to become a vital policy tool. In our view, the inability to quickly supply a set of robust and effective tools in response to the sudden surge in demand in the 1970s is one of the main reasons for the doom of energy analysis in the early 1980s. In perfectly good faith, proponents of energy analysis made promises about marvellous analytical tools which they simply could not deliver. This failure, together with the end of the energy crisis, destroyed the credibility and relevance of energy analysis for policy making.

The quick rise and fall of energy analysis was mirrored by contemporary developments in legislation. A temporary victory of energy analysts was won with the passing of the Federal Nonnuclear Energy Research and Development Act of 1974 (PL 93-577, integrated later on by PL 96-294 title II). This law required the Department of Energy (DOE), at that time still called Energy Research and Development Administration (ERDA), to analyze the potential net energy yields of new energy technologies proposed under the Acts before funding them (GAO, 1982). The need for this law was explained to congress during various hearings by those working in energy analysis (H.T. Odum mentions this fact in his letter to *Science*, 1977, p. 261) and the basic rationale is explained by Long, stating that:

> The government could end up subsidizing research and development on tech-nologies that require more energy (and fossil fuel) than they furnish... government support is often directed at those opportunities whose econom-ics are the most difficult to evaluate and which are, thereby, risky.
>
> (Long 1978, p. 265)

However, history tells us that this experiment of making the use of net energy analysis compulsory failed and backfired. After trying to apply the law, the ERDA refused to do so any further claiming it was impractical, and explained the reasons in a technical report entitled *Net Energy Analysis: Little Progress and Many Problems* (ERDA, 1977). In spite of the complaint of the US comptroller general to the congress reporting that DOE had spent hundreds of millions of dollars on projects without estimating potential net energy yields of new tech-nologies (GAO, 1982), eventually the mandate of using net energy analysis stopped being followed. As remarked by Fraley and McDonald (1978), from the text of PL 93-577 it was not even possible to define in uncontested terms what should be considered as 'an application of net energy analysis' in the first place. For this reason it was difficult to decide whether or not DOE was adhering to the requirement of the Act. The theoretical framework of net energy analysis simply was not robust enough for generating a well-defined policy tool capable of deliv-ering the required applications. Moreover, as explained in Chapter 7, the original framework of net energy analysis was especially problematic when applied to energy systems not based on fossil energy.

The use of energy analysis to generate policy tools was not only at the core of this legal dispute but also generated a heated debate within the academic commu-nity in general, and that of energy analysts in particular. The divide was between:

- those saying that energy analysis can provide a useful understanding of the biophysical roots of the economy and that, therefore, it should be used to *complement* the indications given by economic analysis in policy discus-sions;
- those saying that energy analysis is the only way to get a reliable under-standing of the biophysical performance of the socio-economic process, and that therefore it should *replace* economic analysis in the discussion over sustainability.

The supporters of the latter view suggested the possibility of establishing a 'natural' system of values based on a large-scale energetic view, to be used in long-term sustainability discussions; and an energy theory of value, that is embodied energy of goods and services, for use in local-scale, economic discussions (Odum, 1971; Hannon, 1973). Not surprisingly, this provocative hypothesis solicited a storm of reactions from both economists and non-economists. For instance, Georgescu-Roegen (1979) dismissed this idea as just another attempt at attributing the formation of economic value to just a single scarce production factor (earlier attempts being attributed to Marx with labour). He pointed out that the availability of net energy is just one of the production factors required by the economic process, a necessary but not a sufficient one. Huettner (1976, 1978) attacked the idea from both a theoretical point of view – human preferences, equity issues and intergenerational equity issues cannot be addressed, not even in principle by energy analysis – and a practical point of view – the methodological problems of energy analysis are so serious that it is unthinkable to propose a policy tool based on such shaky ground (see next section on sticky points). Another criticism from economists (Webb and Pearce, 1975) pointed directly to the weak spots of energy analysis. First, on the descriptive side, the dubious claim that it is possible to aggregate different kinds of energy into an overall assessment while maintaining the distinctions of quality attributes associated with their value, and second, on the normative side, the impossibility of handling in a substantive way, using biophysical variables, 'value conflicts' typical of human affairs.

These criticisms from outside energy analysis were backed up by vigorous criticism from within. The provocative title of a famous paper of Leach (1975), an important expert on energy analysis, 'Net Energy Analysis: is it any use?' clearly illustrates the attempt of those working in energy analysis to take distance from the exaggerated claims about its potential:

> From the start there were skeptics, chiefly economists, who often based their attacks on a misunderstanding of the humble aims of Net Energy Analysis as a descriptive science, believing they smelled heresy in the form of proscription and energy theory of value. But more recently skepticism and doubt have spread to net energy analysts themselves, especially in recent months as the tide of studies produced a remarkable variety of methods, assumptions and 'results' which could not easily be explained away as merely the teething troubles of a new discipline.
>
> (Leach, 1975, p. 332)

Other eminent scholars expressed similar preoccupations. For example, Slesser (1977) commented in *Science*: 'I have yet to see a rigorous definition of net energy analysis in the scientific literature, although in our own group we have a precise convention' (p. 261). Before him, a pioneer of energy analysis, Chapman (1974, p. 91) already observed: 'At the present time there are almost as many methods of evaluating the energy cost of a product as there are workers in the field.'

2.3 Systemic methodological problems of energy analysis surfacing in the literature

2.3.1 Back to the epistemological conundrums faced by energy analysis

We list here the classic sticky points that emerged in the discussions about energy analysis in the 1970s (Chapman, 1974; Leach, 1975; Herendeen, 1978). These methodological problems are direct consequences of the epistemological conundrums described in Chapter 1 and lead to a series of specific technical problems of accounting. Even though they were discussed in several dedicated workshops (IFIAS, 1974; IEA, 1975; IGT, 1978), they have remained unresolved:

1   the co-existence of multiple relevant scales (non-equivalent valid representations of the same process) and the resulting arbitrariness in boundary definition (truncation problem);
2   the difficulty of aggregating energy forms of different kinds (e.g. how to account for the difference in quality between electricity and fuels?);
3   the impossible simplification of complex networks of transformations into a clear-cut, input/output analysis (joint production dilemma). This includes the difficulty of dealing with the special characteristics of self-organizing systems, that is they define for themselves what should and what should not be considered as useful energy input.

As we discussed in Chapter 1, it is impossible to define a universally-valid protocol of accounting (one size fits all, once and for all) that can be applied to different kinds of energy defined within non-equivalent narratives. When studying a network of energy transformations in a complex socio-economic system the aggregation of different kinds of energy forms simply cannot be done in a substantive way. It depends on the specific identities of the metabolic pattern (the whole) expressed by an integrated set of elements using these energy forms for different purposes (end uses) at different scales. In practical terms, depending on the type of change we want to describe and depending on the purposes of the analysis, we have to be prepared to use different methods of accounting and combine the results in a meaningful description. For example, a quantitative method useful to assess the rate of depletion of fossil energy stocks (that is tracking the actual consumption of tons of oil) is not reducible to the method useful for assessing the gross energy requirement of a country (calculating the virtual 'tons of oil equivalent').

Whenever we come across a numerical result from an energy analysis of a complex network of energy transformations operating across different scales, we must recognize that numbers not only depend on the characteristics of the observed network but also on a series of pre-analytical choices made by the analyst. Those choices are informed by the analyst's perception of the goal of the analysis, of the relevance of the selected narrative about energy transformations, of the pertinence of the scale used to observe changes and gather data, and finally the specificity of the context in which the energy transformations take place. Both the scientific validity and the usefulness of any quantitative assessment of energy (the numerical results of energy analysis) will depend on the quality of this series of choices, as we will illustrate below.

2.3.2 The truncation problem

The truncation problem refers to the unavoidable arbitrariness of boundary definition in relation to space and time when dealing with complex systems operating simultaneously on multiple scales. It has been neatly described by Chapman (1974) in relation to the assessment of the energy required to produce a loaf of bread. He shows that we can keep enlarging the domain of activities involved in the production of a loaf of bread, which should be considered for the accounting of the energy inputs, from the local process (energy to the oven) in the bakery, to the production of grain, to the making of the oven, to the construction of infrastructures, etc. We can keep expanding the boundary of the analysis to arrive at the whole planet and even outside, if we include the sun as the provider of solar energy.

> It is clearly impossible to determine the proportion of all the production processes in the world needed to produce a loaf of bread or any other single product. Any analysis must be based on a sub-system of the world, a sub-system for which all the inputs and outputs are known. The choice of a sub-system is the first crucial step in evaluating an energy cost.
>
> (Chapman, 1974, p. 92)

But if we focus on just one sub-system of the 'whole', how do we know if we included the most relevant part? How important is the part we left out? This dilemma is called the truncation problem in energy analysis. A system operating simultaneously on multiple scales implies the existence of several non-equivalent descriptions. By default, this indicates that the same entity can be simultaneously perceived and represented as having different boundaries. Hence, the choice of just one of the possible perceptions and representations of the same system (the choice of one specific scale of analysis and related boundary definition) means a loss of potential information (the information associated with the representations obtained using other scales). A change in scale (in the narrative used to define what the system is and what it does) will affect the pertinence of the representation.

A notorious example of the truncation problem regards the assessment of the energetics of human labour (Table 2.1). Considering the huge amount of time and effort dedicated by the community of energy analysts to this subject (for an overview of issues, attempts and critical appraisal of results, see Fluck, 1981, 1992; Giampietro and Pimentel, 1990, 1991, 1992; Giampietro et al., 1993), we may well consider this one of the largest theoretical fiascos of energy analysis.

The literature on the energetics of human labour (reviewed by Fluck, 1981, 1992) shows many different methods (derived by the implementation of different narratives) to calculate the energy equivalent of one hour of labour. Indeed, the assessment of the flow of energy embodied in one hour of labour can refer to:

Table 2.1 Examples of non-equivalent assessments of the energy equivalent of 1 hour of human labour found in scientific analyses

Level	'Grain' and 'Time Horizon' of assessment	NARRATIVE	Range of values	Energy type	Factors affecting the assessment
n+3 Gaia	Centuries Millennia	EMergy analysis of biogeochemical cycles and ecosystems	10–100 GJ	Embodied solar energy	• Ecosystem type • Choice in the representation • Transformities • Choice of ecological services included
n+1 society	1 decade 1 century	Societal metabolism	200–400 MJ	Oil equivalent	• Energy source mix • Energy carrier mix • End uses mix • Efficiency in energy uses • Level of technology • Level of capitalization
n household	1 year 1 decade	Time allocation Technological conversions	2.0–4.0 MJ 20–40MJ	Food energy Oil equivalent	• Quality of the diet • Convenience of food products • Food System characteristics
n-2 body/organs	1 hour 1 year	Physiology	0.2–2.0 MJ	ATP/food energy	• Body mass size • Activity patterns • Population structure (age and gender)

- the metabolic energy of the worker during the actual work only, including (e.g. Revelle, 1976) or excluding (e.g. Norman, 1978) the resting metabolic rate. We deal here with a time scale of hours;
- the metabolic energy of the worker including also non-working hours (e.g. Batty et al, 1975; Hudson, 1975; Dekkers et al, 1978), on a time scale ranging from one day to one year;
- the metabolic energy of the worker and his dependents (e.g. Williams *et al.*, 1975), typically calculated over a time period of one year;
- all embodied energy, including commercial energy, spent in the food system to provide an adequate food supply to the population from which labour supply is derived (Giampietro and Pimentel, 1990), calculated over a time period of one year. This assessment no longer refers to food energy but to fossil energy;
- all the energy consumed in societal activities (Fluck, 1981). Dealing with a time scale of one year and coverage of the whole society. Again, this assessment no longer refers to food energy, but to fossil energy;
- finally, H.T. Odum's Emergy analysis (Odum, 1996) includes in the accounting of the energy embodied in human labour also a share of the solar energy spent by the biosphere in providing environmental services needed for human survival – open in the definition of time. This assessment is no longer based on either food or fossil energy, but on quantities of primary solar energy.

The relative quantitative assessments are given in Table 2.1 (page 40). These numbers show that 'rigorous' scientific assessments of the energy equivalent of one hour of labour found in literature vary from 0.2MJ to more than 20GJ and refer to at least three different types of energy forms. And when we say 'rigorous' scientific assessments we mean it. These assessments are all correct (they are the result of a pertinent analysis) within their own chosen narrative. This clearly shows that the quantification of an energy input required for a given process, or the energetic equivalent of a given output, not only depends on the information gathered at a given scale, but also and foremost on the choice made in the pre-analytical step regarding the boundary definition (Giampietro *et al.*, 2006).

2.3.3 Boundary definitions and the distinction between gross and net energy flows

When dealing with complex systems operating simultaneously across different levels of organization we must recognize that the quantitative information gathered at the local scale is non-equivalent to the information referring to the large scale. Chapman (1974, p. 97) illustrates this principle for copper smelting. Comparing two processes of copper smelting (electric versus fuel-heated furnace) he finds at the local scale that the electric furnace has a better thermal efficiency (61 per cent) than the fuel-heated furnace (27 per cent). However, the local assessment of efficiency considers only the furnace and focuses exclusively on the conversion of energy carriers (electricity and fuel, respectively) into the end use of smelting copper. Enlarging the boundary (scale) of the analysis to also include the energy spent to make the energy carriers (the gross energy requirement of the whole process), Chapman finds that the generation of electricity in the UK (at the time of writing) requires about 4J of primary energy sources (e.g. coal) per 1J of electricity delivered, whereas the making of fuel carries negligible production losses (J of fossil fuel spent to make 1 J of fossil fuel). Thus, at the *local* scale, where energy quantities are considered as *net energy carriers*, we find that the electric furnace is more efficient than the fuel-heated furnace. Whereas at the *large* scale, where energy quantities are considered as the *gross energy requirement* for the given end use, we must conclude that the fuel-heated furnace is more efficient than the electric furnace.

The relevance of boundary definition is particularly evident in the assessment of the performance of electric cars. Some authors are convinced that the electric car is a perfect solution for reducing CO_2 emission, because of the use of electricity rather than gasoline in an internal combustion engine, as well as for saving energy, because an electric engine is more efficient than an internal combustion engine. However, this conviction is based on a local-scale analysis addressing only the conversion of net energy carriers into end uses. Unless the electricity consumed by the electric car is produced with primary energy sources other than fossil energy, such as wind power and/or hydroelectric power, this assessment can be grossly misleading. If the electricity used by electric cars is produced by coal-fired plants, it is doubtful that these cars have a better ecological performance than conventional cars.

Indeed, the distinction between net and gross energy requirement is fundamental in any energy analysis. Slesser (1987, p. 228) states: 'If energy be considered the physical driving force of a developed or developing economy, a distinction must be made between primary energy sources and the net amount of useful fuel entering the economy.' As a matter of fact, at the 1974 IFIAS workshop it was decided to introduce the concept of gross energy requirement defined as: 'The gross enthalpy of combustion released at standard state of all the naturally occurring energy sources which must be consumed in order to make a good or service available' (quoted in Slesser, 2003, p. 2). Note that this definition of the gross energy requirement refers to a clearly specified kind of energy equivalent, 'gross enthalpy' specifically refers to thermal energy.

Nevertheless, at the IFIAS meeting it was not specifically worked out how to further handle this distinction between local and large scale representations. What was suggested though, in relation to the accounting of energy flows at the local scale, and explicitly endorsed by Slesser (2003), is the use of distinct numeraires for quantities of electricity (kWh) and quantities of fuels or heat process (the enthalpic unit, joule). This suggestion points to the problem that electricity and fuel refer to two different kinds of energy: electricity can be considered a form of mechanical energy, whereas fuels are carriers of potential calorific value (see Chapter 3). These two forms of energy have a different quality (see Figure 1.2, page 20).

In conclusion, when accounting instances of energy flows observed at the local scale, we deal with the assessment of quantities of net energy carriers, such as electricity, fuels and process heat, which do have special qualitative characteristics. On the other hand, at the large scale we deal with gross energy requirements, which are expressed in terms of a standard form of reference (joules equivalent) that is, in general, thermal energy.

2.3.4 The problematic aggregation of energy flows of different quality

The problem of aggregation of different kinds of energy was extremely clear to the pioneers of energy analysis. For example, in his overview of the literature to illustrate this point Long (1978) remarks: 'The statement usually made by these workers is that "not all calories are equal"', because a calorie of wood energy will do less work than a calorie of coal energy' (p. 274). It is for a good reason that coal replaced wood as a source of calorific value, that oil has replaced coal, and that natural gas is now replacing oil. Even when considering only energy carriers used for their calorific value, there are qualitative differences affecting the usefulness of a joule, which are related to the characteristics of the conversion process of potential chemical energy into thermal energy. Nevertheless, much more relevant is the case of electricity, which already in the literature of the 1970s was consistently treated as a different kind of energy form from fossil energy (see also Chapter 3 and Appendix 1).

In his description of the importance of the distinction between heat and work, Slesser (2003, p. 3) says: 'It is not heat that drives the economy, but thermodynamic work.' Hence, the observation that 1J of electricity is more valuable than 1J of heat can explain the large investment of thermal energy (heat) into thermodynamic cycles having the goal of generating power (mechanical energy/electricity). In line with this thought, in the energy analysis of the 1970s, quantities of electricity were accounted for by their gross energy requirement (their thermal equivalent), that is the amount of calorific value required to generate the given amount of electricity. In the case of electricity produced from nuclear or hydroelectric power (that is, electricity not requiring the direct consumption of fossil energy during the operation of the power plant) the accounting was done in terms of 'virtual' quantities of fossil energy, that is the famous Tons of Coal Equivalent (TCE) in the 1970s or Tons of Oil Equivalent (TOE) in the 1980s, indicating the equivalent amount of fossil energy that would have been required to produce that same amount of electricity using the standard conversion factor of that time (e.g. Chapman, 1974; Bullard and Herendeen, 1975; Herendeen, 1978).

However, the solution of using a quality factor for aggregating different kinds of local energy flows into a single number was clearly perceived as problematic in the community of energy analysts. For example, Maddox, commenting on the use of a conversion factor based on the thermal equivalent, says:

> Under this standard, then, a gallon of gasoline is equivalent to 36.6 kWh of electricity. However, it can quickly be seen that comparing electricity and

gasoline strictly on their respective enthalpies ignores qualitative distinctions that cannot be directly duplicated by gasoline, and vice versa. As a result, the enthalpies of separate energy forms do not give an adequate equivalence by which to derive a net energy value.

(Maddox, 1978, p. 135)

This brings us back to the impossibility of using hay to feed a car or gasoline to feed a horse (Figure 1.3, page 24).

An additional complication of the aggregation method was flagged by Fraley and McDonald (1978, p. 169), after critically examining 12 studies of energy analysis: 'Electrical input was consistently multiplied by a weighting factor to convert into fossil fuel equivalents. This use of a weighting factor really short-cuts the analysis: the need to find the energy inputs to produce electricity is bypassed.' They are certainly right, but with this method valuable information is lost, since this method converts all the assessments based on direct observations at the local scale (referring to actual flows of net energy carriers – the electric-ity consumed by cars) into quantitative assessments referring to the large scale expressed in gross energy requirement (referring to virtual flows of gross energy requirement – the quantities of thermal equivalent calculated for the energy input). The problem is generated by the fact that the gross energy equivalent depends on the characteristics of the system generating the electricity, which do not have anything to do with the characteristics of the local process (the electric engine of the car). Thus, the original assessment of local energy transformations based on net energy cannot be extrapolated to a larger scale of analysis using this approach.

Concluding his critical appraisal of the various methods of aggregation proposed in literature Maddox states:

> ...these general methods to establish a standard measure by which to conduct net energy analysis fail, and these failures are crucial. They signify that there is no universal net energy calculation, because there is no unam-biguous energy measure that allows one energy form to be compared to another. Energy cannot be treated as a single entity, because its various forms possess irreconcilable qualitative distinctions.
>
> (Maddox, 1978, p. 136)

To make things even more complicated, when discussing a criterion of energy equivalence, it is not only important to look at how a given energy flow is gener-ated (e.g. the making of 1kWh of electricity) but also at how it is used. As observed by Leach (1975, p. 342): '...while electricity, for example, may have a unique thermodynamic value as electricity, its practical value...depends entirely on its end use application...' Generally, electricity is considered to have a higher quality than coal as it can be considered a form of mechanical energy (see Chapter 3). However, if electricity is then used as a source of heat for cooking (an energy carrier used for a specific end use), the superior quality of 1J of electricity is no longer obvious. Indeed, as we will repeatedly stress in this book, it is impossible to define the performance of a given set of energy transformations if we do not consider simultaneously in an integrated way: (i) the set of gross energy flows; (ii) the resulting set of net energy flows; and (iii) the relative set of end uses.

We conclude this section with the advice given by Leach (1975, p. 341), who, like Slesser, endorsed the IFIAS recommendation: 'One approach is to solve the add up problem by avoiding it altogether: the analysis should confine itself to displaying all flows and numbers separately.' This is exactly what we will propose in our approach explained in the second part of this book.

2.3.5 The difference between gross energy requirement and primary energy sources

In the previous section we made a distinction between gross energy requirement (the requirement of energy input of the whole 'black box') and net energy requirement (the requirement of energy carriers of the individual converters within the black box). We saw that the gross energy requirement of the whole system is obtained by multiplying the different energy forms used inside the system with 'ad hoc' conversion factors (quality factors that determine the thermal energy equivalent) and summing the resulting (virtual) quantities of standard energy form (e.g. caloric value of fossil energy expressed in Tonnes of Oil Equivalent – TOE).

Expressing the energy consumption of a country in terms of gross energy requirement (measured in TCE or TOE) was a popular activity in the 1970s and 1980s. In fact, it was used as a normalization method to compare total energy consumption among countries, by 'correcting' for the differences in the mix of energy carriers used in their economies (the relative contribution of electricity) and for the differences in the mix of primary energy sources used to generate electricity (the relative contribution of nuclear and hydroelectric power).

Note, however, that although the use of TOE (or TCE) makes it possible to standardize the quantitative assessment of the gross energy requirement among different countries, it does not map onto their profile of primary energy source use. Where primary energy sources are defined as a set of physical quantities, whose existence is out of human control, which must be extracted (e.g. fossil energy stocks) or captured (e.g. mechanical energy in wind, falling water, or tides, solar energy, nuclear energy) to supply the required flow of energy under human control. The introduction of 'virtual' quantities of fossil energy in the energy accounting implies that we lose track of the actual requirement of material flows. That information is vital in relation to the analysis of environmental limits (e.g. stocks of fossil energy) and environmental impact (e.g. CO_2 emission). In fact, on the supply side we need to know the required profile of primary energy source use to quantify the exact requirement of material inputs (how many tons of coal and oil, cubic meters of natural gas, hectares of land, cubic meters of falling water, tons of uranium, etc.). As regards the environmental sink capacity, we need the profile of primary energy source use to quantify emissions (greenhouse gases, radioactive waste). An accounting of electricity generated with hydroelectric power in terms of thermal energy equivalent is useful to obtain the overall gross energy requirement, but it should be kept in mind that these virtual TOEs do *not* imply a corresponding depletion of oil reserves or CO_2 emission.

In general, the use of energy equivalents or standard conversion factors for aggregating energy forms of different quality results in a loss of grip on the physical side of the energy transformations (Georgescu-Roegen, 1975; Maddox, 1978).

2.3.6 Joint production dilemma

The joint production dilemma refers to the impossibility of simplifying complex networks of energy transformations (notably autocatalytic loops) into a linear representation of energy flows typical of energy input/output analysis. The joint production dilemma was another one of the classic problems of energy analysis surfacing in the 1970s (Chapman, 1974; Leach, 1975; Herendeen, 1978).

For example, imagine that we want to assess in energetic terms the performance of camels living in their natural habitat (Giampietro, 2006). Assuming that the energetic input of a herd of 100 camels over one year can be assessed by calculating the food energy eaten by the camels in the form of biomass, what should we include in the assessment of the 'energetic output' of the herd? We may include among the possible outputs: (i) the supply of meat; (ii) the supply of milk; (iii) the supply of mechanical power; (iv) the supply of wool; (v) the supply of blood to drink in emergencies in the desert; and (vi) the maintenance of valuable genetic information of the species. Then, what logic should we use to associate these different six outputs to the common energetic input (biomass feed) when calculating the corresponding 'energy costs' (output/MJ of eaten biomass)? Can we imagine a substantive criterion that can be used to decide how to assign a share of the energy input to the wool, or the meat or the genetic information? A more detailed discussion of this problem has been given by Cleveland (2010).

There is no simple solution to this epistemological problem, and we can say that it is unavoidable that a simple, linear representation based on an input/output approach gets into trouble when dealing with the perception and representation of a complex self-organizing system. The joint production dilemma is just one of the consequences of the inadequacy of simplistic representations applied to the analysis of complex energy networks. Another example of this systemic problem is represented by the phenomenon of impredicativity (chicken–egg paradox). It is discussed in detail in Chapter 6, where we address the problems faced when trying to carry out a net energy analysis of the quality of primary energy sources.

2.3.7 The neglect of power: the time dimension of energy flows

> The treatment of capital and time in Energy Analysis can be simply stated: there isn't any. That is to say, that there is no mechanism for representing value capital or for representing time.
>
> (Jones, 1989, p. 350)

Before closing this chapter, we want to flag another systemic problem found with the first generation of energy analysis, and that is the neglect of the time dimension associated with energy flows. This problem originates in early developments in classical thermodynamics where the time dimension was purposefully ignored (Appendix 1). However, it is important to be aware that the process of conversion of energy input into useful energy (applied power) requires the existence of a structural organization, that is, power capacity or technical capital, capable of realizing such conversion in a finite time in the first place.

This systemic neglect of the time dimension can be explained by the avoidance of addressing the concept of 'force' in the original field of energetics. This neglect was necessary to avoid the epistemological troubles associated with the issue of scale. In fact both the concepts 'force' and 'power' require us to explicitly address the issue of scale (see Appendix 1). Because of this purposeful avoidance both in the emerging field of energetics and in the more structured field of thermodynamics, both the inputs (quantities of enthalpy) and outputs (quantities of work) are measured in energy units, none of which carry any reference to time dimension.

The neglect of the issue of power in energy analysis is all the more bizarre if we consider that one of the pioneers and most active scientists in this field in the 1970s, H.T. Odum, was an outspoken advocate of the idea that the analysis of the energetics of living systems (including socio-economic systems) should be based on the study of power and not on the study of energy. As observed by Hall and Klitgaard, (2012, p. 243): 'Howard Odum has taken the concepts one step further by arguing that it is not just the net energy obtained but the power, that is, the useful energy per unit of time, that is critical.' As a matter of fact, H.T. Odum suggested that the maximization of power was the guiding principle to explain the evolution of metabolic systems (Odum and Pinkerton, 1955; Hall, 1995). However, following the above-mentioned developments in the field of energetics/thermodynamics, the concept of power was simply discarded from energy analysis.

We examine the theoretical aspects and the practical implications of the issue of power in detail in Chapter 5. The concept of power is central to our proposed approach for multi-scale integrated assessment of societal metabolism, and is formalized in the second part of this book. In our accounting we take the point made by H.T. Odum seriously and we study energy flows (supplied and required) across compartments per unit of human time.

3   The aggregation of energy flows at the national level

In this chapter we address the epistemological challenge posed by the analysis of energy flows at the level of the whole society. Nowhere is this challenge more evident than in the generation of national energy statistics. We will pinpoint important discrepancies in existing national datasets of energy statistics made available to and widely used by the public. We specifically focus on electricity (section 3.1), which is an energy input of exceptionally high quality and demands the use of specific conversion factors when accounting for its production from a given mix of primary energy sources.

The controversial issue of how to aggregate different energy forms in national energy statistics points at the existence of a deeper epistemological problem: the existence of logical bifurcations in the meaning of the relative numbers (section 3.2, page 57). For an accounting protocol to be useful to describe energy flows within a society, it must adopt more than just one *numeraire* to quantify the various relevant aspects of its energy metabolism: the gross energy requirement of the whole (the black box) and the specific net energy requirements of the relevant parts (sectors) operating within.

3.1 The headache of electricity accounting

3.1.1 What is so special about electricity?

When looking for a unified protocol of national energy accounting, one of the major sources of trouble is the challenge of how to account for electricity. As a matter of fact, the term electricity is ambiguous in itself, because it does not correspond to an exact definition of one unique energy form. Associated with the term electricity we find the following semantic categories of energy forms: (i) a particular formalization of kinetic energy (electric current) measured in ampere (A), (ii) potential energy (electric potential) measured in volt (V), and (iii) *vis electrica* or electric power output, which is a combination of the former two energy forms (the given potential multiplied by the given current). This third interpretation of the term 'electricity' is the more common one in energy analysis and can be measured using the formal category of 'electric Watt', a measure of electric power expressed in volt-ampere (VA), or, alternatively, in kWh, a measure of a sort of mechanical energy corresponding to the amount of power output generated over a period of one hour. As regards the distinction commonly made in thermodynamics between the two non-equivalent energy forms of thermal energy and mechanical energy, we can safely state that electricity belongs to the latter.

One of the pioneers of energetics, James Prescott Joule, became famous for proving that it is possible to establish fixed conversion factors between quantities of energy of different forms. That is, we can eventually find conversion factors between quantities of heat (e.g. measured in Btu), mechanical power (e.g. measured in Joule) and electricity (e.g. measured in kWh), after handling the complications related to the distinction between continuous currents and alternating currents. However, one must always keep in mind that the possibility of establishing a conversion factor between two energy forms does not eliminate the fact that the two energy forms still belong to different semantic categories.

As a matter of fact, those who have tried to quantify differences in energy quality among energy forms using thermodynamic narratives have proposed the concept of exergy (see Box 3.1). They are clear that electricity has an extremely high quality as energy form: '*electrical energy is in theory totally convertible to work*' (Dinçer and Rosen, 2007, p. 338). Their conviction is such that in their accounting engineers assume that electricity has the same value as the physical work 'exergy': 'For electricity, the energy and exergy values are identical, since electricity does not carry any entropy...' (Wall, 2003, p. 128).

Indeed, to make the conversion from chemical potential energy to *vis electrica*, fuel has to be converted into heat energy and hence consumed. The resulting heat energy is then converted into mechanical energy using the Rankine cycle, and the mechanical energy is in turn converted into electricity (see Figure 1.2, page 20). For this reason, the generation of electricity from chemical potential energy (fossil energy), via thermal energy, must entail important energy losses. When looking for mechanical energy 'a joule' (a measured quantity) belonging to the semantic category *vis electrica* is more valuable than 'one joule' (a measured quantity) belonging to the semantic category thermal energy (the input of enthalpy in the Rankine cycle), which can be associated with chemical potential energy (fuel input). Accepting the point that *vis electrica* (or electric power) and thermal energy are energy forms of distinct quality, we face the challenge of generating a system of accounting that can handle the co-existence of different flows that are measured all in joules (or Btu of kWh) but have different qualities. Clearly we can sum numerical assessments of these flows referring to different energy forms, all represented in joules, into a single number, but such a summation would obscure the qualitative differences of the different energy forms considered and may generate numbers meaningless for the study of societal metabolism.

3.1.2 Accounting protocols for electricity production in energy statistics

The unsubstantiated claim made by Rankine that in energetics it is possible to establish a series of quantitative equivalences between all types of energy forms within a unique system of accounting has generated the widespread belief that in

Box 3.1 The basic rationale associated with the concept of exergy

Exergy is defined as the maximum amount of work that can be produced before coming to equilibrium with a reference state of the environment (Ertsvag, 2001; Ayres *et al.*, 2005; Al-Ghandoor *et al.*, 2009). When this rationale is applied to the analysis of the quality of an energy input – e.g. a quantity of thermal energy entering as an input in a thermodynamic cycle such as the Rankine cycle represented in Figure 1.2, page 20 – then the concept can be used to define an index of quality for such an input. The classic example used to explain this concept to students (in relation to the concept of thermal entropy) is that the temperature at which a given amount of heat is available does affect its quality. The mantra then says that a given quantity of heat Q available at 300 degrees Celsius (°C) is more valuable than the same quantity of heat Q available at 30°C. The standard explanation for this statement is that the quantity of heat Q if available at 300°C makes it possible to generate steam and operate a turbine, whereas the same quantity of Q at 30°C is of little use – it is a degraded quantity of heat. It should be noted that this neat explanation works only if we take as reference state the environment we are living in, since the thermodynamic definition of exergy makes explicit reference to the characteristics of the environment – 'before coming to equilibrium with a reference state of the environment'. As a matter of fact, the quantity of heat Q at 300°C may result useless to generate work if the process would take place in an environment in which the temperature is 300°C! In addition, the quantity of heat Q at 300°C is useful only if we have a device capable of converting such a heat into an output of mechanical work and if we need such work. Prehistoric human beings or people stranded on a remote island without technology could not make use of such a quantity of heat. A more technical discussion on the impossibility of using the exergy concept to define, in substantive terms, quality indices for energy forms used as input by metabolic systems is given in Appendix 1.

energy analysis it is possible to use generic quantitative assessments (e.g. expressed in joules) to get a unified representation of any network of energy transformations, no matter how complicated.

For instance, the United Nations Technical Report, *Concepts and Methods in Energy Statistics* states:

It is therefore logically permissible and economically necessary to have an overall accounting framework in which all sources of energy – or at least those relevant to the analysis – can be expressed in a single accounting unit so that the flow of each can be traced from its origin in production or imports through transformation to delivery (with or without transformation) to exports or to inland final energy users.

(UN, 1982, section G §13)

We argue that what the UN Technical Report, *Concepts and Methods in Energy Statistics* claims as being 'logically permissible and economically necessary' is actually a mission impossible.

If we want to convert energy quantities referring to the same energy form (e.g. calorific value) but expressed in distinct measurement units (e.g. J, kcal or Btu) we do not face any epistemological problem in making the conversion. For instance, when dealing with quantities of fuel used for generating heat, then 1kcal = 4.186J = 3.9683Btu.

However, the situation is different if we are dealing with the conversion of energy forms of different kinds. A given quantity of energy, e.g. 1J, may refer to different semantic categories (gross energy requirement or energy carrier), or refer to different kinds of energy forms (thermal versus mechanical energy). In the case of electricity generation with a coal fired power plant we may have an assessment referring to one quantity of energy associated with a flow of energy input (gross energy requirement expressed in the form of a requirement of chemical potential energy over a year) and another quantity of energy associated with a flow of electricity output (mechanical energy per hour). This scenario presents a crucial predicament for quantitative analysis. When two quantitative assessments of energy, even if both expressed in joules, refer to different semantic categories (flow of thermal energy versus flow of mechanical energy), the summation of these two numbers is meaningless, even if there is no dimensional inconsistency. They can only be reduced to each other (referring both to the same semantic category), within a specific grammar and using a conversion factor. This conversion factor requires us to consider different pieces of information (data) coming from observations carried out at different scales. That is, when two quantities of energy refer to distinct semantic categories, it is irrelevant that they can be expressed in the same energy unit– e.g. J, kcal, Btu, kWh. In order to be summed one of the two quantities has to be corrected for a quality factor, but then the resulting sum is meaningful only in relation to the criterion chosen to determine the equivalence factor. If we need mechanical energy, then 1J of electricity is more effective than 1J of natural gas. But if we need heat for warming water, then 1J of natural gas is more effective than 1J of electricity. We saw in Chapter 2 that in the 70s the problem of accounting of electricity was solved by converting joules of electricity in their thermal equivalent (the energy required for producing electricity using fuels). However, after performing this operation the quantitative result is no longer a direct measurement of 'energy quantities' carried out at a local scale. That is we can measure a certain quantity of electricity going into a refrigerator in VA, e.g. 100MJ. But then when using the thermal equivalent we obtain a different number, e.g. 300MJ of thermal equivalent (using a conversion factor 3.0/1). This quantity is determined by the choice of production rules made by the analyst. For example, the chosen conversion factor (3.0/1) may reflect the characteristics of the conversion process used as a standard. For instance, we can justify this by saying that 3.0/1 was the average conversion factor thermal energy/electric energy in Greece in 2003. But we could have chosen another standard and therefore another conversion factor, for example the average conversion factor thermal energy/electric energy in Spain in 2003 (2.6/1). Therefore, the resulting quantity of energy (the thermal equivalent) is a gross energy assessment no longer based only on the information gathered at the local scale (the actual flow of electricity measured in VA at the point of use – 100 MJ) but it depends also on the choice of the analyst (the decision of using either 3.0/1 or 2.6/1 for the conversion). This is the reason why, in energetics, we have to discuss carefully the production rules used for quantitative assessments: with each aggregation or correction based on equivalence factors we are reducing the original quality of the data input.

Hence, every time we deal with quantitative assessments of 'energy forms' it is crucial to define whether or not we are dealing with quantities of the same kind and from the same semantic category. According to the Joint Committee for Guides in Metrology (JCGM/WG2, 2008) a measurement unit should be 'a real **scalar quantity,** defined and adopted by convention, with which any other quantity of the **same kind** can be compared to express the ratio of the two quantities as a number' (p. 6, emphasis added). According to this definition, measurement units can only be used for handling the quantification of energy forms of the same kind (potential chemical energy with potential chemical energy, kinetic energy with kinetic energy, etc.). This requires that the two energy forms, measured with the same unit, must share the same measurement scheme. For example, the level of horsepower (measured in a unit of power such as kg.m/s or hp) of horses may be compared to the level of horsepower of engines if we measure for both the mechanical power output with the same measurement scheme, for instance, pulling a weight for a certain distance at a certain speed.

However, if we assess the power output of a car (a system supplying mechanical power) or a light bulb (a system supplying luminous flux) by simply multiplying their 'power levels' measured in Watts (W = J/s) by the time of application (s), we obtain quantities of 'joules' that are derived neither from a direct measurement of mechanical power nor luminous flux. Such a numerical assessment is based on the application of a dubious production rule. What is the meaning of measuring the power output of mechanical power and luminous flux in the same unit? When considering them as power outputs do they have a common measurement scheme?

These questions are important since data reported in the tables of energy statistics are generally referring to: (i) different semantic categories (primary and secondary energy); (ii) energy forms of different kinds: primary energy sources of different kinds, such as fossil energy and crude oil (chemical energy mapping onto thermal energy), wind energy and hydropower (mechanical energy mapping onto electricity); and secondary energy of different kinds, such as thermal energy and electricity. In order to effectively handle this information, we have to establish a flexible grammar. That is, an integrated set of expected relations among the values assigned to energy quantities belonging to the semantic and formal categories used to characterize the various energy forms of different types. Only in this way can we become able to generate appropriate protocols of accounting according to the purpose of the analysis (for a detailed discussion of the concept of grammar in the analysis of metabolic systems, see Giampietro *et al.*, 2011). Indeed, this pre-analytical definition of a flexible grammar is a prerequisite for the production of any set of (national) energy statistics. An example of such a protocol of accounting is presented in Part II.

The accounting of electricity production is invariably central to any grammar willing to characterize the production and use of energy carriers of a country. When electricity is exclusively produced from the conversion of heat, the problem is, in principle, easy to solve – at least, if we are interested in the gross energy requirement. One can use the quantity of thermal energy (associated with chemical potential energy) used to produce a unit of electricity (mechanical energy) as the conversion factor in the accounting of the thermal energy equivalent.

The problem is generated when we also have to deal with what is called in the OECD/IEA-*Energy Statistics Manual* (2004) 'non-thermal electricity', which is defined as: '…the energy obtained from devices driven mechanically by air or water (wind, hydro, wave, tidal, etc.). In almost all cases the mechanical force present in the moving parts of the apparatus is used to generate electricity (there are of course a few exceptions such as pumping water from windmills)'.

In relation to this point, in our view, it is very disturbing that important systemic differences exist in the present accounting protocols for electricity of major international agencies, supplying data sets of national energy statistics. For example, the energy statistics of BP and the US Energy Information Agency use a method that is different from the one adopted by the International Energy Agency (IEA) and Eurostat. These differences are illustrated in Figure 3.1.

The protocol followed by BP statistics is based on the logical criterion of the opportunity-cost method, or partial substitution method. This method boils down to the accounting of virtual quantities (in joules) of primary energy source equivalent (thermal energy form such as tons of oil equivalent) per joule of *vis electrica* (a form of mechanical energy): a flat conversion factor of 2.6/1 is applied to any quantity of electricity entering the system without concomitant consumption of fossil energy sources. In practical terms this method follows the traditional accounting method used by the pioneers of energy analysis in the 1970s. On the other hand, the protocol followed by IEA and Eurostat is based on the logical criterion of the physical energy content method illustrated below. Note that we indicate electricity, a flow of electric power measured in VA or kWh, as *vis electrica* in order to avoid confusion with other possible interpretations of the term electricity and to stress its high quality.

The application of the BP protocol is illustrated in the upper part of Figure 3.1. In this example, we imagine the generation of a total output of 278MWh of electric power (equivalent to 1TJ or 10^{12} J of *vis electrica*). According to the scheme (Figure 3.1), of this electricity 50 per cent is produced by a fossil fuel plant, 20

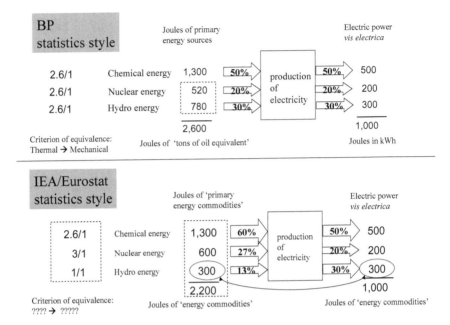

Figure 3.1 The different protocols used to account for electricity in energy statistics

per cent by a nuclear plant, and 30 per cent by a hydroelectric plant. Following the partial substitution method, the accounting of the electric power is based on the consumption of virtual joules of potential chemical energy (the reference for a primary energy source) associated with the production of 1J of *vis electrica* using one given common conversion factor. In this example, we use the conversion factor adopted by BP statistics, determined by the average ratio of efficiency for thermal generation of electricity in the OECD countries (38.5 per cent of the input of thermal energy converted into the output of electricity determining a conversion: 1MWh = 0.086TOE/0.385) entailing a factor of equivalence of 2.6/1. Thus, in Figure 3.1 we see that the production of 1TJ of *vis electrica* is equivalent to the consumption of 2.6TJ of oil equivalent.

In this way, a *common* criterion of equivalence is established to handle the accounting of the non-equivalent non-thermal energy forms (hydroelectric, nuclear, wind, etc.) used to produce electricity. With this protocol we obtain the obvious result that the amount of electricity measured in term of joules of *vis electrica* (1TJ of electric power for society) and that measured in terms of joules of primary energy source equivalent (2.6TJ of oil equivalent) refer to different semantic categories.

Two features of this accounting protocol deserve attention. First, the composition of electricity production in terms of *vis electrica* (in kWh) by source (50 per cent fossil energy, 20 per cent nuclear, and 30 per cent hydroelectric) remains the same whether we express the amount of electricity in joules of gross energy requirement (TOE associated with the thermal equivalent) or in joules of mechanical power for society (the actual supply of *vis electrica* to the grid). Second, both the sum on the left (summing joules of gross energy equivalent referring to thermal energy) and the sum on the right (summing joules of electric power, the mechanical energy) in Figure 3.1 include only addends belonging to the same semantic and formal categories. They properly sum apples with apples and oranges with oranges.

The International Energy Agency (IEA) and Eurostat, on the other hand, have adopted a new protocol of accounting based on the physical energy content method. To this purpose, a logically challenging semantic category (criterion of equivalence) has been introduced for the accounting of energy flows at the national level, 'joules of energy commodities' (OECD/IEA, 2004). Considering the basic principles of energetics, the semantic meaning of this category is anything but clear. In fact, this category is semantically void: it is used to account and sum together both joules of primary energy source equivalent (thermal energy – apples) and joules of *vis electrica* (mechanical energy – oranges). In our view, the use of this category represents a systemic violation of the laws of thermodynamics as it sums joules of chemical energy to joules of mechanical energy without using any conversion factor.

The grammar behind this new accounting system is illustrated in the bottom part of Figure 3.1. We start off with the same amount and composition of *vis electrica* as in the top part of Figure 3.1. Thus, we have on the right a total of 1 TJ of electric power generated by three types of power plants: 50 per cent from fossil energy, 20 per cent from nuclear, and 30 per cent from hydroelectric plants. When coming to the quality factors (grammar) used to account for these energy flows, we discover some rather bizarre production rules.

The grammar of IEA/Eurostat, based on energy commodities as the semantic category of reference, uses the following production rule: 1J of electric power (*vis electrica*) is equivalent to:

- 3MJ of energy commodities, if the electricity is generated by a nuclear plant. This conversion factor relates to the quantity of energy in the form of heat found in the reactor (OECD/IEA, 2004);
- 2.6MJ of energy commodities, that is the actual ratio of thermal energy to electricity production in a given country in a given year, for the electricity generated from thermal conversions. This conversion factor relates to the amount of chemical energy burned in the power plant per joule of electricity produced;
- 1MJ of energy commodities, if the electricity is generated from a hydroelectric plant. No conversion factor is applied in this case: the kinetic energy of the moving or falling water used in the hydroelectric plant is summed as such, because there is no thermal conversion involved.

Using this so-called physical energy content method to assess the total energy use related to the electricity production of a country (Figure 3.1, bottom part), we find some intriguing features. First of all, the supply of 1TJ of *vis electrica* to the grid corresponds to a requirement of energy equal to 2.2TJ of 'energy commodities', whatever the meaning of this semantic category may be. From this fact, one should conclude that at the large scale (the big picture) joules of *vis electrica* are not the same as joules of energy commodities (the assessment on the right is different from the assessment on the left); but then, at the local scale, joules of *vis electrica* generated by hydroelectric power are considered to be equal to joules of energy commodities.

Second, the assessment of the composition of the electric power production by source (type of power plant), when measured in terms of joules of energy commodities, is heavily biased by the choices made in defining the production rules. In fact, in relation to the hypothetical example given in Figure 3.1, we have a situation in which 30 per cent of the actual electric power entering the grid (*vis electrica*) is generated by hydroelectric plants, whereas the protocol of accounting will assign only a mere 13 per cent of the total energy accounted in terms of joules of primary energy commodities to this source (Figure 3.1, bottom part). On the other hand, nuclear energy producing only 20 per cent of the actual electric power (*vis electrica*) would result as accounting for 27 per cent of the total energy measured in joules of primary energy commodities.

In our view, the most worrying feature of this method of accounting is that the reported sum of joules of primary energy commodities in Figure 3.1 (left part of bottom graph) adds joules of chemical energy (1,300MJ referring to calorific value) to those of nuclear heat (600MJ referring to heat in the reactor) and to those of *vis electrica*, which can be assumed to be a form of mechanical energy (300MJ referring to volt-amperes directly delivered to the electric grid). This summing goes against everything known in energetics and thermodynamics (see the discussion of the definition of differences in quality for different energy forms within thermodynamic cycles given in Chapter 1).

The fact that the IEA/Eurostat accounting protocol makes no clear distinction between gross energy (thermal energy used to produce electricity) and net energy (the flow of electricity: an energy carrier, within the system) and between energy forms of different quality (thermal and mechanical) creates ambiguity. Moreover, it causes a bias in the relative importance given to hydroelectric energy (lack of importance) and nuclear energy (excessive importance). Each joule of electricity produced by nuclear plants is accounted as three joules of primary energy commodity. In this protocol it has been assigned a higher weight than the corresponding virtual quantity of fossil energy. On the contrary, each joule of electricity produced by hydroelectric power – the purest quality of mechanical energy – is considered as just one joule of primary energy commodity as if it were a mere joule of coal.

In Figure 3.2 we illustrate the effect of the two different accounting protocols on the assessment of the relative roles of nuclear power and hydroelectric power in the energy mix of Sweden. The upper graphs refer to the partial substitution

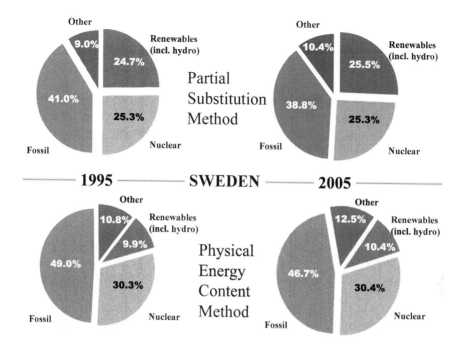

Figure 3.2 The two different assessments of the energy mixes of Sweden (data referring to 1995 and 2005) determined by the use of different protocols of accounting
Source: Sorman, 2011

method (e.g. BP statistics) and we see that when accounting electricity with this method nuclear and renewable energies (where hydroelectric generation of electricity is included) are assigned similar importance (around 25 per cent) in the metabolic pattern of energy in Sweden. On the other hand, if the physical energy content method (IEA/Eurostat) is adopted (lower graphs of Figure 3.2), then nuclear energy seems to be far more important than renewable energies (about 30 per cent versus about 10 per cent), even though this difference does not reflect the actual supply of electricity (*vis electrica*). It is important to remember that, at each year, both methods are representing the pattern of energy use of Sweden starting from the same set of raw data.

3.2 The unavoidable bifurcation within possible energy assessments referring to either primary energy sources or energy carriers

Another problematic feature of existing assessments of energy flows at the national level concerns the distinction between primary energy sources and energy carriers (related to the semantic category of secondary energy). Energy assessments referring to primary energy sources give an external view of the national energy metabolism, while those referring to energy carriers provide a view from within. Both views are essential and important for shaping national energy policy, however we show here that it is impossible to use a method of accounting based on one single numeraire to describe the entire set of relevant energy conversions at the national level.

To illustrate this aspect, we explore in Figure 3.3 (page 59) a detailed representation of the metabolic pattern of energy in Spain in 2003. We adopt here the partial substitution method to assess the requirement of primary energy sources (expressed in joules with oil as a reference). Specifically, we adopt a conversion factor of 2.61/1, which is the actual thermal equivalence calculated as the ratio between the quantity of thermal energy gone into electricity production and the output of electric power in Spain, in 2003.

In our representation in Figure 3.3 we explicitly acknowledge the semantic distinction between primary energy sources, gross energy requirement, energy carriers, and end uses, a distinction that will be discussed at length in the next chapter. In this example we focus on the aggregate pattern of production and consumption of the required quantities of the three types of energy carriers used in the economy: electricity, heat and fuels.

Given the unavoidable losses associated with the conversion of primary energy sources into energy carriers (not only the production of electricity entails conversion losses, but also the production of heat and fuels), it is inevitable that we find a difference in the assessment of quantities of net energy requirement (the local assessment of the mix of energy carriers) and the assessment of gross energy requirement (the total energy which must be controlled by humans in the society to generate the required net supply). For this reason, we necessarily find a logical bifurcation in the quantitative assessment of the 'energy used' in the form of electricity. To obtain such an assessment we must either adopt an external (supply-side) view referring to the gross energy requirement – e.g. measured in Tons of Oil Equivalent (TOE) – or an internal (consumption-side) view referring to the local energy requirement measured in joules of energy carriers (e.g. a mix of *vis electrica,* fuels, and heat).

The external or supply-side view refers to the interface of the whole society, seen as a black box, with its boundaries. If we want to know the amount of primary energy sources (physical gradients) needed to generate the gross energy requirement, then the assessment must necessarily focus on the availability of favorable gradients (primary energy sources) in the environment and/or on the potential to directly import energy carriers.

The internal or consumption-side view refers to the hierarchical level of local conversions of energy carriers into applied power. If we want to know how many joules of energy carriers (defined both in quantity and mix) are needed to guarantee the expression of a given set of functions/end uses, that is the net energy requirement, then the assessment must focus on flows of locally-defined energy inputs that refer to the given mix of energy carriers and the given power capacity in the various compartments of society.

To illustrate this point we represent the various primary energy sources used by Spain on the left side of Figure 3.3. They are grouped into fossil energy sources (oil, coal and natural gas), nuclear energy, and renewable energy sources (wind, photovoltaic, biomass, etc.). These primary energy sources are used in a specific combination (mix) to generate the required supply of energy carriers: a mix of electrical power, chemical energy in the form of fuels, and heat, together representing the net energy available to society. As shown in Figure 3.3 we can represent this external view using a quantitative assessment of the gross energy equivalent (measured in joules of oil equivalent) associated with these primary energy sources. In this way we find a total of 110M TOE. The share of this gross energy requirement that goes into the production of electricity is 36 per cent. On the other hand, using the internal view, the share of the net energy requirement in form of electricity amounts to 18 per cent, assessed in joules of *vis electrica* of the total requirement of joules of energy carriers. Note that in this representation we expressed the quantities of energy carriers in different units (kWh for electricity, MJ for fuels, and kcal for heat).

Thus, if we ignore the existence of the semantic distinction between gross energy and net energy, we face a logical bifurcation (Rosen, 1985) in the quantitative mapping of energy consumption of Spain: 'electricity' represents at the same time 36 per cent and 18 per cent of the total 'energy' used by the country.

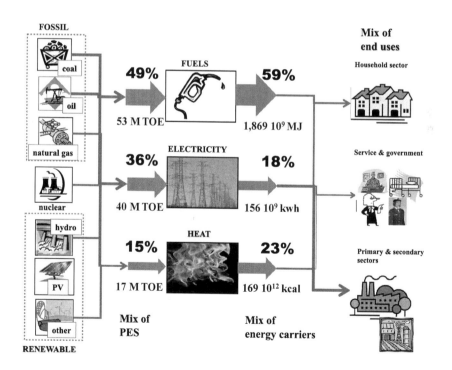

Figure 3.3 The energy metabolism of Spain in 2003 at the national level
Primary data source: Eurostat, 2007

The 'correct' assessment depends on the chosen category used to define quantities of energy, which depends in turn on the level at which we decide to observe the energy flows. At the large scale (the whole society) energy has to be assessed using protocols dealing with gross energy requirement, whereas at the local scale (at the point of use in given sub-sectors or processes) we can only measure flows of energy carriers (net energy requirement) when looking at their requirement or consumption within the various compartments of society.

This logical bifurcation in the quantitative assessment of the relative contribution of electricity is also found when using the physical energy content method (IEA/Eurostat) as protocol of accounting (see Figure 3.1, page 54). Although this protocol pretends that the semantic difference between gross and net energy requirement simply does not exist by introducing the category 'energy commodities'; and that non-reducible differences among energy forms do not exist by summing joules of thermal and mechanical energy without using a conversion factor; the quantitative assessments of energy on the left (gross energy) and the right (net energy) of the accounting scheme illustrated in Figure 3.1 remain non-equivalent.

4 The proper use of semantic and formal categories in energy accounting

In this chapter we first resort to traditional economic accounting (section 4.1) to examine in general the required characteristics of a sound accounting protocol and the criteria for choosing relevant semantic and formal categories. We then apply this information to national energy accounting and define four relevant semantic categories of energy forms, these are: primary energy sources, gross energy requirement, (net) energy carriers, and end uses, each referring to a different scale and narrative about energy conversions (section 4.2, page 67). We then justify our choice of these semantic categories by showing their usefulness in national energy accounting. To this purpose we provide a critical appraisal of several dubious practices common in national energy accounting: (i) linear representations of energy flows (in the form of flow-charts), (ii) use of a single variable for quantifying energy forms belonging to different semantic categories, and (iii) use of a single temporal scale (section 4.3, page 79). Building on the shortcomings of these existing conceptualizations of national energy accounting, we propose a new conceptual approach to energy flow accounting based on the concept of autopoiesis (section 4.4, page 82).

4.1 Learning from accounting in economics

Human beings have a remarkable ability to handle the accounting of complicated monetary transactions. Indeed, it is seldom necessary to explain that different semantic categories of monetary flows cannot be summed. In spite of the fact that both quantities are expressed in the same monetary unit, nobody would add 1,000 US$ of gross revenue to 1,000 US$ of net profit. Similarly, summing monetary assessments belonging to different formal categories is plainly considered a stupidity. Nobody would even think of summing 100 US$ and 100¥ into a total of 200 'monetary units', whatever this latter formal category could possibly mean. Indeed, we all know that it is impossible to study an economic budget using a single category of accounting for monetary flows.

Curiously, the story is quite different when it comes to accounting in energy analysis. As illustrated in the previous chapter, the summing of energy flows belonging to different semantic and formal categories is the order of the day even in official energy statistics. In fact, this erroneous practice has become so deeply rooted that it has profoundly muddled the accounting in energy analysis. For this reason, in this chapter we first point at several basic conceptual distinctions regarding energy flows by drawing on an example of monetary accounting that is easy to grasp, and then analyze the problems found with the conventional linear approach to national energy accounting.

The two basic rules that should be followed when developing an accounting scheme, whether referring to money or energy flows, are:

(1) It is meaningless to sum monetary or energy flows belonging to different semantic categories.

An arithmetic sum simply does not make sense if the addends belong to different semantic categories, even if they are all expressed in the same unit. As already mentioned, 1,000 US$ of gross revenue, 500 US$ of debt, and 300 US$ of net profit cannot be summed into a total of 1,800 US$. Similarly, in energy accounting, we can easily find a caloric equivalent (expressed, for example, in J) for gasoline, horses, orange juice, and slave labour, but it does not necessarily follow that we can aggregate these relative energetic assessments into a meaningful sum. Using the calorific value, we can aggregate items only if they are all associated with the same semantic category 'fuel' and if indeed there is an existing set of energy converters capable of using these items as fuel. Using jargon, we say that we can sum different energy forms only if they fit within a common criterion of equivalence.

(2) It is meaningless to sum monetary or energy flows belonging to different formal categories without using a conversion factor.

Even if we handle quantitative assessments belonging to the same semantic category, for example gross revenue, we cannot simply sum 100 US$, 300 ¥, and 500 €. These three addends refer to different formal categories and, even though each of them is useful in itself to quantify the same semantic category 'gross revenues', in order to sum them we must apply appropriate conversion factors using valid exchange rates (a quality factor required for the conversion). For instance, 1 € was equal to 1.45 US$ on July 4, 2011.

4.1.1 A quantitative analysis of the budget of a charity project

The importance of recognizing and acknowledging these distinctions when developing protocols of accounting is illustrated below with a simple example of monetary flows.

Our example refers to a restaurant that is run within a charity project aimed at financing a housing project for retired musicians. For sake of simplicity and given its charitable status, we assume that our restaurant does not pay any taxes. A simplified accounting scheme of the relevant monetary flows is represented in Figure 4.1.

We start from the lower left box in Figure 4.1, labelled 'cash inflow from customer bills', which shows that a flow of 1,000,000 US$ per year is generated by the clients going to the restaurant. In this accounting scheme this money

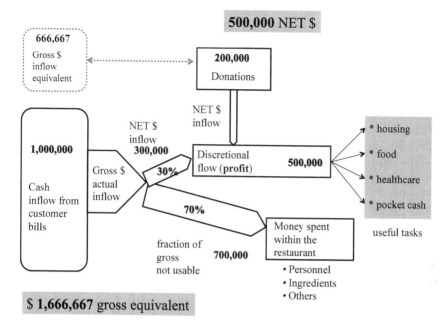

Figure 4.1 An accounting scheme for monetary flows associated with the operation of a charity project using a restaurant to finance a housing project for retired musicians

belongs to the semantic category 'actual gross inflow'. However, only 30 per cent of this flow of money is available to support the housing project (net inflow), as the other 70 per cent has to be invested to cover the operating costs (overhead) of the restaurant and keep the place running.

Independently from the restaurant business, the project also collects donations from people willing to contribute to the cause. This flow of US$ – indicated by the box 'donations' in Figure 4.1 – is readily available: no tax, no overheads, and, therefore, it has a different quality (a much better one) for the charitable cause than the 'cash inflow from customer bills' than US$ belonging to the category 'actual gross inflow'. Thus, in this example the flow of donations (200,000 US$) belongs to the semantic category 'actual net inflow'. Summing the net inflow from the restaurant to that of the donations, the project generates a 'discretional flow' of money (US$ belonging to the semantic category 'net inflow') equal to 500,000 US$, with which the housing project can accommodate fifty retired musicians each year. This discretional (or disposable) flow of money is then used to cover the various useful tasks associated with the assistance of retired musicians, such as providing housing, food, healthcare and pocket money. These useful tasks are analogous to the 'end uses' in national energy accounting.

Undoubtedly one of the questions central to the management of the charity project will be: 'How much money is needed to accommodate 50 musicians in the housing project?' Even with a simple accounting scheme as this one (no taxes, no interests to pay on mortgages), it can be hard to provide one single, unambiguous answer. In fact, it is impossible to give a useful answer to the question using only a single quantitative assessment (sole number). There are several factors involved in answering the question and we need to generate an integrated quantitative representation of the different categories of money flows, considering different semantic and formal categories of reference. In fact, the answer depends on distinct pieces of information: (i) how much money is derived from customer bills; (ii) how much are the overhead costs of the restaurant; (iii) how much money is derived from donations; and (iv) what is the cost of each retired musician?

Consider now the following possible quantitative assessments to answer our question.

Assessment 1

We need 1,200,000 US$/year, referring to the unspecified flow of money into the project in the past calendar year, a sum based on the aggregation of quantities of US$ of gross inflow and net inflow. This amount refers to the overall inflow of money into the restaurant regardless of its source, and summing money referring to different semantic categories: US$ of donations (net inflow) and US$ of customer bills (actual gross inflow). This number may provide useful information in relation to security issues, but it is fairly useless if we want to know more about the number of customers needed or the relative importance of the donations received.

Assessment 2

We need a discretional flow of 500,000 US$. This assessment undoubtedly provides important information on the disposable cash (the overall net inflow) necessary to support the 50 retired musicians (assuming that 10,000 US$/year per retired musician is enough for the purpose). However, this answer still does not provide information about the required number of customers per retired musician.

Assessment 3

We need a 'total gross equivalent' of 1,666,667 US$. For this assessment, we have added an additional semantic category in Figure 4.1, called 'virtual gross inflow' (upper left part of the graph), which converts the amount of money from donations (net inflow) into the corresponding amount of money that would have been spent by 'virtual customers' in the restaurant to generate that same quantity of net inflow ('virtual gross inflow'). To generate this assessment, we use the actual ratio gross/net experienced in the restaurant (the overhead going into the running of the restaurant) on the actual gross flow of money generated by customer bills (200,000/0.30). This procedure is equivalent to the application of the partial substitution method adopted by BP for energy accounting and discussed in the previous chapter, where 1J of electricity (net inflow) is multiplied by a given conversion factor to transform it into joules of primary energy source (oil) equivalent (virtual gross inflow) that would be required to produce that electricity.

Thus, the answer of a 'total gross equivalent' of 1,666,667 US$ is obtained by summing to the actual gross inflow (1,000,000 US$) of last year, the virtual gross inflow (666,667 US$) that would be required to generate the net actual inflow of donations (200,000 US$). Hence, the number 1,666,667 US$ is the 'total gross inflow equivalent' that would be required to generate a net disposable cash of 500,000 US$, if the restaurant were getting its money only from the customers of the restaurant (no donations).

Why would we want to do such a complicated operation? Because in this way, we can express all the monetary flows in a single semantic category of reference: US$ of 'total gross inflow equivalent' (referring to the interaction with customers via customer bills). In this way we can perform a meaningful comparison of our charity project to other projects in different places, where donations may play a more or less important role. This solution may seem elaborate, but it is the only way to compare the performance of different charity projects using a single quantitative assessment. In fact, having fully understood the logic of this mechanism of accounting we can study the differences in performance of various charity projects by looking at specific factors, such as differences in the characteristics of the restaurant (cost of the bill and operating costs) or the relative share of donations. This single semantic category of reference would be meaningless if the charity project were to generate money in different forms – producing fruit preserves or selling second hand books – in different places.

4.1.2 The analogy between economic flow accounting and energy flow accounting

We can reflect now on the analogy between the scheme of accounting of monetary flows in the charity project and the conventional scheme of national accounting of energy flows based on the thermal equivalence of joules of non-thermal electricity. The donations (net inflow) are analogous to the amount of electricity derived from non-thermal sources, e.g. wind power, hydroelectric power, photovoltaic, whereas the gross customer bills are analogous to the calorific value of the energy form of reference (oil) used as a measure for the gross energy requirement (actual gross inflow referring to a economic activity of reference – customer bills of that typology of restaurant). In the analogy, the difference in quality between the two flows, 'actual gross inflow' from customer bills and donations is analogous to the difference in quality between gross energy requirement in thermal energy (measured in relation to the potential chemical energy of oil) and electric energy (the latter is, as discussed earlier, already a form of mechanical energy). Thus, when considering the goal of the charity project –

generating a flow of net profit (disposable net inflow) for the retired musicians –
the dollars of 'actual gross inflows' (customer bills) are less valuable than the
dollars of donations (net disposable cash), because the former entail unavoidable
economic expenses, while the latter can be used as such. Using the analogy we
can say that a flow of thermal energy entails unavoidable losses (the overhead for
running the restaurant) if we want to use it to generate mechanical energy,
whereas the flow of *vis electrica* (electric power) can be considered as mechanical energy.

There is another important observation. The semantic category 'gross inflow'
is important, since it makes it possible to study how much the project is dependent on biophysical flows from its context – the physical flow of customers
entering the restaurant (the outside view). However, the mechanism of aggregation – mixing money from customer bills 'actual gross inflows' and from
donations 'net inflow' into a single category of accounting 'total gross equivalent' – using the category of "virtual inflow equivalent"; implies a loss of
information about the real interaction that the charity project had with
customers. The required number of customers is crucial information, in fact it
determines the quantity of food that has to be purchased, the hours of labour
needed to run the restaurant, the number of tables for seating, the quantity of
rubbish generated, etc. But the use of the category 'virtual gross inflow' hides
the specific role that 'donations' play in reducing the number of required
customers. In fact, customers that give a donation in addition to the payment of
their bill reduce the number of 'required customers' per 'assisted retired musician'. As it will be discussed below, the use of the category "gross energy
requirement equivalent" to generate quantitative assessments muddles the possibility of assigning to a given energy flow a coupled requirement of biophysical
gradients (specific typology of primary energy source). When assessing a given
amount of energy using the category 'Tons of Oil Equivalent' (gross energy
requirement thermal equivalent), we can no longer know whether this amount of
energy is mapping on to real tons of oil, or on to something else equivalent to
the specified number of tons of oil equivalent.

To conclude the discussion of this example, we can say that the overview given
in Figure 4.1 illustrates the basic rationale adopted in the traditional way of
energy accounting established by British Petroleum (BP) statistics in 1951 (BP
2011) and followed by the pioneers of energy analysis in the 1970s.

Note that the discussion of the example of the economic budget in Figure 4.1
only focuses on the distinction between semantic categories. If this charity project were operating in Europe we could keep the same system of accounting (same
semantic categories) but use a different formal category, using Euro (€) instead of
US dollars, to quantify the monetary flows. If a few US customers had paid their
bills using credit card, they would have generated an 'actual gross inflow' for the
restaurant measured in € by those running the restaurant in Europe, and measured
in US$ by those taking out the relative amount from their bank accounts. Indeed,
when remaining within the same semantic category, several formal categories can
be used (as long as the proper conversion factor among numbers is used). In

energy accounting we can choose to use J, Btu, kcal or kWh as long as the protocol is meaningful (we are summing numbers referring to the same semantic category). However, once the unit is chosen, it should be used consistently.

4.2 Different semantic categories for energy accounting

4.2.1 The use of semantic categories translates into a choice of equivalence classes

In addition to the lessons learned from economic accounting and the vigorous debate on this issue in the field of energy analysis in the 1970s (see Chapter 2), several experts have made the point that it is impossible to discuss the quantification of energy transformations without having agreed upon a useful accounting framework and without addressing the existence of different semantic categories useful to quantify different types of energy forms (Cottrell, 1955; Fraser and Kay, 2002; Kay, 2000; Odum, 1971, 1996). In this section, we further build on these arguments and show that whenever we aggregate different energy forms into a single quantitative assessment, using a conversion factor, we do so in relation to just one of the possible criteria of equivalence. Therefore, the price to pay for this aggregation is to neglect other possible attributes of the energy form (other possible criteria of equivalence).

In fact, it should always be kept in mind that the role of a unit of measurement is to define an equivalence class, by providing a criterion of equivalence, which can be used to aggregate different items belonging to the same class. For example, the International Prototype Kilogram (IPK), defined by the International Bureau of Weights and Measures, makes it possible to compare and aggregate kilogrammes of 'apples' and kilogrammes of 'oranges' as they are both compared against the IPK in relation to their common attribute weight. This common attribute (their belonging to the same semantic category) makes it possible to define an effective measurement scheme. Put in another way, the aggregation of apples and oranges is only possible in relation to the specified relevant attribute 'weight' for which the International Prototype Kilogram represents the external referent; it provides a clear definition of an equivalence criterion. However, the fact that 1kg of apples is equivalent to 1kg of oranges in relation to the attribute weight, does not mean that they are equivalent relative to the vitamin C content or relative to their economic value associated with their sales price. So if we are carrying out a quantitative analysis referring to the vitamin C content we cannot aggregate apples and oranges using their mass as the pertinent quantitative variable.

The situation is no different for energy forms. Unless we have a criterion to define an equivalence class as relevant for the quantitative analysis, we cannot aggregate, without having first developed a meaningful system of accounting, 1J of mechanical energy to 1J of electric energy or chemical energy since we do not have a common 'external referent' associated with a meaningful equivalence class. As observed in the previous chapter, using a conversion factor to define a criterion of equivalence between two forms of energy – e.g. expressing a given quantity of hydroelectric energy as being equivalent to a certain quantity of 'oil equivalent' – solves a problem (how to establish an equivalence in relation to a criterion) by generating another one (missing the existing difference between the two forms, when other criteria are considered). In fact, the 'virtual thermal energy equivalent' associated with hydroelectric generation does not generate the same CO_2 emission as the 'actual thermal energy'. Indeed, the widespread belief that 'energy' can be easily measured and aggregated is simply untrue, and this false belief is at the core of the problems plaguing quantitative energy analysis, especially when dealing with complex networks of energy transformations associated with the autopoietic process of socio-economic systems.

Getting back to the example of the analysis of the budget of the charitable project (Figure 4.1, page 63) we can distinguish different pieces of information essential for the analysis:

1 Information referring to the dependence of the project on the context

How many customers are required to operate successfully? How much food is needed by the restaurant? How much waste is generated? This information refers to external referents that are not measured in monetary terms but that are still relevant for the analysis, since these inputs are needed to obtain the gross inflow of money. Therefore, we should expect that an integrated analysis of the charitable project should also include quantitative information dealing with the interface and the interaction that the restaurant has with the rest of the society, providing an 'external view' of the network of monetary flows taking place inside the restaurant. This information is associated with the semantic category of primary energy sources.

2 Information making it possible to handle the difference between gross and net flows (US$ or J belonging to these two semantic categories cannot be summed)

The very nature of any economic venture (based on autocatalytic loops) implies that money has to be invested to get money, and the same applies to energy activities. This implies that both in economics and in nature there are not 'free meals'. For this reason we should be prepared to accept the fact that any assessment of monetary or energy flows entails a logical bifurcation. We can look at the flow using: (i) a larger scale assessment – the gross flow – the overall consumption of energy input required to make available the net flow used in the conversion; and (ii) a local assessment – the net flow – the input used for a given task required for the specific end use. This point is very important for understanding the epistemological problems faced in energy accounting at the national level. When dealing with aggregate quantities of energy expressed in terms of gross energy requirement at the national level we are dealing with quantities of energy that cannot be measured at the local scale. That is, measuring the kWh consumed by our fridge does not tell us anything about the gross energy requirement of the country in relation to the specific quantity of electricity consumed by our fridge. The difference will depend on the losses of generation of electricity (depending on the technology and the mix used in the country to produce electricity), the losses of distributions (depending on the technology, the performance of the grid, the pattern of consumption of electricity in that day), the fraction of electricity imported in the country.

3 Specific information making it possible to handle the analysis of net inflows

What type of monetary flows do we have? What is the mix of the different inflows? What special features can be associated with these different flows? In order to take care of retired musicians the charity project needs a disposable cash flow that can be invested in specific objects or services required for the assistance of the retired musicians. In the analogy with energy analysis this flow is a net supply of energy carriers, which can be used in the different compartments of the society to carry out the required functions. Therefore, this semantic category refers to forms of energy inside the system, which, when observed at the local level, must be compatible with the energy converters used to carry out end uses and in the adequate quantity and quality to guarantee the desirable useful tasks. Moving back to the example of the charity project, depending on the type of assistance required by the musicians, we can imagine that different typologies of economic transactions may be required. In turn this could imply different modalities of payment (e.g. bank transfers, or handing out cash). Thus, even if we can determine the total of net disposable cash to be spent in terms of 'disposable money', depending on the profile of useful tasks to be fulfilled the project has to handle a mix of non-equivalent forms of payment – e.g. 40 per cent of the total disposable money in cash and 60 per cent in bank transfer. In the same way, aggregate quantities of energy expressed in terms of a net requirement of energy carriers – e.g. *vis electrica*, fuels or heat – can be directly measured at the local scale. However, the aggregate consumption of energy carriers of a given industrial sector or the household sector refers to a mix of energy carriers which are measured in quantities of energy referring to energy forms of different kinds (thermal and mechanical), see Figure 3.3, page 59. Again we are in a situation in which we cannot sum as such joules of electricity, fuel and heat without losing valuable information.

4 Information making it possible to analyze how net inflows are used to guarantee the expected final tasks

How are the final tasks guaranteed using the available net inflows? How effective are the net inflows for the final purposes? The information about the set of services that have to be provided by the charity project to the retired musicians, using the net inflow, is essential if we want to study the overall performance of the charity project. However, it is impossible to define a numerical value of either money or energy capable of indicating the performance in relation to the function to be expressed. We can assess the amount of money (or the amount of energy carriers) spent on each task, but 'per se' this does not guarantee that this money (or energy) has been spent effectively. What we can do is define a set of benchmarks that can be used to check whether the characteristics of the pattern of consumption of money or energy in expressing the specific set of end uses are corresponding with the characteristics that would be expected according to previous experience. In general autopoietic systems organize themselves in the form of stable typologies and this makes it possible to look for metabolic patterns expressing predictable characteristics (more on this in Part II).

In the sections below we focus on the conceptual differences between four relevant semantic categories of energy analysis and the different logical criteria associated with the definition of the relative equivalence classes.

4.2.2 Primary energy sources

Semantic definition of the category

According to the first law of thermodynamics energy cannot be created or destroyed. Therefore, in order to be able to generate 'useful energy' for a given purpose, any energy system must have available a favourable physical gradient. These physical gradients are not under human control, that is, they cannot be made by humans. In fact, because of the first and second law of thermodynamics the making of a favourable energy gradient would cost more (in energy terms) than the taking advantage of it. Energy cannot be made. Favourable physical gradients can be either (i) in the form of a given potential for generating trans-formations, such as a chemical potential in a stock of fossil energy, or (ii) a kinetic energy/mechanical form, that is mass in movement such as flowing water or blowing wind (the concept of *vis viva* proposed in ancient times in physics). This difference entails a dichotomy within the category of primary energy sources which has been labelled by UN energy statistics (see Chapter 3) 'thermal primary energy sources' versus 'non-thermal primary energy sources'. Familiar examples of thermal primary energy sources are coal, natural gas, and crude oil (referring to the calorific value determined by potential chemical energy), while examples of non-thermal primary energy sources are waterfalls, tidal waves, or wind.

Using this rationale we can define the conceptual category of primary energy sources in semantic terms as follows. A primary energy source makes it possible to define a mapping between: (i) the quantity of the gross supply of a given energy form of reference usable by society (either thermal or mechanical) and (ii) the requirement of favourable physical gradients making possible the extraction of 'thermal energy' from stocks or the capturing of available mechanical energy from natural sources.

Be aware that when defining in quantitative terms a primary energy source, the quantity of energy associated with the physical gradient represents a gross supply of energy for society, not a net supply. This is a crucial point that we will discuss in detail in Chapter 6, when looking at the theoretical problems of net energy analysis.

For example, 1 TOE represents a mapping between: (i) a quantity of thermal energy (external referent: a quantity of energy referring to the semantic category of thermal energy) under human control; and (ii) a physical quantity (external referent: one ton of oil) whose existence is not under human control – that oil has been produced by natural processes. The quantity of thermal energy can be measured in several ways using different formal categories. For instance, one ton of oil (physical quantity) is considered to be equivalent to 42GJ or 39.8 million Btu or 11,667kWh or 10 million kcal (different formalizations within the semantic category thermal energy quantities). The value of 42GJ is approximate (it is a standard average) as it depends on the quality of the oil. Then this value has been used to define the 'thermal energy equivalent' of 1 TOE. At this point, it should be carefully kept in mind that when we refer to a quantity of 42GJ associated with one ton of oil equivalent we no longer refer to a quantity of primary energy source (we are no longer referring to an actual quantity of oil in the ground), but to an assessment of a gross supply of thermal energy to society. In relation to the example of the restaurant this amount of energy refers to virtual gross inflow and not to actual gross inflow.

For example 42GJ of TOE can be obtained by burning actual tons of oil or by producing with a windmill an equivalent amount of electricity (when adopting the conversion factor). Thus, we can say that when an assessment is expressed in terms of primary energy sources, it is useful to check its compatibility with the external boundary conditions of a given gross energy requirement associated with a given metabolic pattern of society. However, one should be very careful in not confusing assessment of gross energy requirement (amount of energy under human control expressed in primary energy source equivalent) with primary energy sources (a mapping of a quantity of gross energy onto a specified set of physical gradients outside human control).

Formal criterion to define the quantitative assessment of primary energy sources

To fulfil this goal, assessments of primary energy sources should be measured, first of all, in actual physical quantities not expressed in energy units! Common examples of such physical quantities are: tonnes of oil, cubic meters of natural gas, tonnes of uranium, cubic meters of falling water per height and second, solar radiation per square meter.

Using this criterion we can immediately see that Tons of Oil Equivalent are quantities referring to gross energy requirement, but not to PES, in fact, the external referent of 1 TOE is an unspecified quantity of thermal energy (the criterion of equivalence), without any indication to other physical quantities. But accepting this point requires also accepting that primary energy sources belonging to the semantic category of mechanical energy (e.g. falling water, wind power or solar radiation used in photovoltaic) cannot be aggregated with primary energy sources belonging to the semantic category thermal energy. This implies that it is not possible to have a unique quantitative measurement for primary energy sources.

We can only aggregate quantities of primary energy sources of different kinds (mechanical and thermal) by expressing them as gross energy requirement (e.g. tons of oil equivalent), but this implies losing our grip on the biophysical side of it – the characteristics of the physical gradients associated with these PES.

4.2.3 Gross energy requirement (expressed in thermal equivalent)

Semantic definition of the category

The first and second laws of thermodynamics necessitate that in order to control flows of energy we must: (i) have available a certain amount of favourable physical gradients (which are out of human control); and (ii) invest a certain amount of energy flows (under human control) to conduct activities that make it possible to harness a flow of energy carriers. That is, human society, like all other metabolic systems, must invest 'energy flows' to get access to 'energy flows'. Thus, a certain share of the energy controlled by humans has to be invested in producing energy carriers and therefore it is unavailable for discretional activities; it must be used to exploit primary energy sources.

This situation leads to the unavoidable coexistence of non-equivalent definitions of energy requirements for the operation of social systems.

- According to the large-scale or external view, the gross energy requirement, related to the overall quantity of energy (taken from the environment) that must be controlled by society. This includes both the share of energy that must be invested to exploit primary energy sources and the disposable share of energy used for other, discretionary activities (in order to be able to express other metabolic functions).
- According to the local-scale or internal view, the net energy requirement is related to the transformations of energy taking place inside the system (within the parts operating in the black box). An adequate supply of energy inputs must be made available to all internal compartments to guarantee the maintenance and reproduction of the metabolic system.

The aggregate quantity of energy controlled by humans refers to the concept of gross energy requirement. However, as explained before, it is impossible to characterize in quantitative terms such a gross requirement of energy using just a single number. In fact, such an aggregate value can only be calculated by aggregating non-equivalent energy forms (e.g. thermal and mechanical). For this reason, we can only provide an energetic equivalent of the gross energy requirement using conversion factors to correct for differences in quality after having expressed the aggregate value in an energy form of reference (using conversion factors). Indeed, all measurements of gross energy requirement must have the format of 'joules of a specific-form-of-energy-of-reference equivalent'.

Formal criterion to define the quantitative assessment of gross energy requirement

For historic reasons, the standard energy form used for the quantification of the gross energy requirement has always been 'thermal energy'. In particular, the formalization of this semantic category has been and still is based on either the TCE (tonnes of coal equivalent) or TOE (tonnes of oil equivalent). Within the semantic category of reference of thermal energy, both TCE and TOE can be easily converted to each other using their relative calorific value. Another popular unit has been the Btu (British thermal units) and its large-scale equivalent quad (1 quadrillion Btu = 10^{15} Btu). In all these units, the calorific value associated with potential chemical energy is used as the energy form of reference in the measurement. This choice is logical given that for the last two centuries coal and oil have been the main primary energy sources powering human civilization. Not surprisingly then, the BP protocol (partial substitution method) and the pioneers of energy analysis of the 1970s adopted a conversion factor expressing 'non-thermal' joules of electricity (equivalent to injections of mechanical energy into society) to 'virtual joules of thermal energy' (equivalent to a virtual bonus of fossil energy saved by these injections).

4.2.4 Energy carriers

Semantic definition of the category

Energy carriers are the various forms of energy inputs required and used by the various typologies of converters (power capacity) operating in the various sectors of a society in order to execute desirable functions. The sum of quantities of energy associated with the flow of energy carriers represents the net energy required by society. Unfortunately, it is impossible to aggregate different kinds of energy forms (e.g. electricity and fuels) into a single number at the local level. Therefore, the criterion of equivalence associated with the semantic category of energy carrier is determined by the identity of the converter transforming an energy input into a flow of useful energy (applied power) (see Figure 1.3, page 24). The energy carriers of the same type – types of fuels, types of electric power – are 'the same' only for the typology of power capacity using them: gasoline for cars, electricity for refrigerators. For this reason, quantities of energy carriers always have to be measured and defined at the local scale, at a hierarchical level lower than that of the whole society. Using this rationale we can define an energy carrier as follows: An energy carrier is an energy form used, at the local scale, as energy input by a given typology of energy converter (power capacity), which is capable of expressing useful functions (end uses).

For example, 1kWh of electricity represents a mapping between: (i) a quantity of energy input in a usable form (external referent: a measured amount of *vis electrica*); and (ii) the operation of a specific type/class of converter using electricity as input (power capacity) used to generate a flow of applied power (external referent: an electric engine or appliance). This implies that the definition of an energy carrier is impredicative: it depends on the identity of the converter/power capacity operating within the metabolic pattern. For instance, electricity is an energy input in an electric car, while gasoline is an energy input in a regular car.

For this reason, any quantity of energy belonging to the semantic category energy carrier has to be related to the specific identity of the energy converter, which in turn is related to the task to be carried out. In modern societies, we can define three broad categories of energy carriers: (i) energy input in the form of electricity feeding all types of electric converters; (ii) energy input in the form of fuels used to generate applied mechanical power; and (iii) energy input in the form of process heat (e.g. in the home, through industrial processes or in a nuclear reactor).

In addition to the semantic criterion discussed above, there are other important expected characteristics associated with the semantic category of energy carriers.

- Energy carriers not only necessitate the consumption of the physical gradients associated with primary energy sources, but invariably they also require the consumption of a certain amount of other energy carriers for their own production (determining the difference gross → net). That is, the production of energy carriers requires: (i) an input of energy carriers used during their production process (an internal loop of energy carriers to make energy carriers); (ii) a certain investment of capital (power capacity); (iii) a certain investment of human labour (the workers controlling the power capacity during the process); (iv) a given amount of land area, water, stocks of materials, and other environmental services used in the production process (the physical gradients associated with PES); and (v) a certain stress on the environment in relation to the destruction of the favourable physical gradients associated with PES.
- The identity of energy carriers is determined by the identity of the specific energy converters at the local scale. For this reason, when scaling-up the overall assessment of the energy input required by a given compartment (or a given process), it is essential to know the mix of energy carriers required for different purposes within that compartment which in turn depends on the mix of typologies of converters used to guarantee the required power capacity. That is, electricity is energy for a fridge but not for the engine of a jet while the reverse is true for kerosene. Therefore, when moving scale upward, if we aggregate consumption of energy carriers into a single number, we lose a lot of valuable information. Since the functions expressed by the various compartments of society are different, the relative composition of the types of energy carriers required by society is different for different compartments.
- Energy carriers are produced by the energy sector of a society, but they are required and used by *all* compartments or sectors of society, including the energy sector itself. The ratio between the net supply of energy carriers to society and the consumption of energy carriers within the energy sector for its own operation is an important factor determining the quality of PES.

Formal criterion to define the quantitative assessment

Energy carriers can be measured in different measurement units referring to different formal categories useful to define 'energy quantities', all of which can be converted into J, using appropriate conversion factors. For example, the unit kWh is commonly used for electricity, whereas the kcal and Btu are usually used for heat. Note that the distinction between semantic categories of energy forms, such as thermal energy versus mechanical energy, is logically independent from the distinction between the semantic categories gross energy requirement, primary energy sources and energy carriers. Hence, also when operating within the semantic category of energy carrier we still find the same problem as discussed for the category of primary energy sources, namely that the formal assessments of quantities of energy referring to *vis electrica* (mechanical energy) and those referring to calorific value (thermal energy) cannot be summed. As a matter of fact, when operating within the semantic category of energy carriers they cannot be summed not even using a conversion factor (otherwise they would belong to the semantic category of gross energy requirement). As explained before, the possibility of using the same numeraire – e.g. joules – to assess quantities of energy simply does not imply that these quantities are reducible to each other.

To illustrate this point, Table 4.1 has a few examples of different semantic categories of energy forms (left side) and the conversion factors used to move across formal categories (right side).

Table 4.1 Examples of categorization of energy with their conversion factor to joules

Semantic categories of energy forms	Formal categories for quantification	Conversion factor to joule
Electricity (NET) *local scale/mechanical*	kilowatt-hour (kWh)	1 kWh = 3.6 MJ
Heat (NET) *local scale/thermal*	kilocalorie (kcal)	1 kcal = 4,186 J
Heat (NET) *local scale/thermal*	British thermal unit (Btu)	1 Btu = 1,005 J
Mechanical (NET) *local scale/mechanical*	horsepower-hour (HPh)	1 HPh = 2.65 MJ
Aggregate (GER) *large scale/thermal*	tonnes of oil equivalent (TOE)	1 TOE = 42 GJ
Aggregate (GER/NET) *large scale/thermal*	quadrillion Btu (Quad)	1 Quad = 1.055 EJ
Aggregate (GER) *large scale/thermal*	barrel of oil equivalent (BOE)	1 BOE = 5.4 GJ - 6.1 GJ

Looking at the information given in Table 4.1 we can observe again that the fact that different quantities of energy can all be expressed in joules does not imply that they refer to the same logical external referent. In the first item of the list in Table 4.1 we have a form of energy – electricity – measured at the local scale in kWh, having mechanical energy as the energy of reference. In the second and third items of the list we have thermal energy which can be measured at the local scale using different formal categories (either Btu and kcal). Also the fourth item on the list refers to a clearly defined energy form – mechanical energy – measured at the local scale. All these energy quantities are referring to the semantic category of NET energy. They can be seen as a type of information about energy inputs which can be used to carry out specific local tasks.

Starting from the fifth item – Tons of Oil Equivalent – we get a formal category which is used in general for the assessment of gross energy requirement of a large socio-economic system. This is a quantity of energy which is not measured but calculated using conversion factors. Therefore it refers to a large scale assessment: it refers to the semantic category of gross energy requirement. The same description applies to the seventh item – Barrel of Oil Equivalent – which is different from TOE only for the choice of accounting of the physical quantity of oil used as yardstick (difference in the chosen formal category: barrel/volume versus tons/weight). In the case of the sixth item – quad – given the size of the unit (a very large quantity of energy indeed) it is likely that numbers expressed in quads refer to assessment of the gross energy requirement of a large socio-economic system. However, the choice of using a formal category referring to heat implies a certain ambiguity. In fact, as the Btu is a legitimate unit for also measuring flows of net energy (energy carriers belonging to the category of thermal energy), an assessment expressed in Btu could also refer to a large quantity of energy carriers (net energy) – e.g. when assessing the consumption of gasoline over one year of a large socio-economic system.

4.2.5 End uses (useful tasks)

Semantic criterion to define the category

The continuous process of autopoiesis of a given society (as explained in Appendix 1, autopoietic systems are a class of systems capable of producing themselves, as conceptualized by Maturana and Varela (1980)) it requires the continuous reproduction of the existing pattern of activities (structures and functions). This is evident in the maintenance and reproduction of the society through a series of functions expressed across different hierarchical levels: (i) at the local scale, providing the functional/structural coherence of the parts within the black box; and (ii) at the large scale, providing the functional/structural coherence of the whole in its interaction with the context. This maintenance and reproduction can only be achieved by carrying out an integrated set of tasks across the whole and the various compartments, sub-compartments and sub-sub-compartments making up the society, at different hierarchical levels of organization. Within this narrative we can define 'end uses' as the set of useful functions (the useful tasks that have to be performed by society) – defined across different compartments and at different scales – which guarantee a given autopoietic process of society. For these useful functions to be expressed, local flows of applied power (the local conversions of energy inputs via available power capacity and human control into flows of useful energy) must be generated and focused on achieving expected tasks.

Formal criterion to define the quantitative assessment

It is impossible to characterize in predicative and quantitative terms the category of end use using a proxy variable based on energy units (Giampietro and Mayumi, 2004) – see also the discussion in Appendix 2. At times, it is possible to quantify 'typologies of efficiency' for individual simplified tasks, such as hectares tilled, kilometers walked, or tons of water pumped. However, these assessments per se do not provide any specific measure of the (qualitative) value of the performance of the power output for society, unless we are able to assign a "value" to a unit of the biophysical output (the value of tilling one hectare, etc.). Due to the difficulty in quantifying in energetic terms a predicative definition of 'value' of a given task, the assessment of the 'value' of energy services (end uses) for humans has been most often carried out in economic terms (depending on the specific situation) – more in Giampietro and Mayumi (2004).

In conclusion, the category of end use cannot be quantified in substantive terms, when adopting an output/input approach based on the quantification of energy flows, either in relation to the semantic categories of gross and net energy requirements or the categories energy carriers and primary energy sources. As discussed earlier, a biophysical quantification of end uses can only be obtained by checking the characteristics of the pattern expressed by the structural and functional compartments of a given society with the expected characteristics (benchmarks) of a desirable metabolic pattern. However, this approach requires a special tailoring of the chosen quantitative analysis on the specificity of a given situation (as discussed in Part II).

4.2.6 The implications of the existence of different semantic categories

The two conceptual distinctions between gross and net energy requirement on the one hand and primary energy sources and energy carriers on the other hand are extremely important for the analyst to understand as the different meanings of the four semantic categories imply different roles of the relative assessments in the analysis of metabolic patterns. As a matter of fact, the need to distinguish between semantic categories is explicitly acknowledged in the UN Technical Report on Concepts and Methods in Energy Statistics (1982), in which it is stated:

(1) Primary energy should be used to designate those sources that only involve extraction or capture.

(2) Secondary energy should be used to designate all sources of energy that result from transformation of primary sources.

However, the two concepts proposed in the technical report only apparently coincide with our concepts of primary energy sources and energy carriers, respectively. These concepts seem to refer only to the distinction between 'gross energy requirement' (GER) and net energy accounting (NET). As a matter of fact, the technical report only deals with the accounting carried out in energy units. No attention is paid to the problem of how to establish a relationship between the assessments expressed in GER and the associate requirement of physical gradients. As discussed earlier, if we want to provide useful information about the sustainability of the energetic metabolism of a society, when dealing with the assessment of primary energy sources we should track first of all the quantity and quality of physical quantities (either extracted or captured) associated with the mix of primary energy sources considered (e.g. tons of oil, cubic meters of natural gas, tons of uranium, cubic meters of falling water). Then these physical quantities should be coupled to relative quantities of energy that refer to the semantic category 'gross energy requirement'. This confusion in the handling of the semantic categories to which numbers refer can cause a loss of useful information. For example, information which is available to the statistical offices (the required physical gradients associated with PES) is not conveyed to the public when the dataset describing the national energy accounting is provided only in energy units. In fact, the pre-analytical choice of the taxonomy of categories used in the accounting should be based on the following considerations:

1   Can we establish a relation between the required mix of end uses and the corresponding required mix of energy carriers? Which categories of energy carriers are used in the different structural and functional compartments?
2   Can we establish a relation between the required mix of energy carriers and the resulting required gross energy requirement? Which energy carriers are used in the energy sector to exploit primary energy sources? Which categories of energy carriers are supplied by the energy sector to the rest of the society (quantity and mix)?
3   Can we establish a relation between the gross energy requirement and the mix of primary energy sources needed to match the requirement? Which physical gradients (not expressed in energy units) are required by the energy sector to generate the gross supply of energy carriers used by society (quantity and mix of physical gradients not expressed in energy units)?
4   What role do energy imports play in matching the gross energy requirement with net energy requirement? To what extent is the market (imports) of energy carriers (or primary energy sources) used to externalize outside the societal border the effect of internal or external constraints?

At present, we believe that this type of information is available to the statistical offices, but it is not easily accessible when looking at their databases.

4.3 A critical appraisal of the conventional national energy accounting scheme

In this section we examine the epistemological problems associated with the aggregation of energy assessments at the national level (energy balance) on the basis of the conventional, linear representation of energy flows in the form of a flow chart. The purpose of this exercise is to emphasize the importance of organizing the quantitative representation of the metabolic pattern in a way which is compatible with the semantic categories discussed earlier.

Mapping the chains of energy flows in the form of a Sankey diagram or flow chart is the classic way of showing the energy consumption of a nation. An example of such a flow diagram, in which the width of the arrows is proportional to the flow quantity is the classic series of flow charts provided by the Lawrence Livermore National Lab (LLNL, 2011) for the analysis of energy trends in the USA for different years, available at www.flowcharts.llnl.gov/. We want to analyze in detail, here, a specific example of this accounting scheme used by BEES (2008) to illustrate the energy balance of the USA in 2006, shown in Figure 4.2.

The accounting is based on the use of only one semantic category – the gross energy requirement – with thermal energy as the energy form of reference. The formal category chosen for this particular representation for the quantification of energy is the quad, a multiple of the British thermal unit (1 quad = 10^{15} Btu). We focus here on two crucial pre-analytical choices implied by the protocol of accounting used for this representation.

First, since all the assessments are expressed in quads all the energy forms appearing in this diagram are assumed to be of equal quality and, therefore, they are measured using the same unit of energy, supposedly belonging to the same kind of energy form (same semantic and same formal category). Exactly because of this feature, the representation given in Figure 4.2 is also called an energy balance: the sum of the numbers on the very left side of the graph (cumulative width of the arrows entering, that is the gross energy requirement) has to be equal to the sum of the numbers on the very right side (the sum of the widths of the two arrows exiting, that is end uses plus losses).

Second, the Sankey diagram implies a linear representation of the various flows (an input/output approach). This representation is based on the idea that we have a set of energy forms that move through the socio-economic system and during this trajectory, these various energy forms are being converted into *energy* forms of different kinds. Energy enters into the system on the left side (primary energy sources associated to the semantic category of gross energy requirement), then these energy forms are transformed into more useful energy forms (energy carriers associated to the semantic category 'energy carriers') somewhere in the middle, and finally these energy forms are used, on the right side of the graph, to generate energy services (associated with the semantic category 'end uses').

Clearly, these two pre-analytical choices embody both a semantic conflict and a logical inconsistency. In fact during the trajectory the energy flowing through

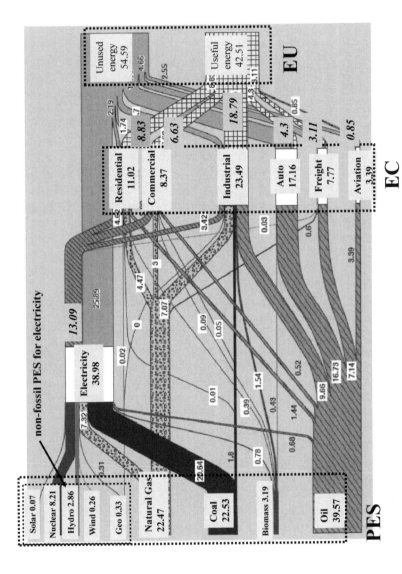

Figure 4.2 The energy balance of the USA in 2006
Source: BEES, 2008; data based on DOE/EIA-0384 (2006) courtesy of Lawrence Livermore National Laboratory and the Department of Energy, June 2007

this diagram changes its semantic identity. The flows change from being perceived and represented as gross energy requirement (on the left), to energy carriers (in the middle), and finally they are converted into end uses (on the right). However, the accounting scheme illustrated in Figure 4.2 ignores this change in quality and treats the quantification of these energy flows as if they were all referring to the same semantic category of 'gross energy requirement – thermal'. In fact, all the energy forms reported in this graph are quantified using quads – as if the same measurement unit could fit all. For example, only 13.09 quads of electricity are entering in the system in the form of energy carriers, whereas 'electricity' is indicated as 38.98 of quads, since it is measured in quads of gross energy coming from the mix of primary energy sources (the reader will recall the logical bifurcation in accounting discussed in Figure 3.3, page 59). This implies that the losses of 25.89 quads in electric generation are referring to quads of gross energy requirement. But then when looking at the second conversion – the movement from 'quads of energy carriers' to 'quads of end uses' we are dealing with losses which are measured in quantities of energy, estimated as a percentage of the quantity of energy carriers used in the generation of useful energy. Therefore, even if these assessments are expressed in quads of energy carriers they refer to 'apples' (losses of gross energy requirement to make energy carriers) and 'oranges' (losses of energy carriers to generate end uses). We argue that ignoring the distinction between the semantic categories of energy flows associated with the structure of the graph (gross energy requirement → energy carriers → end-uses) introduces ambiguity in the quantitative representation. As discussed in the previous section, quantitative assessments of energy forms belonging to different semantic categories can be reduced to each other, but this requires the development of a specific grammar and related, meaningful conversion factors. It requires defining a set of production rules capable of establishing a set of equivalence criteria for the numerical values belonging to different semantic categories.

   An additional problem with this Sankey diagram (Figure 4.2, page 80) is that all the quantitative assessments of energy flows in the accounting scheme are expressed as 'average per year'. This implies that a single scale is used for generating these assessments. Hence, the average values refer to both the whole country (level n) as well as the individual compartments where end-uses are generated. It is logical to assume that the hierarchical level of analysis for studying energy conversions in individual compartments (the flow of energy carriers is defined at the local scale and refers to the category net energy carriers) is different from the scale at which we assess the gross energy requirement of the whole society. For example, the choice of a single scale implies that there is no useful information about the required power capacity in the various compartments of society in order to utilize these energy flows in an effective way. Recall that in order to carry out different functions in different social compartments we not only need specific flows of energy inputs but also specific levels of power capacity. For instance, the industrial sector of a modern society requires a much greater power capacity than the household sector (see the empirical analysis presented in Chapter 9 and more in general Giampietro *et al.*, 2011). Flows of energy inputs are consumed at different paces and in the form of different mixes of energy carriers depending on the specific functions to be expressed. We provide in Appendix 2 a close examination of the accounting protocol used to generate the numerical values given in Figure 4.2. Our analysis shows the logical inconsistency of the choices of semantic and formal categories used in this traditional accounting scheme. In this way we identify the hidden tautological production rule used to achieve success in this mission impossible (including a quantification of the elusive category 'end uses' measured in quads of gross energy requirement). In Figure 4.2 (page 80) assessments referring to different scales, flows of energy of different categories (PES, EC, and EU) and of different kinds (thermal and mechanical) are arranged in a perfect balance using a single set of numbers (everything is measured in quads per year). The price to pay to obtain this result, however, is to presume quads of 'useful energy' (or 'energy services' in other flow charts) and quads of 'unused energy' (or 'rejected energy' in other flow charts) belong to the same category of 'end uses' (more on this criticism in Appendix 2).

4.4 Going beyond the standard linear representation in national energy accounting: looking for a multi-level approach

4.4.1 A multi-level approach requires the integrated use of different quantitative assessments

In this section we show that use of the standard linear representation of energy transformations as used in national energy accounting, based on one single time (year) and space (nation) scale, results in the loss of key information in relation to the possibility of defining expected characteristics (benchmark values) of the various compartments of the socio-economic system. The different functions (end uses) expressed by those compartments in fact can be studied in terms of different requirements of levels of power capacity and different requirements of human activity. In relation to this point, we argue that it is essential to use a multiple-scale approach to generate an energy analysis that is truly relevant for studying the functioning of societies and the feasibility of future trajectories of development. In fact, the qualitative aspects of energy transformations across different levels of organization simply cannot be captured by a pure thermodynamic analysis applied to the society seen as a whole, considered as a black box without any reference to scale or context specificity. These qualitative aspects require an analysis of the metabolic pattern of society across different time and space scales and different functional compartments, and should include:

• The large-scale picture relevant for studying the nature of external constraints: a meaningful assessment of primary energy sources has to deal with the overall conversion of available physical gradients associated with the gross energy requirement, which is in turn used for the production of the required mix of energy carriers.

- The medium-scale picture relevant for studying the nature of internal constraints: a meaningful assessment of energy carriers has to address the nature and the amount of the specific converters employed – the power capacity – in the various compartments of society. The mix of converters used and their respective utilization factors in the different compartments of society will determine both the quantity and composition of energy carriers required for stabilizing the metabolic pattern.

- The small-scale picture relevant for studying the characteristics of specific functional compartments. The analysis of the characteristics of local processes of energy conversions delivering context-dependent specific tasks is required to study the expression of the functions within the various compartments of society. However, the scaling problem implies that the effects of local achievements – the results of improvement in technological coefficients – cannot be translated, as such, up to higher hierarchical levels. For a large-scale quantitative assessment of the effect of changes in end uses we must consider the characteristics of the whole complex network of energy transformations.

As discussed in the previous section and explained in more detail in Appendix 2, if we are serious about a multi-level analysis tracking the flows of energy into the various parts – inside the black box – then we have to consider the difference between assessments referring to gross energy quantity (the energy required at the level of the whole box) and net energy quantities (the energy used in the form of energy carriers within individual compartments). These two assessments are not equivalent, and they require the simultaneous use of different accounting methods.

4.4.2 Debunking the fairy tale of the knowledge-based sustainable economy

In the year 2004, the EU set a strategic goal for the next decade: '... to become the most dynamic and competitive knowledge-based economy in the world capable of sustainable economic growth with more and better jobs and greater social cohesion, and respect for the environment' (European Communities, 2004). This strategic goal implicitly assumes that it is possible to develop and use better technologies, and a more effective knowledge, to obtain a dramatic decoupling between energy use – i.e. gross energy requirement and relative CO_2 emission – and level of economic activity as measured by the economic indicator gross domestic product (GDP).

We argue that belief in this assumption is based on a complete misunderstanding of the biophysical roots of the economic process. Framing the issue in terms of energy analysis, the scientific narrative proposed in the concept of the knowledge economy is based on the misleading idea that technological progress decreases rather than increases the dependence of developed societies on energy and material flows (see also Giampietro and Mayumi, 2009; Giampietro *et al.*, 2011; Murphy and Hall, 2010). Empirical results supporting our argument are presented in Giampietro *et al.* (2011). The concept of the knowledge economy resonates with other fancy concepts (or better ideological beliefs) such as the dematerialization of modern economies and environmental Kuznets curves.

In this section, we try to answer two central questions: Are the numbers currently provided by official energy statistics on national energy flows useful to check the feasibility of the idea of the knowledge-based economy and similar beliefs? What type of information would we need to verify the robustness of such proposed economic strategies?

To this purpose, we illustrate in Figure 4.3 the concept of the knowledge-based economy using the traditional linear representation commonly used in national energy statistics. In this story-telling, energy flows go through a linear set of transformations across different energy forms, as in the energy flow chart in Figure 4.2, page 80, eventually leading to the generation of GDP. The GDP can be interpreted as a quantification and aggregation of final end uses based on an economic narrative. In Figure 4.3, we visualize the underlying idea of the knowledge-based economy. This idea claims that it is possible to achieve a strong decoupling between energy use and GDP thanks to technological progress. According to this vision, if we can dramatically improve the technological efficiency for the first conversion (gross energy requirement → energy carriers) as well as that for the second conversion (energy carriers → end uses), then we can dramatically increase the GDP at the very same moment in which the consumption of primary energy sources and energy carriers is reduced.

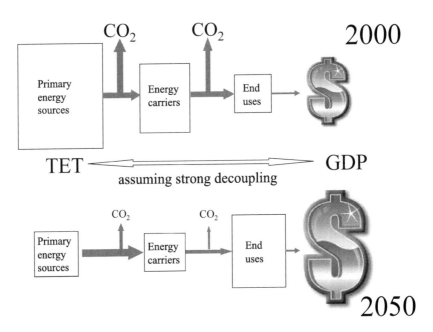

Figure 4.3 The delusion of the knowledge-based economy

What are the different pieces of information that would be required in order to check the feasibility of such a decoupling? To check the validity of the hypothesis of the knowledge-based economy, we should be able to define:

- The feasibility of the knowledge-based economy in relation to external constraints. What is the amount of primary energy sources (physical gradients such as coal, oil, uranium, arable land, falling water), required by this economy?
- The feasibility of the knowledge-based economy in relation to internal constraints. What technical coefficients are required to achieve such a society? This question breaks down into the following ones: What type of supply of energy carriers (electricity, fuels, and heat) will be required – both in overall size and relative composition – to run the knowledge economy? How much power capacity is required? How much human control (hours of labour) is required to run the different sectors of the economy? What end uses are expected in the knowledge economy and how are these end uses different from the present ones?
- The desirability of the knowledge-based economy in relation to internal constraints. What is the set of functions that the society should be able to express in order to achieve a desirable material standard of living? What functions expressed by the knowledge-based economy will be different (and how) from those currently expressed in the post-industrial economy? What currently-expressed functions can be eliminated, without prejudice, to reduce the consumption of energy and resources in the knowledge-based economy?

As argued in the previous sections, the linear conceptualization of energy transformations illustrated both in Figure 4.3 and Figure 4.2 is based on a system of categorization of energy forms and on a representation of their mutual interaction that is not particularly useful for answering any of these three questions, for the following reasons.

First, the ratio gross energy requirement/gross domestic product refers to the whole set of energy transformations (gross energy requirement → energy carriers → end-uses) and therefore does not allow us to distinguish between the losses associated with the first conversion of primary energy sources into energy carriers (the production of energy carriers in the energy sector) and those associated with the second conversion of energy carriers into end uses (the use of energy carriers in the other functional compartments of the society). An analysis of these losses does require heterogeneous inputs of information, which can only be gathered at different hierarchical levels. In relation to the first conversion, we ought to know the technical coefficients of the various power plants (where specific primary energy sources are used to generate a supply of specific energy carriers) as well as the relative composition of primary energy sources currently used for generating the given mix of energy carriers. In relation to the second conversion – that is the efficiency of converters using energy carriers for generating end uses in the various functional compartments of the society – we are dealing with net energy used at the local scale to express specific tasks. For this reason, it is impossible to carry out this analysis by using energy assessments (to find gross energy requirement) which refer to aggregated quantities of energy equivalent defined at the level of the whole country. These losses refer to energy conversions taking place in different compartments, described at different levels and scales and operating under different conditions.

4.4.3 A multi-level approach requires the analysis of autocatalytic loops

Another reason for the weakness of existing energy statistics is that the present taxonomy of categories used to define the sectors of the society associated with end uses does not map onto functional tasks performed by the various compartments of society. In fact the classic representation of energy flows through the economy is based on a division in three sectors: residential and commercial, industrial, and transportation. This selection reflects the traditional expected set of characteristics of the supply of energy carriers to those sectors. The transportation sector requires only liquid fuels, the industrial sector a mix of energy carriers for large industrial plants with the possibility of local cogeneration, and the residential and commercial sector requires energy carriers that have to be delivered to final users. This latter sector includes households, agriculture, commercial buildings, and even the army. Obviously, this sector does not map onto homogeneous functional sets of tasks and activities to be expressed, when considering both the allocation of hours of human activity and power capacity which is required to consume the specific flow of energy carriers.

An overview of the problems related to this traditional choice of end use sectors in the representation of energy flows is given in Figure 4.4. Note that not only do the classic end use sectors not properly map onto relevant functions expressed in society, but they do not even include one of the most crucial functions of society: the generation of energy carriers by the energy sector. As a consequence, when using this representation of the metabolic pattern, it is impossible to define expected benchmark values for required levels of power capacity, labour and required mixes of energy carriers for the expression of functions associated with pertinent compartments (right side of Figure 4.4). Moreover, in this classic representation, there is no detailed information about the consumption of energy in the energy sector beside the losses for the production of electricity.

Again, we see here the historical consequences of the extremely high quality of fossil energy as primary energy source. The original methods of energy accounting were developed for societies based entirely on the exploitation of fossil energy. Fossil energy (and especially oil) is a primary energy source of such high quality (the output/input ratio of energy carriers used in the exploitation is so high) that it was simply not necessary to account for the losses in their exploitation (energy spent in exploring and extracting fossil energy) or refinement to fuels (e.g. the making of gasoline or kerosene). Moreover, since in the vast majority of developed nations the larger share of the oil has always been imported, these losses have never been considered relevant for their national accounting.

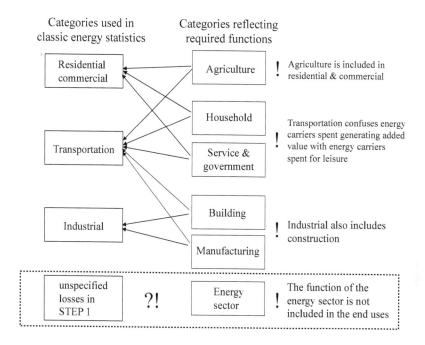

Figure 4.4 The problems with the traditional selection of sectors using energy carriers (on the left side) in relation to functional compartments (on the right side)

4.4.4 Looking at the metabolic pattern of societies as an autopoietic process

Given the systemic problems associated with linear energy accounting, we briefly illustrate below an alternative approach to energy accounting that represents the complex metabolic pattern of developed countries in a more useful way. This more sophisticated representation, which is at the basis of the methodological approach presented in Part II, characterizes four key pieces of information: (i) expected values for the power capacity of the various functional compartments in the socio-economic system; (ii) the quantity and mixes of energy carriers for each compartment; (iii) the quantity and mix of primary energy sources; and, above all, (iv) the nature of the autocatalytic loop associated with the autopoietic process that underlies the reproduction of human society (the metabolic pattern of human societies is generated by energy flows that are stabilizing themselves).

Figure 4.5 shows the various pieces of information required, at different levels of analysis, to provide an effective characterization of the various energy trans-formations associated with the expression of the metabolic pattern of modern economies. It shows how to integrate the information given in Figure 4.2 (page 80) across levels and scales in relation to a process capable of reproducing itself. A detailed discussion of the set of theoretical concepts used to operationalize the

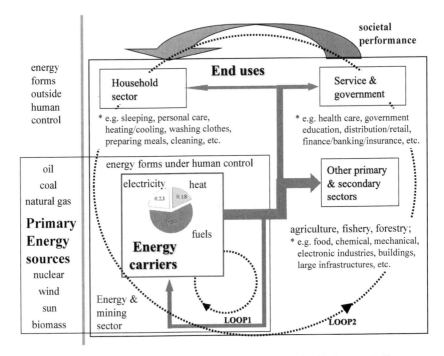

Figure 4.5 An overview of the autopoeitic process associated with the metabolic pattern
of societies

accounting associated with the scheme illustrated in Figure 4.5 has been
presented in Giampietro *et al.* (2011), whereas the specific protocols for quantification are presented in Part II of this book. The main points of our approach,
summarized in Figure 4.5, are:

Point 1

We first characterize the different typologies of primary energy sources, based on
a set of formal categories. In this example, we use the seven categories of primary
energy sources illustrated in Figure 3.3 (page 59) in the analysis of the metabolic
pattern of Spain, but obviously this choice may be changed. This characterization
is done by using a quantification based on both physical gradients (not expressed
in energy units) – e.g. tons of coal, kilos of uranium, tons of water, hectares of
land – and the corresponding gross energy requirement (in thermal equivalent). In
this way it becomes possible to assess the relevance of external constraints – the
biophysical footprint of the energy sector – which may constrain the potential
supply of energy carriers. This information is essential to evaluate energy scenarios that are no longer based on fossil energy.

Point 2

We then characterize the quantities of each type of energy carrier supplied by the various typologies of primary energy sources and the relative performance of the conversions involved. For this purpose, we need to know the connections between individual primary energy sources and the relative flows of energy carriers specified type by type.

Point 3

We then establish a relationship between the mix of primary energy sources and the relative mix of energy carriers. In this type of assessment, we quantify the mix of the required net supply of energy carriers and then establish a relation between this mix and the corresponding gross energy requirement (thermal equivalent). In this way, we can assess the performance of the energy sector relative to the conversion of gross energy requirement (thermal) into net supply of energy carriers. This solution makes it possible to study the characteristics of the internal loop of energy-for-energy (the set of energy transformations taking place in the energy sector) and describe its performance (in terms of required inputs, supplied outputs, power capacity, and labour requirement).

Point 4

We then establish a relationship between the mix of energy carriers, the mix of end uses, the requirement of power capacity, and labour not only at the level of the whole society (level n relative to the black box view) but also at lower hierarchical levels (level n-i), where different compartments and sub-compartments perform the required functions. This analysis of the structural and functional relations of the parts within the black box is necessary to analyze the existence of internal constraints. This result can only be obtained after having defined the taxonomy of expected tasks/functions expressed by the various specialized compartments of society, which can be later on characterized using expected benchmarks. Thus, we need to define a typology of metabolic pattern expressed by the various compartments of society defined across different hierarchical levels.

Point 5

We then calculate: (i) the profile of consumption of energy carriers (mix and amount of each of the carriers); (ii) the requirement of power capacity; and (iii) the labour (or human activity) requirement for each one of the relevant sectors of the economy: household, agriculture, building and manufacturing, service and government, and the energy sector and mining (see Point 6). At this point, the combined use of extensive variables (net energy, power capacity, and human activity) and intensive variables (metabolic rates) makes it possible to define expected benchmarks, for each one of these functional compartments, which can be associated with a desirable expression of required functions. In this way, we can assess the performance of the socio-economic system relative to the conversion of the net supply of energy carriers into end uses.

Point 6

The information about the consumption of energy carriers (mix and amount of each of the carriers) used in the energy sector is crucial for determining the feasibility and desirability of a given metabolic pattern. In turn the consumption of energy carriers in the energy sector depends on the 'quality' of the mix of primary energy sources exploited by the energy sector. This information is essential for the calculation of the energy cost of generating the required supplied of energy carriers in the other compartments. For this reason, the energy consumed by the energy sector should not be considered as a 'generic' loss to be summed to the others. The analysis of the losses taking place in the energy sector is of key importance for understanding the factors determining the quality of alternative energy sources. The flow of energy carriers to be invested in the energy sector in order to guarantee the supply of energy carriers to the rest of the society represents the difference between the gross energy requirement (thermal equivalent) and the net supply of energy carriers. Being related to an internal autocatalytic loop, small differences in this loss may have a non-linear effect on the ratio gross energy requirement/net supply of energy carriers (this is discussed in Chapter 6 and Chapter 7). So we can conclude by saying that the stability of the metabolic pattern depends on the quality of the availability of physical gradients (quality of primary energy sources) and the quality of the technology used in the energy sector for generating energy carriers.

Thus, in conclusion, if we represent the integrated set of energy conversions taking place in modern socio-economic systems over an autocatalytic loop of energy conversions, the categories of energy forms discussed so far have to be referred to the various steps of the autopoietic process, as illustrated in Figure 4.6.

In this way we are no longer representing the metabolic pattern as a set of linear energy transformations, but as an autocatalytic loop of non-equivalent energy forms, which is needed to generate and stabilize the set of structures and functions associated with the operation of modern society. The set of relations illustrated in Figure 4.6 further clarify three important points already mentioned:

1   The semantic category of primary energy sources has ambiguity in its accounting. In fact it requires the simultaneous use of two non-equivalent accounting systems, one referring to physical gradients outside human control and one referring to energy flows under human control. Therefore, an assessment expressed only in energy quantities (e.g. 1TOE = 42GJ) does not belong to this category.

2   If we want to generate a quantitative representation of this metabolic pattern across the various compartments that make up the society and operate at

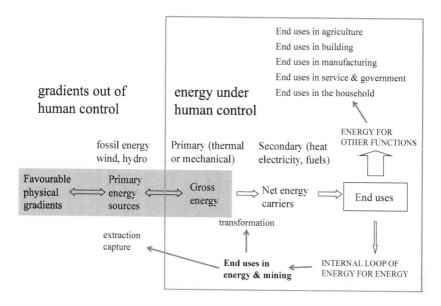

Figure 4.6 The description of the autocatalytic loop of exosomatic energy based on the integrated use of different semantic categories

different hierarchical levels it is essential to address the epistemological challenges implied by this multi-scale analysis. Flows of energy assessed using the semantic category gross energy requirement (semantic category gross energy) cannot be used to study how net energy carriers are used in the various compartments to generate end uses.

3   When studying the viability of the metabolic pattern as an autopoietic process, one immediately realizes that the characteristics of the energy sector, determining the share of the internal loop of energy for energy in the overall pattern of energy uses, are crucial for determining both the desirability and the feasibility of the metabolic pattern. Taking advantage of the gradients provided by primary energy sources, a society has to invest available energy carriers to generate a net supply of energy carriers. At the same time a large fraction of the energy carriers generated in this way is needed to express many other typologies of functions required for both reproducing the society and expressing adaptability outside the energy sector. However, the society can express other activities outside the energy sector only after having established the internal loop of energy carriers used to generate more energy carriers. In spite of the crucial importance of the step of generating energy for energy, not only is the performance of the energy sector not carefully analyzed in energy statistics, but it is not even considered relevant in the overall representation in available data sets.

5 Energy flows under human control

Energy input, power capacity and human labour

In this chapter we abandon the subject of national accounting of energy flows, and focus instead on the energetic analysis of local processes describing transformations of energy flows under human control. In particular, we address the epistemological issues related to the study of general conversions of an energy input into a flow of applied power to fulfil a defined, useful task. Paramount within this local view of energy conversion is the conceptual distinction between energy and power (section 5.1). We show that the unfortunate neglect of this distinction has its historical roots in the early phase of development of the ambiguous field of energetics into the more structured field of thermodynamics, a phase marked by the avoidance of the issue of scale (section 5.2, page 97).

We then argue that, also at the local level (where aggregation practices are of minor importance), acknowledging the issue of the time scale is an essential prerequisite for carrying out a pertinent energy analysis. In particular it requires making a distinction between assessments of efficiency – related only to the direct consumption of energy input – and assessments of the cost of power generation – related to the indirect consumption of energy for the construction and maintenance of power capacity (section 5.3, page 100). For the short time scale it is essential to distinguish between flows of energy input and flows of applied power. The former are generally averaged on a year basis and refer to the extent of the analysis, whereas the latter are averaged on an hourly basis and define the grain of the analysis. We illustrate the importance of this conceptual difference in relation to peak power demands in agriculture (section 5.4, page 101). For the medium time scale it is essential to distinguish between the energy requirement for the building and maintenance of the power capacity required for the conversion (the embodied energy in power capacity or fixed investment) and the energy requirement for the actual conversion of energy input into applied power (the direct consumption of energy input or circulating investment). Another factor that comes into play here is the utilization factor of the power capacity (section 5.5, page 104). In addition to these issues of properly tracking energy transformations across different time scales, we also have to consider the requirement of human labour for process control. In fact, machines cannot operate without supervision. As exosomatic energy conversions invariably require human control, the information on energy input consumption, requirement of power capacity, and utilization factor of power capacity has to be integrated with additional data on the requirement of human labour (section 5.6, page 111). Finally, for a large time scale, the stability of any energy transformation depends on the stability of boundary conditions outside the direct human control (external constraints). An analysis carried out at this large scale requires us to distinguish between renewable energy sources or fund-flows on the one hand and non-renewable energy sources or stock-flows on the other hand (section 5.7, page 115).

5.1 The conceptual distinction between energy and power

> One of the vivid realities of the natural world is that living and also manmade processes do not operate at the highest efficiencies that might be expected of them. Living organisms, gasoline engines, ecological communities, civilizations, and storage battery chargers are examples. In natural systems, there is general tendency to sacrifice efficiency for more power output. Man's own struggle for power is reflected in the machines he builds. In our energy-rich culture, most of our engines are designed to give maximum power output for their size.
>
> (Odum and Pinkerton, 1955, p. 331)

In this passage Odum and Pinkerton make the obvious, but often neglected observation, that in any set of energy conversions aimed at achieving a given purpose, the consumption of energy input is but one of the relevant aspects. Whoever has driven a car knows that it may be possible to consume less gasoline by going slower. However nobody ever opts for going as slow as possible. Actual driving speed is the result of the simultaneous consideration of several distinct aspects, such as safety, speed limit, time pressure, presence of traffic police, cost of petrol, CO_2 emission, etc. Indeed, the dashboard of a car includes several gauges: those providing relevant information related to power (such as the RPM of the engine, the speedometer, and possibly a device to detect radar control) and those providing relevant information related to energy consumption (the petrol gauge). The information related to power (speed) is checked far more often than that related to energy input (petrol level). This example suggests that an integrated characterization of an ongoing process of energy transformation demands something more than a simple energy analysis based on a single quantitative assessment.

In this chapter we claim that a useful quantitative analysis of a given set of energy transformations cannot be based on only a single method of accounting nor on the adoption of a sole quantitative assessment (a number) necessarily referring to unspecified aggregations of flows of energy. A useful quantitative analysis of a given set of energy transformations should be articulated on the basis of semantic and formal categories that generate a useful description of the process and should explicitly address the existing relationship between:

1   Specific local metabolic rates that can be associated to power levels (e.g. how much energy is controlled per hour). These metabolic rates must be defined

and measured at a local scale (e.g. in J/s or MJ/h of energy carriers);

2   Energy input flows consumed over the duration of the analysis (e.g. GJ per capita per year).

Power levels are associated with the internal characteristics of those elements of the system that actually transform energy, that is, the characteristics of the converters of energy input into applied power within the 'black box' and their pattern of use. Power levels deal with questions such as: How many tons of coal can this truck transport in a day over 100km? How fast can this aeroplane travel to Beijing? Assessments of energy input flows, on the other hand, are required to check the compatibility with boundary conditions and are associated with the external constraints faced by the metabolic system. How much energy is required to stabilize the metabolic pattern of New York City during one year? How much food energy is required to feed the crew of this ship during the trip?

Thus, we need to gather two different types of data. An assessment of metabolic rates requires a clear definition of power levels: that is, the rate of the conversion of energy in time which is required locally to generate useful flows of applied power. An assessment of the requirement of energy input requires a clear definition of the type of energy input (electricity versus fuel), the semantic category of energy quantity that we want to measure (primary energy source versus energy carrier), and the time duration of consumption (e.g. the total consumption of energy input over a day, a year or a decade). Here is where the issue of scale sets in. The time scale required to assess flows of applied power is different from the time scale used to assess flows of energy input. Indeed, the time scale is defined by the combination of the time differential (dt) (the grain, related to power) and the time duration (the extent, related to energy input) used in the representation of energy flows.

In our view, neglect of the distinction between power level and energy input flow is one of the major causes of the existing confusion in energy analysis and, therefore, we illustrate here the key importance of properly handling this issue. We want to convince the reader that in order to generate an effective characterization of a given set of energy transformations it is absolutely necessary to adopt an integrated set of assessments that is sufficiently complex to provide all the relevant pieces of information. We start out with a simple example dealing with gender differences in manual labour performance in pre-industrial society. Focusing on the distinction between power level and energy flow, we can detect gender differences in labour performance that cannot be detected when using an assessment based on energy flows alone.

5.1.1 Gender differences in power level and performance of manual labour

It is well known that in pre-industrial societies there is a clear differentiation of labour roles between men and women (Giampietro *et al.*, 1993). In traditional societies men are typically employed for manual activities requiring intense efforts, often for limited periods of time, whereas women and children are predominantly involved in light and repetitive chores. If we try to explain this difference only on the basis of relative energy flows associated with the activities of men and women, neglecting the differences in power level, no justification for this differentiation of roles can be found.

For example, Rappaport (1971), in his energy analysis of the Yanomamö, a pre-industrial society of slash-and-burn cultivators in the forest, writes:

> I found that the performance of men and women in clearing the bush were surprisingly uniform. Although in an hour some women clear little more than 200 square feet and some of the more robust men clear nearly 300 square feet, the larger men expend more energy per minute than women. The energy input of each sex is approximately equal: some 0.65 kcal per square foot.
>
> (Rappaport, 1971)

This quote illustrates the need for using simultaneously non-equivalent quantitative assessments in the energy analysis of human labour. In fact, the uniform performance claimed by Rappaport is based on an assessment of the amount of energy input (food energy used in physiological conversions) consumed per unit of area cleared and averaged over time (work done). This assessment completely ignores the power level at which the work of men and women is delivered, thus missing differences that may be highly relevant for agricultural activities that are typically subject to strong seasonality and bottlenecks in labour supply.

In the following theoretical example (from Giampietro *et al.*, 1993) we show the importance of carrying out an integrated accounting of the energetics of a given task, by simultaneously accounting energy flows in two non-equivalent ways:

- assessment of the energetic cost of a given work (the pace of consumption of energy input); this information is useful to confront the requirement of food energy with external constraints (availability of chemical potential energy);
- assessment of the power output (the power level integrated over a given period of time); this information is useful to compare the actual performance with the required power level of the system (addressing the internal constraints that may limit the generation of the required power output of mechanical energy).

In our example, we consider a task that can be easily quantified using the classic definition of work given in physics: carrying 100kg of sand upstairs, 5m in height. To emphasize the importance of power levels, we consider three different ways to complete this work, each requiring a different power level (see Table 5.1):

1 going 3 times up and down, carrying up one 33.3kg bag of sand each time;
2 going 10 times up and down, carrying up one 10kg bag of sand each time;
3 going 50 times up and down, carrying up one 2kg bag of sand each time.

Table 5.1 The energetics of the same work done at different power levels by men and women

	Case 1 (3 × 33.3kg)		Case 2 (10 × 10 kg)		Case 3 (50 × 2 kg)	
	Men	*Women*	*Men*	*Women*	*Men*	*Women*
	Assumptions					
Physically capable?	Y	N	Y	Y	Y	Y
Physical activity level	7 × BMR	–	4 × BMR	5 × BMR	3 × BMR	3 × BMR
BMR[a]	6.82	–	6.82	5.47	6.82	5.47
Time required (min)	6	–	10	10	30	30
	Estimated energy input					
EI (kJ)	199	–	189.5	190	426	342

Note:
[a] BMR stands for basal metabolic rate. BMR (men) = 0.0485 × Weight + 3.67 (MJ/day) and Weight = 65 kg. BMR (women) = 0.0364 × Weight + 3.47 (MJ/day) and Weight = 55 kg (James and Schofield, 1990)

According to the classic definition of work in physics these three modalities result in the same work done: 100kg of sand lifted up by 5m. However, it is likely that these different modalities are not equally feasible or desirable, either because a specific power level is mandatory – for example, the sand can only be delivered in 33.3kg bags – or because of time constraints – for example, the work must be completed within the shortest time possible.

Indeed, the dataset illustrated in Table 5.1 shows that:

- The three modalities of work entail different time durations for the work to be completed.
- The power level may affect the viability of a given modality. For example, the high power level associated with option A may prevent many women, as well as some men, from performing the task (due to the threshold effect). In this situation, greater physical strength (power capacity) provides a clear competitive advantage.
- Different power levels imply different energy costs for the same quantitative work done (moving up 100kg of sand by 5m). For example, light repetitive effort implying a relatively low power level, as exemplified by option C, gives women an advantage over men in terms of energy cost. Their relatively smaller body size implies a lower overall energy cost (food energy consumption) for the work done. However, this advantageous situation is reversed in situation B, where, according to the equations of physiological conversions, the larger effort required from women compensates for their smaller body size in the overall energy expenditure.

Thus, the modality chosen to perform a given manual task is an essential factor to consider if we want to carry out a meaningful comparison of the energetic performance of the work of men and women. Analyses based only on either an assessment of the work done – which, according to the definition given in classic mechanics, is the same for the three modalities considered in Table 5.1 – or the amount of food energy consumed during the work (see the examples in Table 2.1, page 40) would generate confusion and possibly misleading results.

5.2 Historical roots of the confusion between energy input and applied power

To better understand the existing confusion in the measurement of energy and power we need to go back in time. The first steam engines (such as the engine developed by Thomas Newcomen), operating as early as 1700, had such low efficiency that they could only be used to pump water out of coal mines. Being employed for this task, they obviously operated in the presence of large reserves of available coal and the high rate of energy consumption did not raise any concern. Those that developed better performing steam engines, such as Sadi Carnot and James Watt, worked hard to improve the efficiency of steam engines in order to make them competitive with horses and human workers, and for other possible applications. As observed by Ubbelohde (1955, p. 138): '... if the new steam engines ... were to be sold, their usefulness must be proved to outstrip that of the horse hitherto employed.'

For this reason, many of the experiments of James Watt were aimed at finding an equivalence between the power of a horse – considered a prime mover – and the power of steam engines when performing the same task. In this comparison, horse power (a quantity not referring to an energy quantity but to a force) was used as a reference in comparison with the power of other prime movers, including human workers. This historic setting explains the still widespread use of the horsepower (HP) as a unit of measurement of power, originally expressed in feet-pounds per minute, rather than in the official SI unit, the watt (joule/second). Thus, in its conception the unit of measurement HP was clearly referring to quantities of mechanical energy (applied power) in relation to a given time scale and *not* to quantities of thermal energy (heat) or potential chemical energy (calorific value). By definition, the latter two do not have a time-related component.

The horsepower (HP) was based on the existence of a measurement scheme capable of providing a standard of reference. 'By trials with strong horses used to raise weights, Watt established that a "representative" horse could do mechanical work at the rate of 33,000 feet × pounds per minute' (Ubbelohde, 1955, p. 61). Therefore, Watt's nominal definition of the horsepower reflects the average performance of a representative horse providing an average value of work output per unit of time. This value was then used as a yardstick to assess the power level of other prime movers, just as the International Prototype Kilogram was defined by the International Bureau of Weights and Measures to measure mass.

For example, given that an adult person had to work ten times longer than a horse to achieve the same task, the power level of a human worker (considered as a prime mover) was assumed to be about one-tenth of 1HP. Using exactly the same rationale, the power level of tractors was also derived from a comparison to horsepower. Note, however, that the assessment based on measurement of power output was anything but robust. The relative power output of horses, oxen and camels was not always the same depending on the conditions of work (e.g. the radius of the circles done by the animals as prime movers of a machine) and the factor of equivalence between horsepower and human power was also variable depending on the task to be carried out (Ubbelohde, 1955, pp. 61–62).

Nevertheless, given the historic background, it was perfectly logical that the power capacity of a horse was selected to measure the power capacity of other prime movers doing the same task, thus comparing power capacity with power capacity in relation to a well-defined task (typology of applied power). But, unfortunately, the innocent and legitimate solution to measure power levels in horsepower equivalent not only created a weak yardstick but also generated confusion in the hotchpotch of the emerging field of energetics. The problems were generated by the enthusiasm of the pioneers of energetics who claimed to have found a unifying treatment – including formalizations and accounting schemes – of different energy transformations. With his famous experiments James Prescott Joule determined a factor of equivalence between mechanical energy and heat, two non-equivalent energy forms. He claimed that it was possible to establish a standard conversion factor from a given quantity of output of work in time (a slowly falling weight moving paddle-wheels) into a given quantity of heat flow (the resulting warming up of water in an insulated container). However, this equivalence refers to a set of energy transformation which has as input a given work defined in time and as output a heat flow which must be defined over the same time period. The resulting ratio is calculated on quantities of different 'energy forms' which are flowing in the same time period.

However, if we use this criterion of equivalence without paying due attention to this fact, we can generate dangerous confusion. Since power is defined as a ratio between a quantity of energy and a quantity of time, the horsepower could be converted into Watt (joule/second). For example, using the equivalence of 1HP to 750W, the power level of a human worker (1/10HP) could be expressed as being equal to 75W. This expression of power levels in Watt opened the door to the conversion of assessments of power into assessments of a particular form of energy flow, intended as power output, by merely multiplying the power level, expressed in W, by the time of application, measured in seconds. In this way, after having defined a power output as equivalent to a quantity of energy measured merely in joules, it becomes finally possible to calculate in numerical terms the efficiency of a conversion by using a 'dimensionless' ratio between two quantities of 'energy' (power output/energy input) claimed to have the same dimension. However, the two quantities indicated as output and input are not related to any time dimension and this fact implies a neglecting of the basic nature determining their non-equivalence. So with the establishment of this conversion, a dangerous simplification is introduced by removing the key piece of information about scale associated with the concept of force. As discussed in Appendix 1, an essential goal of the pioneers of energetics and thermodynamics was to get rid of the concept of force, which is clearly associated with the issue of scale.

It should also be observed that Joule's original claim of the existence of a fixed factor of equivalence between thermal energy and mechanical energy is every-thing but robust in relation to the task of generating useful protocols of accounting to be applied to a complex network of energy transformations. In fact, a standard ratio of conversion of mechanical power into heat can only be obtained under controlled settings. As noted at the beginning of this chapter, the equiva-lence is not constant across different power levels. Moreover, the quantitative assessment of the reverse operation – how much heat is required to generate mechanical power? – is much more complicated. As a matter of fact, this second question is the main subject in the analysis of thermodynamic cycles. Exactly because of this problem, classic thermodynamics first of all had to (a forced choice): (i) define a set of ideal transformations (purposely neglecting the issue of time scale) in order to be able to ignore the implications of variation of power levels; and then, later on, (ii) introduce the second law in order to deal with this asymmetry in the transformation of heat into mechanical power and vice versa.

In conclusion, after having accepted the dubious assumption that it is possible to establish a 'substantive equivalence' between joules of power output (joule = watt × second) and joules of thermal energy, the quantitative accounting of ener-getics became increasingly muddled because a single quantitative unit – the joule – was, and still is, being used to handle the accounting of the relationship over two non-equivalent energy forms: power output (mechanical energy which must be transformed at a given power level, the value of which will affect the ratio) and energy input (thermal energy measured in general as an inflow of potential chem-ical energy). In this way, one may decide to ignore the obvious fact that in order to convert quantities of energy input (e.g. 1J of gasoline) into a given quantities of mechanical energy output (e.g. 1J of applied power) you must have first of all a device providing enough power capacity to match (or even better, exceed) the power level at which the conversion takes place. It is here that the concepts of time and power level get back into the picture.

On the other hand, a method capable of establishing a quantitative 'equiva-lence' between applied power (output) and energy input (input) proved very useful for calculating the efficiency of engines. An energy output (expressed in joules of mechanical energy) could be divided by an energy input (expressed in joules of chemical energy/thermal energy equivalent), generating a crisp ratio measuring their efficiency.

Unfortunately, the general acceptance of this equivalence implied that the concept of power capacity was systemically ignored from the quantitative analy-sis of thermodynamic transformations. More details on the historic reasons for the neglect of the issue of scale and the purposeful ignoring of the concept of force in the science of energetics are provided in section A.1 of Appendix 1.

5.3 Exosomatic energy flows under human control and the issue of time scale

Modern societies massively replaced human power with machine power. As a matter of fact, the incredible transformation of society that took place with the industrial revolution is intimately related to the changing role of human activity within the socio-economic process. We find that after the industrial revolution, in contrast to what was going on in pre-industrial society, human activity is no longer used to provide flows of applied endosomatic power – flows of applied power generated by physiological conversions carried out by human muscles. It now has the function of providing control (information flows) over flows of applied power generated by exosomatic devices – machines converting energy input into applied power outside the human body, but still under human control. We will get back to the distinction between exosomatic energy and endosomatic energy when introducing the concept of the exosomatic metabolic pattern in the second part of the book. What is important here is that the massive switch to exosomatic power generation implied a radical change in the role of human activity in relation to both the work done within the economic process (e.g. tilling the soil, processing goods, transporting commodities) and the activities carried out within the household sector (e.g. commuting, preparing meals). In particular it implied an important fact, very relevant for energy analysis. Earlier, in the example of the division of labour between men and women, we saw that when dealing with the endosomatic conversion of energy input (food) into applied power (human labour) there is a fixed relation between: hours of human activity, available power capacity, and requirement of food. The relation between these quantities is given by the physiological characteristics of human beings. After defining the typology of a human being – an adult male of a given body size – we can calculate the power output per hour of activity, the energy consumption, his power capacity. However, when dealing with the generation of exosomatic flows under human control, the situation changes dramatically. The relation between energy input and hour of human activity depends on the level of power that is made possible by exosomatic devices. In the same hour a worker can control a flow of 5MJ of energy input transformed into applied power, or a flow of 5,000MJ of energy input transformed into applied power. The ratio depends on the amount of power capacity controlled by the worker (a mobile phone versus a jumbo jet). So we can say that the generation of useful exosomatic energy flow requires the availability of three factors: (i) an energy input (measured in joules); (ii) power capacity (measured in kW); (iii) human control (measured in hours). However, we cannot define a priority among the relative quantitative relation of these three factors.

For this reason, if we want to study the network of flows of exosomatic energy under human control within a socio-economic system it is important to study the relationship between these three factors. In relation to this task (as illustrated in more detail in Part II) we can define a variable, called exosomatic metabolic rate (EMR_i). EMR_i describes how much exosomatic energy (energy carrier) is going into power generation in relation to a given task *i*, per unit of human activity (HA$_i$), is needed to provide control in relation to that task *i*:

$$EMR_i = ET_i/HA_i$$

In this way it becomes possible to deal with the following questions.

- How much power capacity is required for a given task?
- What are the implications of the existence of possible thresholds of power level that limit the viability domain of a given activity?
- How much human activity is required for controlling a given flow of applied power generated by using this power capacity?
- What are the economic and biophysical costs to produce, maintain and reproduce the required power capacity?
- How much energy goes in direct consumption (energy input locally transformed into applied power) and how much energy is consumed indirectly (embodied) for the construction of the power capacity?

In the rest of this chapter we illustrate a series of conceptualizations that make it possible to deal with this list of questions. We emphasize here that in order to deal with all these questions one must be able to combine information referring to different relevant scales. An assessment of the average requirement of energy input over a year, even if expressed in the form of a quantity of energy divided by time, does not say anything about the power level at which the given energy input must be used, let alone about the stability of the supply of energy input, or the lifespan of the engine associated with the power capacity that is required by the process.

5.4 Energy conversions at the short time scale: facing peak power demand

It is well known that agricultural operations may be subject to seasonal labour bottlenecks depending on the choice of agricultural techniques. In order to study the implications of these peak labour requirements we must adopt a temporal scale for the analysis that is smaller than the year basis that is typically used to calculate average values. Thus, when considering human labour (endosomatic power) we not only need to know the total energy consumption averaged over a year, but also the number of hours of work required month by month for specific tasks.

Consider the case of a small farm that practices a cultivation technique requiring 2,000 hours of human labour per hectare per year. This represents, more or less, the labour of one person over one year (250 work days of 8 work hours each). Assuming that the farm has a total size of four hectares, it will require a total of 8,000 hours of human labour (1,000 labour days) or the equivalent of four full-time farmers. This refers to the requirement of work hours assessed at the scale of a one year period.

Using the power estimates provided by the work of Watt (the power level of a worker is 0.1HP or 75W) and adopting the concept of energetic equivalence based on the power output (power capacity multiplied by time of use), we can express the output of applied power of an hour of human work in joules (75W × 3,600s). According to this approach, we can thus say that an adult worker generates 0.27MJ of applied power per hour. Following through this dubious approach of expressing power output in an energetic equivalent measured in joules (but please remember that 1J of power output does not refer to the same kind of 'energy' as 1J of energy input) one could define the total applied power required on a yearly basis for the cultivation of the four hectares as 2.16GJ (75W × 1,000 labour days/year × 8 hours/day × 3,600 seconds/hour).

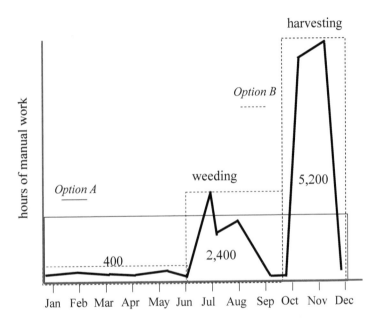

Figure 5.1 The profile of agricultural labour requirement during the year on a hypothetical farm

We now turn to the assessment of the work requirement at the farm on a monthly scale. The profile of farm activities associated with the chosen technique of agricultural production is illustrated in Figure 5.1.

In this case, the profile is characterized by marked seasonality, with two peaks of labour demand for weeding and harvesting: both activities have to be carried out in a determined, limited time window. This profile clearly shows that the yearly labour requirement of 8,000 hours is not evenly distributed over the various months of the year:

- The period from late December to early June (about six months) is characterized by a low labour requirement of less than 2 hours/day. In this slack season a single farmer could easily take care of the four hectares all by himself.
- The summer months, from early June to late August, represent a period with an intense labour demand: 2,400 hours of work in 90 days, related to the weeding season. In this period, about four farmers must be working simultaneously to be able to also cope with the other chores on the farm.
- In autumn, from late September to late November, there is an extreme power peak: 5,200 hours of work to be delivered in 45 days, related to harvesting. This peak requires the presence of at least 15 farmers to secure the harvest and also cope with additional chores on the farm.

How shall we organize the manual labour for operating our four-hectare farm? A first option (A) would be to have the four hectares cultivated by four full time farmers, each working for 250 days/year. Using our quantitative definition above, we find that they generate a flow of applied power of 2.16GJ over a period of one year at an average power level of 300W. A second option (B) would be to have the four hectares cultivated by 15 hired workers working for 67 days/year each, thus generating a flow of applied power of 2.16GJ over a period of one year at a power level of 1,125W.

If we compare the performances related to these two options, we immediately realize the importance of obtaining information about the work to be done at the smaller time scale. Indeed, it is easy to see that the quantitative information of work requirement based on the time scale of the whole year, i.e., 8,000 hours of labour for the four hectares, is pretty useless. In fact, if we adopt a quantitative assessment based on applied power expressed in joules and quantified over one year, the two options would have an identical result (2.16 GJ for 1,000 labour days) even though they are completely different in their ability to cope with power bottlenecks. Option (A), with a maximum power capacity of 300W, would most likely result in the loss of the entire production due to lack of human power in the critical seasons of weeding and harvesting. This scenario also means a huge excess of power capacity in the slack season (see Figure 5.1). On the other hand, option (B), with a maximum power capacity of 1,125 W and a flexible farm labour force, allows the farm to cope with the peak labour demands associated with the techniques of cultivation. The solution of hired work also provides the option (for 14 out of 15 workers) to look for alternative off-farm activities in the slack season. Indeed, for an agricultural society the amount of food produced for society (the energy return of agricultural work) is linked, in a non-linear way, to the ability of that society to harvest an area as large as possible in a limited window of time (as well as to the ability to face other peaks of power demand). The requirement for and availability of power capacity is crucial information.

5.5 The medium time scale: assessing the cost of power capacity

In this section we take a critical look at several aspects of the relationship between the requirement of energy input (e.g. a flow of potential chemical energy in the input) associated with the execution of a given work (task) and the required output of applied power (a flow of power output of mechanical energy) associated with a given power capacity to carry out the given task. As we have seen, assessments of applied power flows refer to internal constraints or characteristics of the converters: to the capability of generating a flow of mechanical energy, and require the adoption of a local scale (descriptions referring to hours, days or months).Whereas assessments of energy input flow refer to external constraints: the availability of an adequate input flow of potential chemical energy, and require the adoption of a larger time frame (average amounts over a year).

5.5.1 Comparing the cost of power generation: living systems versus machines

If we enlarge the time horizon of the assessment we have to consider another relevant flow of energy: the energy required to make and maintain the power capacity required to convert an energy input into a flow of applied power. Thus, a new aspect has to be added to the analysis of the conversion of energy carriers into end uses: the creation and maintenance of the capital fund (e.g. a horse, a tractor) required for energy conversion.

Returning to our farm example, in which we considered thus far only food and human labour (endosomatic power), the energetic cost of power generation would be represented by the amount of food energy required by the workers and their dependents in order to guarantee the required physical labour output over a one year period. As we have seen in Section 2.3.4 (Table 2.1, page 40), when dealing with human labour, this assessment is anything but easy. The exact definition of the cost of power generation is complicated by the epistemological challenge of boundary definitions (leading to the truncation problem) for both the converter (human being) and the set of conversions (see the examples illustrated in Table 2.1, page 40). This issue will be discussed in detail in Chapter 7.

Let's now compare the energetics of power generation of human workers, horses, and tractors in relation to the generation of the power output required by the farm that was used earlier as example (Table 5.2). We adopt a scenario based on the availability of power capacity capable of carrying out the required tasks (15 workers, 4 horses, 1 tractor). For now we intentionally keep using the dubious energy equivalence expressed in joules between assessments of flows of applied power (mechanical energy) and assessments of flows of energy input (chemical energy), in order to clarify key concepts in the analysis of the energetics of power generation.

A comparison of the energetics of horsepower output with that of human power output (Table 5.2) shows that horsepower can generate greater power capacity to carry out the work to be done, translating in a shorter time requirement in terms of hours of work. This difference is especially important when the

Table 5.2 A comparison of the energetics of three kinds of power generation: horse power, human power and machine power

	Human power (15 workers)	Horse power (4 horses)	Machine power (200HP)
Power capacity	1,125 W	3,000 W	150,000 W
Potential applied power (AP) output per year at full capacity	8.1 GJ [a]	21.6 GJ [d]	3,510 GJ [g]
Actual applied power (AP) output per year at given capacity utilization	2.36 GJ [b] capacity utilization 0.29	2.47 GJ [e] capacity utilization 0.11	2.16 GJ [h] capacity utilization 0.0005
Energy input (EI) in GJ per year	87 GJ [c]	92 GJ [f]	15,210 GJ of fossil energy at full capacity [i] 9 GJ of fossil energy at capacity utilization 0.0005 [j]
Cost of power generation (EI/AP) at full capacity	10.7/1	4.3/1	4.3/1
Cost of power generation (EI/AP) at given capacity utilization	36.8/1 capacity utilization 0.29	37.2/1 capacity utilization 0.11	4.3/1 capacity utilization 0.0005 [j]

Notes:

a (15 workers × 250 days × 8 h/day) = 30,000 h/yr, with an energetic equivalent of (30,000 h × 75 × 3,600) = 8.1 GJ/year

b 8,740 h/yr, based on pattern of actual working hours: weeding (90 days × 4 workers × 8 h) = 2,880 h; harvesting (45 days × 15 workers × 8 h) = 5,400 h; other activities (115 days × 1 worker × 4 h) = 460 h. With an energetic equivalent of (8,740 h × 3,600 × 75) = 2.36 GJ/year.

c Based on a population age structure of 65% adults and 35% dependent non-working, and grain consumption of 0.667 kg/day for adults and 0.33 kg/day for dependents, resulting in average per capita consumption of (365 × 0.667 × 0.65) + (365 × 0.333 × 0.35) = (158 + 42) = 200 kg of grain/year; The labour profile in society entails that only 50% of the human food energy consumption can be invested in agricultural work (because of dependent non-working people and alternative activities), therefore the support of 15 workers entails the consumption of '30 people equivalent' of grain supply per year = 6,000 kg of grain, which is equivalent to an energy input (1 kg of grain = 14.5 MJ) of 87 GJ.

d (4 horses × 250 days × 8 h/day) = 8,000 hours/year, with an energetic equivalent of (8,000 h × 750 × 3,600) = 21.6 GJ (over a year)

e 916 hours/year, based on actual working hours: weeding (9 days × 4 horses × 8 hours) = 288 hours, harvesting (17 days × 4 horses × 8 hours) = 540 hours, other activities (22 half days × 1 horse × 4 hours) = 88 hours, with an energetic equivalent of (916 h × 3,600 × 750) = 2.47 GJ (over the year)

f Based on a horse population structure of 85% adults and 15% colts for reproduction, and a grain consumption of 4 kg/day for adults and 2 kg/day for colts. Yearly grain consumption: (365 × 4 × 4) + (365 × 2 × 0.7) = 6,351 kg or 92 GJ.

g Based on 6,500 hours/year (75% of time), with an energetic equivalent of (150,000 W × 3,600 × 6,500) = 3,510 GJ (over a year).

h Actual working hours on crops about 4 hours/year (0.0005 of full capacity), with an energetic equivalent of (150,000 W × 3,600 × 4) = 2.16 GJ (over the year)

i Direct consumption 11,700 GJ/year (3,510 GJ/0.3 – efficiency of conversion) plus indirect consumption (for construction and maintenance, discounted over 15 year life-span) 3,510 GJ/year (15% of the direct energy consumption) ;

j Direct consumption 7.2 GJ/year (2.16 GJ/0.3 – efficiency of conversion) plus indirect consumption (construction and maintenance discounted over 15 year life-span) 1.8 GJ/year (15% of the rate of direct energy consumption).

time dimension is relevant (time is money...) and when human labour can be allocated to other economic activities.

The actual flow of applied power delivery shows that in relation to energy conversion, horses and humans have, more or less, the same ratio of conversion of energy input into applied power (around 36/1). However, it should be noted that this ratio depends on the capacity utilization factor (load factor of the power capacity), which is defined as the fraction of time (in a one year period) that the converter generating power capacity is (since it can be) used for applying power. Animal power becomes really much more convenient when the utilization factor of power capacity is high. Hence, animal power is best used for workloads that are spread in a continuous way over the year, whereas it is not particularly effective for dealing with infrequent and large peaks of work load. This is a problem typical of all living 'prime movers': they need to be fed even when they do not work. As discussed before for the four full-time farmers in relation to Figure 5.1, page 102, both animal and human power are inflexible when having to deal with large variations in requirement of power capacity.

**33HP animal power
(controlled by 5 workers)**

- land for feed
- work for caring them
- smell
- water and soil
- stables

**200HP mechanical power
(controlled by 1 worker)**

- fuel
- maintenance and spare parts
- CO_2 emission
- iron and other materials
- construction of the machine

Figure 5.2 There is no match between animal and machine power for harvesting. A harvester powered by 33 mules versus a 200HP harvester powered by an endothermic engine

Sources: 33 mule harvester picture from the Robert N. Dennis collection of stereoscopic views of Washington state, Wikicommon; the 200HP harvester picture, author 'Rastrojo'

Comparing the energetics of animal power with that of machine power, we find that machine power has a tremendous advantage over animal power. As suggested by the very definition of the machine (a 200HP tractor) a medium-sized tractor can generate the same power capacity as hundreds of horses (Figure 5.2).

Concerning the potential energy cost of power generation (ratio between the flow of energy input consumption, EI, and the flow of applied power, AP), there is virtually no difference between horse power and machine power at full capacity (Table 5.2) when the load factor is 100 per cent – at least in this simplified example based on calculations using the naive energetic equivalence approach. That is, the actual conversion of energy input (expressed in joules) into a flow of applied power (expressed in joules) is similar at full capacity. Note, however, that in the case of horse power the energy input is in the form of food energy (biomass) whereas in the case of machine power it is in the form of fossil energy.

However, a difference in the cost of power generation between animal and machine power becomes plainly evident when the capacity utilization factor (ratio between actual and potential applied power output) changes. As shown in Table 5.2, given the profile of power output requirement of our hypothetical farm, horse power capacity would operate at a capacity utilization ratio of 0.11, whereas machine power capacity operates at a much lower capacity utilization ratio: a meager 0.006 (less than 1/100) of full capacity. However, the effect of a reduced utilization ratio on the cost of power generation is dramatically different in the two cases. In the case of horse power, low capacity utilization implies a major increase in the cost of power generation by almost nine times (from 4.3/1 to 37.2/1), let alone if we consider the requirement of human labour to take care of the animals during the year. In the case of machine power, its under utilization does not generate any difference in the cost of power generation – in this simplified analysis it remains the same: 4.3/1. However, it must be noted that a low utilization factor for agricultural machinery becomes crucial when including economic considerations: due to the low pace of biological flows, the power capacity (machinery) tends to be used for fewer hours per year in agriculture than in the industrial sector, and therefore its economic return tends to be lower (Giampietro, 1997).

Three main points emerge from our comparison between animal and machine (mechanical) power:

1 There is a huge difference in the flexibility of operations

Mechanical power makes it possible to have a very flexible adjustment to serve peak power demand. The advantage provided by machine power capacity lies in the simple fact that we can just switch on the machine when we need it and switch it off when we're done. Once switched off, the machine no longer consumes energy. This is not quite the case with living power generators, such as humans and animals. When facing isolated peaks of power demand during the year – a situation typical of monoculture cultivation – machine power has a tremendous advantage over animal power. As a matter of fact Brody (1945) observed that the population of working horses and mules in the USA dropped from 21 million in 1920 to 14 million in 1945. However, this drop took place only in large farms, whereas animal power remained widely used in smaller farms.

> ...the work of animal power is being replaced by petroleum-power machinery of which about a billion dollars was spent in 1937. While the replacement of horses by machine is rapid on the larger farms, yet perhaps ³/₄ of the US farms – naturally, the smaller units – are operated by horse and mule power...
>
> (Brody, 1945, p. 898)

Large monocultures determine the synchronization in time of activities and thus naturally generate peak power demand (Giampietro, 1997). Paradoxically, this phenomenon, while being a curse for traditional pre-industrial farmers, represents a plus for the highly mechanized farm since it reduces human labour demand. For this reason modern high input farms are naturally associated with a heavy requirement of machine power. On the other hand, as noted earlier, in economic terms, this represents a major burden since the large economic capital is then used only a limited number of hours a year. This explains the systemic need for subsidies for the operation of agriculture in developed countries (Giampietro, 2003; 2008). Still, because of the bonanza of fossil energy (a stock flow energy input), the solution of subsidizing the mechanization of farms is not only possible but also very popular in developed countries.

2 Machine power is the key to economies of scale determining major labour savings

The tremendous power difference between a machine generating 200HP and operated by a single person and an animal-powered device operated by five persons and generating 33HP is illustrated in Figure 5.2, page 106. The power amplification of human labour is 2,000/1 (power capacity of the machine/power capacity of humans) in the first case, and 66/1 (power capacity of mules/power capacity of humans) in the second case. Note that these ratios refer only to actual field operations. When considering the overall average of work on the farm, we have to consider that the maintenance of the machine-powered combine, when out of work, is negligible, when compared with the maintenance of 20 mules during the entire year. Again, we see that it would be absolutely impossible for a single regular-sized household to run a farm of hundreds of hectares – the size of Canadian or US farms – if the power was to be generated only by horses or mules. In particular, it would be impossible to produce corn with less than eight hours of human labour per hectare per year.

3 Machine power is the key to economies of scale determining major land saving

The energy input consumed by animal power is a fund-flow input. This means that a constant and reliable supply of feed for the horse and mule depends on the availability of land, water, fertile soil, sun radiation and favourable climatic conditions. When trying to achieve large power capacity using animal power – e.g. the example illustrated in Figure 5.2 for the USA – the agricultural sector is confronted with a dramatic increase in land requirement for the production of animal feed: '...when the number of farm horses in the United States peaked at 21 million in 1919, at least 20 per cent of the country's farmland was needed to cultivate their feed' (Smil, 2000).

5.5.2 Relevant factors in the study of the cost of power generation

In Box 5.1 we present an example of the various factors that should be considered when analyzing the energetics of a given task: harvesting, using a modern 300HP combine. The analysis shows that an assessment expressed in a sole, plain number – e.g. 4,880GJ/year of energy input consumed in a year – misses a lot of useful information about the energetics of harvesting. A useful characterization should include all the pieces of relevant information associated with the five factors illustrated in Box 5.1.

Box 5.1 An integrated characterization of the energetics of a given task,
     e.g. harvesting, based on the analysis of several factors

In the assessment of the energetics of a given task we must consider both:

* assessments of energy input per year: the averaged request of energy input assessed over a large duration;
* assessments of power capacity: the pace of energy throughput per hour that is required by the particular task to be performed and associated with the specific requirement of power capacity.

Keeping in mind this distinction at all times, we need several pieces of information in order to get a sound energetic assessment:

DIRECT ENERGY INPUT (EI) required for POWER GENERATION

$$EI_{direct} = (PC \times 3,600) \times 1/\eta \times (UF \times 8,760)$$

where:

PC – power capacity of the converter generating power, expressed in Watt or HP
η – conversion efficiency (applied power/energy input)
UF – utilization (load) factor determined by the product of two factors: (i) capacity load – the fraction of the level of utilization of power capacity over the maximal power capacity (averaged over the year); and (ii) operating load – the fraction of the hours of utilization per year

---

INDIRECT ENERGY INPUT (EI) required for POWER GENERATION (for making, maintaining and repairing the required power capacity)

$$EI_{indirect} = PC \times EC/PC \times 1/LEC$$

where:

EC/PC – embodied energy for the construction and maintenance of the converter per unit of power capacity;
LEC – life expectancy of the converter: the discount time used to transform the amount of energy spent in constructing the converter into a flow per year over its lifespan.

TOTAL ENERGY INPUT required for POWER GENERATION = $EI_{direct} + EI_{indirect}$

Note that the direct requirement of energy input is a flow of energy input used by the agricultural sector, whereas the *in*direct requirement is a flow of energy input used by the industrial sector. Hence, these two flows of energy inputs are consumed by different sectors of the economy and may be referring to energy flows of a different nature.

We now provide a numerical example, referring to a harvester of 300HP powered by an endothermic engine fed with fossil fuel with the goal of illustrating our theoretical point:

1 Power capacity: PC = 300 HP = 225 kW;
2 Conversion efficiency: η = 0.3 (only 30% of the fuel is transformed into applied power);
3 Utilization factor: UF = 0.20 (harvester is used for 1,750 hours/year);
4 EC/PC = 6 GJ/HP of PC = 7 MJ/W of PC, based on a requirement of energy for the construction of the machinery, maintenance, repair and spare parts of around 150 GJ/ton of harvester (Giampietro, 2004);
5 Life expectancy of the converter (harvester): LEC = 12 years.

Using these five distinct pieces of information we can calculate the flows of energy input (per year) that are associated to the direct and indirect consumption of energy carriers for power generation:

$$EI_{direct} = (225 \text{ kW} \times 3,600) \times 1/0.3 \times (0.20 \times 8,760) = 4,730 \text{ GJ/year}$$
$$EI_{indirect} = (225 \text{ kW} \times 8)/12 = 150 \text{ GJ/year}$$
Total Energy Input = 4,880 GJ/year

Note that the utilization factor of the power capacity (UF = 0.2 in this example) is an important factor in determining the relation between direct and indirect consumption. The more we use the power capacity and/or the larger is the life span of the converter, the less relevant is the energy spent for its construction.

In the next section we deal with another key factor (in addition to those presented in Box 5.1) in the integrated analysis of the cost of power generation: the requirement of human labour for process control. In fact, the effective use of exosomatic power always requires some type of human control.

5.6 The requirement of human labour to control the use of power capacity

5.6.1 The progressive replacement of human power with machine power

The discussion of the cost of power generation in the previous section clearly explained why modern societies massively replaced human power capacity with machine power capacity in order to gain a tremendous advantage in dealing with peak power demands.

However, as illustrated in section 5.3 still there is a requirement of human activity for controlling exosomatic applied power. In relation to this point we introduced earlier the concept of exosomatic metabolic rate (EMR_i), which can be used to describe the power level at which exosomatic energy is used for power generation, in relation to a given task i, per unit of human activity (HA_i) required for control in relation to that task i. We can measure the unit of human activity in one hour:

$$EMR_i = ET_i/HA_i$$

Now we can write that:

ET_i (energy throughput for task i) = EI_{direct} = (PC × 3,600) × $1/\eta$ × (UF × 8,760)
[as defined in Box 5.1]

HA_i = hours of human activity per year providing control in relation to the task i
[as determined by the type of activity and task]

The variable EMR_i is extremely important to study the desirability and viability of a given metabolic pattern as it allows us to study how the society decides to allocate (i) energy inputs, (ii) power capacity, and (iii) human activity over the set of functions (end uses) required for its own reproduction. In fact, the relation written above establishes a relation over the possible combinations of the three factors: the quantity of ET_i (the energy directly consumed for carrying out a given task i) – an extensive variable; the quantity of HA_i (the hours of human activity required for carrying out a given task i) – an extensive variable; and the value of EMR_i (the power level at which exosomatic energy has to be used in a given compartment in relation to the specific task) – an intensive variable. This basic relation can be applied to the definition of exosomatic energy flows across different hierarchical levels of analysis (and scales) and for this reason is at the basis of the multi-scale system of accounting illustrated in Part II of this book. For the moment we want to simply flag that by introducing this set of relations it becomes possible to interface the analysis of energy flows with other crucial dimensions of analysis, including:

- the economic dimension related to the 'cost' of the production factors involved in the use of energy carriers: (i) power capacity (technical capital) and (ii) labour (human activity in the paid work sector);
- the demographic dimension related to the population structure of society. Of particular interest here is the dependency ratio of a given society, a factor that defines the ratio of 'non-labour hours' (the total hours of children, students, unemployed and retired people, as well as the physiological overhead of workers when out of work) over 'labour hours' (the total hours of human activity allocated to the paid work sector). A large dependency ratio not only implies a relatively low availability of labour hours in general but also a relatively high demand for those available labour hours in the service and government sector (e.g. for education, health care and taking care of older people) and consequently a reduction of the labour hour supply to the production sectors.

As will be discussed in Part II with a more detailed analysis and empirical result, an analysis of the relation over the three factors stabilizing flows of exosomatic energy (energy input, power capacity and human activity) is the key to understanding the relevant characteristics of the exosomatic metabolic pattern of post-industrial society. These societies can guarantee a large production of goods and infrastructure using only a tiny fraction of human activity in the primary and secondary sectors. This is possible only because of: (i) a dramatic decrease in the cost of power generation; and (ii) a dramatic increase in the power levels reached in these economic sectors of society. This metabolic pattern is typically characterized by a population structure determining a dependency ratio of more than 50 per cent (only 50 per cent of the population is of working age). That is the majority of people in post-industrial society are not engaged in the paid work sector. Moreover, those who do work do so for only 20 per cent of their time (e.g. 1,800 work hours/year) (Giampietro *et al.*, 2011). This means that in a typical post-industrial society only one out of 10 hours of human activity is used to control the power capacity in the paid work sector, and that within the paid work sector the economically active population is mainly allocated (more than 65 per cent) to the service and government sector. Indeed, only approximately one out of 30 hours of human activity is used to direct and control the power capacity in the primary and secondary production sectors (energy and mining, agriculture, building and manufacturing). Yet post-industrial society is capable of consuming and producing an impressive flow of resources and goods. This achievement requires the control of huge levels of power capacity (which are orders of magnitude higher than in pre-industrial times) and complex technical infrastructures. A detailed analysis of the metabolic pattern of post-industrial society based on this rationale is presented in the second part of the book.

The dramatic reduction in the cost of power generation, made possible by the combination of technology and fossil energy, brought about important changes also in relation to gender differences in occupation of employment. We saw in Table 5.1 (page 96) that when power capacity is provided by human muscle the energetic of endosomatic power justifies the existence of different work roles between the genders. In this situation typologies of work requiring a high power threshold may give an edge to men. However, in post-industrial society with the changed role of human activity in the socio-economic process from supplier of applied power to supplier of process control, a bias against the labour of women can no longer be justified by biophysical reasons. Whenever the 'value' of human labour is dependent on the flow of information processed during work (driving a 200HP tractor or flying a jet fighter) rather than the flow of applied power delivered, men and women are perfectly equal (Giampietro *et al.*, 1993).

5.6.2 On the concept of energy slaves and excess of stand-by power capacity

As a final consideration referring to the forced and elusive relation between energy input, power capacity and human activity, we briefly touch here upon the concept of 'energy slaves', a popular notion found often in the media to refer to the invaluable role played by machines in modern society (Nikiforuk, 2011). The concept is used to convey the idea that the material standard of living of modern society is supported by virtue of 'virtual slaves', taking the form of machines powered by fossil energy, which guarantee the large supply of energy services delivered to us. We found the following entry on Wikipedia:

> An Energy Slave is that quantity of energy (ability to do work) which, when used to construct and drive non-human infrastructure (machines, roads, power grids, fuel, draft animals, wind-driven pumps, etc.) replaces a unit of human labour (actual work). An energy slave does the work of a person, through the consumption of energy in the non-human infrastructure.
> (http://en.wikipedia.org/wiki/Energy_Slave, accessed June 2012)

Despite this smooth description, so far attempts to quantify the required number of virtual energy slaves per capita resulted in widely differing numbers. Many of the calculations proposed for making this assessment are anything but clear. In some cases the assessment is based on a criterion of equivalence comparing the energy output (a flow of endosomatic energy output) produced by humans to the energy output provided by commercial energy used by machines (a flow of exosomatic energy input – calculated by reducing by a fixed per cent the energy input). However, the assumptions used for such a calculation are far from being credible: human slaves are supposed to work 24 hours a day, 7 days a week and not only do they not require rest, but not even an overhead of dependent population for their replacement. Using this approach the estimated number of energy slaves per person for developed countries is calculated in the range of 100 and 200 (Barker, 2006; Nikiforuk, 2011; World Forum 98, 2012). Buckminster Fuller, the person that to the best of our knowledge introduced the concept of energy slaves in the 50s, developed a more sophisticated method for such an assessment providing a much larger number:

Using Fuller's unit, the average American at the end of the century had more than 8,000 energy-slaves at his or her disposal. Moreover, Fuller pointed out, 'energy-slaves', although doing only the foot-pounds of humans, are enormously more effective because they can work under conditions intolerable to man, e.g. 5,000°F, no sleep, ten-thousandths of an inch tolerance, one million times magnification, 400,000 pounds per square inch pressure, 186,000 miles per second alacrity and so forth.

(taken from: http://www.pbs.org/fmc/book/14business8.htm
Wattenberg, 2012)

But even this assessment of a much larger number of energy slaves per capita necessarily leaves out an important feature. As shown in the example in Box 5.1, power capacity is not the only factor to be considered and defined in order to generate an 'accurate' assessment of the performance of energy slaves. When dealing with exosomatic energy it is not only the actual amount of energy that you are using that matters, but also the 'power' of doing (as much as possible) 'what you want to do, when you want to do it'. A huge amount of stand-by power capacity represented a dramatic boost for the material standard of living of humans in developed countries.

Indeed, putting numbers aside, we can safely state that the truly important contribution of machine power lies in the incredibly large power capacity available to us in our daily life, at our will. This power capacity dramatically reduces the hours of human activity (in form of manual labour) required to carry out specific tasks (e.g. using a washing machine rather than washing clothes by hand, commuting long distances using a car rather than a bike). Therefore, humans can afford to maintain this large exosomatic power capacity and use it only when needed, even if this implies a poor capacity utilization factor. Take the case of a car. A medium-sized car has a power capacity of between 50–200HP (the power of 500–2,000 human slaves based on the equivalence of 0.1 HP) waiting for us to be used. Camper vans or motorboats, used only a few times each year, represent the perfect example of a much larger idle power capacity used at an even lower utilization factor. And there are many other energy slaves waiting for your orders: lifts, air conditioners, water heating, microwaves, televisions, computers – the list goes on. Add to these domestic slaves those providing services outside our homes, for instance in the form of trains, commercial aeroplanes, ambulances whose combined power levels would translate into the equivalence of hundreds of thousands of human slaves. And finally, we should also add the slaves in all other economic sectors who indirectly serve us, that is the power equivalence of the machines used in the industrial sector, the construction sector, and in agriculture and mining, as well as the power plants generating electricity or the tankers carrying crude oil.

The message is that when using the metaphor of energy slaves we should be aware that the extraordinary performance of machine power is not only related to: (i) the increase in the quantity of energy they make possible to use (when using the criterion of equivalence of the consumption of energy input); or (ii) the actual amount of applied power they deliver for us (when using the criterion of equivalence of the work output); but also (iii) the incredible bonanza of potential power capacity waiting for our orders at all times: the associated luxury of a low utilization factor (especially in the household sector). It would simply be unthinkable to make available similar energy services using human beings; the very idea of thousands of human slaves idly waiting for our commands, 24 hours a day, all year long, is absurd unless you were the Emperor of a powerful empire. And even then, it would still be problematic to make a flexible use of the resulting power capacity. Indeed, the potential problems associated with the instability of a large power capacity based on human slaves were clearly evident during the various servile wars of Rome. In the third servile war, the most famous head of rebel slaves, Spartacus, came to lead no less than 120,000 people in a powerful large-scale war against their previous masters. This risk of an organized rebellion is totally absent with mechanical energy slaves.

In fact, the concept of the impossibility of keeping idle a large amount of endosomatic power capacity has been explored by Mendelssohn (1974), in his book *The Riddle of the Pyramids*. Mendelssohn's riddle refers to the fact that the construction of the three pyramids of Giza at a certain point was carried out simultaneously: the ancient Egyptians apparently did not wait for a pyramid to be fully completed or for another Pharaoh to die, to start constructing the next one. According to Mendelssohn's study in Giza, the Egyptians started a new pyramid as soon as the previous one was near completion. The explanation is simple. In the final stage of construction only a small part of the available human (endosomatic) power capacity could be utilized. This required that the large amount of idle human power capacity had to be engaged in doing something else to avoid unrest. Because of the organizational inertia of the Egyptian society, the only possibility to employ this large endosomatic power capacity was the construction of yet another pyramid.

We thus believe that many of the numerical assessments of the energy slaves per capita needed to support the material standard of living of modern society found in literature tend to underestimate the paramount role that both machine power and fossil energy input play in guaranteeing the material standard of living enjoyed in developed societies.

5.7 The large time scale: boundary conditions and the conceptual distinction between fund-flow and stock-flow of energy

When further expanding the time horizon of the analysis we arrive at what is going on outside the black box. At this large scale, we are basically concerned with the nature of the processes generating (or that generated) primary energy sources. At this level we study the stability of existing boundary conditions or the required favourable boundary conditions making possible the supply of the gross flow of energy input consumed by society.

5.7.1 The difference between fund-flow and stock-flow of energy inputs

Building on the concept of metabolic systems, we can say that societies are open systems that can maintain their identity only through a continuous consumption of energy inputs taken from the environment and a continuous disposal of wastes into the environment. Therefore the survival of society depends on the reliability of both the flow of energy input taken from the context (availability of primary energy sources) and the sink capacity referring to the flow of wastes dumped into the context. The availability of an adequate amount of primary energy sources – when considering only the supply side – can be related to a check on external constraints. In relation to this point, the distinction proposed by Georgescu-Roegen (1971) between 'fund' and 'stock' primary energy sources comes in useful. The conceptual difference and its implications are briefly discussed below.

By definition, a fund-flow supply refers to a flow originating from a fund element and that does not entail a change in the characteristics of that fund element. Therefore, the consumption of an energy input coming from a fund primary energy source does not change the boundary conditions experienced by society. For example, we can milk a healthy cow every day, and if we don't overdo it, the cow will remain healthy. If we consider an entire dairy farm producing milk as a fund element, in which there are sufficient calves guaranteeing the replacement of cows and enough pasture for feeding all the cows, then the flow of energy from milk from this self-reproducing dairy farm does represent a stable and reliable supply of energy input for human nutrition. Thus, as long as the fund (the dairy farm) is able to repair and reproduce itself, the resulting flow can be considered a renewable resource.

Completely different is the situation in which we have a stock-flow supply. Consider the consumption of crude oil derived from an underground reservoir. If we start with an oilfield of 1,000,000 barrels and we consume a flow of 10,000 barrels per year, then, after ten years, the stock from which we obtained the input will have changed its identity. After ten years, the original stock of 1,000,000 barrels will have changed into a stock of 900,000 barrels. Therefore, the consumption of a stock-flow of primary energy sources entails a continuous change in the boundary conditions of the system. Hence, when considering both the stock providing the energy input and the system using the energy input, the original representation of the whole system loses its analytical validity in time. Not only the size of the stock changes in time, but also the net amount of energy that can be extracted from the stock (the more the stock decreases the more effort is required to get out the same quantity). For this reason we call an input derived from a stock flow a non-renewable resource.

A cursory reading of this difference might suggest that it is better for us to exploit primary energy sources associated with fund elements rather than stock elements. However, this is not the case. Indeed, for a society it is much more advantageous to exploit stock-flow resources, at least when these resources have high quality (for more on the quality of energy sources, see Chapters 6 and 12). The explanation for this statement lies in the conceptual difference between power and energy (discussed in section 5.1, page 93) and the corresponding internal and external constraints, respectively, that affect the set of energy transformations associated with the metabolic pattern of a society.

5.8 External and internal constraints on the operation of a metabolic pattern

The question we want to answer in this section is the following one: What factors limit the amount of energy that can be used by a society to express a given set of useful functions? We answer this question individuating two classes of factors: (i) factors limiting the total throughput of energy associated with external constraints (both on the supply or the sink side); (ii) factors limiting the total throughput of energy associated with internal constraints (inability to increase or maintain the required power capacity or to control the relative flows of applied power).

5.8.1 External constraints on the set of energy conversions

External constraints refer to the limited availability and/or accessibility of required primary energy sources (e.g. peak oil) and/or the limited sink capacity of the environment to absorb waste generated by energy conversions (e.g. accumulation of GHG in the atmosphere). External constraints are closely linked to the compatibility, or lack thereof, of the biophysical processes expressed by society with the boundary conditions determined by processes outside human control. We face an external constraint when the context can no longer provide what is required from it or is no longer capable of absorbing what is dumped into it. Examples of relevant external factors for the metabolic pattern of society are:

- with regard to fund-flows: shortage of natural resources and ecological services provided by the ecological processes exploited;
- when dealing with stock-flows: the exhaustion of reservoirs of oil, natural gas, or coal on the supply side and lack of absorption capacity on the sink side.

External constraints impose a limit on the amount of energy input that can be consumed by a society. For example, an external constraint is represented by the situation in which a big truck is supposed to carry a large load from Los Angeles to Seattle, but the truck driver cannot fulfill his task because there are no gas stations for refilling the tank.

5.8.2 Internal constraints on the set of energy conversions

Internal constraints refer to the limited capacity of a given society to process available flows of energy input for generating flows of applied power. Internal constraints may be caused by the inability of a given society to process a larger flow of energy, material and resources, should these be available, because of: (i) shortage of technical capital (power capacity) required to keep the overall cost of power generation low; and/or (ii) shortage of human-made capital for providing an adequate control: available technology, know-how, functioning institutions. Thus, internal constraints impose a limit on the amount of applied power that can be generated by society. With regard to our truck driver eager to transport goods to Seattle, an internal constraint would be represented by a situation in which there are plenty of replenished gas stations along the highway from Los Angeles to Seattle, but he does not have a truck big enough to carry our large load or he does not know how to operate the truck.

The distinction between external and internal constraints is essential if we want to carry out an effective energy analysis, given that most countries live through a period of double transition. As explained by Herman Daly:

> The world is moving from an era in which man-made capital was the limiting factor into an era in which remaining natural capital is the limiting factor. The production of caught fish is currently limited by remaining fish populations, not by the number of fishing boats; timber production is limited by remaining forests, not by sawmills.
>
> (Daly, 1994, p. 28)

The development of machine power led to the generation of a huge power capacity with low maintenance cost. This explosion of power capacity was possible because of the concurrent exploitation of fossil energy, an abundant and cheap-to-extract (at least up to the start of the third millennium) form of stock-flow energy input. The lucky combination of these two events lifted, for the richest part of humankind for almost a century, the traditional internal (shortage of power capacity) and external (shortage of energy input based on fund-flow) constraints that previously limited the expansion of human activity on this planet.

Now, in the third millennium, we are living through a situation in which both external and internal constraints are again shaping the trajectory of development of both developed and developing countries, albeit in different ways. Developed countries, with their huge endowment of exosomatic power capacity, presently face the need to curb their overall consumption in an effort to adjust to emerging external constraints, such as peak oil and GHG emission. Much more difficult is the situation for developing countries that still face the need to invest in the generation of additional technological capital – increasing their power capacity in order to ease internal constraints – at the very same moment in which the external constraints are becoming increasingly tangible and they are forced to reduce their overall energy throughput.

In relation to this formidable challenge, we simply do not know what is the optimal strategy to follow; nobody can predict the future when dealing with 'becoming systems' (Prigogine, 1968), which create their own identity in their process of autopoiesis. What we do know, though, is that to understand and deal with this double challenge, it is essential to develop more effective methods of energy accounting capable of characterizing, for various typologies of countries, both (i) the seriousness of the situation in relation to external constraints (e.g. overall requirement of primary energy sources and the resulting types of emissions); and (ii) the seriousness of the situation in relation to internal constraints: the profile of power capacity in relation to the different societal compartments and functions to be performed.

6 Cutting through the confusion in net energy analysis

In this chapter we cut through the confusion existing in the literature around the concept of net energy analysis, in particular with regard to its application to quantify the 'quality' (feasibility and desirability) of alternative energy sources and new energy technologies. In doing so, we build on the various theoretical concepts discussed in the preceding chapters.

In particular, in section 6.1, we start by framing the basic rationale behind the concept of net energy analysis: net energy analysis can only work when there is an autocatalytic loop of energy. Therefore, when looking for quantitative indicators developed within this concept (such as an energy output/input ratio – e.g. the EROI index), it is essential to be sure that both the output flow and the input flow are defined within an autocatalytic loop. However the application of this rationale is often missed when conducting net energy analysis. We use the example of a popular index, the output/input energy ratio of agricultural production, to illustrate the existing confusion about this point.

In section 6.2, page 127 we focus on the key semantic distinctions to make when applying net energy analysis to the assessment of the quality of energy technologies in the form of quantitative indices. We have to make a distinction between: (i) energy quantities associated with primary energy sources (outside human control) and energy carriers (under human control); (ii) energy quantities assessed in joules of gross energy requirement (thermal) equivalent versus energy quantities assessed in joules of energy carriers; and finally (iii) gross supply of energy carriers versus net supply of energy carriers. We present practical applications of indices that have been proposed for the assessment of energy technologies – the energy requirement for energy (ERE) and the energy return on the investment (EROI) – to illustrate possible confusions.

Following on, in section 6.3, page 133, we dig further into technical details. We focus on the epistemological ambiguity found when trying to formalize, with quantitative indices, the rationale of energy analysis. Using practical examples, we show the crucial importance of developing formal protocols capable of handling in an effective way the sticky points of energy analysis: that is, the aggregation of energy flows of different quality and the truncation problem. In particular we stress the peculiar characteristics of a quantitative analysis which has to be carried out on an impredicative loop (chicken–egg paradox).

In section 6.4 we address the implications of the issue of multiple scales, or put it in another way, the implications of the truncation problem for the generation of applications of net energy analysis based on just a quantitative index of quality (e.g. the EROI index). As discussed in previous chapters, when dealing with the analysis of the metabolic pattern of a society – an integrated network producing and consuming energy carriers – it is necessary to generate a family of EROI indices defined at different scales. However, as soon as we abandon the idea of a single indicator, it becomes important to define the criteria for defining the different boundary definitions and the most effective integrated set of indicators to analyze the quality of alternative energy technologies (associated with alternative energy sources).

In section 6.5 we focus on the intrinsic limitations of the use of a single index, within the rationale for net energy analysis, to characterize the desirability and feasibility of an energy technology in relation to the complexity of the metabolic pattern of society. We argue that we cannot possibly expect that a simple output/input energy ratio (a sole number) can provide all the pieces of relevant information referring to the requirement of: (i) external gradients outside human control (outside the society); (ii) energy carriers of different kind (within the society); and (iii) power capacity and human labour (within the energy sector). We show that a thorough energy analysis can only be obtained by carrying out a complex assessment using an integrated set of indicators referring to different criteria of performance and different definitions of boundaries for the observed system.

In section 6.6 we summarize the key points and lessons learned by this critical overview of the applications of net energy analysis in the form of a decalogue for the energy analyst.

6.1 The conceptual foundation of net energy analysis

6.1.1 What typology of energy transformations is required to apply the concept of net energy analysis?

As discussed in Chapter 2, the ultimate motivation of quantitative net energy analysis has always been that of generating quantitative assessments and qualitative indices useful for evaluating or comparing options to inform decision makers. However, given the semantic ambiguity associated with the concept of energy (see Chapter 1) and the epistemological problems inherent in the quantification of energy flows of different kinds across different scales (discussed in Chapters 3 and 4), the various methods proposed for generating quantitative assessments have all been affected by conceptual problems and have contributed to the existing confusion in the field of energy analysis.

The concept of net energy analysis was developed in the 70s as a conceptual tool useful to assess the quality of energy technologies. Herendeen (2004, p. 33) provides the following rationale for net energy analysis based on a loose (i.e. ambiguous) use of the term 'energy': 'Net Energy Analysis – A comparison of the *energy costs* and the *energy produced* by an energy technology such as a coal-mine or photovoltaic panel' (emphasis added). An application of this rationale to the assessment of the quality of primary energy sources and energy technologies has been neatly formulated by Maddox (1978, p. 135): 'The term net energy implies that return on energy investment must be positive for an energy system to be viable. Otherwise, the energy system is an energy sink, consuming more than it produces, and is not beneficial to society at large'.

As an extension, the logical application of the rationale should be that of looking for a net energy limit that defines whether or not an energy supply technology is viable. In this regard, Herendeen (1978, p.145) proposes the following definition: 'Net Energy Limit – the point at which an energy supply technology requires more energy than it produces.' This approach is about looking for a number (a single indicator) capable of providing this valuable information.

About here is where the straightforwardness ends. Indeed, when we get to the actual calculation of the net energy limit, things become fuzzy because of differences in 'quality' among the various energy forms included in the inputs and outputs and the difficulty in defining a clear boundary for the relative assessment. As discussed in the next section society may decide to invest 35kcal of fossil energy (input) to get 1kcal of beef protein (output), as the 'energy form' beef is more valuable to the final consumer than the 'energy form' thermal energy measured in fossil energy equivalent. A similar situation exists with regard to the energy investments in the energy sector to generate electricity. Electricity is actually produced in the face of a negative energy balance. Indeed, a coal-fired plant may use up to 3J of coal per 1J of electricity produced. The difference in quality between the output of joules of electricity (mechanical energy) and the input of joules of fossil energy (thermal energy) explains the willingness to operate with a negative energy output/input ratio.

Thus, a coal-fired plant producing electricity has an energy output/input ratio lower than one, when considering joules of gross energy requirement per joule of electricity, and yet it is one of the most common energy technologies to produce electricity. This fact clearly indicates that we must be extremely cautious in the pre-analytical step in our choice of semantic and formal categories for the calculation of indices of net energy analysis. The strategy of implementing the concept of net energy analysis by calculating the minimum output/input required to have a viable technology is a very treacherous one.

However, before discussing in details the problems faced when calculating an index capable of defining the quality of an energy technology, we should first of all answer the following question: what typology of energy transformations makes it possible to apply the concept of 'net energy analysis'? In relation to this question, we claim that the concept of net energy analysis must necessarily refer to an autocatalytic loop of energy as the one described in Figure 6.1 (the analogous scheme referring to the exosomatic autocatalytic loop of energy in modern human societies is illustrated in Figure 4.6, page 91).

In fact, the first law of thermodynamics prevents the possibility that in a closed set of energy transformation we can get an output larger than the input and the second mandate that it is not even possible to get even. For this reason, it is obvious that other energy flows must be involved in a set of energy transformations generating an output larger than the input. In the example given in Figure 6.1, in order to generate an output/input larger than one we should consider the flows of physiological energy over the internal loop of energy for energy. The output is the total physiological energy generated by the digestion of nutrients made available by food production, and the input is the fraction of physiological energy going into the generation of the endosomatic power going into food production. In fact, it is only when a human society has a surplus of food from labour in agriculture that the society can express other functions outside the agricultural sector.

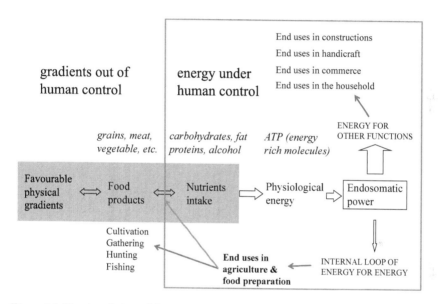

Figure 6.1 The description of the autocatalytic loop of endosomatic energy based on the integrated use of different semantic categories

Cleary, after having identified, within an autocatalytic loop, the basic output/input energy ratio it becomes possible to quantify, by using proxy variables easier to measure: energy in food products per hour of labour in agriculture, such a ratio. This is exactly the type of approach used by those that adopted energy analysis to study pre-industrial society: the reader can recall the example of the study of Rappaport (1971), discussed in Chapter 5, page 92, about the energetic performance of men and women when carrying out agricultural activities.

Getting back to our theoretical discussion on the foundation of net energy analysis, if we admit that net energy analysis should be applied only to an autocatalytic loop of exosomatic energy (Figure 4.6, page 91) then we have to face two important consequences:

1   The quantitative analysis should consider at least two non-equivalent types of energy categories: (i) energy carriers energy under human control (the output and the input); and (ii) primary energy sources, determining the requirement of physical gradients outside human control (what is required to have the output in the first place);

2   The analysis of the energy flows under human control should consider the requirement of the various factors needed for the operation of the energy technology: (i) inputs of energy carriers; (ii) power capacity; and (iii) human labour.

All these issues will be discussed in detail in the rest of the chapter.

6.1.2 What is the meaning of the output/input energy ratio of agricultural production?

According to the previous section we can perform a net energy analysis only having verified that we effectively deal with an autocatalytic loop of energy and after having categorised correctly energy inputs and energy outputs. In relation to this point, before getting into a more technical discussion about applications of net energy analysis, we present here a practical example of the conceptual confusion often found in this field. An application of energy analysis that was very popular in the 1970s and 1980s (see the work of David Pimentel (1979), Vaclav Smil (1991, 2001), and B.A. Stout (1991, 1992)), and is still widely used (e.g. Tyedmers, 2004) deals with the calculation of energy output/input ratios for different typologies of food production in the agricultural sector and fisheries to assess the fossil energy cost of the food supplied. Typical data for energy output/input ratios are listed in Table 6.1.

Table 6.1 Examples of output/input energy ratios in food production
Source: all data from Pimentel and Pimentel, 1996 except for fisheries, Tyedmers, 2004

Food production technique	Output/input ratio (output is expressed in kcal per kcal (calorific value))
Corn, Mexico, using only human power[a]	10.7/1
Corn, USA, with tractors and heavy inputs[a]	2.5/1
Oranges, Florida, USA[a]	1.7/1
Beef, USA, based on feed-lots[a]	0.03/1
Herring/mackerel (purse seine fishing)	0.56/1[a]

Note
[a] Based on the following definition of output and input: 'EROI is the ratio of the energy content of the edible fish protein harvested to the quantity of fossil fuel energy used directly in the harvesting process' (Mitchell and Cleveland, 1993, p. 305)

In these assessments the output is typically measured in kcal of food energy per kilo of food or in kcal of food energy per gramme of protein (see Table 6.1), whereas the input is calculated in kcal of fossil energy. Needless to say that these two energy forms are neither equivalent, nor belonging to the same autocatalytic loop and that therefore the output/input energy ratio should not be considered an Energy Return On Investment (expected to be larger than one). Fossil energy and food energy belong to different autocatalytic loops. Although the two autocatalytic loops do not have anything in common (no shared semantic or formal category in the two definitions of taxonomies of energy forms to be quantified) we can compare the representation of the autocatalytic loop of exosomatic energy described in Figure 4.6 (page 91), and the autocatalytic loop of endosomatic energy described in Figure 6.1.

This implies that the quantities of energy associated with food (kilos of corn, or kilos of beef, or kilos of fish proteins) cannot be reduced within a coherent system of accounting to the quantities of energy associated with fossil energy (tons of oil or cubic metres of gas). The only possible equivalence criteria would be that of the calorific value of the different substances (e.g. 1g of fish protein, 1g of gasoline, 1g of corn) when burned, in a controlled experiment, in a calorimetric bomb. But what would be the usefulness of this criterion of equivalence? The calories associated with corn and fish are not burned by the human body, but digested. As a matter of fact, when considering the energetics of digestion, not even 'kilocalories' of different foods are the same. When considering the physiology of digestion, 1kcal of a protein has a lower return than 1kcal of carbohydrate since it requires more energy to be digested (Westerterp, 2004). In conclusion, we can say that since potatoes, sandwiches and steaks are not burned but digested, quantifying their caloric value using a calorimetric bomb in order to sum them to the caloric value of fossil fuels does not make much sense.

After acknowledging this point, the question is: what does the output/input energy ratio of agricultural production tell us? This energy output/input ratio only tells us something about the dependency of the particular food product on fossil energy for its production. It provides us with a relevant indicator of performance: how many kcal (or joules) of fossil energy are required to obtain 1kcal (or 1J) of a particular food product or nutrient when using a particular technique of production.

Therefore the energy output/input ratio of a particular food can provide a useful indicator for one specific purpose: fossil energy dependence. An indicator often called the 'fossil energy intensity' of a given production. However, being a single indicator it necessarily only provides a small part of the story. If we want to address different criteria of performance we must add other inputs of information and use additional methods of accounting. For example, the production of corn with manual labour in Mexico generates a much higher output/input ratio (10.7/1) than the high-tech production of corn with tractors in the USA (2.5/1). But is this higher energy output/input ratio good or bad news? Certainly, it means that Mexican farmers are less dependent on fossil energy, but we also know that the production of corn using only manual labour does not generate much of an income for farmers.

In the same way, the energy output/input ratios listed in Table 6.1 (page 124) tell us that the production of beef represents a major drain in terms of fossil energy requirement: 35kcal of fossil energy per gram of beef protein. But again, is this the only relevant information for deciding whether or not we shall produce beef? When we produce food (or any other product or service) our ultimate goal is not to maximize the energy return. Indeed, there is no reason to expect that the energy output/input ratio for food production should be larger than 1. The purpose of food production is to supply a varied and healthy diet and make a profit on it (in market economies). In this framework the better quality of 1kcal of animal protein can justify the consumption of large amounts of fossil energy in beef production and fishing. This also explains why US agriculture still bothers to produce oranges, even though the 'fossil energy cost' of 1kcal of oranges is far larger than that of 1kcal of corn (Table 6.1, page 124).

The problem is more general. Can we compare the 'usefulness' of 1kcal of orange juice (source of vitamin C), 1kcal of animal protein (high-quality protein), and 1kcal of corn (carbohydrate source – staple food) using an energetic assessment? The differences in the 'quality' of these different energy forms (when considering their food energy content) – all measured in kcal when calculating the output – make this ratio not particularly useful when dealing with other relevant criteria of performance. Indeed, it is virtually impossible to generate simple quantitative indices capable of providing pertinent comparisons among systems producing different foods and nutrients. Nevertheless, this does not imply that energy output/input ratios are completely useless for comparison purposes. The ratio can be useful to study the different degree of fossil energy dependency for typologies of production techniques in relation to food typologies (animal protein, grains, fruits that are important carriers of vitamin C).

As a matter of fact, if we assess the total amount of fossil energy going into the production of agricultural commodities at world level, we discover that in developed countries the output of food calories is smaller than the input of fossil energy calories (about 1/2), whereas in developing countries the reverse is true (2.2/1) (Giampietro, 2002). But again, the ratio between energy outputs and energy inputs of different quality does not say much *per se* about the desirability of the two options. In fact, the difference in the output/input ratio of agriculture between developed and developing countries is explained by other relevant attributes of performance, as the enormous power capacity used in the agricultural sector of developed countries. This enormous power capacity certainly requires much fossil energy input but allows them to produce their food with only two per cent of their labour force. This strategy generates a low energy output/input ratio for the agricultural sector of developed countries, but it frees up a large supply of human labour for the other (industrial and service) sectors of the economy (see Chapter 9) where economic returns are much higher.

In conclusion, if we do not have a clear idea of the big picture of the network of energy transformations taking place in a society, individuating key autocatalytic loops of energy (associated with the right taxonomy of energy forms), it can be dangerous to focus on the numerical result of a specific analysis – the calculation of an output/input energy ratio – referring to energy quantities belonging to unrelated semantic categories.

6.2 Using net energy analysis to assess energy technologies: the energy requirement for energy (ERE) and the energy return on the investment (EROI)

In relation to the application of net energy analysis to assess the quality of energy technologies, it is important to recognize certain confusion in the proposed approaches for calculating the energy output/input ratio for energy technologies. In order to discuss this point let's introduce two indexes proposed for this purpose: the energy requirement for energy (ERE) and the energy return on the investment (EROI).

6.2.1 The energy requirement for energy (ERE)

The concept of ERE has been defined by Malcolm Slesser, a renowned Scottish energy expert that was asked by the IFIAS to organize a work group on energy accounting conventions (Slesser, 2003, p. 1), using the following two semantic definitions for this index: (i) 'Energy of the resource sequestrated by the energy delivered to point of use divided by energy delivered to point of use' (Slesser, 1975, p. 171), and, later on as the energy that 'must be expended to get at energy' (Slesser, 1987, p. 228). Be aware that according to this definition the ERE looks at an energy input/output ratio rather than an output/input ratio. But again the term used in the definition is a semantic one, 'energy'.

In relation to the formalization of this semantic concept into a quantitative analysis Slesser (2003, p.3) comments: '. . . the alternative, advised by the IFIAS group is to express GER and ERE in terms of energy sources of a *standard quality* – the definition of this being the extent for which the heat of combustion could be turned into work' (emphasis added). Then Slesser (2003, p. 2) defines the ERE as 'GER per unit of enthalpy of delivered fuel' – the acronym GER refers to quantities of energy expressed in Gross Energy Requirement.

Thus, in our terminology, Slesser's technical definition of ERE translates into saying that the ERE is the ratio between: (i) an input defined as gross energy requirement (GER) thermal equivalent; and (ii) an output that should also be expressed in gross energy requirement thermal equivalent. That is, when providing these definitions, Slesser explicitly suggests correcting the quantitative assessments of these two energy flows for quality factors (Slesser 2003, p.2). For example, if the analysis of the ERE refers to a plant producing electricity, then the output of electricity has to be corrected by a quality factor and expressed in thermal equivalent (units of enthalpy). In this way, one avoids the comparison of quantities of energy forms of different quality – output in electricity versus input in thermal energy.

According to Slesser, the homogeneity in the quality of input and output energy flows (both expressed in thermal energy equivalent) is required to assess the overall balance expressed in comparable quantities.

It is important not to confuse the ERE with another index called the 'energy intensity' of a given production technique for a generic product. This index – obtained by calculating a ratio of the gross energy requirement per unit of output – can be used to compare different technologies producing any type of output. The energy intensity is defined as the GER of the net supply of a unit of given product. In this case the gross energy requirement (the input) is expressed in thermal energy equivalent (this is useful since it makes it possible to aggregate different inputs) and it represents the 'aggregate energy cost' of the net supply of a unit of the specified product. This would be similar to the approach used by Pimentel and others in the 1970s to assess the fossil energy required in agriculture per unit of food produced when applied to the same type of food (e.g. fossil energy intensity of 1kcal of fish protein). However, as discussed below, the index of energy intensity is different from the ERE in relation to the choice of the category of energy forms that has to be included in the input (discussed in section 6.2.3, page 130).

6.2.2 The energy return on the investment (EROI)

The energy return on the investment (EROI) is certainly the best-known application of the rationale for net energy analysis to the study of the quality of energy sources. As discussed in Chapter 2, the basic idea was introduced by many authors, including Lotka, Cottrell, and H.T. Odum, but to the best of our knowledge the first use of the label EROI was by Hall *et al.* (1981). Many applications of the EROI can be found in the more recent scientific literature (Cleveland, 1992; Cleveland *et al.*, 1984, 2000; Hagens and Mulder, 2008; Hall *et al.*, 1986, 2008; Heun and de Wit, 2011; Gever *et al.*, 1991; Kubiszewski *et al.*, 2010; Martinez-Alier, 2011; Mansure and Blankenship, 2010; Murphy *et al.*, 2011).

Also in the case of EROI the basic definition of the concept is easy to grasp: 'The ratio of gross energy delivered by an energy production process to input energy required to obtain that gross energy' (Heun and de Wit, 2011, p. 102). Charlie Hall, the father of the EROI, gives the following definition:

> EROI is calculated from the following simple equation, *although the devil is in the details*: EROI = Energy Returned to Society/Energy required to get that energy. Since the numerator and denominator are usually assessed in the same units (an exception we treat later is when quality corrections are made) the ratio so derived is dimensionless...
>
> (Hall *et al.*, 2009, p. 25, emphasis added)

Also in this case the 'easy going' definition is based on the use of the semantically open term 'energy'. However, at this point in the book, the reader should be able to guess: (i) the nature of the devilish details (how to chose pertinent categories), and (ii) that the use of the same unit of measurement in the ratio (kcal/kcal, Btu/Btu, kWh/kWh, J/J) does not guarantee that the energy forms included in this index are of the same kind. So, we can start our analysis by making three important observations about the features of an EROI index:

1   The same EROI ratio can refer to inputs and outputs consisting of: (i) energy carriers of different kinds (e.g. mechanical energy versus thermal energy); (ii) energy flows relating to different hierarchical levels of analysis (gross energy requirement versus net supply of energy carrier); (iii) flows of energy requiring different levels of power capacity and different hours of human activity for control; and finally (iv) primary energy sources associated with different typologies of physical gradients. Put in another way, the same input of energy to the process (1GJ) may require the extraction or the capture of different kinds of non-manmade energy inputs (wind, kilos of uranium, cubic metres of natural gas, etc.).

2   The calculation of an EROI index is based only on 'quantities of energy' associated with formal categories (J, Btu, kcal), which are used to characterize both the input (gross/net energy requirement) and the output (net supply of energy carriers). Thus, the EROI measures only energy flows under human control. For this reason, the index cannot provide any information about the set of physical gradients (whose availability is outside human control) required to generate the output. As noted earlier, the total requirement of fossil energy (thermal) equivalent (the input) does not map univocally onto a direct requirement of physical gradients; the same gross energy requirement can be generated using a different mix of primary energy sources (something which applies also to the ERE index). This simple observation individuates an obvious problem that should be expected with any 'single number' approach proposed for generating as a quantitative assessment of the quality of energy technologies. A single number index simply cannot convey information about all the relevant attributes that would be required for a useful energy analysis. This point is discussed in detail in section 6.4, page 139.

3   The EROI is supposed to be larger than 1 and therefore it must refer to an output/input of energy flows identified within an autocatalytic loop of exosomatic energy. If this is not the case, the assumption that the output of energy (net supply of energy carriers) has to be larger than the 'energy input' would be in conflict with the laws of thermodynamics, as pointed out by Sedlik:

> Net energy, like net profit, implies that a stream of energy 'revenues' is sustained in excess of necessary energy 'expenditures' – i.e. more energy is gained than is spent. For an energy conversions process, the existence of such a positive gain would appear to violate First Law restrictions against energy creation and Second Law requirement of energy degradation.
>
> (Sedlik, 1978, p. 251)

Given that the laws of thermodynamics simply cannot be violated, it is important to understand that the decision of what should be included among the energy inputs and what should be considered as the energy output should reflect some logical definition of semantic categories within the representation of an autocatalytic loop.

6.2.3 The key distinction between energy under human control and energy beyond human control

> If a new technology consumed more energy than it produces so that it had a net energy requirement greater than one, it would not provide any useful contribution to energy supplies and should be dismissed as a net energy sink ... However, such a simple reasoning is not without problems, especially as regards comparing the energy input with the energy output ...
>
> (Mortimer, 1991, p. 376)

As discussed in the previous sections with these two indexes we deal with an apparent thermodynamic paradox: (i) according to the definition of ERE – an input/output ratio in which the input is a flow of gross energy requirement and the output is a flow of net energy supply expressed in gross energy equivalent – it is impossible to generate a net supply of energy; and (ii) according to the rationale of the EROI – requiring that the output produced by an energy technology must always be larger than the input – our expectations seem to violate the laws of thermodynamics. This paradox explains why, at the beginning of this chapter, we claimed that the rationale for net energy analysis means it can only be applied to the analysis of an autocatalytic loop of energy. The positive return is related to an output/input ratio referring to a sub-set of the entire set of energy transformations. Therefore, the question is how to decide whether a flow of energy has to be included or excluded from the accounting of this output/input energy ratio.

In relation to the definition of a technology as either a sink or a net supply of energy, Maddox observes:

> ... this distinction may be lost, depending on whether the natural resource on which an energy system is based is included or excluded from the calculation ... In those cases where natural resources are considered part of the calculation, there is inevitably no net energy production, as the laws of physics state that no system can create energy out of nothing and that there are always losses associated with the supply and use of energy. Consequently, the technical definition of net energy excludes natural resources, treating them as free goods ...
>
> (Maddox, 1978, p. 135)

In a more obscure way, Herendeen (1979, p. 454, emphasis added) makes reference to this same point, with regard to the efficiency of coal-fired power plants: 'We can express the potential of technology to pay back more than it borrows by calculating the ER *without the fuel energy* in the denominator.' Obviously, generating electricity using coal will never provide a positive pay-back in energetic terms, if we include in the input the fossil energy going into the production (the coal burned in the power plant).

According to calculations of Herendeen (1979), in 1979 the energy output/input ratio for coal-fired power plants was 0.31/1. Or, equally, we can say that the energy intensity of electricity was 3.2J of gross energy requirement per 1J of electricity. This assessment includes in the input the fuel (coal) burned for producing the heat used in the Rankine cycle for powering the electric generator. Hence, in order to arrive at an output/input larger than 1, as is expected from an EROI analysis or when using a ERE analysis, one has no choice but to exclude from the accounting the energy content of the coal used to generate the heat of the Rankine cycle. Indeed, according to the rationale of the EROI, one should include in the accounting of the input only the fuel invested in the building of the infrastructure and the extraction and transportation of the fuel. This procedure was also done by Herendeen (1979) in his second calculation: when adopting this alternative assessment the result for coal-fired power plants was an energy output/input ratio of 7.7/1.

Thus, whenever we deal with an energy output/input ratio larger than 1, such as the EROI, a certain amount of energy getting into the process (e.g. the coal used for generating the thermal energy associated with electricity production) has been excluded from the assessment of energy inputs. This energy input – neglected in the accounting – represents a reduction in the availability of primary energy source: a depletion of the stock of fossil energy, which is considered out of human control (outside the black box) and therefore not included as an input. In general, we can define an energy input as being outside human control when it requires neither an investment of power capacity nor an investment of human activity (work) for its generation and storage. Thus, the peculiar status of primary energy sources (also called 'non-manmade energy inputs') implies that we can consider this energy input as free, as it does not require the use of production factors (investments of power capacity and human activity). "...we do not pay Nature for energy, but only the cost of exploiting it" (Hall and Klitgaard, 2012, p. 135).

For this reason, the quantity of energy categorised as primary energy sources beyond human control should, by definition, not be included in the energy accounting of the EROI (but it should be included in the calculation of energy intensity). In the EROI, only the investment of energy carriers required to exploit the primary energy sources is accounted for as energy input. In line with economic thought, the EROI – an analogue of the economic return on the investment – distinguishes between energy forms under human control (energy forms requiring production factors such as power capacity and human activity and therefore an opportunity cost for society) and energy forms outside human control (non-manmade energy inputs). Therefore, as discussed earlier, when expecting an output/input larger than one we must be dealing with an output/input ratio of energy carriers under human control associated with the exploitation of a primary energy source. 'Thus, EROI compares high quality input energies, e.g. the diesel fuel used to run the drill rig, to another high quality energy, the electricity produced...' (Mansure and Blankenship, 2010, p. 1). The EROI index must refer to a ratio of two flows of energy carriers.

6.2.4 The impasse in implementing net energy analysis: The EROI as a case study

The implementation of the EROI index neatly illustrates the general confusion and impasse existing in the field of energy analysis: 'There still does not exist a consistently applied methodology for calculating either the numerator (the energy produced) or the denominator (energy consumed) in the EROI equation' (Mulder and Hagens, 2008, p. 74). In fact, any quantitative application of the EROI, and of any other index of net energy analysis, requires us to address the epistemological challenges associated with the 'sticky points' of energy analysis, that is, the truncation problem, the aggregation of energy flows of different quality, and the need for a multi-criteria assessment. 'Fundamental difficulties in performing EROI include specifying the system boundary and comparing input and output energies at different times and of different thermodynamic quality...' (Mansure and Blankenship, 2010, p. 2).

> The practicality of net energy evaluations rests on one paramount assumption: different energy forms can be equated. If net energy analyses are to work, an appropriate standard of comparison must be found to relate the energy produced to the energy consumed to produce it. Thus the derivation of a net energy number requires that electricity and forms of fuel and of other potential energy be measured on the same scale, and the issue in establishing the credibility of net energy is whether a meaningful scale exists...
>
> (Maddox, 1978, p. 135)

Charlie Hall's own group, in a paper entitled 'Order from chaos: a preliminary protocol for determining the EROI of fuels' (Murphy *et al.*, 2011) acknowledges the existence of the infamous sticky points. However, in our view, the paper does not deliver on the promise given in the title for they do not provide any convincing solutions on how to get out from the chaos. They acknowledge that the choice of boundary is arbitrary and depends on the purpose of the analysis. The solution proposed is that basically 'anything goes', as long as the analysts explicitly declare their choice of boundary. As regards the aggregation of energy forms of different qualities, the solution proposed is that, depending on the circumstances, the analysts should try to do their best choosing among the available options. They further recommend the adoption of a 'price-based aggregation or a Divisa approach for quality adjustments...' (Murphy *et al.*, 2011, p. 1903). We can only observe that an aggregation based on economic variables is something which goes against the basic rationale for developing energy analysis in the first place. They finally provide a table containing a minimum of 15 different possible EROIs, including different choices of possible inputs for inclusion, such as labour, environmental energy costs (?), and indirect costs. However, they do not clarify either the differences in semantic criteria or the difference in the resulting protocols to be used for calculation. We earlier discussed in Chapter 2 (Section 2.3.2, page 39 and Table 2.1, page 40), with regard to the energetic equivalent of human labour, the impossibility of making these calculations when operating across multiple levels of organization, unless we define clearly a set of hierarchical levels of reference and a criterion for integration of the non-equivalent results.

Given this impasse in net energy analysis, in the rest of this chapter we will deal with the following points:

1   Net energy analysis requires the definition of meaningful criteria and clear rules for handling the accounting of energy flows of different quality across scales. That is, before crunching numbers it is essential that we define – in terms of semantic and formal categories – what should be calculated as an input and what should be calculated as an output.

2   Net energy analysis requires addressing the issue of multiple scales and the multi-level nature of metabolic systems in order to properly handle the truncation problem. As observed in the previous chapters, a modern society self-organizes through autocatalytic loops of energy forms operating simultaneously at different scales. This implies that the truncation problem can only be addressed after having individuated key features of the autocatalytic loops that are relevant for organizing the accounting (direct and indirect inputs).

3   Net energy analysis requires the use of an integrated set of indicators and not just a 'number' expressed as a dimensionless ratio. As illustrated by the examples of the output/input energy ratios for food production, when analyzing a set of energy transformations there are different relevant attributes (referring to different relevant criteria of performance), that have to be characterized in an integrated way. For developing such an integrated assessment we should develop a different type of multi-scale energy analysis that would be no longer similar to what is known right now as net energy analysis.

In the remaining sections we provide an overview of the challenges to be faced when generating a quantitative index based on the rationale of net energy analysis in relation to the three sticky points of energy analysis. That is we discuss how to handle properly: (i) the accounting of energy flows of different kinds; (ii) the issue of multi-scale (the truncation problem); and (iii) multi-criteria analysis.

6.3 Handling properly the accounting of energy flows of different kinds

6.3.1 The subtle distinction between the various definitions of energy flows

The distinction between energy forms under human control (requiring production factors such as power capacity and human activity and therefore an opportunity cost for society) and energy forms beyond human control (non-manmade energy inputs) points at the existence of three key distinctions, often missed in applications of net energy analysis:

1 Gross energy requirement versus net supply of energy carriers

The difference between these two quantitative assessments of energy flows, both carried out in energy units (such as J), lies in the scale of assessment. The former is assessed at the large scale using equivalence factors (e.g. 1J of electricity = 2.6J of thermal energy), while the latter is assessed at the local scale observing local conversions of specific typologies of energy carriers (e.g. the petrol consumed per km by a car). Both quantities are measured in energy units, they are both observed from inside the black box, and they both refer to energy transformations under human control.

2 Primary energy sources versus net energy carriers

The former refers to a set of energy forms outside human control (e.g. a barrel of oil still in the ground), which are assumed to be 'free' (zero opportunity cost for society), while the latter refers to a set of energy forms under human control (e.g. 1kWh of electricity in the grid), which are considered an energy investment (associated with an opportunity cost to society). As noted earlier, assessments referring to primary energy sources have to be carried out in physical quantities other than energy, referring to favourable physical gradients that have been generated by natural processes, such as falling water, blowing wind, tidal waves, tons of coal reserves, and cubic metres of natural gas. They refer to observable attributes outside the black box. Still, they may refer to energy forms of different kinds (mechanical energy of the wind or waterfall or the potential thermal energy of coal or natural gas) and this certainly creates confusion when, in the assessment of the gross energy requirement, they are assessed using an energy equivalent. On the other hand, the assessment of energy carriers is carried out only in energy terms, referring to: (i) energy forms under human control; and (ii) specific energy inputs required by specific energy converters (typologies of power capacity) for carrying out specific tasks (electricity, heat and fuels).

3 The distinction between the gross supply of energy carriers and the net supply of energy carriers

The gross supply of energy carriers is generated by the exploitation of a primary energy source and the net supply of energy carriers is generated by the exploitation of primary energy sources (calculated by taking out the input from the gross output). This distinction will be illustrated in section 6.4.2, page 141. As the epistemological conundrum behind these distinctions is as important as it is elusive, we provide two examples of misinterpretation in the next sections.

6.3.2 A controversial net energy analysis of ethanol from corn

In 2006, Farrell *et al.* published in *Science* a comprehensive review of contrasting assessments found in the literature regarding the performance of biofuels.

This paper generated a storm of reactions from energy analysts (Cleveland *et al.*, 2006; Hagens *et al.*, 2006; Kaufmann, 2006; Patzek, 2006). We discuss this study here for the following three reasons:

1   The reputation of the journal in which it was published, *Science*. This is supposedly a prestigious journal that boasts a rigorous review procedure, especially when dealing with controversial and highly-relevant issues;

2   The goal of the study. This study had the explicit goal to cut through the confusion of contrasting assessments thus providing the last word, pronounced by reliable experts, on data and accounting procedures;

3   The degree of sophistication of the quantitative analysis. The study was carried out by the prestigious Energy and Resource Group of Berkeley using an elaborate protocol. The authors analyzed both published scientific and gray literature to check the results presented in six studies illustrating the range of assumptions and data found for the case of corn-based production of ethanol.

According to the protocol of Farrell et al (2006), the energy output/input ratio of ethanol from corn in the USA is greater than 1/1 but smaller than 2/1. In their assessment the output is 1.26/1. Recalling that it is impossible to have a conversion of energy forms generating an output of energy larger than the input (first law of thermodynamics), this result can only be explained if the initial input of primary energy sources required for ethanol generation is ignored and the 'energy input' is only represented by the flow of energy carriers under human control used to operate the energy technology. In the case of ethanol production from corn, the primary energy source is the solar energy fixed into the corn crop in the form of chemical bonds (tons of corn). These tons of corn then make it possible to generate ethanol via fermentation. So the assessment of the output/input is larger than 1 (1.26/1) because the primary energy source (the chemical energy contained in corn) is not included in the accounting of the energy inputs.

But when comparing the production of ethanol with the production of gasoline, Farrell *et al.* arrive at a figure smaller than 1 for the energy output/input ratio of gasoline production, that is, 0.79/1 to be exact. This lower value is not due to a larger use of energy carriers in the internal loop (the production process) but to the choice made by the authors to include the primary energy source (crude oil consumed in the transformation process into gasoline) in the accounting of energy inputs. Rather than ignoring the tons of oil taken from the oilfield (given that the production of this stock has opportunity cost zero for society) – a procedure that would be perfectly in line with ignoring the tons of corn used for fermentation – they sum the energy equivalent of these tons of oil (primary energy source) to the energy consumed in the form of energy carriers in the calculation of the input.

The perplexing result is that the authors thus compare an EROI index (ethanol from corn) with an assessment of the fossil energy intensity of fuel (gasoline from oil). This obviously leads to a grossly misleading conclusion.

6.3.3 A typical study of the EROI of wind power

Another case of confusion in the accounting of energy forms can be found in a study of Kubiszewski *et al.* (2010) in which the authors claim to use the EROI index to assess the quality of wind power. First of all, let's consider the definition of the EROI given by the authors:

> The EROI entails the comparison of the electricity generated to the amount of primary energy used in the manufacture, transport, construction, operation, decommissioning, and other stages of facility's life cycle...Comparing cumulative energy requirements with the amount of electricity the technology produces over its lifetime yields a simple ratio for energy return on investment (EROI)...the EROI = cumulative electricity generated/cumulative primary energy required...
>
> (Kubiszewski *et al.*, 2010, p. 218)

Reading this definition, one remains confused, since the two energy flows compared do not have the same quality: the output is electricity (mechanical energy equivalent) and the input is the gross energy requirement (expressed in thermal equivalent) calculated over the various inputs used in the process. However, the correct exclusion of the mechanical energy input of the wind (primary energy source) from the accounting explains the fact that the output of electricity is larger than the input of gross energy requirement. The authors are also correct in accounting in the quantity of energy going into the input only the fossil-based energy carriers used to build and operate the windmill. However, the use of non-equivalent energy flows muddles the calculation of the EROI. In fact, as observed by Mortimer:

> In the case of electricity, for example, there are sound thermodynamic reasons why one unit of energy in the form of heat cannot produce one unit of energy in the form of electricity and, hence, the basis of the test that the value of the net energy requirement should not exceed one seems fundamentally flawed...
>
> (Mortimer, 1991, p. 376)

This example flags another confusing issue surrounding the analysis of energy flows associated with fossil fuels. Due to the exceptional quality of fossil energy, quantitative assessments of fossil fuels are often carried out by confusing two distinct semantic categories : (i) gross requirement of energy carriers (how much oil – primary energy source in the ground – is consumed because of the flow); (ii) energy carriers (how many joules of energy are associated with the flow of fuels). This point is discussed later on in section 6.4.2 (page 141) and in more detail in section 7.2, page 172. However, we want to flag here that this confusion of the accounting of joules of gross energy requirement thermal (input) with joules of fossil energy fuels thermal (output) has the effect of eliminating the conceptual distinction proposed before between ERE – input assessed in gross energy requirement thermal/output assessed in thermal equivalent – and EROI – input assessed in energy carriers/output assessed in energy carriers. Also this second example clearly illustrates the need for being careful with the definitions of indices and the distinctions to be made among different energy forms.

6.3.4 Ambiguity in the taxonomy of categories for EROI accounting

After this general discussion of the possible sources of confusion when conducting a net energy analysis, we consider now the conventional scheme of accounting proposed for calculating the EROI. Such a scheme, presented in Cleveland (2010) and illustrated in Figure 6.2 introduces some ambiguities in the interpretation of the semantic and formal categories.

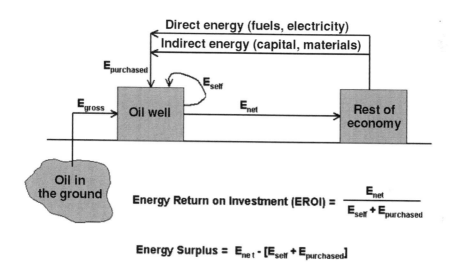

Figure 6.2 The classic EROI scheme of calculation
Source: Cleveland, 2010

In the scheme of Figure 6.2 the label E_{gross} is clearly used to indicate a flow quantified in terms of PES – as indicated by the label explicitly referring to 'oil in the ground'. On the contrary, the flow labeled as E_{net} is not defined in terms of a semantic category for the relative accounting. Within the proposed accounting scheme we find also a flow labeled as $E_{surplus}$, which is defined as E_{net} minus ($E_{purchased}$ + E_{self}). This definition seems to suggest that the flow labeled as E_{net} corresponds to what we called gross output quantified using the semantic category of energy carriers (gross output of EC).

By adopting this interpretation of the labels we can write:

$E_{gross} \approx input_a$ measured in quantity of PES (non-manmade energy input)

$(E_{purchased} + E_{self}) \approx input_b$ measured in quantity of EC (under human control)

$E_{net} \approx output_a$ gross energy supply (energy carriers under human control)

$E_{surplus} \approx output_b$ net energy supply (energy carriers under human control).

$$EROI = E_{net} / (E_{purchased} + E_{self}) = \text{gross energy supply (En.Carr.)} / INPUT_b$$ (En.Carr.)

From this scheme we can notice that there are two different flows of input and two different flows of output. They are all necessary for the establishment of the process, but then the calculation of EROI is done by using only one of the two outputs and one of the two inputs (EROI = $output_a$/$input_b$). As discussed earlier the energy input referring to PES (physical gradients outside human control) is not included in the assessment.

Recalling the theoretical discussions made so far in relation to both energy analysis and net energy analysis, we can say that the scheme of EROI accounting illustrated in the graph of Figure 6.2 lacks a specification of both the semantic and formal categories that should be used to quantify the various energy flows mentioned there. Therefore, we can only imagine that probably the three terms used to calculate the EROI, that is, E_{net}, $E_{purchased}$, and E_{self} have to be assessed in terms of joules of energy carriers (under human control). In this definition the input of PES (tons of oil) and its GER equivalent (the flow E_{gross} measured in TOE – a quantity referring to the category of thermal energy equivalent) should not be included in the calculation of the EROI.

But if this is the case, then, this proposed scheme of calculation does not address properly any of the problems discussed earlier in this book.

1 How to sum together energy carriers referring to different energy forms – e.g. electricity and fuels?

What if the $input_b$ is generated using a mix of the two? If we try to handle the differences in quality among the different energy carriers included in the mix using conversion factors (e.g. the partial substitution method), then the resulting quantitative assessment would be expressed in joules of GER-thermal and no longer in joules of EC. But we need assessments expressed in joules of EC in order to be able to calculate the requirement of power capacity and labour requirement at the local scale in the process of exploitation of the alternative energy source.

2 How to assess the amount of primary energy source required to get a unit of net energy carrier supply, if we use as the only piece of information the output/input ratio?

Moreover, an assessment of the severity of external constraints will depend on the mix of PES used (this is especially true if this analysis refers to a whole country). What if we have a mix of PES including wind power, tons of uranium, tons of falling water and sand tars? Using the information carried out by the EROI index we cannot study the requirement of physical gradients associated with the net supply of energy carrier to society. This calculation can only be applied at the local scale.

3 How to calculate the 'direct' and 'indirect flows of 'energy'?

In the graph of Figure 6.2, the calculation of the input is determined by the sum of two arrows coming back from 'the rest of the economy' labeled 'direct' and 'indirect'. However, there is no clear indication on how to deal with the truncation problem (see Chapter 2). In fact, if we leave the door open for any arbitrary boundary definition of what is embodied in a given energy input, we will undoubtedly discover that socio-economic systems are autopoietic systems, implying that all energy inputs consumed by a society are being used either directly or indirectly to perform its various functions (Giampietro and Mayumi, 2009). Put in another way, not only is this schematic representation too generic in its definition of energy flows, but also it will lead to an infinite regress, a well known 'attractor' for embodied energy analysis (see Herendeen, 1998): it does not provide any criterion on how to deal with the truncation problem.

6.4 Handling properly the issue of multiple scales

6.4.1 Is it possible to apply the rationale of the EROI index across different scales?

In a paper entitled, 'What is the minimum EROI that a sustainable society must have?', Hall *et al.* (2009) address the epistemological challenge of scaling-up net energy analysis from the level of the energy sector to that of society. In relation to this challenge, Hall *et al.* explicitly suggest the possibility of a simultaneous use of multiple boundaries for the calculation of EROI. The proposed solution leads to the generation of a family of EROI indices, each one referring to a quantitative analysis carried out at a different hierarchical level and referring to different external referents.

1   EROI at the point of use = energy returned to society / energy required to get and deliver that energy. According to the authors, this index (calculation includes only energy carriers) should include the direct input used for extracting fossil energy, refinery losses and the energy costs for transportation. In jargon, the calculation of this EROI is based only on the inclusion of the 'direct' input of energy carriers.

2   Extended EROI = energy returned to society/energy required to get, deliver, and use that energy. This index includes also the 'indirect' energy input of energy carriers, which have been used for making power capacity (fixed costs for technical capital) and infrastructures.
3   Societal EROI = summation of the energy content of all fuels delivered/ summation of all the energy costs to get those fuels.

Predictably, the practical details of how to calculate this last index are not given in the text. As discussed earlier, if we want to include all the 'direct' and 'indirect' energy inputs (energy costs for useful activities), we end up discovering that all the energy controlled by humans in society is directly or indirectly used to express functions that have as an ultimate goal that of maintaining (and expanding whenever possible) the existing control on energy flows. Human society is a autopoietic system defining and preserving its own identity through autocatalytic loops of energy, so if we are looking for all the energy inputs 'embodied' directly and indirectly in anything used in a society it is normal to get into an infinite regression; everything is embodied in everything else (Herendeen, 1998; Giampietro and Mayumi, 2009). However, in the paper of Hall *et al.* (2009) there is no clear indication, not even in semantic terms, about the set of criteria that should be used to deal with the truncation problem when calculating the three different EROI indices according to the rationale for net energy analysis. The authors seem to acknowledge the limitations of the existing protocols when they say: "Perhaps we need some way to understand the magnitude, and the meaning, of the overall EROI we might eventually derive for all of a nation's or society's fuels collectively by summing all gains from fuels and all costs from obtaining them (i.e. societal EROI)" (Hall *et al.*, 2009, p.28).

It should be noted that in the 'old times' of net energy analysis, the suggested taxonomy of categories to be used for a quantitative characterization was much richer. However, exactly because of the richness and the diversity of categories to be used in the assessment Leach (1975) concludes that the calculation of a simple index of net energy analysis over the complex set of energy transformations associated with the exploitation of a primary energy source is impractical. A simplified version of the scheme of accounting proposed by Leach is illustrated in Figure 6.3. In his scheme (from which we took out a few additional flows for the sake of simplicity) we can notice that in relation to the accounting of transformation of PES, one should consider that not only the stock of resources exploited is reduced because of the direct extracted flow, but there is an additional reduction implied by the exploitation method.

In this case, the reduction in the availability of the resources not yet extracted takes place in the environment, outside the black box used for the accounting scheme. Therefore, since these processes are not directly under human control, they must be necessarily ignored in the logic of net energy analysis (and the EROI index) dealing only with energy investment and energy return. But even when considering only the autocatalytic loop of energy under direct human control we have to deal with the difference between the energy used directly to extract and

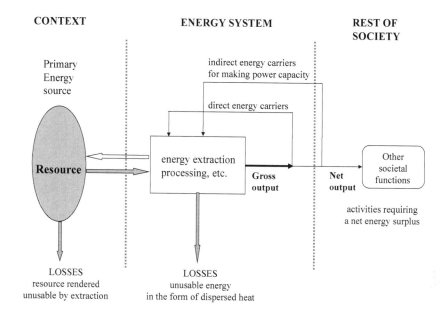

CONTEXT   **ENERGY SYSTEM**   **REST OF SOCIETY**

Figure 6.3 The general scheme of accounting proposed by Leach for net energy
analysis: adaptation of Leach, 1975

process energy (the loop E_{self} in Figure 6.2, page 137) and the energy required for
the making of power capacity. Only after having calculated this indirect input we
can assess the net surplus available to society for expressing additional functions.
In the graph provided by Leach (Figure 6.3) however, there is no reference to the
difference in quality of the flows of energy carriers, in spite of the fact that when
dealing with the large scale (societal level) it is necessary to deal with a mix of
energy carriers referring to energy forms of different kinds (mechanical/electric-
ity and thermal energy).

6.4.2 Acknowledging the issue of impredicativity (chicken–egg paradox)

Another important consequence of the analysis of the autocatalytic loop of exosomatic energy is the resulting need to carry out a multi-scale analysis. This fact
clashes with the standard recipe of reductionism for the assessment of any
production process: the utilization of a linear model to describe the transformations involved. In other words, the classic input/output system of accounting (the
linear view), typical of reductionism, is not applicable to the analysis of autocatalytic loops. In the linear view, the efficiency of a process is captured by a single,
simple number, and the analysis of the exploitation process of primary energy
sources has been no exception to this rule. However, there are two serious

problems with the adoption of a linear model to describe the exploitation process of primary energy sources:

1   The energy flows of the output and input may be of different form (mechanical versus thermal) and hence are not necessarily reducible to one another. This may prevent aggregation procedures.
2   The production of energy carriers is based on an autocatalytic loop: energy carriers are used as input to get energy carriers as output. This introduces impredicativity and at times non-linearity in the resulting quantitative assessment.

To illustrate these complications in the analysis of the exploitation process of a primary energy source, we compare in Figure 6.4 the traditional approach of linear energy analysis (left graph) with a more complex view of the exploitation process based on the concept of autopoietic systems (i.e. systems producing themselves, Maturana and Varela, 1980). The complex view, illustrated in the right graph, forces us to deal with the internal loop of energy for energy and hence with the issue of impredicativity (chicken–egg paradox).

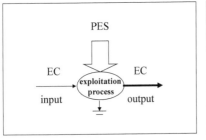 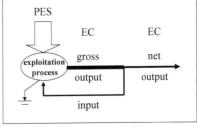

The linear view (simplification of reductionism)	The chicken–egg view (complexity of energetics)

Figure 6.4 The simplistic linear view versus the complex chicken–egg view of the energetics of the exploitation process of primary energy sources

In the linear representation reported on the left side of Figure 6.4, we can see that an unequivocal quantitative energy analysis should be able to make the following two distinctions:

1   The distinction between flows of primary energy sources (non-manmade energy inputs) and energy carriers (energy forms under human control). They refer to different semantic categories and require distinctive quantitative handling. The quantitative assessment of flows of primary energy sources

refers to two external referents: (i) a physical gradient (e.g. tons of coal), and (ii) a quantity of energy referring to an energy form of reference (e.g. thermal energy associated with a ton of coal). The quantitative assessment of energy carriers used as input in the exploitation process refers to: (i) the quantity of energy carriers utilized by available power capacity (electricity, liquid fuels, heat); and (ii) their particular kind of energy form (mechanical versus thermal). The quantification of the output of energy carriers (expressed in a given semantic category of reference, such as chemical energy or electricity) depends on the specific process under analysis.

2 The distinction between joules of output of energy carrier (what comes out from the exploitation process) and joules of input of energy carrier (what is invested in the process). These two flows must belong to the same semantic category of energy carrier under human control, but they can belong to non-equivalent energy forms (electricity or thermal energy).

Thus, in the linear analysis we are dealing with numbers that belong to different semantic categories, primary energy sources (outside human control) and energy carriers (under human control), and most likely, among the energy carriers used as input, to non-equivalent energy forms. As a result we cannot aggregate numbers into a single assessment of 'input flow'.

Basic questions of interest regarding an exploitation process cannot be answered with the information provided by a simple linear representation. For instance, we cannot assess the external constraints to the exploitation process, that is the required amount of primary energy sources (non-manmade energy inputs or biophysical gradients associated with the gross energy requirement). Moreover a ratio of two 'homogeneous' quantities of energy is by definition out of scale: it does not say anything about the tons of material or cubic meters of falling water required. In fact, a given EROI of 10/1 may just as well refer to the energetic analysis of a spider web trapping flies (with an energy output smaller than a few joules per day) as it may to drilling platforms extracting oil (with an energy output in the order of terajoules per day).

Neither does the linear representation allow us to assess the internal constraints of the exploitation process, that is the required size of the investments of: (i) energy carriers, (ii) power capacity, and (iii) human labour in relation to a given net supply of energy carriers. In the linear representation (left side of Figure 6.4), we must assume that the input of energy carriers to be invested in the exploitation process is already available before the exploitation is taking place. However, in practice, this is not the case. In a sustainable process in a quasi-steady state, the input of energy carrier required for the exploitation is obtained as a fraction from the gross output of exploitation – provided the gross output is larger than the required input. Hence, this is the very definition of an autocatalytic loop of energy flows (energy carriers used to produce energy carriers). This idea is represented in the circular or chicken–egg view of the exploitation process, illustrated in the right graph of Figure 6.4.

The circular view of the process of exploitation presents some epistemological challenges. First of all, in this representation the direction of the energy flows (indicated by arrows) suggests that the output of energy carriers comes before the input of energy carriers, which is in violation with the classic reductionist view. Indeed, in the conventional linear representation (left graph in Figure 6.4), first the input (the investment of energy carrier required to get an output) enters into the process of exploitation, then, because of this investment, a gross output results from this exploitation process. This is the classic mantra of reductionism. When considering only the local scale, this gross output can be considered as the return (measured in joules of energy carriers) on the investment (measured in joules of energy carriers). However, when considering a larger scale view (the steady-state view), we get a more holistic view of the process (right graph of Figure 6.4). In this view, it is the output of previous processes of exploitation that is used as an input for the current process of exploitation. When dealing with a multi-level analysis, the output of the process comes both before and after the input flow: a situation of so-called 'complex time' (Giampietro, 2003; Giampietro *et al.* 2006; 2011) or, in popular terms, the chicken–egg paradox (which comes first?). In jargon, we say that we deal with impredicativity, which is typical of any quantitative analysis of an autopoietic system (see Giampietro *et al.*, 2011).

As discussed earlier, a linear analysis of the exploitation process (left graph of Figure 6.4), requires us to make only the following two distinctions in energy flows:

1   primary energy sources (energy input outside of human control) versus energy carriers (under human control);
2   input versus output of energy carriers: these flows belong to the same semantic category of energy carriers, but can belong to different, non-reducible energy forms (mechanical versus thermal energy);

But acknowledging the existence of an autocatalytic loop of energy for energy, we have to introduce a third key distinction:

3   the gross supply of energy carriers (gross output of the exploitation process) versus the net supply of energy carriers to society. As discussed in detail in the next chapter (section 7.2, page 172), the difference between the gross and net supply of energy carriers is determined by the energy output/input ratio of energy carriers (this is the reason why this number is so important) associated with the process of exploitation. This is a relation that may be affected by non-linearity.

We claim that a careful consideration of all these three distinctions is essential for a correct understanding and sound characterization of the exploitation process of a primary energy source. Indeed, if we want to generate an unequivocal quantitative analysis of the various factors determining the overall conversion of a primary energy source into a net supply of energy carrier, we have to develop a protocol of accounting that addresses these three conceptual distinctions. That protocol is presented in the next chapter.

6.4.3 The different scales to be considered to study the quality of alternative energy sources

We can conclude this section by making the following three points.

Some of the narratives used in net energy analysis refer to the flows of energy consumed through the whole of society. These narratives focus on the distinction between the overall quantity of energy consumed by a society, referred to as 'gross energy' (primary energy), and the quantity of EC made available to society referred to as 'net energy' (secondary energy). The difference between the gross and net assessment is due to the losses of energy in the energy sector (energy carriers used to make energy carriers). This internal loop reduces the net supply of EC to society. In this conceptualization, the semantic category 'gross energy' indicates the size of the flow of 'energy' under human control required by the society as a whole (used by the black box in relation to its environment). Therefore this assessment refers to the top hierarchical level of the whole society. On the contrary, the semantic category 'net energy' indicates the size of the flow of 'energy' under human control which is available and used by the parts operating inside the black box at the local scale (the energy carriers used to carry out specific functions by the various compartments of society, excluding the energy sector). Therefore, this assessment refers to lower hierarchical levels within the society. This original distinction indicates the need for considering distinct views referring to distinct hierarchical levels of analysis – the gross energy consumed by the whole black box versus the net energy flows consumed inside the parts across multiple hierarchical levels. These two different analyses require the use of two distinct sets of numbers relevant for the analysis of external constraints (gross energy requirement) at the hierarchical level of the whole society and internal constraints (mix of required energy carriers) at lower levels.

Some of the narratives used in net energy analysis refer to a more specific discussion about technological performance. These narratives use the concept of 'net energy' to characterize and compare the quality of various energy technologies exploiting different typologies of primary energy sources (physical gradients to be extracted or captured). However, in this case, the assessment of net gain refers to a specific process of exploitation of PES (based on the existence of favorable physical gradients outside human control) which is determined by the output/input energy ratio. These processes of exploitation necessarily take place at a local scale, within the black box. Put in another way, this second narrative is about the performance of a specific process taking place within a specialized compartment of society at a much lower hierarchical level (the energy sector is a sub-compartment of another economic compartment). As a result, this type of analysis does not consider the changes taking place in the environment embedding the society. The narrative of an 'EROI index > 1' belongs to this set.

Neither the assessment of the gross energy requirement of the society (referring to the level of the whole society) nor the assessment of the EROI index describing relevant characteristics of specific energy technology can provide the information required to assess the severity of external constraints: the compatibility between the requirement of physical gradients associated with GER and the aggregate impact on the environment of the energy sector. In fact, the same GER can have different physical requirements and environmental impacts depending on the mix of PES used by the energy sector. Moreover, the local environmental impact of any specific energy system cannot be scaled up without considering the big picture of the metabolic pattern as a whole. So, addressing the existence of external constraints requires an 'ad hoc' analytical protocol.

An overview of the relation between these different narratives is given in Figure 6.5.

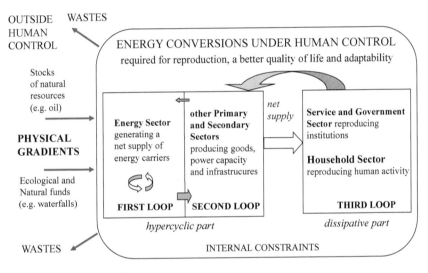

Figure 6.5 Overview of the different narratives that can be used in energy analysis

6.5 When studying the desirability and feasibility of an energy technology a simple number is not enough, we need an integrated (multi-criteria) assessment

6.5.1 How much information can be carried by a single number?

Remaining in a semantic discussion of EROI we can notice that the name of this index is inspired by the concept of return on the investment (ROI) developed in financial analysis. Again, as with the example of the analysis of the budget of the charitable project in Chapter 3 (page 48), we can explore the application of this concept in a simple financial analysis and learn from the experience already available in that field.

Let's imagine that we are asked to evaluate the opportunity to perform an economic investment that will give us a return of 100 per cent. If we use a quantitative index defining the output/input of the monetary flows associated with this investment, this information can be characterized by saying that this investment has a return of 2/1. But then, after having received only the information given by this index – a 2/1 return – can we decide whether or not this investment is worthwhile?

Anybody familiar with economic business immediately sees that the answer to this question is a clear no. In order to evaluate the performance of a proposed investment we need more information. For example, in addition to the information on the ratio of return (2/1) we need to know: (i) the time horizon of such a return. If we are asked to invest 100,000 US$ now in order to get back 200,000 US$ after 50 years, we can conclude that the proposed investment is not particularly attractive; (ii) the scale of the investment. Let's imagine that in order to get such a high return we have to get into a huge financial operation requiring the investment of 300 million US$. If we are just small private investors with an average income we may conclude that this investment is not feasible according to our financial capacity; (iii) how reliable is the assessment of 2/1? If we do not trust the reliability of this information (the seriousness of the people or the stability of the process associated with the financial operation) we may decide to stay away from this investment. From this simple example we can conclude that when dealing with the economic narrative of the return on the investment, a simple number – an output/input ratio – does not provide enough information for generating an informed decision. Moreover the desirability of the investment (the time acceptable to get the given return) depends on the characteristics of both the investor (the goal) and the economy in which the investment is done (the context) and not only on the characteristics of the investment itself.

We can conclude this example by saying that when evaluating an economic investment beside the information about the output/input ratio – the amount of money gained in relation to the initial investment required – we need to consider (at least) four additional pieces of information: (i) the time required for getting the return; (ii) the size of the financial operation – the amount of money that we have to invest in it; (iii) the robustness of the information about the first three factors; and finally (iv) the context against which the performance of this operation has to be evaluated (the same investment characterized using the first three pieces of information may be acceptable in one given situation but unacceptable in another).

Following on from the comparison with financial ROI it is obvious that also when dealing with the analysis of the performance of a set of energy transformations, beside the output/input ratio (an analysis based only on flow elements) an effective analysis of the EROI should be related also to other key factors: (i) the pay-back time of the investment – the power dimension associated with the pace of the flow (the convenience of the investment is justified only if pays back in an adequate time). This implies considering the compatibility with internal constraints (an analysis of the fund elements in charge, within the energy sector, for the generation of energy carriers for the society). A very long pay-back time implies also that the context may change making obsolete the original framing of the analysis (e.g. the problem with nuclear energy). These considerations explain why an analysis of the return on the investment of energy should also consider the requirement of power capacity and the requirement of labour for the exploitation of the given PES (this information is relevant in relation to the analysis of internal constraints). In addition to these two factors, we should also acknowledge that the feasibility of the investment is also related to its overall size, which is associated with a corresponding requirement of natural resources and environmental impact. This is a crucial piece of information for the analysis of external constraints. In theoretical terms we can say that the requirement of physical gradients outside human control is informed by an analysis of the natural fund elements guaranteeing the stability of boundary conditions to the metabolic pattern of the society. It is only when considering this additional information that we can answer the two questions: (i) is a given alternative energy source – and associated energy technology – compatible with the identity of the social system (the societal fund elements determining internal constraints); and (ii) is a given alternative energy source – and associated energy technology – compatible with the boundary conditions provided by the context (the ecological fund elements associated with external constraints)?

6.5.2 When assessing the feasibility and desirability of an energy technology using the EROI index, what is the external referent of the analysis?

In the abstract of their famous paper in *Science* in which they propose to use EROI to explain changes in the performance of the US economy Cleveland *et al.* (1984) say: 'The concept of energy return on investment is introduced as a major driving force in our economy' (p. 890). Later on they state in the text:

> Another important *quality of fuels* is the amount of energy required to locate, extract, and refine them to a socially useful state. This aspect of fuel quality is measured by a fuel's energy return on investment (EROI), which is the ratio of gross fuel extracted to the economy to economic energy required directly and indirectly to deliver the fuel to society in a useful form.
>
> (Cleveland *et al.*, 1984, p. 892, emphasis added)

In this statement there is a clear indication of the external referent used for deciding the quality of the energy source or of the technology. The EROI index assesses 'the quality of fuels'. However, when discussing the relevant attributes to be considered to assess the 'qualities' of fuels Hall *et al.* say:

> These include: 1) sufficient energy density 2) transportability 3) relatively low environmental impact per net unit delivered to society 4) relatively high EROI and 5) are obtainable on a scale that society presently demands.
>
> (Hall *et al.*, 2009, p. 35)

In this quote we see that, when assessing the feasibility and desirability of a fuel for society, the set of relevant qualities includes a set of three different relevant attributes having as an external referent (the 'observable' relevant information for the analysis):

1 The fuel itself

For example, the energy density and transportability of one gallon of gasoline. In our jargon these qualities are relevant attributes of a net energy flow of a given energy carrier observed at a local scale (points #1 and #2).

2 The requirement of physical gradients to generate the gross energy requirement

Once the GER is generated it is transformed later on into a net delivery of fuels to society (point #3). The requirement of biophysical gradients and the associated environmental impact depend on the mix of primary energy sources used by society. In fact, we have to recall here that an assessment of gross energy requirement (and/or net energy requirement) does not map directly onto a resulting demand of physical gradients. Therefore, in order to assess 'the environmental impact of fuels' (the requirement of material to be extracted or the amount of flowing energy to be captured on the supply side and the flow of waste to be absorbed by the environment on the sink side) we need to get additional information, which is referring not to individual fuels (specific flows of energy carriers), but to the special mix of PES which is used to produce them. The same flow of electricity can have a different type of environmental impact if it is produced by a coal-fired plant, a nuclear plant or a hydroelectric plant, the same applies to liquid fuels produced from oil, sand tars or agro-biofuels. Again in order to get useful data about environmental impact we have to consider additional relevant attributes referring to a completely new set of external referents to be observed. The environmental impact associated with either the gross or the net supply of energy carriers can only be considered by studying the interference that the metabolic pattern of society imposes on the metabolic pattern of the ecological systems embedding the society. That is, we have to study the impact that the flows of energy carriers controlled by humans generate on ecological fund elements (the health of rivers, soil, biodiversity, water tables, and the effect of GHG emission on climate and ocean acidification, etc.).

3 'The fuels must have a relatively high EROI and a supply matching the scale that society demands'

Points #4 and #5 on the list given by Hall *et al.* – certainly require putting even more meat on the grill, that is, they require an even more integrated protocol of accounting. In fact, we know that the environmental impact must refer to the mix of PES which is used to generate the gross energy requirement of a fuel. But then if we want to calculate the impact on the environment 'per net supply of energy carrier' we must calculate an additional piece of information: the gross energy requirement/net supply of energy carrier ratio (e.g. right graph of Figure 6.4, page 142). That is, we need additional information which can be obtained only by observing: (i) the energy technology used to extract or capture PES; and (ii) the process adopted to produce the energy carriers from the given PES and make them available for final consumption – e.g. transporting and refining liquid fuels, or making and distributing electricity. This information is required to know the quantity of energy carriers to be invested in the exploitation (the internal loop of energy for energy), that is the difference between gross energy requirement and net supply of energy carriers. If we accept this point, then, the external referent to be observed to get this type of data is no longer only the fuel, but at least two more observables: (i) the characteristics of the technology (or the technologies) used to exploit the primary energy source; and (ii) the pattern of production and consumption of energy carriers in the society. To make things even more difficult, as soon as we get into the analysis of the pattern of consumption of a mix of energy carriers we face another set of relevant attributes to be considered: the specific set of characteristics of 'local patterns of demands of different mixes of energy carriers' in relation to the use of energy carriers of different kinds (if the energy carriers used are in the form of electricity, fuel or process heat). That is, we need to study the pattern of consumption of energy carriers associated with the existing profile of power capacity and human activities allocated at different scales and hierarchical levels across different compartments.

So we can say that the quote of Hall *et al.* 2009 clearly points to the fact that we need a variety of inputs of information to describe the relevant qualities of a fuel or an energy technology in relation to a given society. Needless to say, that if we collapse all these inputs in a single number – the EROI index – we will destroy a lot of this valuable information. As noted earlier, the metabolic pattern of society is an autocatalytic process. Society produces a set of expected functions and reproduces its own structures required for this task. For this reason it is unavoidable to find an impredicative definition of causal relations in the existing set of energy transformations. In the face of this epistemological challenge, the adoption of a linear representation of energy flows – a reductionist approach looking for output/input ratios – can simplify the analysis to a certain extent, but entails a major drawback: it misses this crucial characteristic of the metabolic pattern. Especially critical in this regard is the total neglect of the effects of non-linearity and critical thresholds that determine the feasibility of a given metabolic pattern. If we want to study this key feature of the metabolic pattern we must properly address the existence of a dynamic equilibrium over the requirement and supply of energy carriers. The analysis of this complex equilibrium can only be carried out across different scales and levels and this requires the adoption of a more complex methodological approach.

Finally it should be noted that when looking for an integrated set of answers to be given to different questions, we must adopt non-equivalent quantitative characterizations in our analysis. Virtual quantities of gross energy source equivalent can be useful to sum quantities of electricity generated using different PES in order to make international comparisons – e.g. to generate a comparable assessment of GER expressed in a standardized unit, such as the total use of energy of France versus Germany measured in joules of GER fossil equivalent thermal. However, the virtual tons of oil equivalent associated with the generation of hydroelectric power do not emit CO_2. Hence, a grammar able to properly aggregate different energy forms for one given purpose (e.g. comparing the relative total energy requirement using quality factors to deal with different PES mix) may be totally inappropriate for another purpose (e.g. assessing CO_2 emission and the more general environmental impact on France and Germany). In the same way, what can be useful to assess the effect of changes at the local scale – e.g. changes in consumer behaviour (at the household level) or the effect of improvement in technological efficiency (at the level of industrial plants) – may be completely useless to assess the aggregate effect of these changes for the metabolic pattern of the whole society at the large scale. When dealing with metabolic patterns, local changes have the effect of generating readjustments inside the metabolic pattern, determining a redistribution of energy flows, power capacity and human activity (depending on the relative size of structural compartments) across the various functions expressed by society at the larger level. This fact is at the basis of the well-known phenomenon of Jevons paradox (Polimeni *et al.*, 2008): if a society becomes more efficient in doing something at the local scale, it will not consume less energy as a whole as a result of this fact. Rather it will use the spare capacity generated by the technological improvement in one compartment expressing a given function for doing something else in another compartment in relation to another function. Therefore, unless we are able to check the possible effects that local changes may imply across different levels and scales, the predictive power of simple indices calculated on simplified representations (e.g. the Kuznets' curves hypothesis based on the analysis of changes of energy intensity) remains quite low – for a discussion of this point see Chapter 3 of Giampietro *et al.* 2011. For these reasons, we present in Part II of this book an integrated set of accounting protocols, capable of generating coherent results relevant for studying both internal and external constraints of a given metabolic pattern which can be implemented using a common dataset presenting all the pieces of information gathered at different scales and levels of analysis.

6.6 The decalogue of the energy analyst

Below we provide ten golden rules for the energy analyst who wants to characterize in quantitative terms the performance of socio-economic systems in relation to energy transformations.

Golden rule #1 – When dealing with the quantitative analysis of energy conversions never use the generic concept of 'energy'. When coming to quantitative assessments 'energy flows' defined in generic terms do not exist.

Rather we have to talk of:

- **primary energy sources** – when referring to flows or stocks of energy outside human control. These energy forms are required in order to be able to generate and control useful forms of energy (energy carriers and flows of applied power associated with end uses). The accounting of these PES has to be made in physical quantities (not only in energy units), which can be extracted (e.g. fossil energy measured in thermal energy) or captured (e.g. natural kinetic energy measured in mechanical energy) to produce energy carriers.

- **gross energy requirement** – when referring to the overall amount of 'energy' which must be controlled in order to generate the energy carriers used. Quantities of GER are expressed only in energy units. But because of the differences in quality among different energy forms, the aggregate value of GER requires the use of conversion factors, and therefore the choice of a standard energy form of references. One of the most used solutions is to express GER in quantities of thermal energy equivalent – e.g. Tons of Oil Equivalent. Therefore, assessments of GER do not come from direct measurements (the local scale of reference where flows of energy carriers are observed) but are calculations referring to a larger scale.

- **energy carriers** – when referring to specific forms of energy inputs, compatible with the characteristics of energy converters (power capacity), used to generate flows of 'useful energy' or 'applied power'. These assessments can only be observed and measured at the local scale. Different kinds of energy carriers are measured in non-equivalent forms of energy (mechanical versus thermal). Energy carriers are required in order to generate flows of applied power used by society to carry out the tasks associated with its reproduction and adaptability.

- **end uses** – when referring to the concept of end uses we refer to the set of functions to be expressed at different levels and scales by the society. Because of this multi-scale nature and because of the autocatalytic nature of the process of reproduction of societies, 'end uses' cannot be assessed in quantitative terms using energy units, adopting reductionistic approaches. They require a more complex method of analysis addressing the impredicative nature of the autopoietic process: a holistic multi-scale view.

Golden rule #2 – When dealing with the viability of quantitative analysis of energy conversions we should look for both internal and external constraints. This requires using simultaneously different protocols of analysis.

The existence of a set of energy conversions expressing useful functions for society requires the existence of a structural and functional organization capable of expressing and controlling these energy conversions (internal constraints). At the same time, the expression of these energy conversions must be compatible with boundary conditions and therefore requires the existence of processes outside human control guaranteeing the viability in relation to boundary conditions (external constraints).

When checking internal constraints – in relation to the analysis of the flow of energy under human control – we have to identify the indirect requirements associated with the production factors required to control the energy flows:

- **power capacity** – required to transform the energy input of the process into a flow of applied power;
- **human activity** – required to control the flow of applied power in order to guarantee the expression of the required functions (end uses).

When checking external constraints – in relation to the analysis of the existence of favourable boundary conditions (energy transformation outside human control) – we have to identity:

- **on the supply side** – the availability of the required set of physical gradients: either stocks of inputs (e.g. oil reserves) or natural funds (e.g. natural processes generating useful energy inputs) of an adequate size in relation to the gross energy requirement of a society;
- **on the sink side** – the availability of the required set of physical gradients: either sink capacity (e.g. reservoirs where to sequestrate or store wastes and emissions) or natural funds (e.g. ecological processes recycling the wastes and emissions) capable of absorbing the materials and the heat generated in the conversions determined by the gross energy requirement.

Golden rule #3 – Do not generate an accounting scheme based on only a single scale of analysis (you must use non-equivalent descriptive domains).

Metabolic systems do express relevant patterns simultaneously across different scales and levels of organization. In fact, the conceptual differences between: (i) gross energy requirement (large scale view of the energy consumed) and net energy requirement (local scale view of the consumption of energy carriers); (ii) assessments of flows of energy input (aggregated energy input consumed over the 'extent' of the time scale) and assessments of flows of applied power (local pace of conversion referring to the 'grain' of the time scale); and (iii) assessments referring to energy controlled by humans (the view inside the black box) and the energy available to humans because of processes out of human control (the view of the boundary conditions at the interface of the black box with its context) require addressing explicitly the issue of scale. Therefore, an effective integrated analysis of the overall energetic performance of a socio-economic system can only be observed by looking simultaneously at different factors relevant for describing the characteristics of the interaction of the whole society and its context:

1   the mix of primary Energy Sources used in the energy sector for the supply of gross energy requirement. This mix establishes a relation between the

given GER and the requirement of physical gradients, which must be available;

2   efficiency of the technology used in the energy sector for the generation of energy carriers. This efficiency determines the ratio gross energy requirement/net energy requirement. The effectiveness in using energy carriers to generate energy carriers (gross supply of energy carriers/net supply of energy carriers) can reduce the need of physical gradients for a given requirement of energy carriers;

3   the mix of converters (exosomatic devices providing power capacity) used in the various compartments of the society to guarantee the required functions. The type and mix of converters used in a given society do determine the mix of different kinds of energy carriers used in society – e.g. electric cars versus petrol cars and the efficiency of the conversion (associated with technological performance) at the local scale: the conversion of energy carriers into end uses;

4   the mix of end uses, requiring different intensities of applied power, determines the profile of power capacity and human activity across the different compartments of the society. End uses can be related directly to the characteristics of the socio-economic system – life styles (Americans having large houses and cars), population density (very low population density may prevent the effective use of public transport), climatic conditions (societies living in very cold or very hot weather can require more heating and/or more air conditioning), economic structure (economies based on extractive industries are more energy intensive than economies based on financial operations). Different mixes of end uses, therefore, can explain differences in the pattern of energy uses in different compartments of societies and across societies.

Comparisons made at the level of the whole country using a single quantitative assessment cannot take into consideration the differences in technical performance of individual compartments, which are observable only at the local scale. Therefore a comparison of the energetic performance of different typologies of societies, carried out at the level of the whole country (e.g. assessing the energy intensity of the economy in terms of J/US$), should be considered as a comparison of 'apples' and 'oranges'. In the same way, it is impossible, when making scenarios, to extrapolate the effect of a specific improvement in local efficiency to the whole society if we do not develop first a scaling protocol capable of doing so.

Golden rule #4 – You have to use several semantic categories if you want to measure several relevant attributes and therefore use different formal categories (addressing complex issues requires multi-purpose grammars).

When dealing with complex networks of energy transformations operating across different levels of organization and scale it is impossible to generate a useful quantitative accounting using just a single protocol based on a closed set of semantic and formal categories. As illustrated by our economic example of the analysis of the budget of the restaurant (Figure 4.1, page 63) different semantic categories are required for a proper accounting – e.g. 'gross revenue' versus 'profit' – even when the quantitative assessment is expressed using the same variable – e.g. US$. According to the suggestion of the IFIAS (endorsed later on by several experts of energy analysis) one could imagine adopting an integrated set of different energy variables in the datasets provided for national energy statistics as illustrated in Table 6.2.

Table 6.2 An overview of semantic and formal categories useful for national energy accounting

At the level of the whole country	
Semantic category	*Formal category*
Primary energy sources mix *(outside human control)*	Physical quantities for each PES
Gross energy requirement (thermal) *(under human control)*	Tons of oil equivalent (1 TOE = 42 GJ)
At the local level (observed in compartment$_j$)	
Semantic category	*Formal category*
Net energy throughput (carrier kind$_1$)	$ET_{electric} - kWh$
Net energy throughput (carrier kind$_2$)	$ET_{fuels} - MJ$
Net energy throughput (carrier kind$_3$)	$ET_{heat} - BTU$

When dealing with the concept of desirability we have to deal with the need for contextualizing the meaning of our quantitative indices. We know from economic analysis that a given ratio 'gross revenues/profit' which is acceptable in a given country may not be acceptable in another country. In the same way a certain return on the investment (or a wage) which is judged as very good in a given society could be undesirable in another. For this reason quantitative analysis of socio-economic systems requires the use of benchmark values (expected values for typologies of socio-economic systems) to give meaning to the quantitative assessment. When coming to the analysis of external constraints, the limits imposed by the availability of primary energy sources depends on the local availability of physical gradients. The land requirement of agro-biofuel would be a big problem in China (a very crowded country) but not a problem in Brazil. Using an analysis referring to the local scale, the ratio gross energy requirement/net supply of energy carriers makes it possible to study the performance of the energy sector. However, the specific characteristics of individual energy technologies are muddled because of the effect of different mixes of PES and EC used by different societies. One has to be careful in keeping separated the two types of information: (i) technical coefficients of each energy technology used in the energy sector; and (ii) the overall mix of energy technologies used in energy sectors. The analysis of the performance of an energy sector can become even more challenging because of the imports of energy carriers (importing energy carriers makes it possible to reduce the activities to be carried out in the energy sector of the importing country). Finally, the analysis of local conversions of specific energy carriers into specific end uses makes it possible to study the performance of the various activities. However, again, we must know how to scale this information to the level of the economic sectors at which a mix of different activities is carried out. One has to be careful not to confuse the energy efficiency of individual processes within a given sector and the energy efficiency of the sector as a whole (which depends also on the mix of different processes carried out in it). In conclusion, when applying energy analysis to complex societies we have to develop an integrated set of indicators of performance referring to different semantic categories and different scales calculated within a multiscale analytical framework able to handle such a complex accounting.

Golden rule #5 – Do not make quantitative assessments using 'substantive definitions' (one size fits all) of energy quality, based on thermodynamic narratives.

Thermodynamic narratives are too generic to be applied to the analysis of autopoietic systems (see Appendix 1). This has been clearly stated by Lotka:

> The very fact that they [the laws of thermodynamics] hold independently of substance and form lends their application a catholicity hardly equaled elsewhere in science, and at the same time gives into our hands an instrument of the most extreme economy of thought, since we are relieved, in such application of the necessity of treating each particular case, with all its complication of details, on its own merits, but can deal with it by the shortcut of a general formula. Still, the austere virtue of this impartiality [of the second law of thermodynamics] with respect to substance and form, becomes something of a vice when information is sought regarding certain systems in which mechanism plays, not an incident, but the leading role. Here thermodynamics may be found powerless to assist us greatly and the need for new methods may be felt...
>
> (Lotka, 1956, p. 327)

To fully understand the criticism of Lotka we have to recall here that socioeconomic systems are autopoietic systems, which are self-organizing through informed autocatalytic loops (more in Appendix 1 and in Giampietro *et al.* 2011). This means that they use their own models of themselves when interacting with the external world to guide their action. This implies that what is an 'energy input', what is 'efficiency' and what is 'useful work' within the models used by autopoietic systems depends on their identity and their history (the path-dependent build-up of power capacity and existing institutions providing effective control) – see examples in Chapter 1, pages 12–25. To make things even more difficult the models used by autopoietic systems are different for different typologies of systems, since they are associated with their specific identity, which is evolving in time. This is the reason why qualitative indicators based on substantive thermodynamic concepts – such as entropy or exergy – are unlikely to generate substantive definitions of desirability which can be applied to the diversity of metabolic systems found in our world operating in different and changing boundary conditions. Clearly, thermodynamic analysis represents a very powerful tool when applied to a well-defined process (e.g. industrial trans-formations) for which it is possible to characterize the performance on a pertinent state space (whose validity will not change during the duration of the analysis). We should apply these methods as much as possible, but be aware that often their application becomes problematic.

Golden rule #6 – Do not crunch numbers unless you are sure that the semantics behind them is sound. Do not be worried about doing 'the sum right', but about doing 'the right sum'.

- Do not use standard production rules applied to formal categories (quantities of energy expressed in 'units of measurement') in order to aggregate different energy forms without having checked first the semantic categories to which they refer;
- Do not generate autistic protocols deciding on your own, 'what is the system' and 'what the system does', without having checked the pre-analytical choices with those who will use the model and having checked whether the chosen definition violates logical rules.

Any definition of a semantic category is associated with a corresponding definition of an equivalence classe via the identification of an external referent. We can certainly sum joules of orange juice to joules of gasoline using the equivalence criteria of 'calorific value', but then we have to find someone that would find such a sum relevant for some purpose when considering the two energy carriers (orange juice cannot be used for heating or running engines and gasoline cannot be consumed by humans).

This sixth commandment may seem superfluous, however, we can still find a few applications of aggregation of endosomatic energy (food) summed to exosomatic energy (fossil energy) in literature, also when looking at the work of well-known groups (e.g. the group of social metabolism led by Marina Fischer-Kowalski – Haberl *et al.* 2006). Moreover, as discussed in Chapter 3, prestigious international producers of statistics (Eurostat and IEA) after having introduced the category – Joules of Energy Commodities – adopt a production rule which sums 1J of *vis electrica* produced with hydroelectric power (mechanical energy) with 1J of chemical energy extracted in coal (thermal energy) without using any conversion factor.

Golden rule #7 – When coming to national statistics use always multi-purpose grammars to organize your datasets.

Datasets useful for energy statistics can be based on the adoption of many non-equivalent criteria determining relevant equivalence classes. For example, quantitative assessments may refer to physical quantities to be extracted or captured as in the case of useful information about primary energy sources. These physical gradients all map onto specific quantities of energy (of a given form) – e.g. 1TOE = 42GJ of thermal energy. However, the mapping between physical quantities and their energy equivalent is open to bifurcations (it is impossible to establish a one-to-one mapping between GER and PES). Therefore, a dataset referring to the overall GER of a country has to be based on a specific protocol of aggregation of local flows of energy carriers. In relation to this task, there are different semantic criteria that can be used to define an equivalence class of energy forms and therefore there are different criteria of equivalence which can be used to define quality factors for the aggregation of different energy forms. We can use the category 'thermal energy' or 'mechanical energy' to sum energy quantities referring to these different forms in relation to an equivalence class used as a standard (expressing mechanical energy in thermal equivalent or vice versa). However, depending on the goal of the analysis – e.g. when using 'virtual' tons of oil equivalent in the partial substitution method – quantities of energy which are equivalent in terms of calorific value (useful to assess overall GER-thermal) can appear non-equivalent in terms of CO_2 emissions (useful to assess environmental impact). In the same way quantities of energy which are equivalent in kinetic energy cannot be equivalent in terms of end uses (the same mechanical power can generate different results depending on the efficiency of the power capacity and the specific task to be performed – cooking food with kinetic energy). For this reason, it would be wise to keep separated: (i) a core of data measured using the various categories associated with the external referent (what has been measured at the local scale in terms of biophysical quantities) – e.g. tons of oil, tons of uranium, falling water, primary production of electricity not based on thermal conversion. This is the data used by the statistical offices as input (token-data) for generating indicators; (ii) the set of indicators (statistical products) which are calculated values (names-data) using specified protocols starting from the core data (available tokens). In this way, the users of statistics could know, when carrying out energy analysis, which numbers come from direct measurement (mapping on to external referents) and which are generated by the application of protocols (mapping on to the logical criteria of equivalence chosen by the statistical offices).

Golden rule #8 – When assessing the quality of alternative primary energy sources look always for an integrated set of indicators.

When considering the potential of a resource – the coins found in the sofas of a given country –what is important is not the total amount of coins 'available' in a country, but the amount of coins which are 'accessible': the net supply of coins remaining after having calculated the costs for their collection. When dealing with the exploitation of primary energy sources, the internal loop of energy carriers, which have to be invested to generate a supply of energy carriers, can imply a non linear reduction of the net supply. In turn this internal loop also requires an investment of other production factors such as power capacity and human activity. This problem is especially important when dealing with low quality primary energy sources where the output/input ratio of energy carriers is below 2.5/1. We all know that the amount of solar energy arriving on the planet is huge, but this is not a relevant point. What we have to study is how much concentrated net energy supply we can get when exploiting this PES. Additional relevant attributes include (i) the required investment of the input of energy carriers; (ii) the required power capacity; (iii) the work required; (iv) the resulting output/input of energy carriers; (v) the required physical gradients associated with the PES; (vi) the requirement of material and other natural services (such as land, water) on the supply side; (vii) the pollution associated with the exploitation process on the sink side. As you can see it is an integrated set of information that it is needed.

The EROI index (calculated either as the output/input of energy carriers used in the exploitation of a PES at the local scale or the aggregated output/input of energy carriers at the level of the energy sector) is certainly a crucial piece of information to assess the viability and desirability of exploiting new PES. However, this piece of information has always to be integrated with additional information.

Golden rule #9 – Do not study in isolation either patterns of production or patterns of consumption of energy carriers. Any metabolic system works by integrating the two sides (production and consumption of energy carriers) in an organic whole.

Again, the main implication of the acknowledgment of the existence of a metabolic pattern of society is that the process of autopoiesis of society should be perceived as a dynamic equilibrium referring to an integrated set of transformations producing and consuming energy carriers. When studying the performance and the stability of such a complex system, it is not possible to change just one side (or part) – e.g. the characteristics determining the performance of the energy sector – without affecting the rest (the whole): in a metabolic system everything depends on everything else. If we decide to address the impredicative nature of the metabolic pattern, then we should be aware that when dealing with a complex network of energy transformations it is not possible to optimize 'efficiency' as such in relation to a part of the whole, described in isolation. Any formalization of efficiency must be based on a simplification – the chosen representation within a given boundary in space and time. Every time we focus on a simple output/input ratio we must necessarily refer to just one aspect (a single function) and just one part of a larger system. For this reason, we should always expect that an 'efficiency gain' referring to one part of the system represented in relation to a given perspective will entail an 'efficiency loss' in another part of the system when considering a different perspective of the useful functions to be expressed.

Golden rule #10 – Do not overestimate the importance of energy analysis.

When analyzing energy transformations in human systems, one should always remember that energy conversions and energy efficiency are only a part of the story. There are a lot of other key dimensions of analysis that matter and many of these dimensions are unknown. In fact, when dealing with complex autopoietic systems it is not possible to predict the future, no matter how complicated the model we are using. This means that we cannot know all the attributes of performance that are relevant now and will be relevant in the future. For this reason, it is not possible to define the best thing to do, no matter how much discussion and participation we do at the moment of the quantitative analysis. Energy analysis can be used to get a better understanding of the situation, to share meaning when discussing and negotiating possible compromise solutions and to eliminate from the discussion options which are outside the feasibility domain – i.e. individuating what is not possible according to known laws of thermodynamics. But in any case, a full evaluation of the performance of a social system should consider too many factors (many of which unknown). Therefore, the energetic performance will always be just one of many other attributes of performance. In relation to this point, the father of thermodynamics, Carnot, warned in person against an excessive simplification of the energetic analysis based on a naïve representation of the efficiency of the conversions of heat into mechanical power and vice versa. In the closing paragraph of his *Reflections on the motive power of fire, and on machines fitted to develop that power,* he states:

> We should not expect ever to utilize in practice all the motive power of combustibles. The attempts made to attain this result would be far more harmful than useful if they caused other important considerations to be neglected. The economy of the combustible [**efficiency**] is only one of the conditions to be fulfilled in heat-engines. In many cases it is only secondary. It should often give precedence to safety, to strength, to the durability of the engine, to the small space which it must occupy, to small cost of installation, etc. To know how to appreciate in each case, at their true value, the considerations of convenience and economy which may present themselves; to know how to discern the more important of those which are only secondary; to balance them properly against each other; in order to attain the best results by the simplest means; such should be the leading characteristics of the man called to direct, to co-ordinate the labours of his fellow men, to make them co-operate towards a useful end, whatsoever it may be.
>
> (Carnot, 1824, p. 59)

According to this beautiful piece, what is important is to develop a sound energy analysis and be able to integrate it with other relevant analysis.

Part II

Proposing a solution

7 In search of a richer, integrated and multi-scale accounting protocol

As discussed in the first part of this book, there is a big gap between the characteristics of existing protocols of energy accounting based on the concept of net energy analysis and the desired characteristics of an integrated multi-scale protocol of energy accounting suitable to analyze complex autopoietic systems such as human society. In this chapter we sketch out the general features of an innovative approach that we propose to generate a more effective energy analysis of the metabolic pattern of modern society.

This chapter starts with an overview of the general features that an integrated accounting of energy flows should express in order to generate a useful energy analysis of the autopoietic pattern of modern societies (section 7.1). We emphasize that 'the making of itself' through autocatalytic loops of energy – typical of modern society – can only be analyzed by describing such processes simultaneously at different scales. We distinguish three different levels (scales) for this purpose: (i) the level of the energy sector at which energy carriers are used to produce energy carriers, while exploiting primary energy sources; (ii) the level of the primary and secondary economic sectors (the hypercyclic part of the autocatalytic loop), where the society expresses the function of supply of goods and infrastructures (physical transformation activities); (iii) the level of the whole society, where the characteristics of the given set of 'end uses' can be used to study the desirability of a given metabolic pattern in relation to the expectations of a given socio-economic system. This fact requires the integration of non-equivalent characterizations into a coherent framework.

At the scale of the energy sector (section 7.2), we can carry out an analysis of the performance of energy technologies after individuating the relevant characteristics of the process of exploitation of a primary energy source. This involves studying the loop through which energy carriers are used to generate a net supply of energy carriers using an appropriate protocol of analysis. Practical examples are used to flag key features of this analysis, such as the choice of semantic and formal categories, and the existence of non-linear effects when dealing with low-quality primary energy sources.

In section 7.3 we expand the scale of the analysis to study how the functional parts of the socio-economic system interact. We distinguish between the hypercyclic and the purely dissipative part of the metabolic pattern. The hypercyclic part provides the elements generating the positive autocatalytic loop of exosomatic energy. It comprises the primary and secondary production sectors providing a net supply of energy carriers, material inputs, and power capacity for the rest of society. The purely dissipative part, consisting of the service and government sectors and the household sector, supplies transaction activities to society and reproduces humans (thus guaranteeing the supply of human activity). We show that both the characteristics and the functions of these two macro-compartments are intricately interwoven and that they cannot exist one without another. We outline the principles of the dynamic energy budget of society and of the sudoku effect.

In section 7.4, we define the criteria to be used for boundary definitions in relation to the assessment of direct and indirect inputs for net energy analysis (dealing with the epistemological challenge associated with the truncation problem) and establish a relation between the characteristics of these two concepts with the overall feasibility and desirability of the metabolic pattern of modern society.

7.1 Basic features of an integrated accounting of energy flows across scales

In this section we show how the following integral features of the metabolic pattern of society are included in the model that we propose, in the next chapters, for an integrated accounting of energy flows across scales:

- the impredicative nature of the metabolic pattern associated with the existence of autocatalytic loops of energy flows;
- the issue of multiple-scales in the quantitative representation.

Essential to the handling of both of these issues is a pertinent structuring of the analysis. That is to say that we need to carefully choose the compartments (sectors and sub-sectors) used for the representation of our socio-economic system and the semantic categories used to represent the energy flows going through the system.

7.1.1 Addressing the impredicative nature of the metabolic pattern of energy

In their discussion of the key importance of the quality of primary energy sources for sustained economic growth, Hall and Klitgaard (2012) use the 'cheese slicer' model (presented already in Hall *et al.*, 2008) and illustrated in Figure 7.1. In their representation, the economic process is powered by a flow of energy (bottom arrow) used to generate the GDP (the concentration of arrows on top). The flow of added value generated is then used for investments and consumption. Hall and Klitgaard (2012) explain that when the cost of energy is only a negligible fraction of the GDP, as was the case in 1970 – upper graph – society must invest only a small fraction of the GDP in energy acquisition (indicated by the first top arrow from the left). Moreover, a developed society, having already built up a considerable level of power capacity and infrastructure, can afford to invest only a tiny amount of its GDP in the maintenance of infrastructures and replacement of power capacity (second top arrow from the left). This situation makes it possible to (i) allocate a fair share of the total GDP to other investments (discretionary spending) in the economy, such as expanding new economic activities through research and development and guaranteeing better services, and (ii) to allocate a significant fraction of the total GDP to final consumption. This final consumption can be further divided into two flows: (i) staples (non-discretionary household spending) and household discretionary spending.

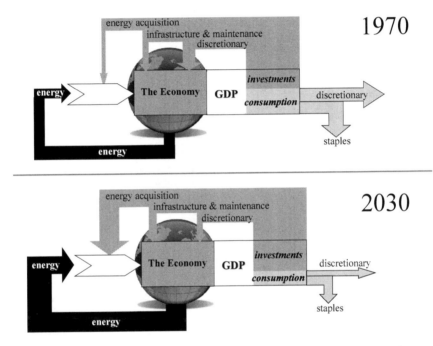

Figure 7.1 Looking at the bio-economic process as an autopoietic process driven by autocatalytic loops of energy: adaptation of Hall *et al.*, 2008

Illustrating the possible consequences of reaching peak oil and a reduced quality of primary energy sources, Hall and Klitgaard also provide a different, future characterization of this same society – lower graph. In this 2030 scenario, the same society will require a much larger energy throughput to operate. However, this increase in energy use results neither in a larger fraction of final consumption nor in a larger flow of discretionary investments in the economy. On the contrary, given the structural changes in the internal loop of energy carriers consumed to produce energy carriers, the energy sector will consume a larger share of the GDP just for its own operation. And that is not all. More power capacity and infrastructures will be required in the energy sector, just to make available the same net supply of energy carriers consumed in the past. For this reason a much lower fraction of the goods and services produced by the economy will be available for final consumption.

Our Multi-Scale Integrated Analysis of Societal and Ecosystem Metabolism (MuSIASEM) approach, which we will gradually unfold in the following chapters, shares the basic rationale behind the loop of energy for energy mentioned by Hall and Klitgaard and illustrated in Figure 7.1. The basic idea of the representation obtained with our approach is illustrated in Figure 7.2.

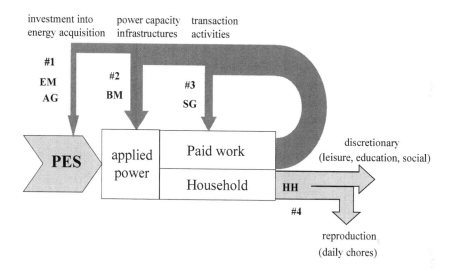

Figure 7.2 Looking at the bio-economic process as an autopoietic process driven by autocatalytic loops of energy: the MuSIASEM representation

Important differences of our approach relative to the cheese-slicer model are:

Simultaneous accounting of several distinct flows

Our model can accommodate the simultaneous accounting of several distinct flows, such as energy, added value, water and waste, within the same definition of 'what the system is' and 'what the system does'. In particular, we can track simultaneously both the flows of energy and added value across different functional compartments and calculate their corresponding throughput rates per hour or per hectare (see Chapter 9). Thus, in our approach, there is no need to separate the accounting of energy from the accounting of GDP as done by Hall and Klitgaard (2012) and shown in Figure 7.1 (page 164). This is possible because in our approach, after having defined the relevant compartments of society both in functional and structural terms, we directly analyze the use of energy flows (and/or of any other relevant biophysical flows) in the various compartments of the economy and the associated economic performance. This makes it possible to couple the economic and biophysical reading across scales using as external referents the different socio-economic sectors and sub-sectors.

Inclusion of power levels and human time allocation

In regard to biophysical flows, our approach not only provides assessments of energy flows, but also of power levels (power capacity/technical capital) and the related profile of allocation of human activity (labour requirement/supply) across the different hierarchical levels of an organization. The inclusion in our model of the assessment of the profile of human time allocation over the difference sectors of the economy is of paramount importance as it allows us to evaluate politically-relevant demographic and socio-economic questions (Giampietro *et al.*, 2011).

As regards to the sticky point of energy analysis, the MuSIASEM approach can:

- characterize the flows of energy using simultaneously two semantic categories: gross energy requirement and net supply of energy carriers;
- keep separated the accounting of energy carriers of different forms (mechanical, thermal, process heat) across the various compartments;
- characterize power levels across the set of considered compartments (making possible an analysis of the required profile of power capacity); and
- characterize the profile of human time allocation across the set of considered compartments (allowing an analysis of the congruence between the requirement for and supply of labour hours across the various sectors of the economy).

7.1.2 Structuring the analysis: choosing a pertinent taxonomy of semantic categories

Of course, the first step of our MuSIASEM approach is to define using semantic categories 'what the system is' and 'what the system does' within our chosen perception of society as an autopoietic (self-organizing) process. This pre-analytical step consists of defining a finite set of semantic categories that maps onto the diverse functions carried out by the various compartments (sectors and sub-sectors) of the socio-economic system. Such semantic definition of the 'skeleton' is an essential aspect of MuSIASEM because effective structuring is a pre-requisite for a sound quantitative analysis. A simplified example of what is called the taxonomy and the grammar in the MuSIASEM jargon is given in Figure 7.3. In the figure we recognize the standard economic sectors (primary, secondary, tertiary) that are generally used for the quantitative analysis of economic performance of a socio-economic system. In our model, the definition of the various sectors and sub-sectors of the socio-economic system is strictly based on the functions they express. The scheme of Figure 7.3 also reflects the functional relations among the various sectors that determine the series of auto-catalytic loops illustrated in Figure 7.2 (and Figure 4.5, page 88). Given this 'skeleton', we will now follow the energy flowing through the metabolic pattern, organized through autocatalytic loops:

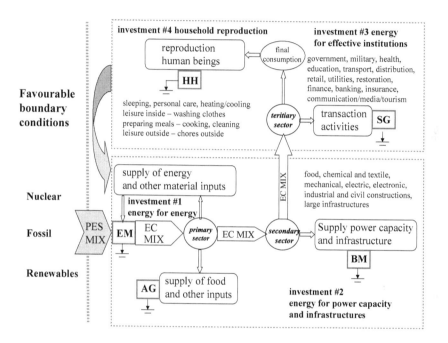

Figure 7.3 The selection of functional categories linked to structural elements (taxonomy) and their expected relations (grammar) in the autopoietic process

- STEP #1: The primary sectors are in charge to make available to society the various flows (energy carriers, food, and other raw materials) required by society for expressing its metabolic pattern. Two very important sub-sectors included here are: Energy and mining (EM), the sub-sector that provides society with the required input flows for its exosomatic metabolism, and agriculture and fisheries (AG), the sub-sector that provides society with the required input flows for its endosomatic metabolism. The primary sectors use a fraction of the available production factors (energy carriers, power capacity and human activity) to express their functions.
- STEP #2: The secondary sector uses another fraction of the available production factors (energy carriers, power capacity and human activity) to express

their own specific functions. In our grammar this sector is called 'building and manufacturing' (BM) and it is in charge of the production and maintenance of power capacity and its related infrastructures.

- STEP #3: The tertiary sector, which in our terminology is called '"service and government' (SG) uses a third fraction of the overall availability of production factors (energy carriers, power capacity and human activity) to express its specific function: to guarantee transaction activities. We include within this term the activities required for reproducing and stabilizing the institutions of the socio-economic process. As explained by North (1990), keeping transaction costs low is an essential function for developed societies.

- STEP #4: The final consumption or household sector (HH) uses the remaining fraction of the overall availability of production factors (energy carriers, power capacity and human activity) to reproduce the invaluable fund element (humans) needed to provide the required supply of human activity to the other compartments and to foster creativity and diversity in the society.

Even if the simplified semantic representation of the socio-economic process shown in Figure 7.3 does not make it possible as such to directly generate a quantitative analysis of energy flows in formal terms, it does allow us to identify a few systemic properties of the metabolic pattern.

First, the metabolic pattern is an autopoietic process characterized by the presence of autocatalytic loops ('chicken–egg processes') that generate impredicativity. Two autocatalytic loops can be identified in relation to the production and consumption of energy carriers (see also Figure 4.5).

1   the first one is taking place in the energy sector itself – energy carriers used to generate energy carriers;
2   the second one is taking place in society as a whole – the various functional sectors of the society make it possible to reproduce structures or institutions and express adaptability. However, the possibility of establishing this second loop depends on the ability of the primary and secondary sectors to guarantee the supply of material inputs, goods, power capacity and infrastructure needed to express the whole metabolic pattern.

Second, the functions expressed by the various compartments of society all compete for the same endowment of production factors: (i) energy carriers (generated by the energy sector), (ii) power capacity (generated by the building and manufacturing sector), (iii) human activity (generated by the household sector), and (iv) an effective institutional setting guaranteeing a low cost for transaction activities (generated by the service and government sector). This autocatalytic loop at the large scale (society as a whole) implies that an alteration or adjustment of the characteristics in any one of the various compartments is almost certain to trigger a change in the characteristics of the other compartments. This complex re-arrangement within the socio-economic system as a whole cannot be predicted in a deterministic way. However, by adopting a multi-scale integrated approach it is possible to study the viability of combinations of these four production factors.

The third systemic property is that the characteristics and the behaviour of the socio-economic system at the level of the whole are not easily mapped onto the characteristics and behaviour of lower-level compartments. There is a certain degree of freedom in relation to the possible adjustments in the profiles of investment of energy carriers, power capacity, human activity, and transaction activities across the lower-level compartments of society. Within the viability domain (the set of all feasible states), human preferences and values as well as random events will eventually determine just one of the possible configurations of the metabolic pattern. Nevertheless, the degree of freedom for selectively choosing 'from within' a specific form of metabolic pattern is limited by the existence of mutual constraints on admissible changes of either the parts or the whole. The required viability of the pattern as a whole dictates that adjustments have to be done in an integrated way, respecting the congruence imposed by biophysical and thermodynamic laws on the network of energy transformations.

As a matter of fact, the existence of a forced set of expected relations over the values of key characteristics determining the viability of a given metabolic pattern is similar to the constraints governing the placement of numbers in a sudoku puzzle. When considered in isolation, a given compartment of the metabolic pattern is affected only by a limited number of constraints. However, if we also consider (i) the rules determining the possible interactions among parts, and (ii) the characteristics of the various parts interacting with the whole, we discover that the characteristics of the parts and those of the whole are constraining each other in an impredicative way. As a result, the emergent property of such complex system is associated with a set of expected relations between the characteristics of the various components. The implementation of the concept of sudoku in the quantitative analysis of the metabolic pattern of modern society is presented in Chapters 10 and 12.

7.1.3 Addressing the issue of multiple-scales: the three levels of analysis (border definitions) in MuSIASEM

An analysis of the energetics of a complex, modern society cannot be obtained by simply summing all the costs and all the benefits associated with the production of energy carriers into a societal EROI index. Socio-economic systems express different functions at different scales, using different combinations of production factors – energy, materials, power capacity, human control, and transaction activities of different kinds – within their autocatalytic loops. Moreover they invest these production factors both when generating a supply of energy carriers and when using them to express functions. It is impossible to collapse this richness of information into a single numerical index defined at one scale only. A sound analysis must acknowledge the complex and integrated pattern of production and consumption of energy carriers across different compartments, operating at different scales, which jointly express an integrated set of functions resulting in a viable metabolic pattern characterized by adaptability and resilience. In fact, the ability to express a viable (and hopefully desirable) metabolic pattern is an emergent property of the whole determined by the successful integration of different tasks coordinated across different levels of organizations. The analysis of such a complex pattern requires a protocol capable of generating a multiple reading over multiple scales and levels. A single index will not do the job. The chosen integrated representation must convey the meaning of the functional compartments – answering the 'why' question – and at the same time characterize the functioning of structural compartments – answering the 'how' question.

Thus, if we want to scale up our analysis from the local level (which characterizes energy flows at the level of a specific energy technology) to higher levels, we must first of all define a logical criterion of accounting for handling the truncation problem. After having defined a set of different levels of analysis we must be able to combine non-equivalent protocols of quantitative analysis within a single coherent framework. We explain here the criteria used by the MuSIASEM approach for achieving this result.

The MuSIASEM approach defines the following three relevant non-equivalent levels of analysis to deal with the integrated characterization of the metabolic pattern of modern society: (i) the autocatalytic loop of energy for energy in the energy sector, (ii) the hypercyclic part of the metabolic pattern in charge of producing the integrated set of inputs required to establish the autocatalytic loop of exosomatic energy, and (iii) the overall autocatalytic loop of society as a whole in its process of self organization.

The level of analysis of the energy sector

The first level of analysis corresponds to the autocatalytic loop of energy for energy taking place in the energy sector. This internal loop has been illustrated in Figure 4.5 (page 88) and is indicated as investment #1 in Figure 7.2, page 165. This analysis can be related to the accounting scheme of EROI discussed in Chapter 6 and discussed below in section 7.2. The analysis of the set of energy transformations taking place at this level is crucial for obtaining information about the quality of energy technologies in relation to both external and internal constraints. The information related to external constraints is associated with the analysis of primary energy sources used in the energy and mining sector – energy input outside human control (non-manmade energy input) – essential to assess the amount of natural resources (favourable biophysical gradients) needed to guarantee a given throughput of energy carriers. This information is relevant to both the supply side (e.g. to address questions such as depletion of fossil energy stocks) and the sink side (e.g. emission of greenhouse gasses). The information related to internal constraints is regarding the amount of 'production factors' required to be able to effectively use the given amount of energy carriers in the energy and mining sector. This information is essential to assess the amount of both power capacity and human labour that must be allocated to the energy sector for producing the required net supply of energy carriers. Once allocated to the energy sector, these production factors are no longer available for the expression of useful functions in other compartments.

When dealing with this integrated analysis of external and internal constraints, the output/input ratio of energy carriers associated with the exploitation of a given primary energy source becomes a crucial piece of information. In fact, it characterizes the quality of the process of generation of energy carriers (the quality of the energy technology) in relation to both external and internal constraints.

The level of analysis of the hypercyclic compartment

The second level of analysis corresponds to the hypercyclic part of the metabolic pattern in charge of producing the integrated set of inputs required to establish the autocatalytic loop of exosomatic energy (the whole box including the primary and secondary sectors in Figure 7.6, page 183). This autocatalytic loop must be able to generate a net surplus of the two production factors power capacity and disposable energy carriers plus additional flows of inputs such as food, fibres and minerals. In the MuSIASEM approach the characteristics of this hypercyclic part are measured by an index that we call the strength of the exosomatic hypercycle (Giampietro and Mayumi, 2009; Giampietro *et al.*, 2011) – discussed in the following chapters. The existence of a hypercyclic part is a mandatory feature of any stable self-organizing system and therefore this concept plays a key role in the biophysical analysis of the economic process (Giampietro *et al.*, 2011).

Even though Hall and Klitgaard (2012) never mention the concept of the hypercyclic part or the idea of a dynamic budget of the metabolic pattern, whose characteristics depend on the sharing of a given endowment of production factors to be distributed across different functional compartments, when they talk of the role of energy in shaping the activities of human society, they come out with this description:

> ... the issue is not simply whether there is surplus of energy but how much, what kind (quality), and at what rate it is or was delivered. The interplay of those three factors determines net energy and hence the ability of a given society to divert attention from life-sustaining needs such as growing sufficient food or the attainment of water toward trade, warfare, or luxuries, including art and scholarship.
>
> (Hall and Klitgaard, 2012, p. 41)

Even if the proposed EROI index cannot provide this information, Hall and Klitgaard seem to share our claim that a useful energy analysis should not only assess energy flows, but also the profile of requirement of power capacity, making a distinction between two types of activities: (i) those aimed at fulfilling life-sustaining needs; and (ii) those aimed at expressing more elaborate functions (learning, adaptability, enjoyment of life).

If we want to study in quantitative terms the relation among these different characteristics we need to establish a criterion for making a distinction between what should be considered as a 'surplus' (something which can be considered as a discretionary investment) and what should be considered as the basic 'subsistence' needs. The ability to invest a larger fraction of productive factors on activities related to the well-being of humans, innovations and creativity is obviously related to the ability to generate the maximum 'surplus' in the exosomatic autocatalytic loop of the hypercyclic compartment. In relation to this point the index called 'strength of the exosomatic hypercycle' (SEH) measures exactly the amount of surplus that can be used by the society (in terms of power capacity, human activity and energy carriers) per unit of labour in the primary and secondary sectors (the sectors in charge for guaranteeing the establishment of the exosomatic autocatalytic loop). Therefore, it represents a biophysical measure of productivity of labour (see also Giampietro and Mayumi, 2000). We describe the semantic and formal categories used for a quantitative analysis of the dynamic budget of supply and requirement of production factors within the autocatalytic loop of exosomatic energy in section 7.3.

The level of analysis of the whole society

The third level of analysis corresponds to a large scale appraisal of the characteristics of the overall autocatalytic loop of society seen as a whole reproducing itself. At the level of the whole society making itself, it is no longer possible to apply the principles of net energy analysis; all the energy carriers are produced and used to do something relevant for society. Still, a quantitative analysis of the characteristics of the energy metabolism (e.g. the relative size of investments in the hypercyclic part versus the purely dissipative part) can provide useful information about the desirability of the resulting metabolic pattern for the people living in society. There are metabolic patterns that are associated with a high material standard of living (a large production and consumption of goods and services per capita) and others that are associated with poverty and suffering. This type of analysis of the coherence of the metabolic pattern in relation to the expression of a complex set of functions at the level of the whole society, as perceived by the people living inside the society, is illustrated in detail in Chapter 10.

The integration of the three levels

An overview of how to combine the non-equivalent quantitative analyses generated at these three different levels is presented in section 7.4. The detailed analysis of this integration is given in Chapter 12.

7.2 The quantitative analysis of the autocatalytic loop of energy carriers for producing energy carriers within the energy sector

In this section we present an approach to the quantitative analysis of primary energy sources based on the theoretical discussions presented in Chapter 6. The goal of this quantitative analysis is to characterize the quality of primary energy sources using a set of benchmark values making it possible to compare the characteristics of an energy technology (producing a net supply of energy carriers) to the characteristics of the pattern of consumption of energy carriers in the other compartments of the society. In order to be considered of 'high quality' a primary energy source has to have a low requirement of production factors (energy carriers, power capacity and human activity). In fact an energy sector requiring a negligible fraction of production factors makes it possible for the hypercyclic compartment to generate an adequate surplus for the autocatalytic loop (at the second level). In conclusion the quantitative analysis discussed here makes it possible to characterize the primary energy source – at the level of the energy sector – in a way that can be integrated in the MuSIASEM approach, bridging this information with other information referring to different levels and scales.

7.2.1 The proper taxonomy of categories when assessing the exploitation of primary energy sources

As argued in Chapter 6, the performance of an exploitation process of a primary energy source should be quantified using a set of different quantitative indicators and not just a single index such as an energy output/input ratio. Indeed, a sound protocol for quantification should be able to establish an unequivocal relation between: (i) the opportunity cost of operating such technology (requirement of power capacity and labour) in relation to internal constraints; (ii) the requirement of natural resources (physical gradients) out of human control in relation to external constraints; and (iii) the net supply of energy carriers for society. We illustrate these relations for the production of biofuel (energy carrier) based on the exploitation of agro-biomass (which can be considered a proxy for solar energy and considered as the primary energy source of the process of production of biofuels) in Figure 7.4.

The upper part of Figure 7.4 characterizes the production process of ethanol from corn in the USA, whereas the lower part characterizes the production process of ethanol from sugarcane in Brazil (data are from Giampietro and Mayumi, 2009). As shown, in both cases we assume that the input of energy carriers to the process is covered by a fraction of the gross ethanol produced. Thus, we assume that the two production processes do not require any fossil energy input (operating with zero emissions).

For instance, as regards the ethanol-corn system (upper graph of Figure 7.4), the standard assessment found in the literature that the production of 1GJ of ethanol requires about 120kg of corn (equal to a production of 66GJ ethanol per hectare/year), is grossly misleading. That is, if we operate under the hypothesis that a fraction of the gross output must be used to cover the required energy input in order to have a self-sustaining, zero-emission bio-fuel system, then we will have to face a massive requirement of natural resources (external constraints). In fact, because of the internal loop of energy for energy, we must produce 11GJ of ethanol (gross supply of energy carrier) to obtain 1GJ of net supply of ethanol (energy carrier) (66GJ: 6GJ in Figure 7.4). Hence, the actual requirement of corn

Ethanol Production from Corn (USA) – 1 hectare

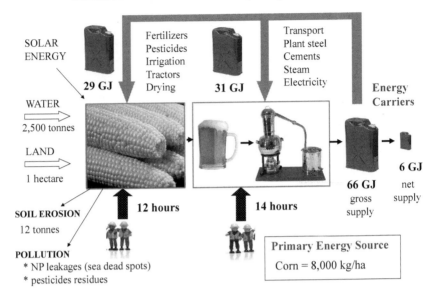

Ethanol Production from Sugarcane (Brazil) – 1 hectare

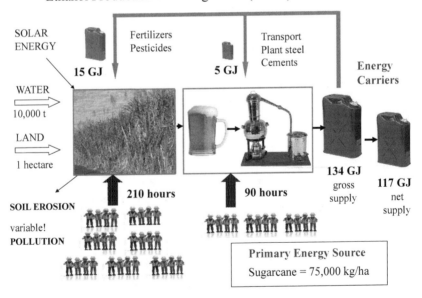

Figure 7.4 The process of exploitation of agro-biomass (primary energy source) for the production of a net supply of biofuels (energy carrier): US corn-ethanol (upper graph) and Brazilian sugarcane-ethanol (lower graph)

(the primary energy source) is 1,333kg (8,000kg/6GJ) per 1GJ net supply of ethanol. This is 11 times the average assessment of the corn requirement found in the literature.

As regards the requirement of power capacity and human labour, the internal loop of energy carriers in the production of ethanol (Figure 7.4) clearly presents a dilemma: (i) one can either use a high level of power capacity (technical capital) in the exploitation of available primary energy source (corn) thus saving on the labour requirement, as is the case in US ethanol production from corn, or (ii) use a large amount of human labour to reduce the requirement of machine-based power capacity, as is the case in Brazilian ethanol production from sugarcane. As we can see in Figure 7.4, the first alternative is not without problems. In fact, carrying out virtually all the operations with machine power rather than human labour demands a large investment of energy input (60GJ/ha) in making, maintaining (indirect energy inputs), and operating (direct energy input) this power capacity. This is what determines the low output/input ratio of energy carriers for US ethanol production from corn. Nevertheless, the second option also has its drawbacks. It is simply incompatible with the high labour productivity associated with the metabolic pattern of a developed country (more on this in Chapters 8, 9 and 10).

The production of ethanol from sugarcane in Brazil, with an output/input ratio of energy carriers of about 7/1 (Figure 7.4), implies a relatively small difference between gross and net supply of energy carrier. This does reduce the requirement of environmental services (e.g. water and arable land) and environmental impact per GJ of net supply of energy carrier compared to ethanol production from corn in the USA (Figure 7.4). However, the problem with Brazilian ethanol production from sugarcane lies with the internal constraints, in particular the high demand for human labour. The low level of mechanization of the system is exactly what keeps the energy output/input ratio high in the Brazilian system. Indeed, a low power capacity entails a lower consumption of energy carriers in the process of exploitation, but a much higher demand of labour instead. In the Brazilian system, 2.6h of labour are required for producing the net supply of 1GJ of sugarcane-ethanol (Figure 7.4), which corresponds to a labour productivity of 0.38GJ/h. This is almost 50 times lower than the labour productivity required from an energy sector of a typical developed country (18GJ/h) (see Chapter 12; Giampietro and Mayumi, 2009; Giampietro et al., 2011). In fact, despite the respectable output/input ratio of energy carriers of 7/1, ethanol production from sugarcane in Brazil generates too weak an exosomatic hypercycle to guarantee sufficient production factors for the rest of society. An energy sector based on a massive production of ethanol would absorb too large a fraction of the labour force, leaving too few labour hours for the operation of other economic sectors (see Giampietro and Mayumi, 2009). A more detailed discussion of this issue is given in Chapter 12.

In conclusion, in order to study the feasibility and desirability of the exploitation of a potential alternative primary energy source we need to gather an integrated set of data and organize the information on the basis of a pertinent set of categories for energy accounting: (i) primary energy sources; (ii) energy carriers (e.g. energy carrier as output and – possibly – other energy carriers as input in the process); (iii) gross supply of energy carriers; (iv) net supply of energy carriers; (v) requirement of hours of human labour; and (vi) power levels (flows of energy carriers controlled per hour of human activity) and corresponding requirement of power capacity.

In order to evaluate external constraints related to the primary energy source, a quantitative characterization of an exploitation process must also be able to establish a relation between the gross energy requirement/supply (in this case fuel), expressed in a given energy form of reference (thermal energy), and the required primary energy sources expressed in physical quantities (e.g. either tons of maize or sugarcane).

As regards the energy carriers we must be able to establish: (i) the internal requirement of energy carriers for the exploitation process (closely associated with the requirement of power capacity and labour); and (ii) the net supply of energy carriers delivered to society (which should meet the requirement of society). It is important to recall that if we deal with different types of energy carriers as input in the process of exploitation (e.g. a mix of fuels and electricity), we cannot simply sum the energy quantities into an overall assessment of input expressed in joules of energy carriers, because they refer to non-equivalent types of energy carrier.

Finally, in order to deal with the internal constraints we have to examine the requirement of human labour and power capacity, to check the aggregate requirement of these two production factors in the energy sector. The larger the requirement of labour and power capacity in the energy sector, the lower the quality of the exploited primary energy source.

In the next section we will closely examine the relation between the gross and net supply of energy carriers and the energy output/input ratio, as well as the implications of the non-linear relation between the gross and net supply of energy carriers for low-quality primary energy sources.

7.2.2 The non-linear relation between gross and net energy supply when dealing with alternative energy sources of low quality

As illustrated in the examples of Figure 7.4, the relation between the requirement of primary energy source (PES), relevant for the definition of external constraints, and the net supply of energy carrier (NSEC), relevant for determining the viability of the supply of energy carrier, is of prime interest for society. This is especially true when the primary energy source is limited in quantity or not easily accessible. Using the chicken–egg scheme on the right of Figure 6.4, we can relate this ratio to the relative value of gross supply of energy carrier (GSEC) and net supply of energy carrier (NSEC):

PES/NSEC = (PES/GSEC) × (GSEC/NSEC)

It is important to realize that the ratio PES/NSEC may be affected by non-linearity, the degree of which depends on the range of values of the output/input ratio of energy carriers: where: (i) the output of energy carrier is represented by GSEC; and (ii) the input of energy carriers is represented by (GSEC – NSEC).

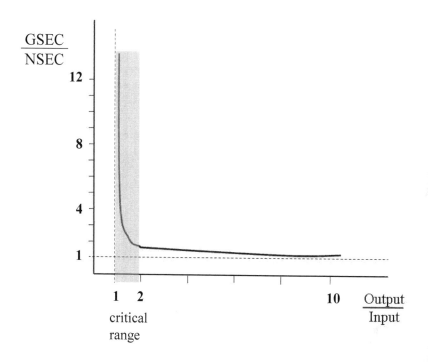

Figure 7.5 The non-linearity between gross output of energy carriers and net output of energy carriers in relation to the classic output/input ratio
Source: Giampietro and Mayumi, 2009, used with permission from Earthscan

To show this point we can write the output/input ratio of energy carriers (Figure 7.5) as:

output/input ratio = GSEC/(GSEC – NSEC)

We can then write the relation between GSEC and NSEC as:

GSEC/NSEC = output/input × [1/(output/input – 1)]

The existence of non-linearity in the relation between the GSEC/NSEC ratio and the classic output/input ratio of energy carriers is illustrated in Figure 7.5. When dealing with high-quality primary energy sources (output/input ratio greater than 5/1), we see that the value of the ratio GSEC/NSEC is close to 1, and therefore the difference between GSEC and NSEC is negligible. In this case we can assume that the ratios PES/GSEC and PES/NSEC are similar. Thus, when exploiting a high-quality primary energy source, such as oil, the internal loop of energy carriers required to make energy carriers can be considered negligible in the assessment of the resulting net supply of energy carriers. Moreover, in this case the internal loop of energy for energy will not significantly affect – at least in the short term – the relation between the speed of depletion of primary energy source stocks and the pace of consumption of energy carrier derived from that stock.

For instance, when the output/input ratio is greater than 10/1, the consumption of 100 barrels of oil in the form of a net supply of energy carriers (NSEC) can be considered as more or less equivalent to the depletion of 100 barrels of oil in the reservoir (PES). A difference of more or less 15 per cent in the value of the various flows may very well be inside the error bar associated with the quantitative assessments. Probably this explains why the distinctions between (i) joules of primary energy source (fossil energy) versus joules of gross energy carriers (fossil energy); and (ii) gross energy carriers (fossil energy) versus net energy carriers (fossil energy) have not been recognized, so far, as being relevant by most of those working in the field of energy analysis. This may also explain why the work of Sedlik (1978), who as early as 1978, proposed the basic concept presented here, has been completely ignored.

The situation becomes completely different when dealing with primary energy sources other than fossil fuels. When dealing with low-quality primary energy sources (output/input ratio lower than 2.5/1), we see that the energy output/input ratio is either close to or inside the critical area of non-linearity illustrated in Figure 7.5. An example of such a case is the corn-ethanol production system in the USA discussed earlier (Figure 7.4, page 174). In this situation, any small reduction in the energy output/input ratio may cause large increases in the GSEC/NSEC ratio. That is, any additional or unforeseen internal loss of energy carriers in the exploitation process causes a non-linear increase in the difference between gross and net supply of energy carrier. This, in turn, has its repercussions with regard to the external (required natural resources and sink capacity) and internal constraints (requirement of power capacity and labour) of the exploitation process. In fact, when facing a relatively large GSEC/NSEC ratio, we require: (i) a greater amount of primary energy source in order to obtain the same net supply of energy carriers (NSEC) (in the example of corn-ethanol 11ha are required to generate the net supply equivalent of the gross supply of 1ha), and (ii) more power capacity in order to handle soaring investments of energy input needed to replace human labour to obtain the same net supply of energy carriers (NSEC). In the corn-ethanol case heavy investments of machinery are required to reduce the labour demand for cultivating large areas. This may result in a clash with, respectively, external and internal constraints, eventually leading to stock depletion and/or environmental damage and lack of economic viability of the process (a more detailed discussion of the case study of agro-biofuels is discussed in Giampietro and Mayumi, 2009).

Below the threshold of 2/1 for the energy output/input ratio, the large internal consumption of energy carrier is likely to make the exploitation process of the primary energy source in question no longer viable. Many of the alternative primary energy sources that are currently proposed do have a low output/input ratio, and the message of Figure 7.5 is extremely relevant for any assessment of their viability.

7.2.3 Integrating existing indices of energy analysis into a more complex set of indicators

It is certainly true that the classic output/input ratio of energy carriers in the exploitation process of a primary energy source (what Charlie Hall calls EROI index at the point of use) is a relevant piece of information to assess the quality of an energy technology. Perhaps not so much in itself, but because of the fact that it allows us to calculate benchmark values to study the severity of external and internal constraints. As regards the external constraints, we can compare the specified set of physical gradients outside human control (availability of natural resources and sink capacity) that are required for generating a given net supply of energy carriers against the actual availability of those physical gradients. As regards the internal constraints, we can compare the set of production factors required for producing a net supply of energy carriers against the actual power capacity and human labour available for investment in the energy sector by society.

However, in order to integrate in this way this 'EROI at the point of use' into the bigger picture, it is essential that the energy inputs are calculated in a consistent manner. We already touched upon this topic in Chapter 6, page 120. We clarify this further with an example based on the assessment of the EROI of an oil shale by Cleveland and O'Connor (2011). We select this example because the authors specifically address the semantic ambiguity in the definition of the EROI and propose several non-equivalent EROI indices for the same process of exploitation.

In particular, the authors focus on the logical bifurcation in the calculation of the EROI represented by the choice whether or not to include 'internal energy' among the inputs. In this case the authors refer to the energy directly taken from the oil shale (in the form of thermal energy) as internal energy, that is used *in situ* to heat the material underground, making it possible to pump it to the surface. Because this is an internal consumption of thermal energy, paid for by a depletion of the stock of primary energy source, there is no doubt in our interpretation that it should be included as an input of the process. According to the rationale presented in Chapter 6 this internal consumption of energy must be considered among the inputs. In fact, the process of heating the material *in situ* not only entails the consumption of a natural resource (on the supply side) and additional CO_2 emission (on the sink side), thus making it relevant in relation to the external constraints, but it also requires some form of control by humans (it is an energy transformation under human control) and therefore it implies an opportunity cost for society, thus making it relevant also in relation to the internal constraints. If we define the criteria of how to calculate the 'EROI at the point of use' in this way, it becomes much easier to individuate the pertinent semantic and formal categories at the moment of developing a protocol of accounting.

In conclusion we believe that in order to take advantage of the information provided by the output/input energy ratio (or EROI at the point of use) we have to feed such information into a more complex method of characterization of the metabolic pattern of the society; provided of course that the calculation method is in accordance with the selected semantic and formal categories of the larger framework of the accounting protocol. In any case, things become more difficult if we want to scale-up from the local analysis of an individual set of energy transformations (the exploitation of a given energy source) to a more aggregate view of the metabolic pattern of society – e.g. the entire energy sector, the hypercyclic compartment, the whole society.

7.3 Scaling up: the hypercyclic and the purely dissipative part of the metabolic pattern

7.3.1 The hypercyclic and purely dissipative parts of society

The phenomenon of hierarchical organization of flows of energy and matter in natural ecosystems and in general in dissipative networks is one of the topics addressed by theoretical ecology (e.g. Margalef, 1968; E.P. Odum, 1971; H.T. Odum, 1971, 1996; Ulanowicz, 1986, 1997). This type of analysis is justified by the foundations of non-equilibrium thermodynamics applied to the process of self-organization of metabolic systems (Schneider and Kay, 1994; Kay, 2000) (see also Appendix 1). The MuSIASEM approach adopts the theoretical conceptualization as proposed by Ulanowicz (1986) for the analysis of aquatic ecosystems. This conceptualization is closely associated with the basic rationale for net energy analysis. According to this conceptualization, the network of matter and energy flows making up an autopoietic or metabolic system (such as a socio-economic system) can be divided into two functional parts: a part generating a so-called hypercycle (a positive autocatalytic loop) and a purely dissipative part.

The part generating the hypercycle has a positive net return in energetic terms when considering its interaction with the context. Indeed, it expresses a set of activities aimed at gathering energy inputs (primary energy sources) from the context and making critical inputs available to the rest of the system. Its operation has a cost that is necessarily lower than the return. This part thus makes available to the system more energy carriers, power capacity and material flows than it consumes for its own operation (for reproducing its own structures and expressing its own functions). In fact, the hypercyclic part provides a surplus of energy and material inputs as well as production factors to the rest of the system for expressing other types of structures and functions. The functional role of this part (in relation to the whole) is to drive and keep the whole system away from thermodynamic equilibrium while guaranteeing its biophysical viability (the concept of hypercycle was introduced by Eigen, 1971). That is, a positive auto-catalytic loop is required to preserve a set of metabolic structures and functions that can only be stabilized by a continuous flow of inputs taken from the context and a continuous flow of wastes dumped into the context. Note, however, that the hypercyclic part is not only a source of positive return for the whole system, but also a major liability. When hypercycles operate without a coupled process of control (and damping), they do not survive for long, they 'just blow up' (Ulanowicz, 1986, pp. 56–57). The process of control is provided by the purely dissipative part of the system.

The dissipative part of the system has – as its name suggests – a purely dissi-pative nature. This part is made up of elements expressing a net consumption of energy carriers, power capacity and material flows. However, this part is certainly not useless for the system. On the contrary, it is essential for its long-term sustain-ability. The dissipative part makes it possible to better direct and use the available surplus provided by the hypercycle, thus providing adequate control on the expression of the metabolic pattern and, at the same time, exploring new possible structures and functions (Giampietro, 1997; Giampietro *et al.* 1997). Indeed, the dissipative part is the part in charge of the adaptability and flexibility of the meta-bolic system in the long run (e.g. through reproduction, education, and social relations); qualities that are crucial for its sustainability (Conrad, 1983; Ulanowicz, 1986; Kampis, 1991; Holling, 1995).

Note that a metabolic system made of a hypercyclic part alone could not be stable in time. Without the stabilizing effect of the dissipative part, the positive feedback of the hypercycle would be reflected upon itself without attenuation, and eventually the upward spiral would exceed any conceivable bounds (Ulanowicz, 1986, p. 57). For this reason, when analyzing an autopoietic or meta-bolic system we should always look for an expected set of functional relations established over its internal parts that are directly associated with the rationale for net energy analysis. Indeed, it is a general characteristic of any metabolic pattern that the long-term stability of the system depends on the wise coupling of a hyper-cyclic part to a purely dissipative part. The two parts depend on each other: they complement each other in guaranteeing the functionality of the system as a whole. This rationale provides us with a useful logical criterion to deal with the trunca-tion problem in the quantitative analysis of complex energy networks characterized by impredicativity (chicken–egg logical paradoxes). We will address this issue in section 7.4. First, in the following sub-sections (sections 7.3.3 and 7.3.4) we will see how the dichotomy of the metabolic pattern as one hypercyclic and one purely dissipative part relates to the standard classification of economic sectors and sub-sectors, and how it provides the basis for analyzing the dynamic energy budget of society.

7.3.2 Transformation and transaction activities

Reference to a functional specialization among different compartments of socio-economic systems, other than the classic primary, secondary and tertiary economic sectors, can also be found in economic theory. For instance, Nobel Prize winner Douglass North (1990) suggests that the activities expressed by a socio-economic system can be divided into two classes: (i) transformation activities, which are related to the effective handling of biophysical processes, and (ii) transaction activities, which are related to the effective handling of information required to operate effective institutions. Transaction activities are required for the successful integration and amplification of production and consumption processes and for developing adaptability.

The classification of transformation and transaction activities proposed by North roughly corresponds to the hypercyclic and dissipative compartments, respectively, proposed by Ulanowicz (1986). We will refer to both classifications in our MuSIASEM approach (for a more detailed discussion of this point see Giampietro *et al.* 2011).

7.3.3 The structural and functional organization of society in its process of self-organization

Following the conceptual distinction proposed by Ulanowicz (1986), it is possible to group the classic economic sectors of a society into two large functional units corresponding to the hypercyclic and purely dissipative parts, respectively, of the metabolic pattern. This is illustrated in Figure 7.6.

The hypercyclic part includes the classic primary and secondary economic sectors, including the agricultural sector (AG), the energy and mining sector (EM), and the building and manufacturing (BM) sectors. This part of the socio-economic system, although consuming energy carriers, material, power capacity, and infrastructure for its own operation, generates a net supply of energy carriers, other inputs and production factors for the rest of the system (required for expressing the functions of the purely dissipative part). The primary sectors (energy and mining and agriculture) produce the required metabolized flow of energy carriers, food, and other inputs such as minerals. The secondary sector (building and manufacturing) provides the basic goods, infrastructures and machinery for the system. This macro-compartment makes it possible to establish a positive autocatalytic loop of exosomatic energy, that is, of energy carriers and power capacity that allow the production of more energy carriers and more power capacity. Not surprisingly the hypercyclic compartment requires a significant fraction of the total input of energy carriers.

The hypercyclic compartment, consisting of the primary and secondary sectors, guarantees the transformation supply activities associated with the production of input flows, goods, and infrastructures required by society.

The purely dissipative part, on the other hand, is represented by the service and government (SG) sector and the household sector (HH). In modern society, these two sectors entirely depend on the energy carriers, food, products, power capacity and infrastructures generated by the hypercyclic compartment (the primary and secondary productive sectors). As noted earlier, the label of 'purely dissipative activities' does not imply that this macro-compartment does not

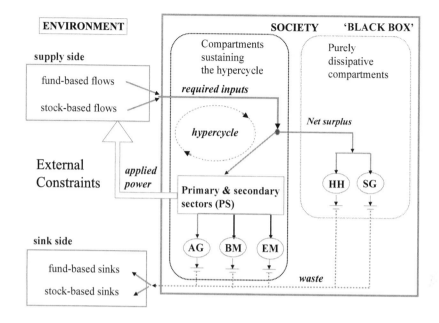

Figure 7.6 The dynamic energy budget associated with the metabolic pattern: the forced coupling of the hypercyclic and the purely dissipative parts

express key functional activities. In fact, the purely dissipative part expresses a series of organized structures and behaviours able to keep in check the potentially explosive effects of the hypercyclic part by flaring the surplus of energy input and production factors into activities that do not amplify back in terms of additional supply of energy carriers and power capacity. Moreover, the purely dissipative part must generate, stabilize and expand effective institutions that are required for controlling the reproduction of the complex metabolic pattern, by developing anticipatory systems and fostering the learning and adaptability of the whole.

Thus, the purely dissipative part is crucial in guaranteeing transaction activities and final consumption activities. Without these, a society could not possibly express a metabolic pattern. In particular, these activities are essential for the reproduction and operation of the following institutions:

- households: individual human beings are reproduced in biophysical terms at the level of households. They are key for producing a net supply of human labour for control;
- social institutions: social organizations are required to guarantee the proper functioning of social institutions. These are essential for lowering the transaction costs.

The energy security and stability of the metabolic pattern of a society depends on its ability to match the requirement of energy flows and power capacity across these two macro-compartments (Giampietro *et al.*, 2011). We will address this in detail in the following section.

7.3.4 Basic features of the dynamic energy budget of society

The rationale of the dynamic energy budget is at the basis of the MuSIASEM approach (see Giampietro, 1997; Giampietro *et al.*, 1997; Giampietro and Mayumi, 2009; Giampietro *et al.*, 2011) and will be presented in detail in the next chapter. We present here, the basic features of the dynamic energy budget, focusing on the exosomatic hypercycle and the purely dissipative compartment following the schematic illustration of the simplified dynamic energy budget given in Figure 7.6.

When considering the socio-economic system as a whole (level n), we can define a given aggregate requirement (demand) in terms of (i) flows of energy carriers, and structural elements, most notably (ii) power capacity (for expressing functions) and (iii) human labour (for control). As its name suggests, the dynamic energy budget focuses on flows of energy carriers, but the analysis can just as well be carried out for material flows, such as water or waste.

We can then characterize the interaction among the various compartments (parts) of the socio-economic system at lower hierarchical levels (n-1, n-2, etc.) by considering that these compartments use (i) a certain share of the total input of energy carriers, and (ii) a certain share of the total endowment of power capacity and human activity (labour when invested in the paid work sector – AG, EM, BM, SG). Thus, the metabolic pattern of each specific compartment of society (at lower hierarchical levels) is characterized by its relative share of the overall input of energy flows and of the overall endowment of power capacity and human activity. It follows that if a specific compartment (e.g. the household sector) increases its share of use of energy carriers, then other compartments will have to compensate and reduce their consumption of energy carriers. The same is true for power capacity. The profile of human labour reflects two distinctions: (i) human activity in the paid work sector (HA_{pw}) versus human activity spent in the household sector (HA_{HH}); (ii) the profile of allocation of human activity in the paid work sector on lower level compartments (AG, EM, BM and SG). Put in another way, within any given metabolic pattern there is an internal competition among the various compartments for the aggregate amount of energy carriers, power capacity and human activity, and the profile of distribution of these production factors can be used to study the viability and desirability of the exosomatic metabolic pattern (this is explained in the remaining chapters of this book).

What is particularly relevant here is that the hierarchical, forced relation between the characteristics of the whole and the characteristics of the parts makes it possible to define expected functional relations within the metabolic pattern. For instance, the energy security and stability of the metabolic pattern of society depends on its ability to match the requirement of energy flows and production factors to be divided among the hypercyclic and purely dissipative macro-compartments (Giampietro *et al.*, 2011). Indeed, the existence of a dynamic energy budget associated with the expression of the metabolic pattern entails the existence of mutual constraints determined by the characteristics of these two macro-compartments.

The biophysical-technological identity of the hypercyclic compartment (the primary and secondary production sectors) defines (i) the flow of energy carriers and the power capacity that can be supplied by the hypercyclic compartment to match the overall demand of society (at level n), including its own demand (at level n-1) per hour of human activity invested there, and (ii) the surplus of energy carriers, power capacity per hour of human activity in the hypercyclic compartments that must be allocated (level n-1) to the purely dissipative compartment (services and government sector and household sector) because of the characteristics of its components. Note that the biophysical-technological identity of the hypercyclic compartment is determined by the available technology and know-how in relation to the mix of specific energy carriers required by society for its various end uses, as well as by the quality of natural resources available (the mix of accessible primary energy sources).

As suggested by North (1990), in developed societies, transaction activities are essential for guaranteeing the proper functioning of socio-economic institutions, which in turn are essential for an efficient functioning of transformation activities (Giampietro *et al.*, 2011). Industrialization and economic growth mean a contin-uous expansion of the diversity of structural organizations and functions expressed in the purely dissipative parts and increased complexity of the system of control (Giampietro *et al.*, 2011). In conclusion we can say that a continuous improvement in the material standard of living (final consumption) translates into a continuous increase in requirement of transaction activities, which in turn requires a greater net supply of energy carriers, power capacity and material (the surplus in the autocatalytic loop) from the hypercyclic part. This leads to a constantly growing labour productivity and investment of power capacity in transformation activities in the hypercyclic part (Giampietro *et al.*, 2011).

The viability of the dynamic equilibrium between the hypercyclic and the dissipative compartment can be verified by looking at the congruence of two crucial parameters: the strength of the exosomatic hypercycle and the bio-economic pressure.

The strength of the exosomatic hypercycle is defined as the energy throughput supplied to society per hour of human labour in the hypercyclic compartment (primary and secondary production sectors). This number represents the level of biophysical productivity actually achieved per unit of human activity invested in the hypercyclic compartment, given its biophysical-technological characteristics.

The bio-economic pressure is defined as the required energy throughput per hour of human labour allocated to the hypercyclic compartment. This number defines the threshold of biophysical labour productivity that is forced upon the exosomatic hypercycle by the characteristics of the metabolic pattern of society as a whole.

In conclusion, the two macro-compartments, the exosomatic hypercyclic and the purely dissipative part, can only change their characteristics simultaneously in an integrated way. This forced compatibility between the characteristics of the metabolism of the various compartments, defined at different hierarchical levels, forms the basis of the sudoku effect, which provides a powerful tool to study the viability of changes in the metabolic pattern of modern society in relation to the dynamic equilibrium of the whole. The quantitative application of the sudoku effect is presented in Chapter 10.

7.4 Moving over hierarchical levels of analysis, boundary conditions and the truncation problem

The co-existence of non-equivalent narratives about energy investments and energy returns referring to different hierarchical levels require non-equivalent definitions of system boundaries (e.g. recall the example of the co-existence of many legitimate boundary definitions for the analysis of the energetics of human labour described in Chapter 2, page 12). In particular, if we want to carry out calculations according to the rationale for net energy analysis we may deal with any one of the following three hierarchical levels discussed in this chapter:

1   the autocatalytic loop of energy carriers for producing energy carriers in the energy sector (the idea behind the EROI at the point of use);
2   the dynamic equilibrium between the hypercyclic and purely dissipative compartments of the metabolic system that establishes a forced relation among their metabolic characteristics;
3   the emergent property of the metabolic pattern as a whole that determines the 'degree of desirability' for living inside that socio-economic system. This characteristic cannot be studied using the net energy analysis rationale, because at the level of the whole society, all the forms of energy used are re-invested – there is no net energy gain. At the level of the whole society we can only look at the set of functions expressed by society and use benchmark values to describe the relative performance of the metabolic pattern compared to other socio-economic systems or to desired characteristics.

In this chapter we have seen a series of theoretical concepts and semantic criteria that are useful to handle the epistemological ambiguity associated with the existence of the various hierarchical levels and the related definitions of boundary conditions (to deal with the truncation problem) and to develop a sound, integrated, quantitative analysis of the metabolic pattern of society.

A schematic representation of the rationale of the MuSIASEM approach explained using these concepts is provided in Figure 7.7. When dealing with the analysis of the external constraints we deal with the analysis of energy inputs (left side of Figure 7.7). Considering society as a whole (top of Figure 7.7), we can define the overall gross energy requirement of the socio-economic system and check whether it is compatible with available boundary conditions; that is, the

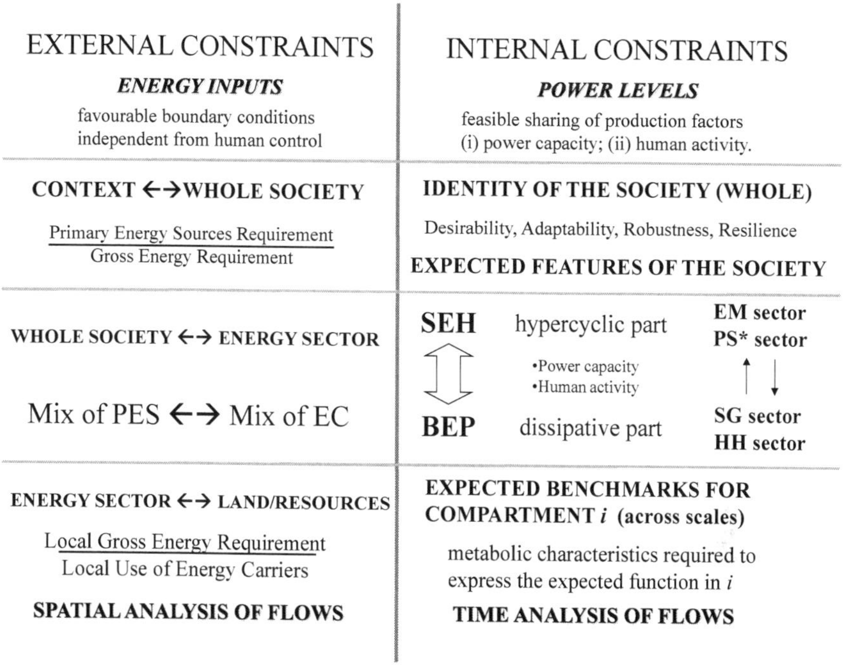

EXTERNAL CONSTRAINTS	INTERNAL CONSTRAINTS
ENERGY INPUTS	***POWER LEVELS***
favourable boundary conditions independent from human control	feasible sharing of production factors (i) power capacity; (ii) human activity.
CONTEXT ←→ WHOLE SOCIETY	**IDENTITY OF THE SOCIETY (WHOLE)**
Primary Energy Sources Requirement Gross Energy Requirement	Desirability, Adaptability, Robustness, Resilience **EXPECTED FEATURES OF THE SOCIETY**

WHOLE SOCIETY ←→ ENERGY SECTOR	**SEH**	hypercyclic part	**EM sector** **PS* sector**
		•Power capacity •Human activity	↑ ↓
Mix of PES ←→ Mix of EC	**BEP**	dissipative part	**SG sector** **HH sector**

ENERGY SECTOR ←→ LAND/RESOURCES	EXPECTED BENCHMARKS FOR COMPARTMENT *i* (across scales)
Local Gross Energy Requirement Local Use of Energy Carriers **SPATIAL ANALYSIS OF FLOWS**	metabolic characteristics required to express the expected function in *i* **TIME ANALYSIS OF FLOWS**

Figure 7.7 Relevant factors for studying internal and external constraints of a metabolic pattern at different levels of analysis

primary energy sources available. This may refer either to the availability of resource stocks (to assess the life expectancy of the reserves), or renewable resources and the related demands of other biophysical inputs (land, water, etc.), or a combination of both. In order to develop a robust system of accounting we have to establish a relation between the assessment of the gross energy requirement (the total amount of energy under human control) and the total energy throughput expressed in terms of energy carriers (divided by typology such as electricity, fuel, and process heat). This analysis has to be carried out across the various compartments of the society. It requires moving down the hierarchical structure, analyzing the characteristics of lower level compartments. Alternatively, when discussing scenarios, one can also work in the opposite direction starting from the bottom up. In that case, expected technical coefficients of local processes are used to calculate the overall consumption of energy carriers and the resulting requirement of primary energy sources.

When addressing the analysis of the internal constraints to the metabolic pattern, we deal with power levels (right side of Figure 7.7). In this case, we shall examine the relative amount and combination of the two production factors, power capacity and human activity, invested in the various compartments of society. At the larger level (top of Figure 7.7) we see that the identity of the society (the set of functions associated with the metabolic pattern) will define the desirability of the autopoietic process. Moving down the hierarchy to the macro-functional compartments of the exosomatic hypercycle and the purely dissipative part, we can check the feasibility (viability) of the dynamic energy budget of society. The performance of these two macro-compartments in turn depends on the characteristics of each of the sectors making up these macro-compartments. Therefore, we have to characterize each one of these sectors (even if referring to different levels) using an integrated set of characteristics relative to the energy input and power level.

The scheme given in Figure 7.7 is based on a set of expected semantic relations. In order to put this theory into practice we need a system of accounting capable of formalizing all these relations across different hierarchical levels and scales in quantitative terms. The MuSIASEM approach has been conceived to do this. We illustrate our methodological approach in detail in the following Chapters 8, 9, 10 and 11. The specific application of MuSIASEM for assessing the quality of alternative energy sources is discussed in Chapter 12.

8 Concepts, ideas and representations underlying the multi-scale integrated accounting of society's energy metabolism

In this chapter we introduce and explain the concepts, ideas, and representations on which we have built our multi-scale, integrated accounting of the energy metabolism of society. Most of these have been briefly touched upon in the preceding chapters. Here we try to be more exhaustive in our explanations and show how they fit our model, using examples to make our case. We particularly focus in sections 8.1, 8.2 and 8.3 on the common features of the endosomatic and exosomatic energy metabolisms; in section 8.4 on the central role of human time allocation and the mosaic effect, which is used to reveal the relations between human time allocation and exosomatic energy flows; in section 8.5 on the allocation of human time and power capacity to the various compartments of human society defined at different levels; in section 8.6 on impredicative loop analysis used to individuate threshold values for the characteristics of key compartments of the socio-economic system that determine the viability of the dynamic energy budget; and finally, in section 8.7 on the simultaneous use of top-down and bottom-up approaches.

8.1 The energy metabolism of the human body

In recent years, the term 'metabolism' has gained much popularity in the field of energy and material flow analysis of society. Its literal meaning, according to the online Oxford dictionary is: 'the chemical processes that occur within a living organism in order to maintain life'. In this sense, the entire socio-economic system can – we believe justifiably – be considered as a living organism. We like this analogy. But it should be applied consistently (unfortunately, as we will see, this is not always the case). In this section, we analyze in detail the energy metabolism of the human body (endosomatic energy metabolism), so as to lay a solid basis for drawing the analogy with the energy metabolism of socioeconomic systems (exosomatic energy metabolism). But first we show below why a familiar example like the metabolism of the human body may help us to put things in perspective.

8.1.1 Calling for some common sense

Few people would believe that professional football players, such as Leo Messi, can maintain their top performance, if they were to start eating consistently only half the usual amount of food, inhale consistently only half the amount of oxygen, and/or produce consistently only half the usual amount of urine, faeces and CO_2 exhaled. This scepticism derives from our solid or sometimes intuitive knowledge of the energy metabolism of the human body. Indeed, scientists have established the expected (typical) size and metabolic rate for various organs making up a human being. For instance, an average adult liver weighs 1.8kg and consumes 9.7W/kg of energy, an average adult brain weighs 1.4kg and consumes 11.6W/kg of energy, and an average heart weights 0.3kg and consumes 21.3W/kg (Durnin and Passmore, 1967). The size of other organs (such as skin, bones, and skeletal muscles) depends on the total body size, while the metabolic rate of certain organs will depend on the physical activity performed (notably by skeletal muscles). Given this knowledge, we may logically expect that a given human body with a given physical activity pattern must dissipate a determined amount of food energy and emit a determined amount of CO_2 in order to remain in steady state (not depleting its own body mass as energy source). We have sufficient information about the relation between the organized structures and relative functions within the human body to assess pretty accurately the food energy requirement (and associated material flows) for carrying out a specified set of physical activities while maintaining the original body weight and composition. Thanks to this knowledge, we know that nobody would even think about consistently cutting the food energy intake of Leo Messi or other professional football players by half.

But, strangely enough, nobody seems to object to the ambitious targets for reductions in CO_2 emission launched at international conferences on climate change. In the 2009 Copenhagen Climate Summit, proposals have been put forward to reduce the CO_2 emissions of industrialized countries by 50 per cent, 70 per cent, and even 80 per cent within a time frame of only a few decades. From the considerable worldwide approval that this conference drew, we have to conclude that at present there exists a generalized consensus on the idea that altering the metabolic pattern of complex socio-economic systems is far easier than changing the metabolic pattern of professional football players.

We do not share this belief. As a matter of fact, the metabolic pattern of modern society is incredibly complex and subject to powerful internal constraints and lock-in mechanisms that resist change. Any ambitious CO_2 emission reduction target implies a concomitant change in energy use and a re-adjustment of the functioning of the entire socio-economic system. The basic questions 'Is a large reduction in the CO_2 emission of industrialized countries feasible?', and 'Which existing functions will be affected by such a reduction?' touches upon the very core of energy analysis.

Because the human energy metabolism is familiar to almost all of us, we illustrate here a simple multi-scale assessment of the metabolic pattern of the human body (endosomatic metabolism). The mechanism of the assessment is not different for the metabolism of a modern socio-economic system (exosomatic metabolism).

8.1.2 A multi-scale assessment of the metabolic pattern of the human body

A quantitative representation of the metabolic pattern of the human body is shown in Figure 8.1. As shown on the left side of this figure, the metabolic pattern of the human body as a whole, in a steady state, can be quantified in terms of three variables: (i) the total body mass (in kg), and (ii) the total flow of food energy metabolized on a local scale (in kcal/day or W). From these two variables, we obtain a third one, (iii) the average flow of energy metabolized per kg of body weight (in kcal/kg/day or W/kg).

These three variables can be used to describe the metabolic pattern of specific functional parts of the body, such as individual organs (heart, lungs, brain, liver, skeletal muscles, etc.) in relation to the metabolic pattern of the whole body. In fact, if we characterize all the organs making up the human body (Table 8.1), in a way that provides closure over the total body mass, then we can establish a relation (a weighted sum) between the metabolic characteristics of the parts (at level n-1) and those of the whole (at level n) (Giampietro *et al.*, 2011).

The amount of energy (W) metabolized by any one element, be it the whole or any one of the parts, is visualized in Figure 8.1 (right graph) by the area of the grey rectangles, where the width represents the size of the element (in kg) and the height its metabolic rate (in W/kg). In this way, we can establish a relation between the metabolic characteristics across two different levels of organization: (i) the energy metabolized by the whole body (upper right part of Figure 8.1), as determined by the total body mass (70kg) and average metabolic rate (1.2W/kg), and (ii) the energy metabolized by the various parts making up the body (lower right part of Figure 8.1), as determined by the organ-specific masses and metabolic rates (in W/kg).

Table 8.1 The dual characterization of the metabolic pattern of the whole and parts making possible the scaling for a typical adult man of 70 kg of body mass

Functional compartments of human body	Body mass kg (year)	Metabolic rate W/kg	Energy flow W
Liver	1.8	9.7	17.4
Brain	1.4	11.6	16.2
Heart	0.3	21.3	6.4
Kidneys	0.3	21.3	6.4
Muscles	28.0	0.6	16.8
Other	32.8	0.5	17.0
Whole body	**70.0**	**1.2**	**81.0**
	Total body mass	Endosomatic metabolic rate	Total endosomatic energy

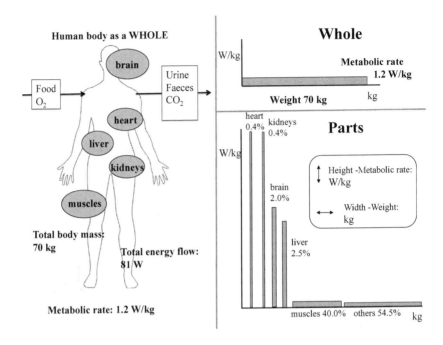

Figure 8.1 Multi-scale analysis of the metabolic pattern of the human body: endosomatic energy metabolism

Note that the mechanism of scaling between levels (the mosaic effect linking the parts to the whole) works only: (i) if we can define the expected metabolic rates of the individual organs independently from the information obtained at the level of the whole body (the characteristics of lower-level elements must map onto so-called external referents or attributes observable at that level), and (ii) if the sum of the masses of the lower-level elements equals the mass of the whole body, i.e., if we have a *closed* representation (Giampietro *et al.*, 2011). Only when these two conditions are met can we establish a relation between the metabolic characterization of the whole (at level n) and the metabolic characterization of the parts (at level n-1). In this situation: (i) the sum of the areas of the rectangles describing the parts (level n-1) is equal to the area of the rectangle describing the whole (level n), and (ii) we have an impredicative definition of the relation between the characteristics of the parts and the whole, in the sense that changes in the characteristics of the whole entail *and* are determined by changes in the characteristics of the parts, and vice versa.

8.2 Useful concepts for generalizing the analysis of the energy metabolism

Several important theoretical concepts are behind this method of decomposing and accounting in an integrated way the characteristics of a metabolic system. A full theoretical discussion of all the concepts required to carry out this multi-scale analysis of a metabolic pattern has been given in Giampietro *et al.* (2011). Here we illustrate just the most important ones that will help us to generalize the multi-scale accounting of the energy metabolism of the human body to that of any metabolic system, notably a socio-economic system.

8.2.1 Holons and holarchies

Arthur Koestler (1968, 1969, 1978) proposed the concepts of 'holarchy' and 'holon' to address a key epistemological challenge associated with the perception and representation of complex systems. The term holarchy was coined to indicate the special nature of metabolic systems that are organized in nested hierarchies. Indeed, it refers to a form of organization based on a cascade of hierarchically organized holons. For example, in the case of human beings we see that cells are parts of tissues, tissues are parts of organs, organs are parts of human bodies, human bodies are part of households, households of villages, etc.

The term holon stresses the dual nature of the elements of a holarchy: they are expressing simultaneously the nature of a whole and a part. That is, a holon can be viewed as a part expressing a function, which is defined as useful by its higher hierarchical level (e.g. the function expressed by the brain for the human body), or as a whole, which provides meaning for its own parts at the lower hierarchical level (e.g. the brain structure and function explains the role of neurons and their connections inside the brain) (Giampietro *et al.*, 2006). Thus, the term holon underlines that what is special about the organization of living systems is the systemic coupling of a functional (the role) and a structural (realization of an organized structure) type in relation to higher and lower levels of organization.

The idea of holarchy and holon is essential for the analysis illustrated in Figure 8.1 because it makes it possible to:

- adopt a functional criterion to define the parts of the body. The total mass of the human body can be divided into different parts (liver, brain, kidney, etc.) using distinct functional categories to account for the kilograms;
- define a quantitative measure of the size of the structure that is associated with the expression of each particular function indicated by the categories, for example 1.4kg of brain or 1.8kg of liver;
- provide a closure on this accounting by establishing a relation between the expression of the function of the whole at level n (survival and reproduction) and the function of the parts at level n-1 (the ability of the various parts to provide the entire set of functions required by the whole while respecting the lower-level constraints determined by the parts of the parts at level n-2).

8.2.2 Autopoiesis and autopoietic systems

Autopoietic systems are a class of systems capable of reproducing themselves, as conceptualized by Maturana and Varela (1980, 1998). Autopoiesis literally means 'self-production' (from the Greek *auto* for 'self' and *poiesis* for 'production'). The term autopoiesis describes the fundamental and complementary roles of structural and functional types found in biological and social systems. In this sense, we can see the metabolic pattern of the human body as the expression of an autopoietic process based on an autocatalytic loop of energy forms as illustrated in Figure. 4.6 (page 91) and Figure 6.1 (page 123).

As discussed earlier, a quantitative analysis of a human metabolism must be based on a clearly defined lexicon of energy forms and material elements to be useful. For example, when dealing with the endosomatic energy metabolism of human beings – Figure 6.1 (page 123) –we must distinguish between:

- Primary energy sources: these are food items such as grain, meat, milk and vegetables, and are measured in physical units (such as kg or l) that can be associated (converted) either to energy flows (in kcal or J) or material flows (such as g of protein or mg of vitamin C).
- Energy carriers: in human physiology, energy carriers are represented by energy-rich molecules, such as ATP.
- End uses: these are the purposeful activities associated with human metabolism (functions expressed across scales by cells, tissues, organs, organ systems, and the whole body).

Looking inside the human body, we have to define a correspondence between the lexicon of food intake (chemical composition of food items) and the lexicon of human physiology, cellular biology and biochemistry (e.g. amino acids, nucleotides, ATP). By establishing this bridge we can analyze the existence of internal constraints. How is the functioning of the parts affecting/being affected by the functioning of the entire body?

For a large-scale analysis of the interactions of the body as a whole with its context, we have to focus on the category of end uses. As a matter of fact, the study of human metabolism would be meaningless without a coupled analysis of the activity associated with (the functions expressed by) such metabolism, especially the set of activities producing the food required for human survival.

Thus, in order to gather the data required for a pertinent quantitative representation of human metabolism, we have first of all to select a set of relevant narratives and a useful set of external referents. Then the choice of a grammar becomes possible because of the existence of a closed set of impredicative) relations: food supply (critical end use) → food energy (primary energy source) → ATP energy (energy carriers) → behaviour (mix of end uses) → food supply (critical end use).

8.2.3 Georgescu-Roegen's flow-fund model for representing metabolic systems

Georgescu-Roegen (1971) proposed a flow-fund model for representing the economic process. He provides the following epistemological explanation for fund and flow elements.

Flow elements are those elements that are either produced or consumed during the analytical representation. They reflect the choice made by the analyst when deciding what the system does and how it interacts with its context. In the case of the human body, an example of a flow element is the flow of food energy required to utilize the power capacity of both the organs and the whole body and the flow of applied power that humans use to interact with their environment.

Fund elements are elements whose identity remains the same in the chosen analytical representation. This definition reflects the choice made by the analyst when deciding what the system is and what the system is made of in relation to the given time duration of the analysis. In the representation of the economic process, human labour, capital equipment and Ricardian land are three fund elements (Georgescu-Roegen, 1971). In the case of the human body, both the whole body and the organs are taken to be fund elements; they are supposed to be maintained and they are supposed to remain 'the same' over the time period of the analysis. If the person passes away or if there is an organ failure then the set of expected relations over functions and structures described on the right side of Figure 8.1 (page 192) will no longer be valid.

8.3 The exosomatic metabolic pattern of socio-economic systems

Lotka (1956) first introduced the distinction between endosomatic and exoso-matic metabolism in relation to the power capacity of society, that is, the mechanical conversions of energy under human control. Indeed, the exosomatic metabolism of societies became tremendously important after the industrial revolution, as the impressive accumulation of technological capital implied a dramatic increase in the power capacity available to boost the productivity of human activity (Cottrell, 1955; Hall *et al.*, 1986). Lotka explicitly suggested that a hierarchical level of organization higher than that of the individual ought to be used to describe the flow of exosomatic energy in modern society: '... it has in a most real way bound men together into one body: so very real and material is the bond that society might aptly be described as one huge multiple Siamese twin' (Lotka, 1956, p. 369).

The distinction between exosomatic and endosomatic energy conversions was later proposed by Georgescu-Roegen (1975) as a working concept for the ener-getic analyses of bioeconomics and sustainability. We provide here the following definitions, based on the work of both Lotka and Georgescu-Roegen.

- Endosomatic metabolism: physiological conversions of different types of energy inputs (food items) into end uses that take place inside the human body.
- Exosomatic metabolism: energy converted outside the human body with the goal of amplifying the output of useful work associated with human activity (e.g. the use of tractors, the melting of metals, air transport). Exosomatic metabolism entails the adoption of a mix of: (i) energy input; (ii) power capacity; and (iii) human activity required for controlling the generation and use of applied power for fulfilling tasks.

- The exosomatic metabolic rate (EMR): the rate of exosomatic metabolism per hour of human activity (measured in joules/hour). Specific values of EMR can be calculated, across different hierarchical levels, for the various compartments making up a socio-economic system. The EMR_i of any particular element 'i' (average value per year) is a function of: (i) the power capacity, (ii) the power utilization factor, and (iii) the efficiency of the energy converters – determining the value of energy throughput (ET_i) – and (iv) the hours of human activity (HA_i) invested in the element.

On the basis of these definitions we can describe the functional compartments of a socio-economic system as holons, which we can then define in terms of:

- fund elements: (i) hours of human activity (functional side) and (ii) power capacity provided by exosomatic converters of energy (structural side); and
- flow elements: (i) energy carriers consumed to generate applied power; and (ii) other relevant material flows and monetary flows (which are not considered in this book – examples of this analysis are given in Giampietro *et al.* 2011).

In this way, the autopoietic process of the socio-economic system can be described as an autocatalytic loop of exosomatic energy (and material) transformations. In the analogy with the endosomatic metabolism of human beings we can identify an autocatalytic loop as shown in Figure 4.6, page 91 – and then develop an effective grammar capable of studying the metabolic pattern of modern society that describes the structural and functional compartments in charge of establishing the metabolic pattern – Figure 4.5 (page 88), Figure 7.3 (page 167).

The size of the socio-economic system and 'its organs' can be defined in terms of the amount of hours of human activity dedicated to these various functional parts (Figure 8.2).

An example of this approach is illustrated in Figure 8.2 for the metabolic pattern of Catalonia (an autonomous region of Spain) using the categories described in Figure 7.3, page 167. Note that the size of human society and its compartments is defined by the amount of human time allocation rather than the number of people. The central role of human time allocation in our model is discussed in the next section.

Using the same method as for the analysis of the endosomatic metabolism (Figure 8.1 and Table 8.1, page 191), we can express the metabolic pattern of the individual compartments of society and the whole society in terms of both size (human time allocation) and energy throughput. This is illustrated in Table 8.2.

8.4 The central role of human time allocation in the multi-scale integrated analysis of the exosomatic energy metabolism

The profile of allocation of human time (activity) across the different compartments of society (defined at different hierarchical levels) stands out as a key

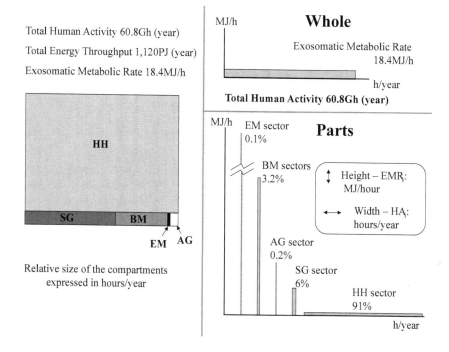

Total Human Activity 60.8Gh (year)

Total Energy Throughput 1,120PJ (year)

Exosomatic Metabolic Rate 18.4MJ/h

HH

SG   BM

EM   AG

Relative size of the compartments
expressed in hours/year

MJ/h   **Whole**

Exosomatic Metabolic Rate
18.4MJ/h

h/year

Total Human Activity 60.8Gh (year)

MJ/h   EM sector   **Parts**
        0.1%

BM sectors
3.2%   ↕ Height – EMR$_i$:
                    MJ/hour

                 ↔ Width – HA$_i$:
                    hours/year

AG sector
0.2%
            SG sector
            6%
                    HH sector
                    91%

h/year

Figure 8.2 A multi-scale analysis of the metabolic pattern of Catalonia 2005: exosomatic
energy metabolism
Source: data from Ramos-Martin *et al.*, 2009

Table 8.2 The dual characterization of the metabolic pattern of the whole and parts for
Catalonia, 2005
Source: data from Institut d'Estadística de Catalunya (IDESCAT), 2011

	Functional compartments of Catalonia		
	HAi Gh (year)	EMRi MJ/h	ETi PJ (year)
EM sector	0.06	2,000	120
BM sector	1.95	331	547
SG sector	3.60	75	270
AG sector	0.15	175	27
HH sector	55.1	2.8	155
Society	60.8 THA Total human activity	18.4 EMR$_{SA}$ Exosomatic metabolic rate (societal average)	1,120 TET Total (exosomatic) energy throughput

factor in our model for studying the feasibility and desirability of a given meta-bolic pattern of society (Giampietro *et al.*, 2011). At the level of the whole society (level n) there exists a direct, linear relation between the population size of society expressed in number of people (the more conventional approach) and that expressed in hours of total human activity per year (THA):

$$THA_n = \text{number of people} \times \text{hours in one year (8,760)}$$

Thus, in the year 2005, Catalonia had a size of 60.8×10^9 hours per year of human activity (THA) determined by its population size (6.9 million people) and the number of hours in one year (8,760). The profile of allocation of the fund element human activity over the various compartments in society, defined at different hierarchical levels, can be neatly represented by a dendrogram, as illus-trated in Figures 8.3 and 8.4 (pages 198 and 199).

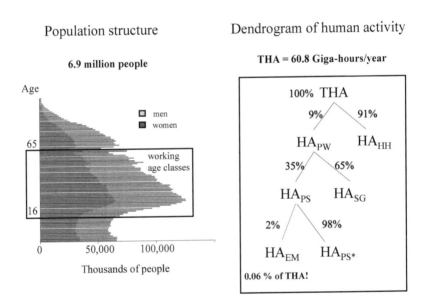

Figure 8.3 A multi-scale analysis of the profile of allocation of human activity in Catalonia 2005 across different compartments operating at different levels

The dendrogram in Figure 8.3 starts with the total human activity (for one year) at level n, the level of the whole society. For instance, in the case of Catalonia, in 2005, the population of 6.9 million people corresponded to a total human activity (THA) of 60.8 Gigahours/year. Then, moving to level (n-1), the total hours of human activity are split between two compartments: (i) the paid work sector (HA_{PW}), which in Catalonia, in 2005, absorbed 9 per cent of total human activity; and (ii) the household sector (HA_{HH}) which in 2005, in Catalonia, accounted for 91 per cent of THA (see also Figure 8.2, page 197). Moving further down to level (n-2) in Figure 8.3, we see that the hours of human activity allocated to the paid work sector (HA_{PW}) are split between the primary and secondary sectors (HA_{PS}) on the one hand (accounting for 35 per cent of HA_{PW}) and the service and government sector (HA_{SG}) on the other hand (accounting for 65 per cent of HA_{PW}). Eventually, depending on the purpose of the analysis, we can define a lower level – level (n-3) – by further splitting the hours of human activity allocated to the primary and secondary sectors between the energy and mining sector (HA_{EM}) and the other compartments in the primary and secondary sectors (HA_{PS*}). We thus see that, at the end, a mere 0.06 per cent of the total hours of human activity of society is allocated to the energy and mining sector.

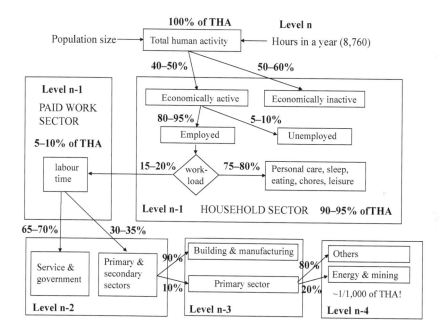

Figure 8.4 The allocation of human activity across the different compartments of a modern society based on typical benchmark values

The profile of distribution of the hours of human activity across the various compartments of a society strongly depends on the demographic and socio-economic characteristics of that society. As illustrated in Figure 8.4, this is especially true for the division of the hours of human activity among the household sector and the paid work sector. An important demographic variable in this context is the dependency ratio, defined as the ratio of the economically inactive population and the economically active population. The dependency ratio depends on the population age and gender structure as well as on socio-economic variables, such as life expectancy, access to education, and retirement age. The link between demographic structure and the allocation of human activity over the various economic sectors is also illustrated in Figure 8.3.

Other important variables in this context are the work load and the unemployment rate (see Figure 8.4). It is important to realize that 80 per cent of the activity (time) of the employed population still ends up in the household sector, because people simply do not work 24 hours a day. With a typical work load of less than 2,000 hours/year, less than 20 per cent of the time of an average employed person is allocated to the paid work sector.

8.5 The mosaic effect: an integrated analysis across hierarchical levels

When generating a multi-scale analysis, the advantage of expressing the size of the whole society and the various functional compartments defined at different hierarchical levels in terms of hours of human activity becomes evident. In fact, it allows us to capture the two key features of our model outlined before, for the assessment of the endosomatic metabolism (Giampietro and Mayumi, 2000; Giampietro et al., 2011).

- The dendrogram of human time allocation makes it possible to keep coherence among non-equivalent descriptions referring to different hierarchical levels of analysis with regard to the amount of energy input required for both the whole society and the individual parts.
- The time element allows us to assess the power level at which the different compartments are metabolizing energy across levels. This characteristic provides us with additional information about the requirement of power capacity in the various parts of the system defined over different hierarchical levels.

Indeed, the metabolic pattern expressed by any of the various compartments (holons) integrated into a functional whole (holarchy) can be characterized using the following triplet of variables (Table 8.2, page 197):

1   The hours of human activity (fund element) in compartment i (HA_i, expressed in hours), illustrated by the width of the gray bars in Figure 8.2, page 197 (right side);
2   The amount of exosomatic energy (flow element) used in compartment i (ET_i);
3   The exosomatic metabolic rate (ratio between flow and fund element) in compartment i (EMR_i, expressed in MJ/h), illustrated by the height of the gray bars in Figure 8.2, page 197 (right side).

The relation between the profile of allocation of total human activity (THA) and that of total energy throughput (calculated according to a given protocol) defines a profile of requirement of power capacity across the compartments. This is illustrated in Figure 8.5, showing the simultaneous use of the two dendrograms (of total human activity and total energy throughput) based on the same definition of compartments across hierarchical levels.

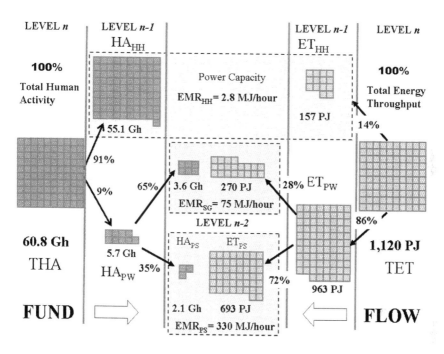

Figure 8.5 The coupled dendrograms of allocation of human activity and energy throughputs in Catalonia 2005 determining a profile of power capacity requirement across compartments

As shown in Figure 8.5, we thus have a so-called 'mosaic effect' and with this we can conduct an integrated analysis of the characteristics of the parts and the characteristics of the whole across the levels (for more on this method see Giampietro *et al.*, 2011). The set of expected relations that can be established across levels in this way is as follows:

$$THA = HA_{HH} + HA_{EM} + HA_{PS*} + HA_{SG}$$
$$TET = ET_{HH} + ET_{EM} + ET_{PS*} + ET_{SG}$$
$$EMR_{SA} = TET/THA \text{ (at level n)}$$
$$EMR_i = ET_i/HA_i \text{ (at level } i\text{)}$$
$$EMR_{SA} = \Sigma \left[(HA_i/THA) \times EMR_i \right]$$

HA stands for human activity (time), ET for energy throughput, EMR for exosomatic metabolic rate, which is proportional to the requirement of power capacity, and compartment i is defined at levels lower than n. The specific metabolic rates expressed by the various compartments (holons) defined at the lower levels (determined by the triplet of values of ET_i, HA_i and EMR_i) have to be congruent with the constraints dictated by the whole socio-economic system (holarchy) to which the compartments belong (TET, THA and EMR_{SA}).

As explained in detail in Giampietro *et al.* (2011), the existence of a set of forced relations over the various fund and flow elements within and across levels implies the existence of a set of internal constraints limiting the possibility of dramatic changes taking place in individual compartments. Indeed, for any changes to take effect, they have to be consistent with both: (i) internal constraints, referring to the compatibility over the change in the relative requirement and supply of fund and flow elements (human activity, power capacity, and energy input) within the hierarchical structure, and (ii) external constraints, referring to the compatibility of the aggregate flows associated with the functioning the whole society with boundary conditions (an adequate supply of input and sink capacity for wastes). A way to assess the desirability and viability of the metabolic pattern of modern societies, considering these relations and constraints, is presented in Chapter 12.

The existence of constraints in the organization of the socio-economic system is visible in the representation of the different 'sizes' of the various sectors in Catalonia using either hours of human activity (HA_i) or energy throughput (ET_i) for the description. Catalonia is a typical modern society in that the number of hours of total human activity invested into the production of primary flows: exosomatic energy carriers, food and minerals, is extremely small (less than one per cent of the total human activity) (see Figure 8.3, page 198). Indeed, in most developed countries, the combined number of workers engaged in energy and mining, agriculture, and fishery accounts for less than five per cent of the economically active population (Giampietro *et al.*, 2011). Thus, for every hour of human activity allocated to the primary production sectors, about 200 hours are allocated elsewhere. This explains why the power capacity of the primary production sectors (energy and mining and agriculture) must be extremely high: powerful exosomatic devices are used in these sectors to boost the productivity of human labour. As we will discuss below, the exosomatic metabolic rate EMR_{EM} in the energy and mining sector (EM) is extremely high compared to the corresponding value of EMR_{HH} in the household sector (HH) and of EMR_{SG} in the service and government sector (SG).

When studying the potential effects of proposed structural changes in the economy, it is essential to be aware that different functional sectors have different energy requirements per hour of human activity. Eliminating 10 per cent of labour hours in the service and government sector has a completely different effect on the metabolic rate of the economy than eliminating 10 per cent of labour hours in the primary production sectors. The same applies to the creation of new jobs in compartments having large differences in their EMR_i. Creating a job in the primary production sectors requires a larger investment of power capacity (technical capital) than creating a job in the service and government sector.

8.6 Impredicative loop analysis and the importance of power capacity

8.6.1 The forced relation between power levels and investments of production factors across compartments

In the previous section we illustrated that it is possible to define the exosomatic metabolic rate (EMR_i) for each compartment i on the basis of the size of the fund element HA_i (hours of human activity allocated to compartment i) and the size of the flow element ET_i (exosomatic energy flow in compartment i), using a standard relation valid across hierarchical levels: $EMR_i = ET_i/HA_i$. At the same time, the EMR_i can also be related to the power capacity available in compartment i using the relation explained in Chapter 5, page 92, ($ET_i = PC_i \times \eta \times UF_i$):

$$EMR_i = (PC_i \times \eta_i \times UF_i)/HA_i$$

Where PC_i is the power capacity (in Watt), η_i the conversion efficiency (applied power/energy input) and UF_i the utilization factor. Adopting this integrated view of energy flows, we find that at the level of the whole society the average metabolic rate (EMR_{SA}) depends on two factors: (i) the values of the various metabolic rates of the parts (EMR_i), and (ii) the relative size of the parts, measured using the values of the couplets ET_i and HA_i. In turn this requires a profile of allocation of power capacity capable of maintaining asymmetric dendrograms such as those typical of modern societies. For example, we see in Figure 8.5 that only 9 per cent of THA goes in paid work, but it has 86 per cent of exosomatic energy throughput! To make things even more asymmetric, in the next split only 35 per cent of the human activity of PW goes into the PS compartment, whereas 72 per cent of the exosomatic throughput of PW is used by PS. These asymmetries in the two coupled dendrograms can only be handled by allocating different levels of investments of power capacity in these different compartments. These investments result in the different EMR_i found in the different compartments.

An overview of the set of forced relations between the size of fund and flow elements determining the metabolic pattern of a society is illustrated for Catalonia in Figure 8.6. The set of forced relations within such a hierarchical structure puts in evidence the impredicative relation between the characteristics of the parts and those of the whole. Indeed, we cannot change the values of the benchmarks of the whole (THA, TET and EMR_{SA}) without changing the characteristics of lower-level elements (HA_i, ET_i and EMR_i) and vice versa.

The various characteristics of the components of the metabolic pattern of Catalonia have already been quantified in the dendrograms shown in Figure 8.5, page 201. But there are two new aspects introduced in Figure 8.6. First, a different order of splits in the dendrograms: the primary and secondary production

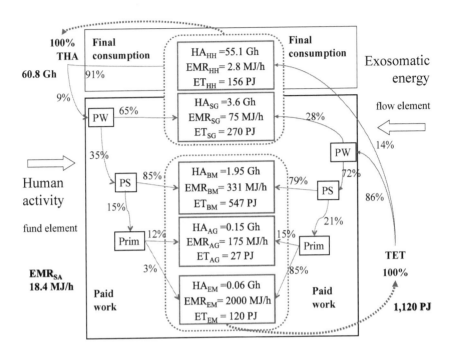

Figure 8.6 The two integrated dendrograms of fund elements and flow elements
determining the metabolic pattern of Catalonia in 2005

sector is divided into building and manufacturing (BM), the compartments
making power capacity and infrastructures, and agriculture (AG) and energy and
mining (EM) – indicated by the label used in Figure 8.6 for primary sectors (Prim
for short) – the compartments guaranteeing the input of material flows. Second,
Figure 8.6 shows two autocatalytic loops determining the feasibility of the metabolic pattern.

The first loop refers to the amount of exosomatic energy invested in the energy
and mining sector (EM, 120PJ), which must be able to stabilize the total supply
of exosomatic energy used by society (TET, 1,120PJ) in order to guarantee the
entire set of functions expressed by the various compartments. Thus, the energy
and mining sector has to guarantee the stabilization of the entire flow of input of
exosomatic energy whilst using only 0.1 per cent of the total human activity
(THA) and only 11 per cent of the total exosomatic energy throughput (TET).

The second autocatalytic loop refers to the hours of human activity invested in
the household sector (HH: 55.1Gh) that must be able to reproduce the entire fund
human activity (THA: 60.8 Gh) so as to generate enough human activity to be
invested in the paid work sector (PW: 5.7 Gh). In relation to this autocatalytic
loop we can interpret the hours spent in final consumption (HH) as the overhead
that the fund human activity requires for its own reproduction.

From a cursory look at the set of quantitative relations illustrated in Figure 8.6 and the resulting characterization of the metabolic pattern of the various compartments in terms of a given triplet of values HA_i, ET_i and the resulting EMR_i it is easy to grasp that none of the metabolic characteristics of any element within the system (the specific mix of production factors human activity, power capacity and energy throughput), can be changed without changing at the same time some characteristics of other elements. In this scheme all numbers depend on each other. We also see that within the metabolic pattern of modern societies there is a competition for a series of limited resources (in economic jargon these are called production factors):

1   The hours of human activity for providing control (defining and limiting the functional capability of the various compartments) are available in a given amount (THA) and then have to be wisely invested across the different structural compartments – either in the PW or the HH sector – to guarantee the expression of the required functions.
2   The power capacity associated with exosomatic energy converters, which defines and limits structural capability, is available in a given amount (determining the profile of EMR_i in the different compartments) and has to be wisely invested across the different structural compartments to guarantee the required functions.
3   The energy and material flows, which define and limit the possibility of expressing functions in the various compartments, are available in a given amount (TET) and have to be wisely invested across the different structural compartments to guarantee the required functions.

This internal competition among functional and structural compartments for the same set of production factors becomes even more evident if we adopt a representation based on the narratives of theoretical ecology. For example, using the graph language developed by H.T. Odum (Odum, 1971) and adopting the functional definition of compartments discussed earlier, we can represent the interaction among the different compartments of a modern society as illustrated in Figure 8.7. Note that the energy and mining sector (EM) has been singled out so that we can better focus on an adequate supply of energy carriers (both in terms of quantity and composition) to society. The PS* sector thus represents the primary and secondary production sectors without the energy and mining sector: building and manufacturing (BM) and agriculture (AG).

In this numerical representation we have rescaled the quantitative assessment over the scale of one year (duration) and one hour (grain) and normalized the value per capita per year. This representation shows the importance of considering power levels in the analysis. In fact, it is obvious that in this metabolic pattern the PS sectors do operate using only a tiny fraction of human activity. The different levels of power capacity requirement in different sectors are determined by the asymmetries in the dendrograms of split between THA and TET illustrated in Figure 8.5, page 201. These asymmetries can result in tough constraints for the

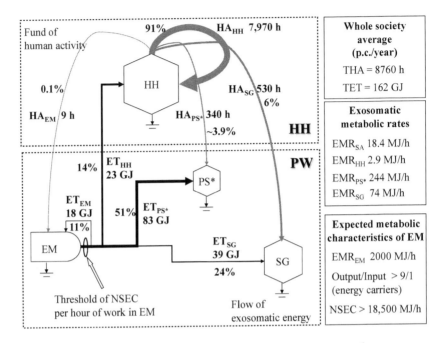

Figure 8.7 The expected characteristics of the energy sector to guarantee the
autocatalytic loop of energy carriers in Catalonia 2005

benchmarks set for individual compartments. For example, the metabolic pattern
of Catalonia, illustrated in Figure 8.7, is feasible only if the performance of the
energy and mining sector (EM) matches the following characteristics: $EMR_{EM} \approx$
2,000 MJ/h; output/input of energy carriers > 9/1; net supply of energy carrier per
hour of labour (NSEC/h) > 18,500 MJ/h.

We get back to this point, when talking about how to carry out an integrated
analysis of the quality of alternative energy sources, in Chapter 12.

8.7 Combining top-down and bottom-up assessments

Thus far, we have employed a top-down approach to assess the flows of energy,
human activity, and power levels over the various compartments of society
defined at different hierarchical levels. Indeed, the use of dendrograms to work
our way down the hierarchy presumes that we start off with data (energy statistics) defined at the level of society as a whole, and then by dividing the data about
human allocation and the data about energy use (extensive variables), we calculate the exosomatic metabolic rate (intensive variables, reflecting the
characteristics of local energy conversions). However, there are other ways to
assess power levels and related energy flows.

Indeed, we can look directly at the set of exosomatic energy converters used for providing the required power capacity in specific sub-compartments at lower hierarchical levels. For instance, we can assess the electricity consumption at the household level by looking at the set of exosomatic devices used in this sub-compartment to express the required functions. Starting from the potential set of exosomatic devices available for expressing the relative functions (see Figure 8.8), we can define household typologies associated with the use of specific subsets of exosomatic devices. For example, a standard household of medium income, living in a developed country, may use the following combination of electric appliances: washing machine, dryer and iron (at a known utilization factor). Then for this typology of functional/structural sub-compartment we can estimate the value of $ET_{electricity}$ using bottom-up information (technical coefficients and utilization factors), rather than using the top-down approach based on statistics of energy consumption for the household sector. In Figure 8.8 we give a few examples taken from the website of General Electric, 'How much power does each appliance use in Watts?' (http://visualization.geblogs.com/visualization/appliances/). The same can be done for power capacity requiring the consumption of liquid fuels. For this purpose, we can look at the characteristics of typical car(s) used by that particular household type (see Figure 8.8) and depending on the system of heating also at the power level of the heating system.

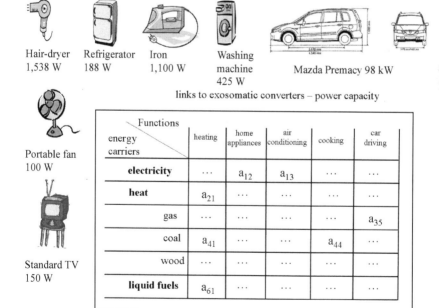

| Hair-dryer | Refrigerator | Iron | Washing machine | Mazda Premacy 98 kW |
| 1,538 W | 188 W | 1,100 W | 425 W | |

links to exosomatic converters – power capacity

Functions / energy carriers	heating	home appliances	air conditioning	cooking	car driving
electricity	...	a_{12}	a_{13}	...	...
heat	a_{21}	...	...	...	...
gas	...	...	...	...	a_{35}
coal	a_{41}	...	...	a_{44}	...
wood	...	...	...	...	...
liquid fuels	a_{61}	...	...	...	...

Portable fan 100 W

Standard TV 150 W

Figure 8.8 An example of a taxonomy of exosomatic devices (home appliances) available for expressing functions at the household type level

This additional way of estimating energy flows in lower-level compartments is essential for generating a more robust protocol of analysis (and scenario making). In fact, in this way we can integrate two different methods of assessment in energy analysis:

1   The top-down approach, assessing the consumption of energy carriers based on data sources from energy and socio-economic statistics; and
2   The bottom-up approach, assessing the consumption of energy carriers by using our knowledge of power capacity and utilization factors for specific compartments and of the relative size of these compartments.

This integrated assessment carried out on multiple-scales makes it possible to increase dramatically the reliability of energy assessments and the robustness of scenarios.

However, we should always remember that when measuring energy flows at the level of individual households, industrial plants, or economic sub-sectors (bottom-up approach), we can only measure flows in quantities of energy carriers, for example, kWh of electric power or gallons of petrol. The quantification of these energy flows, which is based on information gathered at low hierarchical levels, is not equivalent to the quantification of these 'same energy flows expressed in gross energy requirement at level n. For this reason, we must establish a bridge across scales, between quantitative assessments of energy flows expressed at the local scale (in energy quantities of energy carriers – referring to the bottom-up approach) and quantitative assessment of energy flows expressed in quantities of primary energy sources (at the level of the whole society – referring to the top-down approach).

Indeed, thus far we have used in our assessments a generic reference to energy throughputs (energy flows) without addressing the issue of how to quantify them (with which semantic and formal categories). The quantification of these quantities of energy flows is problematic, as we are dealing simultaneously with overall assessments (at the national level: gross energy requirement) and specific, local assessments linked to technical coefficients (at the local level: net energy carriers of different forms). We will take up this argument in the next chapters.

9 Dual accounting of energy flows and the characterization of the metabolic pattern across hierarchical levels

In this chapter we illustrate our proposed method of energy accounting built upon the various concepts presented in Chapters 7 and 8. More specifically, section 9.1 illustrates, using an empirical study referring to a multi-scale analysis of the energy metabolism of 14 countries of the European Union, the importance of adopting a dual accounting of energy flows, one referring to quantities measured in gross energy requirement (GER) and the second in quantities measured in net energy carriers (NEC). We show that when studying the characteristics of individual compartments of modern economies we obtain a different picture depending on the selected method of accounting.

Section 9.2 illustrates a protocol of accounting based on vectors and a multi-level matrix, which can be used to generate a dual reading of the quantities of energy used by a society as a whole and across its compartments defined at different lower levels. In particular, this method makes it possible to avoid the ambiguity associated with the mixing of energy forms of different types discussed in Part I. In this way, it becomes possible to characterize energy quantities across hierarchical levels while maintaining the two crucial distinctions between: (i) gross energy requirement versus net energy carriers; and (ii) energy carriers of different natures. That is, the information about the mix of energy carriers is preserved in the accounting.

Section 9.3 introduces an innovative method of accounting a multi-level arrays dataset capable of characterizing the metabolic pattern across different compartments and hierarchical levels while taking into account the requirement of production factors. This approach makes it possible to establish a relation between the quantities of energy flowing in the metabolic pattern (described at different levels) and the requirement of power capacity and human activity. This information is extremely important to study the existence of internal constraints and it will be used in Chapter 10 to develop an analytical method to study – adopting a view from 'inside the black-box' – the viability domain of the metabolic pattern of modern societies.

9.1 The strengths and problems of the analysis of the metabolic pattern of exosomatic energy across levels: a case study

In this section we present the results of an empirical study of the energy metabolism of 14 countries of the European Union (the classic set of EU15 minus Luxembourg), over the period 1992–2005 (for more details see Giampietro *et al.*, 2011). This study is relevant in relation to our discussion of the metabolic pattern for two reasons.

1   It demonstrates the existence of robust compartment-specific benchmark values for required power capacity and energy inputs.
2   It shows the need for a dual accounting when carrying out a multi-scale energy analysis.

9.1.1 The metabolic pattern of the EU14 countries

In order to understand the implications of changes in the metabolic pattern taking place with economic growth, one has to look at both: (i) the changes of the characteristics of individual sectors; and (ii) the changes in the relative size and role of the sectors within the economy as a whole. The concept of metabolic pattern makes it possible to do so by using benchmarks. In this way, we can study trends of change in the characteristics of both the economy as a whole and the specific characteristics of the sub-sectors. In particular, after having defined an integrated set of benchmarks referring to different compartments, it becomes possible to study how changes in the characteristics of the parts affect and are affected by changes in the characteristics of the whole.

In our EU14 study (presented in detail in Giampietro *et al.*, 2011) we establish a link between the biophysical and the economic reading of the performance associated with a given metabolic pattern. Indeed, our characterization not only represents the rate at which energy is metabolized per hour of human activity in the different compartments, but also the rate of generation of the monetary flow (added value) associated with activities carried out in the paid work sector. In this integrated analysis, we represent each sector (considered in the analysis within the paid work sector) as a disk on a plane, whose characteristics are determined by three pieces of information (Figure 9.1).

- The exosomatic metabolic rate (EMR_i):, the MJ of 'energy' metabolized per hour of labour in compartment i (vertical axis);
- The economic labour productivity (ELP_i): the euro (€) of added value produced per hour of labour in compartment i (horizontal axis);
- The hours of human activity allocated to compartment i (represented by the size of the disk).

Sector-specific performance is easier to characterize when analyzing the relevant sectors of all EU14 countries together (Figure 9.1). In this way, we can clearly see

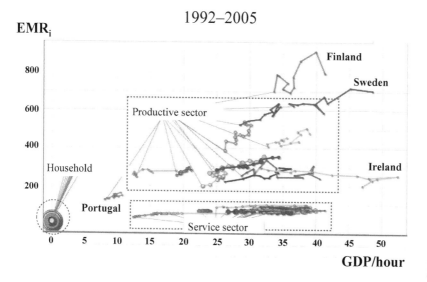

Figure 9.1 Sector-specific energy consumption per hour and economic labour
productivity (GDP/hour) for the EU14, 1992–2005
Source: Giampietro *et al.*, 2011, used with permission

the existence of clusters of values for the exosomatic metabolic rate (EMR) of the
household (HH), service and government (SG) and primary and secondary
production (PS) sectors:

- EMR_{HH}: 2–8 MJ/h
- EMR_{SG}: 30–100 MJ/h
- EMR_{PS}: 130–1,000 MJ/h

Indeed, the primary and secondary production sectors (PS) consistently have the
highest values of EMR_i, and the values tend to increase over time. The service and
government sector (SG) has intermediate values of EMR_i that remain more or less
constant over time, while the household sector (HH) exhibits the lowest values of
EMR_i. A more detailed analysis of these values and trends is given in Giampietro
et al. (2011). Note that when considering the exosomatic metabolic rates (EMR_i),
the differences among sector-specific values (for HH, PS and SG) within countries are more pronounced than the range of values found for each specific sector
among countries.

On the other hand, the rate of generation of added value (GDP/hour or ELP_i)
is similar (12–45€/h) for the service and government and the primary and secondary production sector. Note that by definition the corresponding value for the
generation of added value in the household sector is zero for all EU14 countries
(see Giampietro *et al.*, 2011). When analyzing changes in the energy intensity in

this way one can immediately realize that the indicator usually used for this task – the ratio gross energy requirement per year (total exosomatic throughput) divided by the GDP per year – is totally useless (see Chapter 3 of Giampietro *et al.* 2011). In fact, the overall change in this value (at the level n) can depend on many factors (change in the relative mix of PES, change in the relative importance of the PS sector versus SG in the paid work sector, changes in the ratio EMR_i/ELP_i of individual compartments and sub-compartments, changes in the relative size of individual compartments and sub-compartments). In particular, in Figure 9.1 we can see that the continuous reduction of the size of the PS sector in comparison with the size of the SG explains this phenomenon much better than the effect of technical changes within these sectors the change in the rate of energy use per hour of human activity in the two sectors.

9.1.2 How to assess quantities of exosomatic energy?

The analysis of the metabolic pattern at the scale of lower-level compartments and sub-compartments is seriously hampered by the existing confusion in energy assessments expressed either in joules of net energy carriers or joules of gross energy requirement (let alone joules of 'energy commodities'). Previously, we defined the indicator EMR_i as the MJ of exosomatic 'energy' metabolized per hour of labour in compartment *i*. However, what semantic and formal category should we use to assess this quantity of 'energy'? In the empirical study reported in Figure 9.1, all the values have been calculated in terms of joules of gross energy requirement (thermal equivalent).

However, if we express the EMR_i in terms of joules of gross energy requirement (thermal) required by a given compartment operating at the level (n-2), the provided information is potentially misleading regarding:

- **The profile of power capacity** The energetic converters used in that given compartment do not necessarily process that entire amount of gross energy in the form of energy carriers. For instance, an electric motor using 1MJ of electricity will be reported as having a consumption of 2.2MJ (IEA protocol of accounting) or 2.6MJ (BP protocol of accounting) of primary energy source, when expressing the consumption in joules of gross energy requirement. In the same way, the quantity of energy consumed in the final (household) compartments is overestimated when using joules of gross energy requirement as it includes the energy losses, which occurred in the energy sector, required to make the energy carriers. In a way, the use of gross energy requirements makes it possible to individuate those functions responsible for a given fraction of total energy use. However, these numbers are useless to assess local efficiencies or the requirement of local levels of power capacity.
- **The profile of associated emissions** The emissions attributed to the activities carried out in a given functional compartment do not map exactly onto assessments of either ET_i or EMR_i. In fact, as noted earlier, a certain fraction

of the joules of gross energy requirement (expressed in tons of oil equivalent) did not generate any emission. For instance, the three virtual joules accounted for each joule of electricity produced in nuclear power plants (when adopting the IEA approach), or the joules of virtual tons of oil equivalent accounted for each joule of electricity produced in hydroelectric and photovoltaic plants and wind energy farms (when adopting the partial substitution method) are not generating the CO_2 emission associated with the real burning of oil;

- **The spatial and temporal location of energy losses** The physical location of the energy conversion of energy carrier into end use is not coincident with the physical location of the energy conversion of primary energy source into energy carrier (gross energy requirement → net energy carrier). Losses related to the latter conversion take place in the energy sector (e.g. the production of electricity), whereas losses entailed by the (in)efficiency of power capacity take place at the level of other specific (sub)compartments and depend on the characteristics of the functions expressed in the given metabolic pattern. The spatial and temporal information related to both the size and quality of these two different types of losses can be very relevant. The use of a single accounting of energy transformations in terms of only gross energy requirement makes it impossible to handle all this information.

To illustrate this problem, we describe the metabolic pattern (compartment-specific EMR_i in MJ/h and ELP_i in €/h) of the EU14 for 1990 and 2007 for two compartments: the production sectors (PS) (Figure 9.2) and the service and government (SG) sector (Figure 9.3, page 216), using two different quantitative assessments referring to two non-equivalent semantic categories of reference (Giampietro *et al.*, 2011): joules of gross (thermal) energy requirement (GER assessment) and joules of net energy carriers (NEC assessment) summed together as such without using quality factors. We know that this operation should not be done, but for the moment we provide this assessment to make our point (we discuss how to deal with this problem in the rest of the chapter).

As regards the productive (PS) sector, illustrated in Figure 9.2, the vertical axis represents the energy metabolic rate (in MJ/h) calculated as both: (i) joules of gross energy requirement, thus including also the energy losses for generating electricity, fuel and heat (top graph), and (ii) joules of net energy carrier, considering only the energy carriers used in the sector to generate useful work (bottom graph). On the horizontal axis of each graph, the economic labour productivity is expressed in terms of €/h of labour. The size of each disk indicates the total number of hours allocated to this specific PS sector.

As expected, the energy intensity of the productive sectors (the ratio MJ/€ for this specific compartment) is lower when the EMR_i is measured in joules of energy carriers (EMR_{ECi}) than when measured in joules of gross energy requirement (EMR_{GERi}). In fact, when assessing the throughput in joules of energy carriers in PS we are not charging the productive sectors for all of the energy losses associated with the generation of energy carriers. That is, we are not

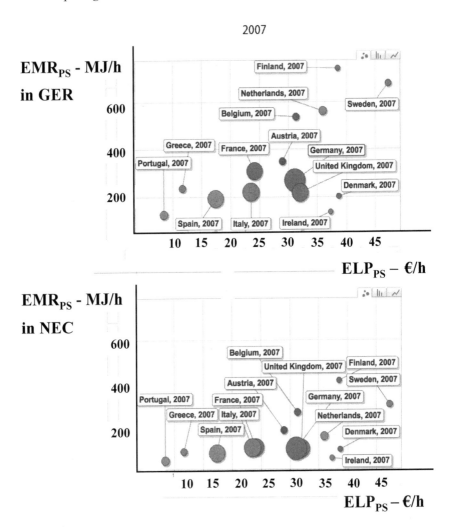

Figure 9.2 Energetic metabolic rate (EMR$_{PS}$) and economic labour productivity (ELP$_{PS}$) of the productive sectors of the EU14 in 2007: based on gross energy requirement (GER) accounting on the top and net energy carrier (NEC) accounting on the bottom
Source: Giampietro *et al.*, 2011, used with permission

accounting for the energy carriers spent for making energy carriers used by the compartments other than the energy sector.

This potential confusion in the assessment of the energy throughput of the production sector shows once again the risk of providing (and using) only one single quantitative assessment of the type 'one size fits all'. It is possible to do an accounting that attributes to the production sector only the losses referring to its own operation (using an accounting of flows of NEC). However, this can be done only if at the same time we have another, non-equivalent accounting that assesses where the actual losses are taking place (referring to the losses for the transformation of GER into NEC). When comparing countries operating with different mixes of primary energy sources and energy carriers and different sizes of import and export of energy forms, it is simply impossible to provide a useful characterization by using only one single set of energy assessments. A striking example of this failure is the attempt to use the semantic category 'energy commodities' by IEA and Eurostat (see Chapter 3, page 48).

The same dual accounting of the metabolic pattern is illustrated in Figure 9.3 for the service and government sector. Note that the values of EMR_{SG} are much lower than the values of EMR_{PS}, to a point that the scale on the vertical axis for the service and government sector in Figure 9.3 is approximately half of that used for the productive sectors in Figure 9.2. Also, for the service and government sector, we see a clear difference in EMR between the two accounting methods. Notably, the differences in the values of EMR_i among countries are much less pronounced when expressed in joules of energy carrier than when expressed in joules of gross energy requirement. Especially clear is the clustering around a common value of EMR_{PS} (50–60 MJ/h expressed in joules of energy carrier). In fact, in the PS sector different mixes of activities (e.g. forestry and pulp industry, heavy metallurgy, industrial production, versus textile and computer industry) for countries operating in different biophysical contexts (e.g. Finland and Sweden) do entail differences in the intensity of the use of energy carriers. On the contrary, in the SG sector the tasks to be performed are more or less similar among countries. Moreover, the technology used in this sector is increasingly becoming uniform, as indicated by the fact that the EMR_{SG} of the various EU countries are converging around a value of 50–60 MJ/h, when measured in joules of net energy carrier (NEC).

Nevertheless, as shown in Figure 9.3, when assessing the value of EMR_{SG} in joules of gross energy requirement we do find a rather diversified set of values for the EU14 countries. This is because an assessment of EMR_{SG} expressed in joules of gross (thermal) energy requirement encompasses the effect of differences in the mix of primary energy sources used to generate energy carriers, that is, it includes the energy losses for electricity generation.

9.2 A multi-level matrix for generating a dual assessment of energy flows in the metabolic pattern

To avoid confusion, from now on we will make a distinction between:

1   the notation ET_i –indicating a quantity of generic exosomatic throughput, without reference to the semantic and formal category;
2   the notation EC_i – indicating a quantity of exosomatic throughput expressed in joules of net energy carriers (requiring a specification of the type of energy carrier);

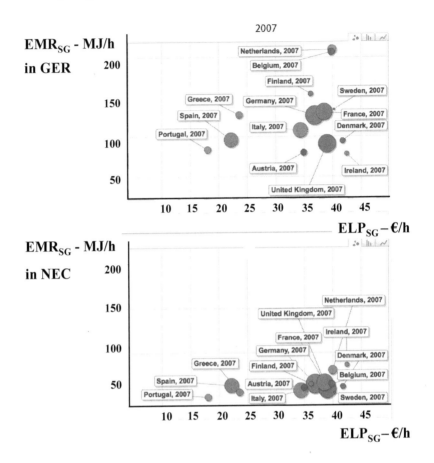

Figure 9.3 Energetic metabolic rate (EMR$_{SG}$) and economic labour productivity (ELP$_{SG}$) of the service and government sectors of the EU14 in 2007: based on gross energy requirement (GER) accounting on the top and net energy carrier (NEC) accounting on the bottom
Source: Giampietro *et al.*, 2011, used with permission

3   the notation GERi – indicating a quantity of exosomatic throughput expressed in joules of gross energy requirement (requiring a specification of an energy form of reference – e.g. thermal).

9.2.1 The mix of three types of energy carriers

At the hierarchical level of individual economic sectors, we can represent the simultaneous consumption of different energy carriers in a three-dimensional graph. Each point on the graph indicates the relative composition of the energy carriers consumed (electricity, heat and fuels) and the absolute consumption of energy carrier mix in a year is indicated by the size of the sphere having that point as the centre. This type of representation is illustrated in Figure 9.4 for the agricultural sector of our EU14 countries (Giampietro *et al.*, 2011).

The three-dimensional representation shown in Figure 9.4 allows us to observe country-specific peculiarities in the use of energy carriers. We see, for example, that the Netherlands uses much more heat in agriculture than other countries because of its massive use of greenhouses in the production of high-added-value agricultural products.

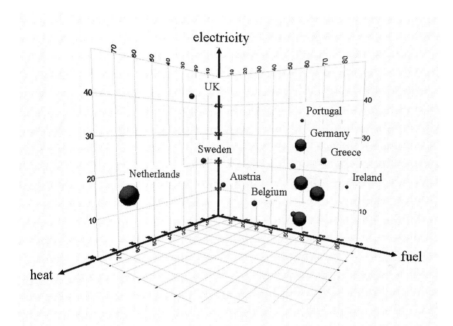

Figure 9.4 Three-dimentional graph showing use of three different energy carriers in the agricultural sector for the EU14 countries
Source: data from Sorman, 2011

But how can we handle the information provided by this three-dimensional representation using numbers? In the graph we characterize the net energy carrier consumption of a given compartment/sector by combining two pieces of information: (i) the total amount of net energy carrier consumed, and (ii) the relative composition of the net energy carriers consumed. For example, the overall consumption of net energy carrier in the household sector EC_{HH} (old ET_{HH} measured in EC) of Spain, in 2003, is the sum of the energy quantities referring to the flows of electricity, heat and fuels:

$(EC)_{HH} \leftrightarrow$ 197 PJ of electricity + 382 PJ of heat + 514 PJ of fuels

As discussed in our decalogue of the energy analyst (Chapter 6, page 120), we cannot simply sum the three terms on the right into:

$(EC)_{HH} \times$ 1093 PJ_{ECmix}

Incorrect step, obtained by aggregating non-equivalent energy forms!

Therefore, to convey all the relevant information we can use a vector of three elements in which the total amount of energy carrier is expressed by the existing relations among the different quantities of energy carriers (the mix). That is, for each compartment i of the society (including the whole country) we can write a vector of the net energy carriers defined as follows,

$NEC_i = (X_{1i}, X_{2i}, X_{3i})$

Where
X_{1i}: net energy carrier in the form of electricity;
X_{2i} : net nergy carrier in the form of heat; and
X_{3i} : net energy carrier in the form of fuels.

In the example of the household sector of Spain such a vector would be written as (the numbers are expressed in PJ/year):

$NEC_{HH} = (197, 382, 514)$

Using the same approach we can use the same vectoral notation to express the NEC consumption of the whole of Spain (using the suffix societal average) in PJ/year:

$NEC_{SA} = (860, 1400, 1776)$ defined at the level n

Or the NEC consumption of the SG sector, in PJ/year:

$NEC_{SG} = (224, 92, 1003)$ defined at the level n-2

Then using a set of conversion factors between the quantity of a given type of energy carrier NEC_j (e.g. 1 joule of electricity) and the amount of gross energy requirement (thermal) GER required to produce it (e.g. 2.6 joule of thermal energy) we can convert the quantities of energy expressed in NEC into quantities of GER equivalent.

For instance by using the following set of conversion factors (GER/NEC_j) for Spain – e.g. (i) 2.61, for electricity; (ii) 1.1, for heat; (iii) 1.38, for fuels – we can calculate the total aggregate of Gross Energy Requirement of that country. To do so, starting from the definition of the consumption of the different energy carries for the whole society: $NEC_{SA} = (860, 1400, 1776)$ – defined at the level n – we can calculate, using the three conversion factors, the following sum expressed in PJ of GER thermal equivalent:

$$GER_{SA} = (860 \times 2.61) + (1400 \times 1.1) + (1776 \times 1.38) = 6234$$

In general terms we can say that a conversion vector for each compartment i can be defined where each element y_{ji} represents the ratio between gross energy requirement of energy carrier j and X_{ji}.

The value of y_{ji} depends on the conversion characteristics of compartment i. For example, consider the following 5×3 matrix describing the mix of NEC (j: 1=electricity; 2=heat; 3=fuels), expressed in PJ, across the different compartments (i:1=SA, 2=HH, 3=SG, 4=PS*, 5=EM of Spain in 2003:

$$\text{NEC (Spain) } 5 \times 3 = \begin{pmatrix} 860 & 1400 & 1776 \\ 197 & 382 & 514 \\ 224 & 92 & 1003 \\ 366 & 907 & 81 \\ 73 & 19 & 178 \end{pmatrix}$$

By knowing the conversion factors calculated as average for the whole country GER_{ASA}/X_{jSA} (GER_{ASA} is the total aggregate GER for the whole country), we can convert the information carried by the first row into an assessment of the GER for the whole country. If we knew for each of the compartments included in the matrix the specific conversion factors GER_{ji}/X_{ji} (GER_{ji} is GER of j energy carrier for compartment i), we could generate a similar assessment in GER equivalent for the various elements.

Alternatively, we can obtain an approximate evaluation of the amount of GER that should be assigned to each compartment by using the average of the country within the various compartments. In formal terms we can express this approach as follows.

In the more general case, when it is possible to define conversion factors specific for each compartment i across levels, we can write a conversion vector for compartment i as follows:

$$Y_i^t = (y_{1i}, y_{2i}, y_{3i})$$

where t signifies transpose.

Then we can obtain the total aggregate of Gross Energy Requirement GER_{Ai} for compartment i as follows,

$$GER_{Ai} = NEC_i \times Y_i$$

Whenever this option is not available, we can use a single set of the conversion ratios (averages for the country) defined at the national level, then we can suppress the index *i* and call the conversion vector *Y* rather than Y_i

In order to keep the distinction between the different energy carriers within GER_{Ai}, we can use a diagonal conversion matrix Y_{Di},

$$Y_{Di} = \begin{pmatrix} y_{1i} & 0 & 0 \\ 0 & y_{2i} & 0 \\ 0 & 0 & y_{3i} \end{pmatrix}$$

When adopting a standard set of conversions factors for the whole country the subscript *i* of Y_{Di} and in the matrix Y_{Di} will be suppressed and we can use Y_D.

Then we can obtain a vector of each type of gross energy requirement for compartment *i* as follows,

$$GER_{Vi} = (GER_{1i}, GER_{2i}, GER_{3i})$$

where
GER_{1i}: gross energy requirement attributable to electricity;
GER_{2i}: gross energy requirement attributable to heat; and
GER_{3i}: gross energy requirement attributable to fuels.

Then we can obtain GER_{Vi} as follows,

$$GER_{Vi} = NEC_i \times Y_{Di}$$

We provide an example of this approach in Figure 9.5, applied to the analysis of Spain, in which this method is used to establish a relation between the two different forms of quantification of energy flows (GER and NEC). On the top part of the figure the approach is used to provide a general assessment of the GER of the various compartments by aggregating the quantities required for the production of the various carriers in a single quantitative assessment: GER_{Ai}. Whereas in the lower part of the figure we illustrate the means to quantify gross energy requirement by typology of energy carrier used in the different compartments defined at different hierarchical levels and scales: GER_{Vi}.

9.2.2 An example of dual accounting of energy flows: the metabolic pattern of Spain

In Figure 9.6 we present a visual representation of the dual accounting of energy flows, based on the correspondence between an assessment expressed in PJ of GER_{Ai} and PJ of NEC. We apply this quantitative characterization to the semantic definition of structural and functional compartments illustrated in Figure 7.3, page 167 (reflecting the basic rationale of the 'cheese slicer' presented in Figure 7.1, page 164 and the analysis based only on energy flows illustrated in Figure 7.2, page 165). Using this visualization, we briefly revisit the logical bifurcation found in the quantitative accounting of energy, generated by the co-existence of

Net energy carriers   GER/NEC$_i$ Gross energy requirement

$$
\begin{array}{c}
\text{SA}\\ \text{HH}\\ \text{SG}\\ \text{PS*}\\ \text{EM}
\end{array}
\begin{bmatrix}
860 & 1400 & 1776\\
198 & 382 & 514\\
224 & 92 & 1003\\
366 & 907 & 81\\
73 & 19 & 178
\end{bmatrix}
\times
\begin{bmatrix}
2.61\\ 1.10\\ 1.38
\end{bmatrix}
=
\begin{bmatrix}
6234\\ 1641\\ 2074\\ 2062\\ 457
\end{bmatrix}
\begin{array}{c}
\text{SA}\\ \text{HH}\\ \text{SG}\\ \text{PS*}\\ \text{EM}
\end{array}
$$

electricity heat fuel   conversion factors   GER$_{Ai}$ thermal

Net energy carriers   GER/NEC$_i$ Gross energy requirement

$$
\begin{array}{c}
\text{SA}\\ \text{HH}\\ \text{SG}\\ \text{PS*}\\ \text{EM}
\end{array}
\begin{bmatrix}
860 & 1400 & 1776\\
198 & 382 & 514\\
224 & 92 & 1003\\
366 & 907 & 81\\
73 & 19 & 178
\end{bmatrix}
\times
\begin{bmatrix}
2.61 & 0 & 0\\
0 & 1.10 & 0\\
0 & 0 & 1.38
\end{bmatrix}
=
\begin{bmatrix}
2244 & 1540 & 2450\\
513 & 420 & 708\\
586 & 102 & 1386\\
952 & 998 & 112\\
190 & 21 & 246
\end{bmatrix}
\begin{array}{c}
\text{SA}\\ \text{HH}\\ \text{SG}\\ \text{PS*}\\ \text{EM}
\end{array}
$$

electricity heat fuel   conversion factors   electricity heat fuel
GER$_{Vi}$ thermal

Figure 9.5 Correspondence of assessments of energy flows (quantified in PJ/year of GER and NEC) across levels in Spain 2003: GER$_{Ai}$ (top graph); GER$_{Vi}$ (lower graph)

two non-equivalent valid narratives for defining energy throughputs (see Part I, Figure 3.3, page 59).

The data used for this assessment are based on the quantitative characterization presented in Figure 9.5. The use of four significant digits could suggest to the reader an extreme accuracy of the relative assessments. Obviously, this is not the case. All the numbers presented here (and in general found when discussing this type of energy accounting) are affected by large doses of indeterminacy (as we will discuss in more detail in Chapter 11) that would require the adoption of two significant digits. However, we keep the four significant digits only to make it possible for the reader to recognize and keep track of the different sets of numbers used across levels in the dual quantitative characterization.

By looking at the data of Figure 9.6 we can better understand the difference between the two narratives associated with the use of GER or NEC quantitative assessments.

The first of these narratives concerns the local-scale view. It considers energy assessments carried out at the level of individual compartments, by measuring actual energy flows of net energy carriers. In this narrative, all the transformation losses in making and distributing carriers (that is, the difference between GER$_{Ai}$ and NEC, accounting for 2,198PJ in Figure 9.6) are attributed to the energy and mining sector. The other sectors are considered to only consume the direct net supply of energy carriers allocated to them.

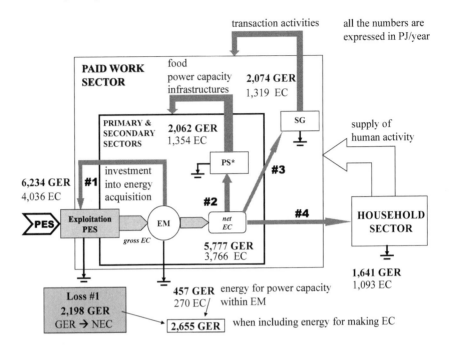

Figure 9.6 An example of dual accounting in terms of gross energy requirement and energy carriers of the metabolic pattern across compartments of Spain in 2003

The second narrative is the whole-society view. This societal view should be used if we want to assess the share of gross energy requirement (measured in thermal equivalent – e.g. TET_{GER}) that is associated with the various functions expressed by society, which can only be guaranteed because of the energy metabolism in the various compartments. Within this narrative we have to attribute the specific share of transformation and distribution losses needed to generate the energy carriers used by compartment i to that same compartment i – GER_{Vi}. This share will depend on the particular mix of energy carriers used by compartment i.

In Figure 9.6 we see, for instance, that the household sector (HH) uses 1,093PJ of energy in the form of net energy carriers. However, there are an additional 548PJ of energy associated with this flow, which are used in energy and mining (considering the local scale) for the production of these energy carriers. Nevertheless, these additional 548PJ of energy are consumed by 'the society' to express the activities of the household sector. Therefore, when considering the hierarchical level of the whole society (second narrative) and when measuring flows in gross primary energy thermal equivalent, we should consider this fraction of the total flow of GER-thermal equivalent as the quantity of energy of this type required for guaranteeing the functions expressed by the household sector: GER_{VHH}. In this second narrative, the society has to allocate 1,641PJ of

GER-thermal equivalent to the household sector to reproduce and generate the activities of this sector. The narrative adopted here refers to a definition of structural and functional boundaries according to which each compartment has to fulfil its own role within the societal metabolic pattern.

Because it is inevitable that we will face logical bifurcations when defining the profile of energy use in a society operating across multiple levels of organization, the only solution is to provide a dual assessment that characterizes all the shares of energy throughput in the various compartments, as shown in Figure 9.6. For example, for the PS* compartment (productive sectors minus energy and mining) we have the following two assessments:

1   Local-level view: 1,354PJ of net energy carrier. This quantity of energy refers to a vector, the elements of which refer to joules of energy carriers of different kinds. The local-level view assesses the direct consumption of energy carrier by type at the local level of the power capacity in PS*. This number is useful to study the efficiency of the local energy conversions (the technology), the requirement of power capacity and labour hours to operate the sector;
2   Whole-society view: 2,062PJ of gross energy requirement (thermal equivalent) – GER_{VPS*}. This number refers to the indirect energy requirement associated with the pattern of consumption of net energy carriers in the PS* compartment, the relative composition of the corresponding mix of primary energy sources consumed to produce these energy carriers, and the technology determining the ratio GER/NEC. This number is useful to assess biophysical constraints at a larger scale, in particular with regard to the relation between external constraints and the expression of (selected) societal functions.

If we want to study possible alternative metabolic patterns, based on a different profile of allocation of energy carriers (mix and relative quantities) and a different profile of allocation of human activities (requiring a readjustment in the profile of levels of power capacity), we should always opt for a dual reading to 'visualize' simultaneously both types of information.

9.2.3 How to derive conversion factors

If we want to convert the information on the quantities of energy carriers contained by the vector $(NEC)_i$ into the corresponding amounts of gross energy requirement, we must apply a conversion vector containing a specific conversion factor for each energy carrier. That is to say that we have to calculate, for each one of the energy carriers, the gross energy requirement in the energy and mining sector per unit supply of energy carrier. This specific ratio of the gross energy requirement and net supply of energy carrier gives us an energy carrier-specific, flat conversion factor. We can thus define a conversion vector $Y_i = {}^t(y_{1i}, y_{2i}, y_{3i})$, where y_{1i} is the conversion factor $(GER/NEC)_i$ for electricity generation, y_{2i} for heat generation, and y_{3i} for fuel generation. For example, we saw before that by using 2003 data from Spain, we can define the following conversion vector: $\mathbf{Y}_{SA} = [2.6, 1.1, 1.4]_{SA}$.

However, the generation of conversion factors requires us to choose a criterion of equivalence. As discussed in Part I it is possible to define conversion factors for specific energy carriers – e.g. electricity – by defining standard factors of equivalence. We described the 'partial substitution method' (the BP approach) or the 'physical energy content method' (the Eurostat approach) generating flat conversion factors, which are then applied across the different compartments (Figure 3.1, page 54).

On the other hand, we can calculate the conversion factors, starting from actual measurement of the overall losses due to: (i) the efficiency of the electricity production process from fossil energy sources (coal, natural gas and oil); and (ii) the distribution losses. Conversion factors calculated in this way are more accurate. They may be calculated for a specific process (e.g. in the case of co-generation), or for a particular geographic location (close to or distant from power plants) or a particular technology (depending on the efficiency of specific power plants). The problem with this second approach is that conversion factors calculated in this way become time and space specific: they have to be assessed for every country and every year or in the case of local assessment, their value cannot be used in a different place and in a different year. Just to give an idea of the possible changes in time and across countries, we report in Table 9.1 the conversion factors (ratio GER/NEC) for the production of electricity for 1990 and 2007 for the EU14 countries in Table 9.1.

Table 9.1 The ratio gross energy requirement to net energy carrier for the production of electricity in 1990 and 2007 for the EU14 countries
Source: data from Sorman, 2011

Country	1990	2007
Spain	2.95	2.36
France	2.88	2.86
Sweden	2.83	2.88
Belgium	2.87	2.64
Finland	2.75	2.76
Germany	3.21	2.80
Netherlands	2.52	2.46
UK	2.88	2.50
Austria	2.87	2.82
Denmark	3.09	2.73
Greece	3.36	3.14
Ireland	2.90	2.36
Italy	2.66	2.41
Portugal	2.94	2.47

As we will discuss in more detail in Chapter 11, in energy analysis it is impossible to avoid confronting the dilemma of accuracy versus relevance. If we use average values associated with expected benchmark values as flat conversion factors, we must accept the consequence: in this way we are generating quantitative assessments affected by a certain dose of approximation (loss of accuracy). On the other hand, if we want to use extremely accurate data based on direct observations at the local scale reflecting specific circumstances, we must accept the consequence: in this way we are generating quantitative assessments which are 'special' and therefore not particularly relevant for other situations. We can recognize in this dilemma the core of the issue of scale, how to scale up special local characteristics (required to gain accuracy) without losing the relevance of the information for discussions referring to events and phenomena described at a much larger scale.

9.3 The multi-level characterization of the metabolic pattern across levels

9.3.1 Introducing a representation based on a multi-level arrays dataset

In this section we introduce 'something completely different'. Even though we keep using a multi-level matrix composed of different arrays of data, we want to flag to the reader that what we present below has nothing to do with the conventional use of vectors and matrices (e.g. the representation given in Figure 9.5, page 221) or an input/output matrix, often used to study the interaction of economic sectors (e.g. Leontief, 1986).

Our approach goes against Occam's razor (the principle stating that, other things being equal, a simpler explanation is better than a more complex one), as it aims to introduce redundancy in the representation of the metabolic pattern across different levels, so as to take advantage of the effect of mutual information (what we call the sudoku effect). The accumulation of mutual information is an expected feature of autopoietic systems operating through autocatalytic loops across levels (Giampietro *et al.*, 2011). In these systems the characteristics of the various parts must be compatible with the characteristics of the whole and vice-versa. In order to allow for this redundancy, we start by expressing the mathematical relations determining the dual reading of energy flows illustrated in the previous section. This time we abandon the vector notation and we express the relations in scalar terms.

For example, starting from the information contained in the vector describing the pattern of net energy carriers consumption in the service and government of Spain:

$$NEC_{SG} = (224, 92, 1003) \text{ [the vector } NEC_i = (X_{1i}, X_{2i}, X_{3i})]$$

We can adopt a scalar characterization summing the three quantities of energy carriers (electricity, heat and fuel) without using any quality factors.

$EC_{SG} = 224 + 92 + 1003 = 1{,}319$ (the sum of the three elements of the vector NEC_{SG})

In formal terms we can express the definition of the scalar sum of EC as:

$$EC_i = \sum_{j=1}^{3} X_{ji}$$

As discussed earlier, this sum in a scalar number should not be used to assess an overall flow of energy carriers, since it refers to a mix of carriers of different qualities. For this reason we have to add additional information to it in order to keep the relevant information about the difference in quality in the mix of energy carriers. To this purpose we specify the composition of the mix using the three elements of EC_{SG} which refer to electricity, heat and fuels, respectively. That is:

(1) $0.17_{1SG} = 224/1{,}319$; (2) $0.07_{2SG} = 92/1{,}319$; (3) $0.76_{3SG} = 1003/1{,}319$;

In formal terms we can describe this operation as follows. Starting with the given vector of energy carriers – $NEC_i = (X_{1i}, X_{2i}, X_{3i})$ – we can derive the mix of energy carriers defined as $X_i = (x_{1i}, x_{2i}, x_{3i})$ as follows:

$$X_{ji} = \frac{X_{ji}}{\sum_{j=1}^{3} X_{ji}} = \frac{X_{ji}}{EC_i}$$

At this point we can write down the information about the consumption of energy carriers in the SG sector using an array of 4 elements:

array of 4 elements:	$1{,}319\ EC_{SG}$;	0.17_{1SG} ;	0.07_{2SG};	0.76_{3SG}
in formal terms:	EC_i	X_{1i}	X_{2i}	X_{2i}

With this method we can retrieve the information given by the 3 element vector by using the information given by this 4 element array:

3-element vector: $(224, 92, 1003)$　　　　　　　　➜ $NEC_i = (X_{1i}, X_{2i}, X_{3i})$
4-element array: $1{,}319\ EC_{SG}$; 0.17_{1SG} ; 0.07_{2SG}; 0.76_{3SG} ➜ EC_i; x_{1i}; x_{2i}; x_{3i};

To move to a quantitative assessment expressed in GER, we have to use the set of conversion factors – GER_{jSA}/X_{jSA} for Spain – represented by the set of 3 elements. In this way we generate an array of 7 elements carrying the required information:

7-element array ➜	2.61,	1.10,	1.38,	1,319	0.17,	0.07,	0.76,
formal definition ➜	y_{1i},	y_{2i},	y_{3i},	EC_i,	x_{1i},	x_{2i},	x_{3i},

By combining the information given by the first 3 elements with the information given by the last 4 elements, we can calculate the amount of joules of gross energy requirement (thermal) associated with the metabolism of the service and government sectors – GER_{Vi}:

(1) amount of GER attributed to EC electricity = $1,319 \times 0.17 \times 2.61 = 586$ PJ
(2) amount of GER attributed to EC heat = $1,319 \times 0.07 \times 1.10 = 102$ PJ
(3) amount of GER attributed to EC fuel = $1,319 \times 0.76 \times 1.38 = 1,386$ PJ

That is we can generate another element to be added to the array by summing these three quantities of GER referring to the requirement of three energy carriers (GER_{Vi}) into an aggregate quantity (GER_{Ai}). We can do that without losing meaning since these numbers are all expressed in gross energy requirement (thermal).

$$(ET_{GERA})_{SG} = 586 + 102 + 1,386 = 2,074 \text{ PJ}$$

We can obtain this result by using the conventional vector matrix algebra (using the approach illustrated in Figure 9.5) by defining the following vector:

$$EC_{Vi} = (EC_i, EC_i, EC_i) = (\sum_{j=1}^{3} X_{ji}, \sum_{j=1}^{3} X_{ji}, \sum_{j=1}^{3} X_{ji})$$

From which we can obtain:

(1) $GER_{Ai} = EC_{Vi} \times Y_{Di} \times X_{Di}$; and
(2) $GER_{Vi} = EC_{Vi} \times Y_{Di} \times X_i$

As an alternative, we can also obtain the same result using a classic spreadsheet. In fact, what is relevant for our scope is to show that it is possible to express, using an array of 8 elements, all the information required for carrying out all these calculations. This array can therefore provide a dual characterization of the energy throughput of any compartment of a country. In our example the exosomatic throughput of the service and government compartment of Spain (ET_{SG}) can be characterized using the 8-element array as follows:

8-element array → 2,074; 2.61; 1.10; 1.38; 1,319; 0.17; 0.07; 0.76
formal definition → GER_{Ai}; y_{1i}, y_{2i}, y_{3i}, EC_i, x_{1i}, x_{2i}, x_{3i}

But we increase the level of internal redundancy of the information about the exosomatic energy throughput further by adding more information about: (i) the requirement of human activity; and (ii) the resulting exosomatic metabolic rate (linked to the requirement of power capacity). In this way we are addressing the existence of a set of forced relations over the characteristics of the metabolic pattern across the various compartments due to the existence of the mosaic effect. The dendrograms of allocation of human activity and energy flows across levels constrain the congruence of the resulting profile of exosomatic metabolic rates (power capacity and human activity) allocated among the various compartments (Figure 8.5, page 201).

We thus add two pieces of information to the array of 8 elements presented above: (i) the amount of human activity (hours of HA_i) allocated to compartment i; and (ii) the power level (EMR_i) in the compartment i, according to the relation: $EMR_i = ET_i/HA_i$ discussed in Chapter 8 (page 189). Because of the dual reading of energy flows (GER_{Ai} and EC_i) discussed in the previous section, for each compartment we may have two different values for the same semantic definition of EMR_i:

> 1 $EMR_{GERAi} = GER_{Ai}/HA_i$ – when quantifying the quantity of energy using the semantic category gross energy requirement; and
> 2 $EMR_{ECi} = EC_i/HA_i$ – when quantifying the quantity of energy using the semantic category energy carriers.

However, when dealing with the analysis of technical coefficients – when analysing efficiency and power capacity at the local level it makes sense to use assessments of EMR_i referring only to quantities of energy referring to the semantic category of energy carriers. In fact this information is naturally related to the requirement of power capacity in the compartments (local scale assessments). For this reason, we do not include the value of EMR_{GERAi} among the elements added to the array.

In conclusion, we can use an array of 10 data elements to get an exhaustive quantitative characterization of the metabolic pattern of compartment i (MP_i) which can be defined and observed at different levels (and scales):

$$MP_i \rightarrow GER_{Ai}; \quad y_1; \ y_2; \ y_3; \quad EC_i; \quad x_{1i}; \ x_{2i}; \ x_{3i}; \quad EMR_{ECi}; \qquad HA_i;$$
$$\quad\quad GER \quad (GER/NEC)_i \quad NEC \quad Carriers\ mix \quad Power\ level \quad human\ activity$$

Note that eight of the ten elements of this dataset array have to be entered as primary data (tokens), these include y_1, y_2, y_3, EC_i, x_{1i}, x_{2i}, x_{3i}, and HA_i. The other two elements (GER_{Ai} and EC_i) are numbers resulting from production rules (names in the jargon of software makers). However, the definition of a variable as a token or a name is not rigid. For instance, when studying a scenario we may impose a minimum or a maximum acceptable power level for a specific compartment (EMR_{ECi}). In this way, a hypothesis can be used as a token in a given scenario analysis thus making it possible to check the value required by other variables to obtain congruence. This approach is at the basis of the sudoku analysis proposed in Chapter 10. An overview of the application of this approach to the characterization of the metabolic pattern of the various compartments of Spain in 2003, based on the data of Figure 9.5, is given in Figure 9.7.

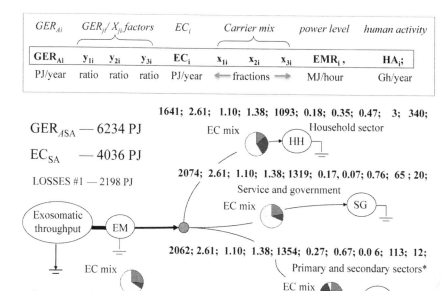

GER_{Ai}	GER_{ji}/X_{ji} factors			EC_i	Carrier mix			power level	human activity
$\mathbf{GER_{Ai}}$	$\mathbf{y_{1i}}$	$\mathbf{y_{2i}}$	$\mathbf{y_{3i}}$	$\mathbf{EC_i}$	$\mathbf{x_{1i}}$	$\mathbf{x_{2i}}$	$\mathbf{x_{3i}}$	$\mathbf{EMR_i}$,	$\mathbf{HA_i}$;
PJ/year	ratio	ratio	ratio	PJ/year	← fractions →			MJ/hour	Gh/year

1641; 2.61; 1.10; 1.38; 1093; 0.18; 0.35; 0.47; 3; 340;

GER_{ASA} — 6234 PJ

EC_{SA} — 4036 PJ

LOSSES #1 — 2198 PJ

2074; 2.61; 1.10; 1.38; 1319; 0.17, 0.07; 0.76; 65 ; 20;

2062; 2.61; 1.10; 1.38; 1354; 0.27; 0.67; 0.0 6; 113; 12;

457; 2.61; 1.10; 1.38; 270; 0.27; 0.07; 0.66; 900; 0.3;

Figure 9.7 A characterization of the metabolic characteristics of the compartments of Spain in 2003 using a ten-element array dataset.

9.3.2 The characterization of the metabolic pattern of society using a multi-level matrix

The use of dataset arrays is extremely helpful to describe the metabolic pattern of a country as they can convey heterogeneous information based on observations and measurements expressed in different units and carried out on multiple levels at different scales. Indeed, a dataset array allows us to convey a dual reading of the metabolic pattern across hierarchical levels, in terms of both joules of net energy carrier and joules of gross energy requirement. In Figure 9.8 we show the general structure of the dataset array describing the metabolic pattern of a society in general terms – upper part – and an actual application of this method of representation (a 10-element-array dataset) making it possible to characterize the metabolic pattern of Spain across different hierarchical levels (and associated compartments) in the year 2007, based on the structure – bottom part.

The quantitative characterizations provided by the rows in the multi-level matrix shown in Figure 9.8 refer to sets of energy transformations taking place simultaneously in different compartments defined at different hierarchical levels (level n, n-1, n-2, n-3, and n-3 again, respectively). Therefore, they refer to observation protocols and measurement schemes that are non-equivalent and non-reducible to each other within conventional mono-scale models. All the same, the required biophysical congruence over the autopoietic process of energy metabolism entails that the existence of mutual information determining (in an impredicative way) the forced characteristics of the various elements, has to be congruent in relation to the establishment of the overall metabolic pattern. That is, the characteristics of the whole (the first row) must be congruent with the characteristics of lower-level compartments (when imagining a top-down causation) and the characteristics of the individual compartments expressing specific local metabolic patterns must be congruent with the characteristics of the whole (when imagining a bottom-up causation).

The formalization of the 10-element-array multi-level matrix

GER_{ASA}	y_1	y_2	y_3	EC_{SA}	x_{1_SA}	x_{2_SA}	x_{3_SA}	EMR_{EC_SA}	THA	n
GER_{AHH}	y_1	y_2	y_3	EC_{HH}	x_{1_HH}	x_{2_HH}	x_{3_HH}	EMR_{EC_HH}	HA_{HH}	$n-1$
GER_{ASG}	y_1	y_2	y_3	EC_{SG}	x_{1_SG}	x_{2_SG}	x_{3_SG}	EMR_{EC_SG}	HA_{SG}	$n-2$
GER_{APS*}	y_1	y_2	y_3	EC_{PS*}	x_{1_PS*}	x_{2_PS*}	x_{3_PS*}	EMR_{EC_PS*}	HA_{PS*}	$n-3$
GER_{AEM}	y_1	y_2	y_3	EC_{EM}	x_{1_EM}	x_{2_EM}	x_{3_EM}	EMR_{EC_EM}	HA_{EM}	$n-3$

The dataset characterizing the metabolic pattern of Spain in 2007

6439	2.36	1.10	1.28	4338	0.23	0.32	0.45	12	354	n
1801	2.36	1.10	1.28	1250	0.21	0.33	0.47	4	316	$n-1$
2270	2.36	1.10	1.28	1545	0.19	0.07	0.74	64	24	$n-2$
1834	2.36	1.10	1.28	1182	0.29	0.58	0.13	126	14	$n-3$
534	2.36	1.10	1.28	361	0.23	0.26	0.52	1091	0.3	$n-3$

Figure 9.8 Multi-level matrix (based on 10-element-arrays) characterizing the metabolic pattern of a society: formal definition (top) and practical application (bottom)

It should be noted that the multi-level matrix made up of 10-element arrays can be used to characterize the metabolic pattern of any set of compartment *i* defined using the semantic categories presented earlier. For example we could express a data set including a 10-element array characterizing the PW sector (the sum of the PS and SG sector) at the level n-1, or the AG (agricultural sector) a subsector of the PS sector, isolated at the level n-3 instead of the EM sector. These two compartments are not included in the example of analysis given in Figure 9.8. That is, a quantitative analysis based on the adoption of this multi-level matrix organized in a spreadsheet makes it possible to tailor the selection of compartments analyzed for the specific goal of the study. For this task, we can use the mosaic effect for aggregating or splitting the various compartments to be included in the analysis, depending on the goal. For instance, we can stop the disaggregation at level n-1 (by aggregating all the sub-compartments of PW into averages values for that compartment) and work with a multi-level matrix of only 3 rows. Alternatively we can add new 10-element arrays to the matrix, if we are interested in specifying the characteristics of relevant sub-sectors, further expanding the number of rows.

A second important characteristic of this method is that by wisely choosing the set of compartments included in the multi-level matrix we can generate redundancy in the information space. This redundancy makes it possible to study the existence of mutual constraints in the characteristics of the elements described within the same metabolic pattern. For example, looking at the dataset indicated in the lower part of Figure 9.8 we can notice that in the first column (the values of the exosomatic throughputs calculated in GER) the value written in the first row (societal average) is the sum of the values written in lower elements of the same column. The same forced relation applies to the elements of the fifth column (the values of the exosomatic throughputs calculated in NEC) and to the elements of the tenth column (the values of hours of human activity). This forced congruence is due to our choice of compartments included in the multi-level matrix. We selected all the compartments found on one side of the bifurcations of the dendrogram plus the first and the last compartments (the societal average and the two compartments of the last split). In this way, the sum of exosomatic throughputs and the sum of hours of human activity invested into lower level compartments is equal to the starting amount of both the total exosomatic throughput and the total human activity assessed at the level of the whole society. In the same way there are constraints over the values of exosomatic metabolic rates (given in the ninth column) defined, row by row, by the relative value of EC_i and HA_i.

This set of forced relations of congruence over the given representation makes it possible to check admissible values within the various arrays of the multi-level matrix, just like in the popular sudoku puzzles. This can prove very useful in the case of a scenario analysis to check the viability of different metabolic patterns associated with a claim that it would be possible to express an alternative combination of structural and functional compartments of the society. In particular, this method of analysis makes it possible to analyze the effect of changes in extensive variables (e.g. population size) and intensive variables (e.g. technological improvements) in relation to the concepts of mosaic effect and impredicative loop analysis (introduced in Chapter 8).

The mosaic effect makes it possible to check the congruence of values across the dendrograms of both THA and TET. This implies a forced relation over the values of the elements defined on different hierarchical levels (rows) in the same columns (ET_i and HA_i) of the dataset array. The forced relation between the relative size of the fund element HA_i and the flow element ET_i (expressed here as EC_i) defines the power level EMR_i, in each single row of the dataset array.

Therefore the profile of power levels EMR_i cannot take on any value (token definition); it is subject to the following rules: (i) it must provide an adequate power capacity: a characteristic that is defined and observed at the local scale i; and (ii) it must be able to express the required function: a characteristic that can only be observed at the larger scale. The horizontal constraint operating in each single row ($EMR_{ECi} = ET_i/HA_i = EC_i/HA_i$) obviously entails that the values of EMR_i across the rows must be congruent with the relative values of ET_i and HA_i in relation to TET (EC_{SA} in this accounting) and THA, which in turn are affected by vertical constraints (the congruence across the columns).

Impredicative loop analysis consists of checking the congruence among different characteristics of the hypercyclic and the purely dissipative part of the metabolic pattern. Impredicative loop analysis studies the forced congruence between the metabolic characteristics that define the overall requirement of inputs of flow elements (energy, food, materials) and fund elements (power capacity and human activity) at the hierarchical level of the whole (level n) as well as the metabolic characteristics of the various compartments guaranteeing this supply (PS) or determining the demand (SG and HH), at lower hierarchical levels. The rationale for this type of analysis (not based on vectors) has been presented in Figure 8.7, where we defined the expected characteristics of the energy and mining sector of a developed country in relation to the characteristics of the other compartments, described within the metabolic pattern. The internal competition for production factors (power capacity, human activity and energy throughput) implies that the investment of these factors into the dissipative side must leave an adequate amount of investment to operate the hypercyclic side. How to use the multi-level matrix representation to carry out an impredicative loop analysis (the sudoku approach) to check the desirability and feasibility of the metabolic pattern of modern societies is explained in Chapter 10.

A last feature of the multi-level matrix is that it offers the ability to establish a link between: (i) a quantitative analysis of external constraints – studying the requirement of primary energy sources required to generate the gross energy requirement (expressed in terms of thermal equivalent) – presented in Chapter 11; and (ii) a quantitative analysis of internal constraints – studying the competition over production factors: net energy carriers (both in mix and quantity), power capacity, and human activity among the various compartments – presented in Chapter 10. In this way, it becomes easier to individuate the factors and understand the related constraints determining the desirability and the feasibility of alternative energy sources. The desirability and feasibility can be checked by considering simultaneously the specific implication of a given metabolic pattern on: (i) the expected characteristics of the compartments studied from inside the black box; and (ii) the characteristics of boundary conditions studied from outside the black box. This integrated analysis is presented in Chapter 12.

10 Studying the feasibility and desirability of the metabolic pattern of society from within

In this chapter we focus on the quantitative analysis of the internal constraints on the metabolic pattern of society. We provide an innovative quantitative method that can be used to analyze the desirability and viability of a given metabolic pattern. This method is based on a description of the network of energy transformations from within the societal system. The chapter is organized into four sections. In the first two sections, we provide empirical support for the hypothesis that economic growth can be associated with a series of expected transformations in the metabolic pattern. In the last two sections we focus on the technical details of how to use our protocol of MuSIASEM. More specifically:

In section 10.1, we introduce the pioneering work of George Kingsley Zipf on the existence of predictable characteristics of the metabolic pattern of socio-economic systems. We back up Zipf's theories with an empirical analysis of the socio-economic structure of 14 EU countries. In section 10.2 we illustrate, on the basis of an empirical analysis of 82 countries world-wide, that economic growth is associated with an expected pattern of structural changes, which in turn determine predictable changes in the metabolic pattern of modern societies. We focus here in particular on the functioning of the two macro compartments defined earlier, the hypercyclic (composed by the primary and secondary production sectors) and the purely dissipative compartment (composed by the household and the service and government sector), and the required equilibrium between their meta-parameter, the strength of the exosomatic hypercycle (SEH) and the bio-economic pressure (BEP).

In section 10.3 we illustrate the use of the 'sudoku strategy' to characterize the internal constraints on the metabolic pattern of society. Using a multi-level matrix characterizing the metabolic pattern of society from the inside, we can define a series of congruence rules over the values of the elements in (i) columns (referring to allocation of energy flows of determined form and human activity over compartments); (ii) rows (describing economic sectors at various hierarchical levels); and (iii) the two sub-matrices that determine the meta-parameters SEH and BEP. The values of all the elements of the multi-level matrix must be congruent *simultaneously* in relation to *all* criteria. In section 10.4 we summarize the main findings of the chapter.

10.1 The internal coherence of the metabolic pattern

In this section we provide empirical support for the hypothesis that the expression of a robust metabolic pattern by modern societies can be explained by the existence of an increasing effect of mutual information among the metabolic characteristics of socio-economic compartments interacting across scales within a complex autocatalytic process. The coherence found in the expected relations among the values of the elements of the multi-level matrix underlying our MuSIASEM approach justifies the use of benchmark values for the analysis of the desirability and feasibility of a given typology of metabolic pattern.

10.1.1 The pioneering work of Zipf

One of the pioneers of quantitative analysis of the internal constraints of modern societies is certainly George Kingsley Zipf. In his rather unconventional scientific career, Zipf moved from the quantitative analysis of regularities found in the letters used in the words of different languages, to that of regular patterns in the characteristics of modern society. He put forward that, when looking at some of the characteristics of their components, complex modern societies show clear signs of critical self-organization. As a matter of fact, the law describing the critical organization of complex systems is called Zipf's law in his honour.

In his seminal book, *National Unity and Disunity: the nation as a bio-social organism*, he presents his investigation of the structure of nations and the existence of clear patterns in the resulting quantitative representation:

> ... if the reader will consult the census for the United States for 1930 he will note a very curious relation between all the communities that contain at least 2,500 inhabitants. Thus he will find that New York was first in size of population; that the second largest city had $1/2$ as many inhabitants as New York; that the third largest city had $1/3$ as many inhabitants as New York; that the fourth had $1/4$ as many; the fifth $1/5$ – indeed, that the nth largest community had $1/n$ as many inhabitants as New York...
>
> (Zipf, 1941, p. iii)

Zipf uses this expected pattern of the relative size of cities within countries as a benchmark for comparison. For instance, in Chapter 4 of his book, he points out that colonial empires manifest an aberrant pattern relative to this benchmark. Capital cities of the dominant colonizing countries (e.g. United Kingdom, France) are larger than the expected size, while capital cities of the subjugated colonized nations are smaller than the expected size. According to Zipf's data, in 1930 London was far larger than double the size of the second largest British city, whereas New Delhi was far smaller than double the size of the second largest Indian city. Zipf explains that London, being the capital of the mother country of the empire, had to assume far more functions than the capital of an ordinary nation, acting as capital not only for the UK but also for the rest of the British

Empire, India included. It thus required more people (human activity) for control (transaction activities in our jargon) than similar European countries without colonies. For the same reason New Delhi needed far less human activity for control than the capital of an organic nation, as most of the operations were taken care of in London.

According to Zipf, the internal socio-economic organization of a nation is so strong as to lock in existing structural and functional relations among the parts of society. The resulting metabolic pattern tends to remain coherent. In order to have a transition to an alternative pattern a sort of collapse is needed, followed by a re-structuring of the profile of allocation of human activity among different economic compartments. Explaining the restructuring of the US economy after the Great Depression he comments:

> Expressed differently, in 1929, the United States discovered a new 'raw material': leisure time, which in a way, is just as much a 'raw material' as coal, oil, steel or anything else, because for many types of human activity, leisure time, is an essential prerequisite...
>
> (Zipf, 1941, p. 324)

Having invested in more power capacity in the paid work sector, a society can only produce more if it also invests more human activity in consuming! In this way, Zipf explains the brittleness of the metabolic pattern (fully saturated in its possible path of becoming) that led to the economic collapse associated with the Great Depression. This collapse forced a restructuring of the US society onto a different metabolic pattern with a different profile of allocation of power capacity, human activity and flows of energy and material over the different compartments of the socio-economic system.

Zipf's pioneering work on the quantitative analysis of emergent properties of the socio-economic organization of countries did not get the attention it deserved. Unfortunately, and still today, few people in the field of energy analysis are famil-iar with his work. In line with Zipf's thinking, we show here that we can indeed perform quantitative analyses that identify emergent properties of complex meta-bolic systems. In fact, MuSIASEM is useful to reveal the existence of internal biophysical constraints on the metabolic pattern expressed by a given society, indicating its viability.

10.1.2 The internal biophysical constraints represented by coupled dendrograms

In this section we illustrate the existence of forced relations between the structural and functional characteristics of the compartments making up a society (the set of internal hidden relations illustrated in Figure 8.6, page 204 and Figure 8.7, page 206, identified using the multi-level matrix shown in Figure 9.8, page 230). Notably, the profiles of distribution of power capacity and human activity across the various compartments are intricately interwoven and mutually constrained.

The set of expected relations translates into the expression of a coherent metabolic pattern, which is especially robust and surprisingly uniform for the wealthier EU economies. This phenomenon is known as 'convergence'; the various countries of the EU tend to converge toward a common set of expected characteristics.

As a matter of fact, we illustrated in Chapter 9 that EU14 countries show a consistent set of values of exosomatic metabolic rates (EMR_i) – especially when using quantitative assessments based on energy carriers – of individual compartments. These values can be used as benchmark to predict with a certain approximation the characteristics of compartments of EU14 countries without looking at the specific data. Here we further analyze the nature of this systemic property. For this purpose, we propose an analysis based on dendrograms of fund and flow elements across hierarchical levels, as illustrated in Figure 10.1.

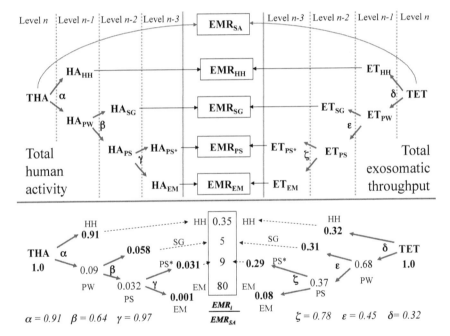

Figure 10.1 The distribution of human time and energy throughput over the various compartments of society and the resulting metabolic pattern, represented in general terms (upper part) and quantified for the EU14 (lower part)
Source: Giampietro *et al.*, 2011 used with permission

With regard to the dendrogram showing the profile of allocation of human activity (HA) across levels and compartments (Figure 10.1), we see that at each level we have a coefficient (dimensionless) determining the distribution of human activity: α determines the split of THA in HA_{HH} and HA_{PW}; β determines the distribution among HA_{SG} and HA_{PS}; and γ determines the distribution among HA_{PS*} and HA_{EM}. We have the same for the profile of allocation of energy throughput (ET) across levels and compartments (Figure 10.1): δ determines the division of TET into ET_{HH} and ET_{PW}; ε determines the distribution among ET_{SG} and ET_{PS}; and ζ determines the distribution among ET_{PS*} and ET_{EM}.

In the upper part of Figure 10.1, we define the characteristics of the metabolic pattern of the various compartments that make up a society in terms of HA_i, ET_i and EMR_i. As can be seen, the values of these three are intricately linked to the identity of the two dendrograms defining the profile of allocation of human activity and energy throughput over these same compartments. In the bottom part of Figure 10.1, we quantify the coefficients α, β, γ, δ, ε, and ζ, and the resulting relative metabolic pattern for the EU14. The values shown are averages over the EU14 countries, referring to the year 2003, and the relative metabolic rates shown for the various compartments can be expressed in relation to the metabolic rate of the entire society (EMR_i/EMR_{SA}). We have thus obtained a 'blue print' of the metabolic pattern for EU countries.

From our blueprint we clearly see that the various socio-economic compartments in EU societies are operating at widely different power levels (EMR_i). For instance, the power level of the energy and mining sector is approximately 80 times the average level in society ($EMR_{EM}/EMR_{SA} = 80$), and approximately 230 times the average power level in the household sector (EMR_{EM}/EMR_{HH}). These differences result from the asymmetric shape of the dendrograms of human activity and energy throughput. For instance, 91 per cent of the total human activity but only 32 per cent of the total energy throughput is allocated to the household sector.

The between-country variation in our EU14 sample with regard to the coefficients α, β, γ, δ, ε, and ζ, is fairly small, especially for those referring to the profile of allocation of human activity (a data set presenting a multi-level characterization of the metabolic pattern of EU14 countries is provided in Sorman, 2011).

In Table 10.1 we compare the metabolic pattern of the USA and China with our EU benchmark. Examining these numbers, we can individuate where and how much the USA and China are 'different' from the EU. Looking at the profile of

Table 10.1 Comparison of the benchmarks defining the metabolic pattern of the EU with the metabolic pattern of the USA and China

	α $HA_{HH} - HA_{PW}$		β $HA_{SG} - HA_{PS}$		γ $HA_{PS*} - HA_{EM}$		δ $ET_{HH} - ET_{PW}$		ε $ET_{SG} - ET_{PS}$		ζ $HA_{PS*} - HA_{PS}$	
EU14	91%	9%	64%	36%	97%	3%	32%	68%	45%	55%	78%	22%
USA	90%	10%	**83%**	**17%**	92%	8%	**41%**	**59%**	52%	48%	71%	29%
China	**82%**	**18%**	**33%**	**67%**	N.A.		30%	70%	**7%**	**93%**	N.A.	

Note: Numbers reported in bold are 'outliers'

allocation of human activity, we see, for instance, that China has a much higher percentage of its total human time allocated to paid work (α) (this can be attributed to a much lower dependency ratio) and a completely different distribution of its labour time among economic sectors (β); notably it has a poorly developed service sector compared to the EU. Looking at the profile of distribution of energy throughput, we see disequilibrium between transaction and production activities in China (ϵ), which shows that the power capacity of the country is invested mainly in producing.

The situation in the USA is completely different. It has a relatively high percentage of its labour time invested in the service sector (β), and a very large share of its energy throughput is accounted for by the household sector (δ) (larger houses, more driving).

It should be noted that these quantitative assessments (and relative benchmarks) of the values assigned to the semantic terms 'exosomatic throughput' (TET and ET_i) and 'exosomatic metabolic rate' as discussed in Chapter 9, can be quantified in different ways (e.g. using an assessment of GER thermal – scalar – or in EC using a vector). To make things more complicated the numerical value depends on the definition of the compartments used in the grammar (the protocol adopted in Table 10.1 is presented in Giampietro *et al.* 2011). However, the choice of the specific protocol used to quantify these semantic concepts is not the relevant point to be made here. The point is that after having agreed on a protocol of accounting, it is possible to find systemic differences in the relative characteristics of the compartments generating a metabolic pattern.

10.1.3 The metabolic pattern of the purely dissipative part of society: the bio-economic pressure

Before we present a method to quantify the bio-economic pressure (BEP) using a multi-level matrix representation we briefly explain why the concept of BEP and its counterpart, the strength of the exosomatic hypercycle (SEH), are required to generate a sudoku effect.

Using the information provided by the dendrograms of human activity and energy throughput, we can combine the two sectors of final consumption (household sector and service and government sector) into one macro-compartment: the purely dissipative compartment of society – Figure 7.6, page 183. Examining the metabolic pattern of the purely dissipative compartment in relation to that of the whole society, we can assess the bio-economic pressure exerted on society.

When looking at the benchmark values for the metabolic characteristics of individual compartments – Figure 9.1, page 211 – we can notice that the clustering around a common value is particularly evident when considering the metabolic characteristics of the household and service and government sector (the values of EMR_{HH} and EMR_{SG}). Moreover, this clustering is even more evident if the characteristics of these two sectors are quantified expressing the energy throughput in quantities of energy carriers – Figure 9.3, page 216. So when looking at the situation of an EU14 country we can use the average values of EMR_{HH}

and EMR_{SG} as a standard of 'desirability' perceived from within. These are values that can be associated with a metabolic pattern that is worth striving for. The hypothesis that the value of BEP can be used as indicator of material standard of living has been confirmed by an empirical analysis over 84 countries (presented in Giampietro *et al.* 2011), when considering modern countries operating within the market economy.

The information provided by these benchmarks makes it possible to use a characterization of the societal metabolism of the type presented in Chapter 9 – based on a multi-level matrix made of data arrays – to assess the performance of a given metabolic pattern in terms of end uses. That is, we can say that the various end uses expressed by an exosomatic metabolic pattern must guarantee a desirable material standard of living in the SG and HH sectors. This result can be quantified by saying that the metabolic pattern should guarantee to the SG and HH sectors a quantity of human activity and energy throughput as large as possible. Using a bio-economic jargon we can say that economic development tends to increase the amount of flows and fund elements making up the society as much as possible, which can then be allocated to the purely dissipative compartments (within the range of the value of BEP), while remaining in the viability domain (within the range of feasible values of SEH). In relation to the concept of the dynamic energy budget, any increase in BEP requires an adjustment of the profile of distribution of the production factors (power capacity, human activity and energy carriers) across the various compartments. In fact, using the theoretical concepts illustrated in Chapter 8, it is clear that an increase in BEP leads to an increased asymmetry in the dendrogram of split of total human activity (more human activity in consumption and transaction activities and less human activity in the PS sector). This in turn affects the pace of consumption of energy carriers of the whole society, since the metabolic pattern requires much more power capacity (and energy input) in PS in order to be able to handle the effects of the resulting asymmetries in the dendrograms.

10.2 Structural changes in the metabolic pattern associated with economic growth

10.2.1 Indicators characterizing the metabolic pattern of nations

In order to concisely describe and compare the metabolic patterns of different countries, we introduce here three quantitative indicators developed for this purpose within our MuSIASEM approach (Giampietro *et al.*, 2011): the exo/endo energy ratio, the ratio THA/HA_{PS}, and the bio-economic pressure (BEP).

The exo/endo energy ratio

The indicator exo/endo is simply defined as the ratio between the total exosomatic energy flow metabolized by the various sectors of the economy and the total endosomatic energy flow (or food energy) metabolized by its population. This indicator reflects the extent of technological capitalization of the economy or the so-called exosomatic power capacity of society. Pastore *et al.*, 2000, analyzing a large sample of countries, report a minimum value of 5/1 for the exo/endo energy ratio for societies where exosomatic energy is still largely in the form of natural energy conversions, such as biomass burning and animal power, and a maximum value of 90 for developed countries. These assessments are based on national statistics of consumption of exosomatic energy and on a flat value of endosomatic metabolism of 10 MJ/day per capita. Given this method of calculation, the exo/endo ratio is closely related to the exosomatic metabolic rate (EMR_i). For example at the level of the whole country (SA = societal average), we find:

$$(Exo/Endo)_{SA} = ExoMR_{SA}/EndoMR_{SA}$$

while for the other, lower levels we can write:

$$(Exo/Endo)_i = ExoMR_i /EndoMR_i$$

It should be noted that when coming to the formal quantification of these semantic definitions we have to decide which category of reference will be used to express quantities of energy. In the past, the data produced by our group and used in this section were expressed in joule of gross energy requirement (thermal) – the data available using energy statistics. When adopting this formalization of the concept of exosomatic throughput our empirical analyses have shown that differences in the values $exo_i/endo_i$ closely reflect differences in the values of $ExoMR_i$, because the denominator ($EndoMR_i$) is fairly constant for the different sectors of developed societies, fluctuating slightly around 0.4 MJ/h or 10 MJ/day (Giampietro *et al.*, 2011).

The ratio THA/HA_{PS}

The indicator THA/HA_{PS} is defined as the ratio between the total human activity (THA in hours) in a society and the absolute amount of labour hours allocated to the primary and secondary production sectors of the economy (HA_{PS}). It can also be written as $[(HA_{PS} + HA_{HH+SG})/HA_{PS}]$. Thus, it reflects the distribution of human activity between the hypercyclic (HA_{PS}) and purely dissipative part (HA_{HH+SG}) of the socio-economic system. Using North's terminology (1990), it reflects the relation between (i) transformation activities (HA_{PS}), comprising the productive sectors energy and mining, agriculture, and building and manufacturing, and (ii) transaction activities (HA_{HH+SG}), comprising the household sector and the tertiary sector. Changes in the value of the ratio THA/HA_{PS} reflect changes in: (i) demographic characteristics, such as life expectancy; (ii) socio-economic characteristics, such as work load, unemployment, level of education, and retirement regulations; and (iii) structural changes in the economy, such as the relative size of the primary and secondary production sectors versus the service and government sector (see Figure 8.3, page 198 and Figure 8.4, page 199).

Bio-economic pressure (BEP)

The indicator BEP, or bio-economic pressure, is formed by the above two indicators and is defined as follows:

$$BEP = EMR_{SA} \times THA/HA_{PS} \, (\text{in MJ/h})$$

In the empirical analysis presented below we use the dimensionless proxy variable, used in earlier research, defined as $BEP = (Exo/Endo) \times (THA/HA_{PS})$.

The value of BEP increases (i) when the exosomatic energy throughput (EMR_{SA}) of society increases, and/or (ii) when the fraction of hours of human activity allocated to the primary and secondary production sectors of the economy decreases, generating an increase in the ratio THA/HA_{PS}. In practical terms, an increase in the EMR_{SA} means that more exosomatic energy is used by the given size of society (THA) for expressing its functions. This increase in energy use usually takes place both in the hypercyclic and in the purely dissipative compartments. More complex are the implications of a decrease in the ratio HA_{PS}/THA: increase in THA/HA_{PS}. In fact, if a share of human activity is transferred from the hypercyclic (EM + AG + BM) to the purely dissipative compartment (HH + SG), with a concomitant increase in the supply of energy, food, and goods produced and consumed (typical of economic growth), then we must allocate more power capacity and energy to the hypercyclic compartment so as to boost the strength of the exosomatic hypercycle (SEH), that is the physical labour productivity in the hypercyclic compartment. This larger investment of power capacity and energy carriers is required to compensate for the reduction in labour input. The result of this continuous boosting of the physical labour productivity is especially clear in the primary production sectors (EM and AG): all the exosomatic energy carriers consumed per person in one day in a typical developed society are made available by less than two minutes of human labour in the energy sector (Giampietro and Mayumi, 2009). In the same way, the total amount of food consumed by a US citizen in one year is made available by less than 20 hours of work in the US agricultural sector (Giampietro, 2003).

Thus, we have yet another example of non-linearity across compartments involved in the stabilization of the metabolic pattern of a society undergoing economic growth. Indeed, we cannot expect that the trend of continuous growth of BEP can go on forever. As power levels in the hypercyclic compartment reach very high levels (as is the case at present), it becomes increasingly difficult to achieve further increases (to further boost the strength of the exosomatic hypercycle) without affecting the remaining sectors of the economy. Put another way, in fully industrialized socio-economic systems the hypercyclic compartment experiences a decreasing marginal return on the investments aimed at making available more surplus of power capacity, energy carriers and hours of human activity for the purely dissipative sectors. To make things more difficult, in a 'full world' the accessibility of natural resources per capita is decreasing which reduces the effectiveness of investments of technical capital in the hypercyclic compartment. For this reason in the last two decades developed countries, in order to keep their high values of BEP, have switched to another strategy, one based on massive import of goods and on increasing debts (Giampietro *et al.*, 2011).

10.2.2 Modern countries evolve toward the expression of a similar metabolic pattern

With the MuSIASEM grammar it is possible to generate a biophysical reading of the process of economic growth that is no longer based on economic variables. The first validation of this idea has been obtained with a large empirical study, completed more than a decade ago. In that study (Pastore *et al.* 2000) the value of the bio-economic pressure was proposed as an indicator of development, and the study showed that such an indicator correlates (like the economic indicator GDP p.c.) with all the indicators of economic development used by the World Bank over a sample of 107 countries including more than 90 per cent of world population. In a more recent study using the MuSIASEM grammar (Giampietro *et al.*, 2011) we have individuated an expected pattern of change over the relations between structural and functional compartments of socio-economic systems taking into account the relative size and importance of these compartments in the economy. The trajectory of expected transformations is exactly the same if these changes are observed either using the indicator GDP p.c. or the indicator BEP developed in our grammar. That is, our empirical analysis over a sample of 84 countries in the period 1980–2007 confirms that hypothesis that structural changes follow a familiar evolutionary pattern associated with an expected readjustment of the relative size and characteristics of the various compartments included in the grammar, when the value of BEP increases. Through the analysis already done we could individuate three typologies of socio-economic systems:

1   Those operating at low values of BEP (societies with a low GDP) – these societies have a large fraction of human labour (and economic activity) in agriculture (endosomatic metabolism is still important as a source of power capacity). The most striking structural and functional change that takes place in these societies during a period of rapid economic growth is the progressive urbanization of the population. The phenomenon of urbanization systematically reduces the agricultural labour force in favour of other economic sectors, and reduces the economic importance of the agricultural sector in the economy. As a matter of fact, this phenomenon is so marked that both the percentage of GDP from the agricultural sector and the percentage of farmers in the labour force are excellent indicators of economic growth: the lower the values of these two indicators, the higher the GDP per capita (Giampietro, 1997). As soon as societies increase their value of BEP (shifting production factors from the agriculture sector to other compartments of society) the overall endowment of power capacity, energy throughput and the level of economic activity tends to increase and move away from agriculture,

which loses its importance. Exosomatic power replaces endosomatic power. These changes require structural adjustments (changes in the dendrograms determining the profile of investment of power capacity, energy inputs and human activity).

2   Those operating in a range of medium values of BEP (societies with a medium GDP) – these societies invest their production factors into the development of the building and manufacturing sector. What they need is a rapid increase in the availability of power capacity (which translates into an increased consumption of energy input). Again this requires an additional set of structural adjustments, in relation to economic activities: the importance of the BM sector grows for intermediate values of BEP or GDP. As a matter of fact, in the study provided in Giampietro *et al.*, 2011, it is possible to observe a change in the trajectory of development followed by developed countries in the past. In the last decade we can detect a sort of specialization with countries having a much larger size of BM (e.g. China producing and exporting goods) than the fraction expected for developed countries, and others having a much lower size of BM (e.g. USA and EU countries more specialized in consuming).

3   At high values of BEP – societies with a very high GDP – these societies move the bulk of their economic activity to service and government. Post-industrial societies tend to concentrate their economy on transaction and consumption activities. In fact, increased industrial activity sooner or later unveils the importance of lowering unit transaction costs, which is, the key role of functional economic institutions in a modern economy (North, 1990). In other words, to enhance the use of power capacity in the industrial sector, we must invest more human activity and power capacity in the service and government sector. This is especially true if demographic changes (e.g. progressive ageing of the population and longer education) entail an increased requirement of labour in those services taking care of the growing dependent population and the greater need for education and research and development. The takeover of the SG sector in developed economies is evident when looking at its relative share in the economy. The service and government sector accounts for 20–30 per cent of the GDP in less developed countries and more than 60 per cent of the GDP in developed countries.

This increased importance of the service and government sector in the economy is even more pronounced in terms of allocation of the labour force to this sector (see the data referring to the HA_{SG} sector of USA in Table 10.1, page 237). In this respect, it is certainly relevant that jobs in the service and government sector are easier to generate because they require less capital investment and are less dependent on energy throughputs than jobs in other economic sectors.

10.2.3 The metabolic pattern becomes more robust with economic growth

In this section we detail the results of our recent empirical study of a sample of 84 countries over the period 1980–2007 (Giampietro *et al.*, 2011). In this study we looked at the overall movement of these countries in a three-dimentional space defined by parameters developed within the MuSIASEM grammar (THA/HA$_{PS}$, Exo/Endo, and BEP or GDP), and individuated a clear attractor (a viability domain for the possible combinations of structural adjustments in these parameters) determining an expected trajectory associated with economic development.

According to our working hypothesis, the trajectory of economic growth is associated with a progressive reallocation of human activity and power capacity from the primary and secondary production sectors, in charge of transformation-production activities, to the dissipative part of the economy, that is the household and service and government sectors, in charge of transformation-consumption and transaction activities. Note, however, that for such reallocation to take place, society must increase the absolute size of the investments of power capacity and direct energy use (energy carriers) in the primary and secondary production sectors.

In general terms we can say that economic growth requires first of all an increase in the capability of carrying out transformation activities (producing and consuming more goods), as reflected by the exo/endo ratio. This can only be obtained by reducing the number of farmers, who in pre-industrial society account for more than 80 per cent of the labour force (Giampietro, 2003). In the traditional paradigm of economic development the reduction of the number of farmers, in charge of the generation of endosomatic energy flows, is linked to a development of the industrial sector, required to expand the generation and use of exosomatic flows.

However, as soon as a society increases its capability of producing and consuming goods there is also the necessity of decreasing the transaction costs per unit of goods produced and consumed (North, 1990). Hence the SG sector must gain weight within the economy otherwise the development of the industrial sector would be hampered by high transaction costs, a problem typically experienced by developing countries (North, 1990). For this reason, after a certain threshold, economic growth needs a progressive increase in both the share of: (i) labour activity invested in the service sectors (North, 1990), and (ii) human activity invested in consuming (Zipf, 1941). According to this hypothesis, we should find a progressive increase in the ratio THA/HA$_{PS}$ with economic growth.

Our analysis of integrated structural changes in the economy of 84 countries between 1980 and 2007 has shown the emergence of a well-defined metabolic pattern onto which virtually all developed countries converge (Giampietro *et al.*, 2011). We here visualize the trajectory of changes using two similar representations:

1   A three-dimensional space defined by monetary (GDP per capita) and biophysical variables (exo/endo and THA/HA$_{PS}$), as illustrated in Figure 10.2, page 246;

2   A three-dimensional space using only biophysical variables (BEP, exo/endo, THA/HA$_{PS}$), as illustrated in Figure 10.3, page 246.

Note that the sample does not include some important countries, such as Russia, due to lack of a consistent set of data over the chosen period, or the main producers of oil in the Middle East (outliers excluded on purpose).

Comparing the trajectories in the two three-dimensional graphs, we see a more consistent pattern in Figure 10.3, where only biophysical variables are used for the representation. This comes as no surprise, given the auto-correlation among the three biophysical variables used (BEP is the product of the other two factors). In fact, the basic goal of the comparison between Figure 10.2 and Figure 10.3 is to explore: (i) the similarity of the figures when using GDP rather than BEP; and (ii) the relation between exo/endo and THA/HA_{PS}, that is, whether an increase in the pace of exosomatic metabolism entails a forced change in the profile of allocation of human activities over the various sectors of the society.

In conclusion we find that economic development is associated with the convergence of the metabolic pattern of societies toward a well-defined attractor that is subject to: (i) external constraints related to the availability of supply and the capacity to absorb the flows metabolized by the various economies (food, energy and material), and (ii) internal constraints related to the capability of expressing the various functions associated with the various compartments of the economy while competing for the aggregate amount of fund elements (human activity and power capacity) and flow elements (energy, food and material). In particular, we find that the overall consumption of resources is not only determined by 'technology' (an abstract idea assumed to be determining the efficiency of all the conversions taking place in an economy at the level of the whole society), but rather by: (i) the profile of the different technologies used in the different compartments, which are specific for the various functions to be expressed, and (ii) the relative size of the various compartments. Moreover, the characteristics of the whole can be heavily affected by the terms of trade.

10.3 A quantitative characterization of the dynamic energy budget: the sudoku effect

So far we have been presenting quantitative analysis about the value of an indicator we call bio-economic pressure defined within the MuSIASEM grammar. This indicator can be defined in semantic terms ($BEP = EMR_{SA} \times THA/HA_{PS}$) but at the moment of its quantification we can only measure it in scalar terms using the semantic category of gross energy requirement (thermal). As discussed in Chapter 9 it would be much better to study the internal relations among compartments of society expressing the metabolic pattern using a quantitative analysis based on quantities of energy referring to the category of energy carriers. As discussed in Chapter 9, if we want to do so, then we have to adopt a vector notation or our alternative method of characterization based on a multi-level matrix composed of different arrays of data. In this section we provide an overall scheme of analysis for the assessment of the feasibility and desirability of the metabolic pattern in relation to internal constraints using our method of characterization. We show how the representation of the metabolic pattern based on a multi-level

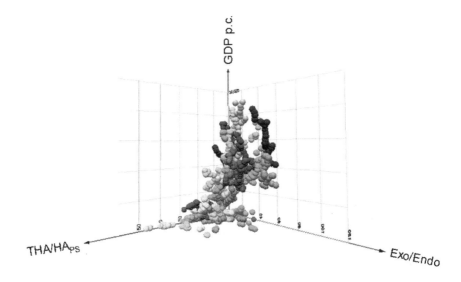

Figure 10.2 The trajectory of structural changes (1980–2007) in the economy of a large
sample of countries represented in a three-dimensional space: GDP p.c.,
Exo/Endo, THA/HA$_{PS}$
Source: Giampietro *et al.*, 2011, used with permission

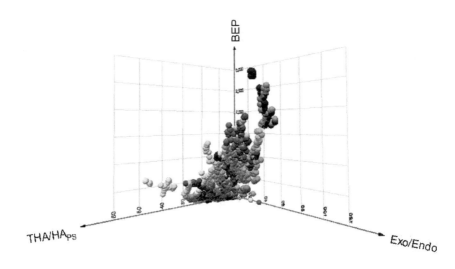

Figure 10.3 The trajectory of structural changes (1980–2007) in the economy of a large
sample of countries in the three-dimensional space: BEP, Exo/Endo,
THA/HA$_{PS}$
Source: Giampietro *et al.*, 2011, used with permission

matrix can be used to detect the set of mutual constraints associated with the over-all viability of the dynamic budget.

The desirability and feasibility of the dynamic budget associated with the metabolic pattern can be analyzed by focusing on the compatibility between the characteristics of the hypercyclic compartment of society (the productive sectors) on the one hand, and the characteristics of the whole society (the metabolic pattern of the hypercyclic and purely dissipative compartments combined) on the other hand. This forced relation can be studied from two different points of view: (i) by looking at the value of BEP from the requirement side, and (ii) by looking at the value of the Strength of the Exosomatic Hypercycle (SEH) – the value of BEP from the supply side when considering the dynamic exosomatic energy budget.

The former characterization is useful for assessing the desirability of the metabolic pattern in terms of material standard of living. This view 'from the inside' is not concerned with the severity of external constraints, but only with the compatibility of power levels among the compartments (the profiles of distribution of power capacity, energy throughputs and human activity). Using the multi-level matrix this characterization can be obtained by looking at the characteristics of the purely dissipative compartment of society (the two arrays of data describing the HH and the SG sectors) in relation to the characteristics of the whole (the array of data describing the characteristics as societal average).

The latter characterization, the value of BEP from the supply side, is useful for assessing the feasibility of the metabolic pattern in terms of internal constraints (technology and know-how) required to guarantee the resulting asymmetry in the dendrograms. In the jargon of MuSIASEM this dual reading of BEP is called SEH, indicating the value of the strength of the exosomatic hypercycle capable of matching the value of BEP. The hypercyclic compartment must be able to deliver the required amount of energy carriers, foods, materials, power capacity and infrastructures using only a limited amount of human activity (HA_{ps}). Using the multi-level matrix this characterization from within can be obtained by looking at the characteristics of the hypercyclic compartment of society (the two arrays of data describing the PS* and the EM sectors) in relation to the characteristics of the whole (the array of data describing the characteristics as societal average).

Therefore when adopting a multi-level matrix of data arrays characterizing the metabolic pattern across the various compartments, the dynamic equilibrium can be interpreted as a relation of congruence between:

1   those internal characteristics of the metabolic pattern determining the value of the bio-economic pressure defined at the level of the whole society and the HH and SG compartments on the requirement side;
2   those internal characteristics of the metabolic pattern determining the strength of the exosomatic hypercycle at the level of the whole society and the PS* and EM compartments on the supply side.

We now define a multi-level matrix useful for this task, starting from the basic multi-level matrix defined in Figure 9.8, page 230, by making the following adjustments.

1   Since this is a view of the metabolic pattern taken from the inside of the society all the energy values are assessed in terms of net energy carrier. This requires us to take out the reference to gross energy requirement and the relative conversion factors. In practical terms this means removing the first four columns of the multi-level matrix defined in Figure 9.8, page 230 (GER_{Ai}, y_{1i}, y_{2i}, y_{3i}).

2   In order to focus on the internal characteristics of the metabolic pattern, the values of human activity and energy are given on the per capita and per year basis. Therefore, $THA_{p.c./ySA}$ (societal average) is equal to 8,760 hours, and $TET_{p.c./ySA}$ (societal average) is equal to the amount of NEC (summed without any quality factors). As a consequence the value of $TET_{p.c./ySA}$ must always be used together with the information about the corresponding mix of energy carriers, EC $(x_1; x_2; x_3)_{SA.}$

3   Two additional columns – representing: (i) the values of $ET_{p.c./yi}/TET_{p.c./yi} = \tau_i$ (the fraction of TET used in the compartment) calculated for various compartments (on the left); and (ii) $HA_{p.c./yi}/THA_{p.c./yi} = \eta_i$ (the fraction of THA used in the compartment) calculated for various compartments (on the left) – are added to the original matrix.

The final result is indicated in Table 10.2. Since the quantities of both exosomatic energy throughput ($EC_{p.c./yi}$) and human activity ($HA_{p.c./yi}$) used in this multi-level matrix are defined per capita, it is important to add the size of the population, in order to make possible the conversion to aggregate quantities for the whole country.

Table 10.2 The normalized multi-level matrix of data arrays characterizing the metabolic pattern across compartments per unit of population

Population – number of people					BEP_{EC} ⟵ ⟶ SEH_{EC}			
1	$EC_{p.c./ySA}$	x_{1AS}	x_{2AS}	x_{3AS}	EMR_{ECSA}	1	$THA_{p.c./ySA}$	Level n
τ_{HH}	$EC_{p.c./yHH}$	x_{1HH}	x_{2HH}	x_{3HH}	EMR_{ECHH}	η_{HH}	$HA_{p.c./yHH}$	Level n-1
τ_{SG}	$EC_{p.c./ySG}$	x_{1SG}	x_{2SG}	x_{3SG}	EMR_{ECSG}	η_{SG}	$HA_{p.c./ySG}$	Level n-2
τ_{PS*}	$EC_{p.c./yPS*}$	x_{1PS*}	$x_{2\,PS*}$	$x_{3\,PS*}$	EMR_{ECPS*}	η_{PS*}	$HA_{p.c./y\,PS*}$	Level n-3
τ_{EM}	$EC_{p.c./yEM}$	x_{1EM}	x_{2EM}	x_{3EM}	EMR_{ECEM}	η_{EM}	$HA_{p.c./yEM}$	Level n-3

By normalizing the values of THA and TET per capita per year, we can better focus on the characteristics determining the internal coherence of the pattern when comparing countries of different size of population. In fact, when adopting the characterization given in Table 10.3 the large population difference between Germany and the Netherlands is no longer affecting the characterization of their metabolic pattern. In this way we can compare countries of different population size. Whenever needed, one can always multiply the column of $HA_{p.c/yi}$ by the population size (and then re-scale the flows of EC) in order to move back to the original characterization given in the matrix represented in Table 9.2.

An example of this characterization (using our dataset of EU14 countries) is given in Table 10.3 for Spain.

Table 10.3 The metabolic pattern of Spain (using the template of Table 10.2) 'the view from the inside'

Population of Spain – 44,475,000

τ_i	$EC_{p.c/yi}$	x_{1i}	x_{2i}	x_{3i}	EMR_{ECi}	η_i	$HA_{p.c/yi}$	
1	108,500	0.229	0.316	0.455	12	1	8,760	SA
0.285	30,900	0.206	0.327	0.466	4	0.893	7,825	HH
0.352	38,200	0.189	0.069	0.742	64	0.068	598	SG
0.281	30,400	0.303	0.631	0.068	93	0.038	329	PS*
0.082	8,900	0.227	0.256	0.516	1091	0.001	8	EM

The set of numbers organized in this table are affected by different typologies of constraints similar to the integrated set of constraints found in the popular sudoku game. A self-explanatory illustration of this fact is given in Figure 10.4.

We can consider the typologies of constraints in Figure 10.4 in the following ways.

Constraints within columns

We have two redundant definitions of constraints referring to the required closure across hierarchical levels. They refer to:

(i) Fund elements $\sum HA_{p.c/yi} = THA_{p.c/ySA}$; and ($\Sigma \eta_i = 1$); and
(ii) Flow elements $\sum EC_{p.c/yi} = EC_{p.c/ySA}$; and ($\Sigma \tau_i = 1$);

Constraints within rows

We have two definitions of constraints referring to: (i) the required closure of the definition of $EC_{p.c/yi}$ in relation to the mix of energy carriers: $\sum_j x_{ji} = 1$; and (ii) the required relation between $EC_{p.c/yi}$ and $HA_{p.c/yi}$ linking, row by row across levels generating the resulting power levels ($EMR_{ECi} = EC_{p.c/yi} / HA_{p.c/yi}$). Again we reiterate that this relation can only be established using a multi-level matrix since the quantity of $EC_{p.c/yi}$ is obtained by summing energy carriers of different kinds.

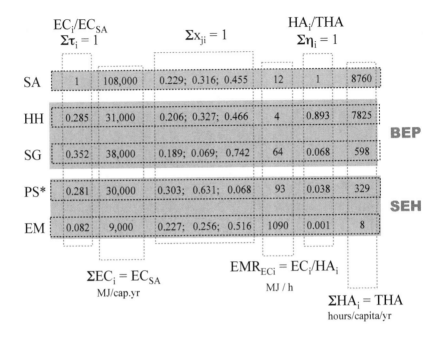

Figure 10.4 The set of different typologies of constraints on the viability of the dynamic
        budget when representing the metabolic pattern with a multi-level matrix
        for Spain, 2007

Constraints over subsets of numbers (submatrices) within the matrix

Another type of constraint is determined by the mutual information contained in
the functional and quantitative definitions of the different parts of the society.
That is, the whole society is expressing a given metabolic pattern, which is characterized, at the level *n*, using the information contained in the first row of the
matrix (SA). Within this metabolic pattern, the characteristics of the SG and HH
sector – represented in the second and third rows of the matrix – determine a
given profile of allocation of both energy carriers and human activity on what can
be considered as the purely dissipative part of the society (the upper compartment
in the matrix). Using the definition given earlier we can say that by coupling the
characteristics of the first row with the characteristics of the second and third
rows, we can have an integrated characterization of BEP (bio-economic pressure)
from the requirement side. As described earlier, the characteristics of the metabolic pattern illustrated in the fourth and fifth rows refer to the functions
expressed by the PS* and EM sectors. Therefore, they reflect the characteristics
of those compartments guaranteeing the supply of energy carriers, food, material
inputs, power capacity and infrastructures. Again by coupling the characteristics
of the first row with the characteristics of the fourth and the fifth rows we can

obtain an integrated characterization of the value of SEH (strength of the exoso-matic hypercycle).

We can better describe the nature of this additional constraint, illustrated in the matrix of Figure 10.4, page 250, by constructing two sub-matrices of the matrix illustrated belows shown in Table 10.4 and Table 10.5.

Looking at the information needed to define BEP from the requirement side

The characteristics of the metabolic pattern of society – defined at the level n – combined with the characteristics of the HH compartment – defined at the level n-1 (second row) and the SG compartment – defined at the level n-2 (third row) – can be used to define the value of the bio-economic pressure. That is, using the expression:

$$BEP = EMR_{ECSA} \times THA/HA_{PS} - \text{defined on the multilevel matrix}$$

After writing the sub-matrix illustrated in Table 10.2, page 248, we can get the information:

* EMR_{ECSA} from the first row by $[EMR_{ECSA}; .x_{1AS}; x_{2AS}; x_{3AS}]$;
* THA/HA_{PS} from the second and third row: : $[1/\{1 - (\eta_{HH} + \eta_{SG})]$.

Therefore the information about BEP (defined across different levels) can be retrieved from the submatrix illustrated in Table 10.4.

Table 10.4 The sub-matrix characterizing the desirability of the pattern: bio-economic pressure

Population – number of people				$BEP_{EC} = EMR_{ECSA}/[1 - (\eta_{HH} + \eta_{SG})]$		
1	$EC_{p.c./ySA}$	x_{1SA}	x_{2SA}	x_{3SA}	EMR_{ECSA}	1	$THA_{p.c./ySA}$
τ_{HH}	$EC_{p.c./yHH}$	x_{1HH}	x_{2HH}	x_{3HH}	EMR_{ECHH}	η_{HH}	$HA_{p.c./yHH}$
τ_{SG}	$EC_{p.c/ySG}$	x_{1SG}	x_{2SG}	x_{3SG}	EMR_{ECSG}	η_{SG}	$HA_{p.c./ySG}$

Looking at the information required to define SEH from the supply side

In the same way, we can define another sub-matrix, illustrated in Table 10.5, by adding to the first row of the matrix illustrated in Table 10.2, the remaining two rows (fourth and fifth rows), referring to the metabolism of lower-level compartments (PS* and EM), where the entire set of functions of the PS sector are carried out.

In this way, we can look at the supply side of the dynamic budget, and see which characteristics of the PS sector (in relation to the whole society), are required to match the value of BEP (on the demand side).

$$SEH = EMR_{ECSA} \times THA/HA_{PS} \text{ defined on the multi-level matrix}$$

Table 10.5 The sub-matrix characterizing the feasibility of the pattern: strength of the exosomatic hypercycle

Population – number of people					$SEH_{EC} = EMR_{ECSA} / (\eta_{PS\bullet} + \eta_{EM})$		
1	$EC_{p.c./ySA}$	X_{1SA}	X_{2SA}	X_{3SA}	EMR_{ECSA}	1	$THA_{p.c./y}$
$\tau_{PS\bullet}$	$EC_{p.c./yPS\bullet}$	$X_{1\,PS\bullet}$	$X_{2\,PS\bullet}$	$X_{3PS\bullet}$	$EMR_{ECPS\bullet}$	$\eta_{PS\bullet}$	$HA_{p.c./y\,PS\bullet}$
τ_{EM}	$EC_{p.c./yEM}$	X_{1EM}	X_{2EM}	X_{3EM}	EMR_{ECEM}	η_{EM}	$HA_{p.c./yEM}$

By comparing the two sub-multi-level matrices illustrated in Table 10.4 and Table 10.5 we can appreciate that by adopting a multi-scale analysis it becomes possible to avoid a tautology in the quantitative analysis. The two terms BEP ←→ SEH are defined in the same way at the level n: '$EMR_{ECSA} \times THA/HA_{PS}$'. However, when considering the integrated set of characteristics of the metabolic pattern determining this value across different hierarchical levels we can express their value using non-equivalent data: (i) the set of elements determining the value of BEP in Table 10.4 are defined over a given combination of hierarchical levels – level n, level n-1 and level n-2; whereas (ii) the set of elements determining the value of SEH in Table 10.5 are defined over a different combination of hierarchical levels – the level n and the level n-3.

In the two assessments the information about EMR_{ECSA} is given by the first row [EMR_{ECSA}; x_{1SA}; x_{2SA}; x_{3SA}], the aggregate consumption coming from the various sectors, which is common for the two characterizations. However, the assessment of THA/HA_{PS} is obtained using the information contained in the second and third rows: $1/\{1 - (\eta_{HH} + \eta_{SG})\}$ – when looking for BEP – and in the fourth and fifth rows: $1/(\eta_{PS\bullet} + \eta_{EM})$ – when looking for SEH.

Then when establishing a relation between the values of the various elements of the two sub-matrices shown – in Table 10.4 and Table 10.5 – we can see that the forced overall congruence of the values in the two sub-matrices characterizing different aspects of the same metabolic pattern can be seen as an effect of 'mutual information' on the admissible values of the elements organized in the matrix described in Table 10.3, page 249. A self-explanatory illustration of this fact, based on the analogy with the sudoku game, has already been given in Figure 10.3, page 246. The forced congruence of the characteristics of various elements belonging to the same metabolic pattern, but operating across different hierarchical levels, explains the existence of this mutual information.

This mutual information is required to guarantee the compatibility of the characteristics of the structural and functional elements operating at different scales within the same metabolic pattern. This mutual information has been generated in the evolution of the autopoietic process by the existence of an integrated set of constraints on the viability and desirability of the metabolic pattern operating across scales within the process of autopoiesis. The growing importance of this mutual information on the expression of the overall metabolic pattern explains the increased robustness of the pattern for high values of BEP ←→ SEH as illustrated in Figure 10.2, page 246 and Figure 10.3, page 246.

Using the information given by these two multi-level matrices in a spreadsheet we can study the feasibility and the desirability of possible scenarios of changes in the metabolic pattern in modern societies. For example we can carry out 'stress tests' on the possibility of a quick decarbonisation of the economy of developed countries operating at very high values of BEP – can a developed country remain in the viability domain of its dynamic budget if the quantity of fossil energy throughput is dramatically reduced?

10.4 Wrapping up

In this chapter we have illustrated the application of an innovative protocol of energy accounting which makes it possible to generate a useful characterization of the network of energy transformations taking place within modern societies. In order to achieve this result the integrated protocol characterizes an expected set of relations (defined in semantic terms) over the characteristics of energy transformations taking place within a coherent metabolic pattern formed across different hierarchical levels (in formal terms), using different scales; while keeping separated the accounting of energy forms of different types and addressing the complication associated with the existence of autocatalytic loops (impredicative loop analysis).

These different pieces of information are combined into a coherent information space by using a protocol of accounting based on multi-level matrices of data arrays. In this chapter, we have first described the protocol in formal terms and then we have illustrated it using numerical examples. Three main points to be driven home from the material presented in this chapter are:

1   The characteristics of lower-level elements (energy transformation of energy carriers transformed into end uses within the compartments of society) can be described in quantitative terms using two accounting categories – gross energy requirement and net energy carriers. In the first part of the chapter we showed that useful information can be obtained by describing the structure of the metabolic network using the first category. However, if we want to observe the technical coefficients of the various compartments (how energy carriers are used to express functions) at the local scale we have to use assessments expressed in energy carriers.

2   A multi-level integrated characterization of the metabolic pattern of modern societies provides an internal redundancy in the information space used in the representation. This redundancy makes it possible to define a set of expected relations over the values taken by the various variables used in the protocol (mosaic effect over the values of columns and rows). By choosing wisely the definition of compartments to be included in the multi-level matrix we can analyze the viability of the dynamic budget of the metabolic pattern (BEP ←→ SEH) by defining a relation of congruence over sub-multi-level

matrices (impredicative loop analysis). This integrated representation of the metabolic pattern across scales is a key feature for the generation of robust analysis and scenarios. The complexity of this information space defining coherence across characteristics of elements observed across different levels and scales cannot be used to predict the future (of course!), but it can be used to predict what is not possible and define conditions of feasibility and desirability.

3   The resulting integrated characterization of the metabolic pattern across different levels and compartments based on vectors and matrices can only be used to check the desirability and the viability of the metabolic pattern in relation to internal constraints. Getting back to the discussion over the possibility of radical changes in the metabolic pattern of modern society, if the goal is to cut 50 per cent or even 75 per cent of CO_2 emissions in a couple of decades, we can start an informed discussion about questions like: what type of changes would be required inside the society (re-organization of organs) to cut 50 per cent of the actual energy consumption? After defining a minimum threshold of desirability of the metabolic pattern – which can be associated with a given level of services and power capacity for the various functions to be expressed – what type of changes in technology would be required to guarantee the viability of the resulting dynamic budget? It is important to acknowledge that by using the protocol of analysis described in this chapter we can only develop quantitative characterizations in relation to what happens inside the black box.

Getting back to the conclusions of Part I, the protocol of accounting presented in this chapter addresses the problem of how to deal with two conundrums of energy analysis. In fact, it represents a method of quantitative analysis capable of: (i) providing a dual reading of the requirement of energy of a society referring two different (and not reducible) semantic categories gross energy requirement and net energy carriers across different hierarchical levels; (ii) providing a quantitative characterization of the pattern of consumption of energy carriers across different hierarchical levels while preserving the distinction between energy carriers of different quality (electricity, fuels and heat). Therefore, this system of accounting is qualitatively different from the protocol of energy accounting used right now for national energy accounting. Given the explanation in the first part of the book, we claim that this approach generates information about energy transformations taking place in national economies, which is much more useful than available datasets on energy accounting in relation to the goal of making and analyzing scenarios.

However, there is another challenge of energy analysis that cannot be dealt with using the multi-level matrices presented in this chapter: how to establish a relation between the gross energy requirement for expressing the metabolic pattern (under human control) and the requirement of favourable biophysical gradients (primary energy sources beyond human control). The matrices illustrated in this chapter can only provide the perception from within the system and therefore necessarily study internal constraints. In order to carry out an analysis of external constraints we must interface this information with another type of information referring to the characteristics of the context; we need an additional approach as discussed in the next chapter.

11 Using the MuSIASEM approach to check the external constraints on the metabolic pattern of modern societies

In this chapter we address the issue of how to establish a relation between: (i) the gross energy requirement (GER) of the whole society and (ii) the requirement of favourable boundary conditions – an adequate supply of primary energy sources (PES) outside human control required for the expression of the metabolic pattern of society on the supply and sink side.

Section 11.1 briefly recaps why the quantitative assessment of GER is not useful to study external constraints. In fact, the concept of GER refers to a quantity of energy under human control that must be compatible with internal constraints of societal metabolism: it must guarantee the desired production and consumption of a given mix of energy carriers for fulfilling useful functions. Unfortunately, this quantity 'per se' does not say anything about the requirement of PES (favourable gradients). Using quantities of energy measured in thermal equivalent we cannot know the overall requirement of PES associated with the expression of the metabolic pattern of a given country.

In section 11.2 we present the basic rationale for our analysis. We introduce the concept of environmental impact matrix useful for indicating the overall requirement of physical gradients (both on the supply and sink side) needed to guarantee the required supply of energy carriers consumed by society and therefore to guarantee the expression of the metabolic pattern. The proposed framework is neat in theoretical terms, but it is not easy to implement: we have again to deal with a lot of details hosting all forms of devils. The data that would be required to implement this approach are not easy to calculate in the majority of the cases.

Section 11.3 addresses the nature of the problems found when trying to implement the analytical framework presented in section 11.2. The massive quantity of imports used to supply the required flow of energy carriers to modern societies complicates the analysis of the conversion factors determining a requirement of PES per unit of NEC consumed within a society. In fact, the massive import of energy carriers externalizes to the exporting countries the requirement of favourable physical gradients of the importing countries. When framing the analysis of the metabolic pattern in this way, it becomes evident that modern societies enjoyed a double bonus in relation to their supply of energy carriers: (i) the supply is based on stock-depletion (this provided the possibility of economies of scales in the technology used in the energy sector and a temporary emancipation from land requirement); and (ii) the supply is based on imports (this provided an additional bonus whenever imports are paid for by making debt). This combination made it possible for developed societies, so far, to get a huge supply of energy carriers at negligible biophysical and economic costs.

11.1 Why an assessment expressed in gross energy requirement is not enough

As discussed in theoretical terms in Part I and with practical examples in Chapters 8 and 9 it is impossible to characterize the total amount of energy used by a society (total energy throughput) using a single number. We can calculate a quantity of required energy called gross energy requirement (GER), that can be used to provide an assessment of the overall amount of energy under human control. However, in order to obtain this result we have to measure this quantity in an energy form of reference –thermal equivalent – using conversion factors.

We saw that this assessment is not good to study internal constraints, since numbers expressed in GER do not map, when looking at the local scale at actual flows of energy carriers used in the compartments operating inside the black box. An assessment of the use of electricity or fuels in local transformations is not directly related to the resulting assessment expressed in gross energy requirement.

The method of dual accounting based on vectors and multi-level matrices presented in Chapter 9 is a step forward in generating an integrated analysis of the metabolic pattern. In fact, we saw in Chapter 10, by using an analysis based on flows of energy carriers we can carry out a quantitative analysis inside the various components of the society. In this way, we can bridge the characterization of the whole (the data arrays representing the metabolic pattern at the level n) to the characterization of elements operating at lower levels (lower-level data arrays). In this chapter we explore how to combine this internal characterization with an analysis of the external context of the society.

Building on the notation for the dual energy accounting introduced in Chapter 9 we can make a distinction between: (i) a quantitative assessment of gross energy requirement in aggregate terms compartment by compartment – GER_{Ai}; or (ii) a quantitative assessment of the Gross Energy Requirement by type of energy carrier – GER_{Vi}. That is, for a given compartment i – e.g. the service and government sector of Spain –we can calculate the breakdown of the aggregate GER – $GER_{Ai} = 2,074$ PJ – into the three gross energy requirements attributable to the generation of the required typology of energy carriers – the three elements of the vector GER_{Vi}. For example, using the data given in Figure 9.5, page 221 we can write down the following assessments:

$$GER_{1SG} = 1,319 \text{ PJ} \times 0.17 \times 2.61 = 584 \text{ PJ}$$
$$GER_{2SG} = 1,319 \text{ PJ} \times 0.07 \times 1.10 = 104 \text{ PJ}$$
$$GER_{3SG} = 1,319 \text{ PJ} \times 0.76 \times 1.38 = 1,386 \text{ PJ}$$

However, as noted earlier there is a price to pay to obtain this neat result. The choice of using a flat conversion factor GER/NEC (e.g. as is done in the partial substitution method) has the effect of introducing virtual quantities of energy expressed as thermal equivalent into the assessment. This choice generates two evident problems.

First, an overall assessment of exosomatic throughput expressed in GER-thermal makes it possible to assess an overall requirement of primary energy equivalent – energy forms under human control – after defining a standard yardstick. That is, we can use this analysis to compare the energy use of different countries: is China consuming more GER-thermal equivalent than the USA? However, this standard yardstick is obtained by a quite simplistic set of assumptions. This method cannot assess the severity of external constraints – the mix of physical gradients beyond human control that is required by society in order to stabilize a given supply of energy carriers.

Second, the choice of tons of oil equivalent as the GER-thermal energy form of reference for modern energy analysis has historic explanations: it reflects a frozen accident associated with the birth of the oil based civilization – how the past experience is affecting present accounting. It has been adopted due to the extraordinary high quality of fossil energy, when it was available in abundant supply. As a matter of fact, as discussed in section 7.2, page 172, so far, the output/input of fossil energy carriers has been so high that nobody ever bothered to study in detail the factors determining the difference between the quantitative assessment referring to their gross supply and net supply. On the other hand, if we want to study the feasibility of an alternative metabolic pattern no longer based on fossil energy we face the risk of experiencing a dramatic increase in the internal losses of energy carriers for energy carriers. This is especially likely if these energy carriers will have to be generated by exploiting a fund-flow primary energy source characterized by a low output/input energy carrier ratio. For this reason it is extremely important to develop a system of accounting which no longer uses fossil energy – a stock-flow energy supply based on potential chemical energy – as the standard energy form of reference (the yardstick). Put in another way, a quantification of GER requirement expressed in tons of oil equivalent is totally useless for discussing the biophysical feasibility of future alternative scenarios. We need innovative tools to describe the present predicament in order to make scenarios of an energy future without fossil energy.

For this reason, in order to carry out an effective analysis of external and internal constraints determining the desirability and viability of the metabolic pattern, we have to integrate the method of accounting illustrated in the previous chapters with an additional protocol of quantifications, based on different narratives about what are the relevant attributes to be considered in order to gather a different type of useful information needed for the analysis of external constraints.

11.1.1 Moving from an analysis of gross energy requirement to an analysis of the primary energy sources mix requirement

Remaining with the vision of the metabolic pattern from the inside of the black box (the type of analysis carried out in Chapter 10), we can obtain a quantitative characterization of the overall requirement of energy carriers in the different compartments of the society. According to the analysis of the internal metabolic pattern of the society – e.g. using the information given by the multi-level matrix presented in Table 10.3 – we can describe the flows of energy carriers through the society using a different definition of compartments:

1 $ET_{EM} - EC_{EM}$ in formal terms – expressing the function of generating a net supply of energy carriers for the rest of the society. This flow of energy called ET_{EM} in semantic terms can be formalized using a data array notation describing the three energy carrier types – EC_{EM} x_{1EM}; x_{2EM}; x_{3EM} – characterizing the flow of energy carriers required by the energy sector to express its function;

2 ET_{SA*} (total throughput excluding EM) – EC_{SA*} in formal terms – expressing all the other functions expected by the other compartments of the society. This flow of energy called ET_{SA*}, when assessed using quantities of energy expressed in EC becomes – using the notation introduced in Chapter 9 – $EC_{SA*} = EC_{HH} + EC_{SG} + EC_{PS*}$. Using a data array notation we can characterize the three energy carrier types going into the compartment SA* as follows – EC_{SA*} x_{1SA*}; x_{2SA*}; x_{3SA*};

3 ET_{SA} referring to the semantic concept of total energy throughput – EC_{SA} is the quantity of energy carriers require to express all the functions of the society. In formal terms this is the sum of the energy carriers consumed by all the compartments included in the analysis: $EC_{SA} = EC_{HH} + EC_{SG} + EC_{PS*} + EC_{EM}$. The relation between these three flows is illustrated in Table 11.1, where we can calculate the values of the elements of the third data array starting from the values of the two upper data arrays.

Table 11.1 The energy carriers used in the energy and mining sector and in the rest of society

1	EC_{SA*}	x_{1SA*}	x_{2SA*}	x_{3SA*}	Outside energy and mining
2	EC_{EM}	x_{1EM}	x_{2EM}	x_{3EM}	Energy and mining
3	EC_{SA}	x_{1SA}	x_{2SA}	x_{3SA}	Societal aggregate

Why is it important to make this distinction? Because many of the energy losses to be faced in order to make energy carriers – e.g. exploration of potential PES, search for new reserves, capturing and exploiting PES, production of energy carriers, distribution losses – do not take place within the border of a given country. When adopting the multi-level matrix representation these quantities of energy carriers are not included in the energy used by society to generate energy carriers. This becomes problematic at the moment of calculating the PES requirement of a given country. Looking at the overall requirement of energy carriers for a society the total energy throughput measured in Table11.1 by the data array EC_{SA} cannot be used for estimating the total requirement of PES.

Therefore, we have to conclude that if we want to calculate the amount of primary energy sources required to stabilize the metabolic pattern of a modern society we cannot use: (i) the 'gross energy requirement thermal' (GER_{Ai}), since it is calculated by applying flat conversion factors to the quantities of energy carriers used in the society; or (ii) the total amount of energy carriers used in the country EC_{SA} obtained by summing together the consumption of the various compartments of the society (EC_{SA*}) and the indirect consumption of energy carriers in the energy and mining sector (EC_{EM}).

For energy importing countries the assessment of the quantity of energy carriers used in the energy sector (EC_{EM}) may be a major underestimate of the actual requirement of energy carriers to generate the overall EC_{SA}. In the same way, for energy exporting countries the same quantity could represent an overestimate of the actual requirement. The same problem applies to the calculation of the conversion factors of the type GER_{Ii}/X_{Ii} (for the production of electricity) of a given country. When trying to calculate this factor using a top-down approach – e.g. looking at the actual flows of energy carriers consumed for electricity production and at the electricity consumption in the country – Sorman (2011) found out that countries importing electricity tend to have a value of this ratio lower than the value that would be obtained using a bottom-up approach (the technical conversion losses at the power plant). In fact, importing countries have access to flows of electricity which have been produced elsewhere requiring a lower energy input from the energy sector. In the same way, countries producing either electricity or fossil energy carriers have a much larger consumption of energy for energy in their energy sectors than countries importing these carriers.

This point is important, since the analysis of the external constraints affecting the feasibility of a given metabolic pattern requires the ability to individuate the mix of 'PES' (both in quantity and quality) needed to generate the gross supply of energy carriers required for the generation of the net supply of energy carriers. However, this type of assessment would require a sort of life cycle assessment of the various energy transformations leading to the final consumption of energy carriers in a particular society. That is, what we really need to know is the amount of total gross energy carriers ($GSEC_{SA}$) that is required for generating the metabolic flow of a specific country expressed using the data array EC_{SA}. Unfortunately, as discussed below, this value is very difficult to obtain in most of the cases.

In the rest of the chapter we first present (section 11.2) a theoretical framework that can be used, under the assumption that the value of $GSEC_{SA}$ could be known, to carry out the analysis of external constraints characterizing the quantity and quality of biophysical gradients. Then (in section 11.3) we analyze the possible strategies to be followed in order to deal with the fact that the value of $GSEC_{SA}$ is difficult to obtain in practical situations.

11.2 A logical framework for the analysis of 'feasibility' of the metabolic pattern in relation to external constraints

11.2.1 Presenting the theoretical framework

In this section we illustrate an analytical framework establishing a link between: (i) a multi-level matrix representation useful to study internal constraints (the matrices illustrated in Chapter 10); and (ii) an impact matrix made of a set of relevant indicators of compatibility with external constraints.

In order to achieve this result we can imagine the calculation of a biophysical footprint matrix associated with the mix of primary energy sources used by the energy sector and the quantity of each item in this mix. This solution makes it possible to study scenarios in which we can specify which typologies of PES will be used to generate the required gross supply of energy carriers used by a given society (EC_{SA}).

In this case, we can define such a matrix as:

- a given number of p typologies of PES type l (l = 1, 2,...p) – e.g. (1) coal, (2) oil, (3) natural gas,... nuclear... geothermal... **imports(*)**;
- three typologies of energy carriers (j = 1, 2, 3) – e.g. (1) electricity, (2) heat, and (3) fuels;
- the total gross energy carriers ($GSEC_{SA}$) requirement – defined in relation to the three typologies of energy carriers ($GSEC_{1SA}$, $GSEC_{2SA}$, $GSEC_{3SA}$).

When adopting this analytical approach we should consider imported energy carriers as if they were coming from a 'special' type of PES. As discussed in the following section, we have to observe that in relation to the definition of a biophysical impact matrix, the 'openness' of the metabolic pattern of societies associated with 'imports' complicates the possibility of tracking actual biophysical transformations at the local scale.

After having obtained this information we can define the profile of production of the particular energy carrier j by PES type l. For this purpose, we introduce the following notations:

a_{jl}: the total amount of energy carrier type j (j=1,2, and 3) derived from PES type l (l=1,2,,,,p) where $GSEC_{jSA} = \sum_{l=1}^{p} a_{jl}$;

d_{jl}: the amount of PES type l required for producing one unit of energy carrier type j.
in reality d_{jl} depends on the place from where energy carrier type j comes.

Then we can calculate the total amount PES type l required for producing the total amount of energy carrier type j as $z_{jl}=a_{jl} \times d_{jl}$.

Amount of PES type l used to have $a_{jl} \longleftrightarrow z_{jl}=a_{jl} \times d_{jl}$

According to the very definition of the category 'PES' – for each one of the forms of PES we must provide an expected mapping between a quantity of energy

Table 11.2 The 3 × (p+1) matrix $\text{GSEC}_{\text{jSA}}/z_{\text{ji}}$ needed for generating the biophysical footprint of the energy sector

	Amount	Coal	Natural Gas	Nuclear	Geothermal	Imports
Electricity	GSEC_{1SA}	z_{11}	z_{12}	z_{13}	z_{1l}	z_{1p}
Heat	GSEC_{2SA}	z_{21}	z_{22}	z_{23}	z_{2l}	z_{2p}
Fuel	GSEC_{3SA}	z_{31}	z_{32}	z_{33}	z_{3l}	z_{3p}

(a_{jl}) and a biophysical quantity outside human control (z_{jl}). In this way, we can establish a bridge between requirement of energy flows and requirement of biophysical gradients.

In general terms, by adopting this approach we can establish a relation between:

1   the dual characterization of the energy metabolism expressed in terms of NEC inside the black box when looking at the interaction among parts; and
2   a characterization of the relation between energy quantities expressed in terms of typologies – *PES type l* – and the resulting biophysical footprint, the set of relevant attributes to check the compatibility of external constraints – PES_{BF}, when considering the interaction of the black box with its context.

An overview of the series of expected relations between the PES mix and the energy flows coming from different PES types (fund-flow, stock-flow) is illustrated in Figure 11.1:

Profile a_{jl} ←→ $q_l = \Sigma\ (z_{jl})$ ←→ Profile PES type l ←→ Profile PES_{BF}

The scheme presented in Figure 11.1 illustrates the steps needed to establish such a link. We briefly sketch below the theoretical framework to be adopted to achieve this result and then we provide a practical example of application (in Figure 11.2).

Starting from the top of Figure 11.1, after knowing both the given profile of required supply of a_{jl} and the typologies of PES used for producing them – the value of z_{ji} it becomes possible to calculate the profile of quantities of PES type l – needed to generate such a supply.

θ_1 is a vector consisting of quantities of PES type l derived from the relation Σ (z_{jl}). We can divide the p typologies of PES into two types: (i) h stock-flow types (e.g. potential chemical energy forms); and (ii) *(p-h)* fund-flow types (e.g. other non-thermal forms of primary energy sources).

Then we can associate the profile of quantities of PES *type l* to a set of biophysical conditions of viability – the biophysical footprint of the energy sector – that consists of *m* attributes (indicators of viability) – variables to be measured in relation to benchmarks determining a viability domain.

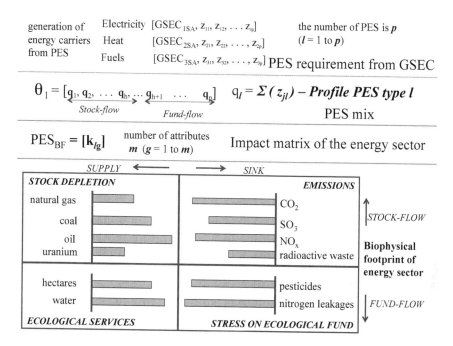

generation of   Electricity $[GSEC_{1SA}, z_{11}, z_{12}, \ldots z_{1p}]$ the number of PES is p
energy carriers   Heat $[GSEC_{2SA}, z_{21}, z_{22}, \ldots, z_{2p}]$ ($l = 1$ to p)
from PES   Fuels $[GSEC_{3SA}, z_{31}, z_{32}, \ldots, z_{3p}]$ PES requirement from GSEC

$\theta_1 = [\underbrace{q_1, q_2, \ldots q_h,}_{\text{Stock-flow}} \underbrace{\ldots q_{h+1} \ldots \quad q_p]}_{\text{Fund-flow}}$ $q_l = \Sigma(z_{jl})$ – ***Profile PES type l***

PES mix

$PES_{BF} = [k_{lg}]$ number of attributes   Impact matrix of the energy sector
m ($g = 1$ to m)

Figure 11.1 The steps leading to the quantitative characterization of a biophysical footprint of the metabolic pattern of a modern country (checking external constraints)

An example of a simplified impact matrix $[k_{lg}]$ with p types of PES type l ($l = 1$ to p) and m types of impact attributes ($g = 1$ to m) is given in Table 11.3.

The impact matrix $PES_{BF} = [k_{lg}]$ defines the set of biophysical gradients – the biophysical footprint, which can be characterized using a set of indicators – which must be available in order to be able to express the metabolic pattern. The set of m attributes to be considered in the analysis of the biophysical footprint has to be defined within a chosen taxonomy: they must result useful to check the compatibility of the metabolic pattern of society with existing boundary conditions (e.g. availability of natural resources and sink capacity).

In the lower part of Figure 11.1, page 263 we indicate four semantic criteria which can be used to define the categories of impact for the chosen indicators:

1   stock-flow PES (e.g. stocks of coal, oil, natural gas, uranium, etc.) referring to the supply side – speed of stock depletion (in relation to the total available stock);

2   stock-flow PES (e.g. fossil energy and nuclear) referring to the sink side such as CO_2, SO_x, nuclear waste – waste flows (in relation to the total sink capacity);

Table 11.3 The impact matrix associating the biophysical footprint showing indicators of impact in the columns; and PES typologies in the rows

		Depletion 1	CO_2 2	SO_3 3	[...]	visual impact m
Coal	$(PES_{BF})_1$	κ_{11}	κ_{12}	κ_{13}	[...]	κ_{1m}
Oil	$(PES_{BF})_2$	κ_{21}	κ_{22}	κ_{23}	[...]	κ_{2m}
Natural gas	$(PES_{BF})_3$	κ_{31}	κ_{32}	κ_{33}	[...]	κ_{3m}
Hydroelectric	$(PES_{BF})_4$	κ_{41}	κ_{42}	κ_{43}	[...]	κ_{4m}
Nuclear	$(PES_{BF})_5$	κ_{51}	κ_{52}	κ_{53}	[...]	κ_{5m}
Wind	$(PES_{BF})_6$	κ_{61}	κ_{62}	κ_{63}	[...]	κ_{6m}
...						
Import(?)	$(PES_{BF})_p$	κ_{p1}	κ_{p2}	κ_{p3}	[...]	κ_{pm}

3 fund-flow PES (e.g. wind, hydroelectric, biomass) referring to the requirement of environmental services such as arable land, solar radiation, flowing water size of the fund element required to guarantee the flow;

4 fund-flow PES (e.g. wind, hydroelectric, biomass) referring to the stress on the ecosystems implied by human exploitation such as pesticides residues, soil erosion, destruction of habitat – stress on the sink capacity of the fund elements supposed to absorb the waste flows.

11.2.1 Using an example of practical application to individuate the problems

Just for the sake of illustration we provide an example of an impact matrix – the biophysical footprint of the energy sector of Spain – in Figure 11.2. As explained in more detail in the next section, the numerical values presented in this example are not the relevant part of this figure. They are just provided to illustrate the type of information which can be generated in this way and its organization.

We want to flag to the reader that in this type of analysis the final quantitative result is not the most important outcome. Rather, in our view, an important aspect of this approach is that it makes it possible to carry out, in a participative way, an integrated quality control on both: (i) the process leading to the definition of this matrix (the choice of criteria of performance behind the indicators). This first step requires discussing the semantic validity of the chosen taxonomy; and (ii) the calculation of the quantitative values (the choice of data and assessment procedures) – on the formal side (Giampietro *et al.* 2006). In our view, this forced discussion of the pre-analytical choices adopted in order to crunch numbers is the most important feature of the approach we are proposing in this book.

The need for discussing explicitly 'the semantics' which are behind the pre-analytical choices of the protocol of accounting makes it possible to introduce a procedure for quality assurance to be applied to this type of analysis. As discussed in Part I, in energy analysis it is essential to acknowledge the fact that any quantification requires an open discussion and even a negotiation in order to reach an agreement on the protocol and the data to be used. We claim that the mandatory requirement of a process of quality control on the process chosen to generate quantitative information in energy scenarios would dramatically improve their robustness and usefulness in policy discussions.

The worst case for energy analysis, and in general for any type of biophysical analysis applied to the issue of sustainability, is a situation in which scientists having different opinions generate data based on the adoption of non-equivalent protocols, and then start 'throwing numbers at each other over the fence' – a nice expression coined by Jeroen Van de Sluijs (personal communication). When generating quantitative energy scenarios it is unavoidable that we produce specific quantitative assessments which are only relevant in relation to the specific issue definition behind their formalization. Therefore the usefulness of the quantitative results depends on the pre-analytical choice of narrative about what is relevant made by the analysts. In this situation, conventional approaches based on the adoption of just a single scale, and a long series of 'ad hoc' simplifications, written in a given protocol, are very unlikely to preserve their original meaning when used in a more general discussion made by different analysts, let alone when including social activists carrying legitimate, but different points of view about the problems to be solved.

PES	GER (EJ)	depletion	CO2 (Mt)	SO2 (Mt)	Radioactive waste	Water (Mt)	Land (1000 ha)	Pesticide (tonnes)
Oil[a]	2.94	70 Mtonnes[g]	289 [i]	-	-	55 [p,q]	negl.	-
Coal[a]	1.23	42 Mtonnes[h]	113 [i]	2.7 [n]	-	206 [p,r]	negl.	-
Natural Gas[a,b]	1.33	42 Billions m³ [b]	82 [i]	-	-	130 [p,q]	negl.	-
Nuclear (0.2EJ)$_{EC}$[a,c]	0.50	1,244 Tonnes U [l]	3.5 [k]	-	160 Tonnes[o]	160 [p,s]	negl.	-
Hydro (0.3 EJ)$_{EC}$[a,d]	0.28	-	0.00015[i]	-	-	160,000 [t]	negl.	-
Wind (0.3 EJ)$_{EC}$[a,e]	0.25	-	0.00022 [i]	-	-	-	-	-
Biodiesel (fossil) [a,f]	0.01	4 Mtonnes[w]	>1 [m]	-	-	160[y]	400 [v]	1,800[x]
Biodiesel (no fossil) [a,f]	0.01	-	-	-	-	930[z]	2,320 [z]	10,440[x]
Imported Electricity		negl.	negl.	negl.	negl.	negl.	negl.	negl.
		externalization of PES requirement to the exporter country						

Figure 11.2 The impact matrix and the biophysical footprint of the metabolic pattern of Spain in 2003

Box 11.1 Notes to Figure 11.2.

a. data from: http://epp.eurostat.ec.europa.eu/portal/page/portal/eurostat/home/ accessed 21/01/2010; **b**. 1,333,703 cubic meters (1 cubic metre natural gas = 31.8MJ); **c**. actual production of electricity 198PJ transformed in GER equivalent using the conversion 2,61/1; **d**. actual production of electricity 30,349TWh (109PJ) transformed in GER equivalent using the conversion 2,61/1; **e**. actual production of electricity 27,211TWh (98PJ) transformed in GER equivalent using the conversion 2,61/1; **f**. actual production of biodiesel 301,000 tons transformed in GER equivalent using the conversion 37.3GJ/tonne; **g**. 1,000 tonnes = 42TJ; **h**. 1,000 tonnes = 29.4TJ; **i**. using average values for new plants and a lifespan of 40 years, according to Yan *et al.*, 2011, assuming 0.161 tons of uranium per MW, and 7728 Mwe of nuclear power installed, according to UNESA, 2011; **j**. IPCC default factor, from Herold 2003, for coal we use coking coal emission factor; **k**. Using average values from both Sovacool 2008, and Lenzen 2008; **l**. for wind: low range value (for windmills larger than 1MW); for hydro: average, exluding flooded land – source: Raadal *et al.* 2011; **m**. using the assessment 3.21 g of CO_2 per gramme of net biodiesel (Ulgiati, 2001), but it should be noted that although the CO_2 emissions due to indirect effects of land use are not considered, these emissions can be huge: Fargione *et al.*, 2008; Searchinger *et al.* 2008; **n**. CORINAIR 1994 according to the IPCC Emission Factor Database (EFDB), http://www.ipcc-nggip.iges.or.jp/EFDB/main.php; **o**. according to the Nuclear Energy Institute (NEI 2011); **p**. average value from Water & Sustainability (Volume 3) EPRI 2011; **q**. 2,268 liters/MWh (EPRI, 2011); **r**. 2,646 liters/MWh (EPRI, 2011); **s**. 3,000 litres/MW/year with a power capacity of Spain of 7,728 MWe; **t**. assuming 5.5 MTonnes per TWh; **u**. this number is not significant, since assuming an output/input of 1.21/1 (Ulgiati, 2001) this system produces a supply of 0.01EJ but it implies the consumption of an amount of 0.008EJ of fossil energy, that would not be needed if this production of biodiesel did not take place; **v**. assuming a production of 750kg of biodiesel/ha (using fossil energy inputs in production); **w**. assuming 10 tonnes of soil per hectare per year (Ulgiati, 2001); **x**. assuming 4.5kg of pesticides per hectare in production (Ulgiati, 2001); **y**. assuming a consumption of 400 tonnes of water per hectare (Ulgiati, 2001); **z**. assuming a 1.21/1 output/input ratio, we have a ratio gross supply of energy carrier/net suppy of energy carrier of 5.8/1. This implies that the land requirement calculated in the raw above has to be multiplied by such a value.

Getting back to a discussion of the typology of data provided in an impact matrix of the type illustrated in Table 11.3, page 264, we can divide the primary energy sources (PES) used to generate energy carriers into two categories: (i) 'fund-flows'; and (ii) 'stock-flows' (basically fossil energy). In Figure 11.2

this distinction is made by using a grey background for indicating stock-flow type primary energy sources – fossil energy and nuclear energy. Over a cursory look at this figure we can realize that this type of PES, especially when dealing with fossil energy, is almost entirely imported by the majority of developed countries. As mentioned earlier, this fact represents another boost in the already high quality of fossil energy for the society using it. In fact, for developed countries, this massive import has three types of positive effects:

1   A large fraction of the investment of 'energy for energy' to produce the carriers is not taking place within the country, but elsewhere. This implies that a certain fraction of the investment of energy carriers required for the exploitation is not carried out by the energy sector of the importing country. Looking at a distinction made earlier between the different flows of consumption of energy carriers in the society – Table 11.1, page 259 – the investments (power capacity, human activity and PES) used for EC_{EM} represent only a fraction of the investments that would be needed to guarantee the required EC_{SA^*} if the supply of energy carriers were to be produced without imports. This keeps low the overall value of EC_{SA}.

2   The environmental impact of the 'energy for energy' of imported carriers is felt elsewhere. In fact, the depletion of stocks and the environmental impact of extraction is taking place in the exporting countries, whereas, on the sink side, the accumulation of GHG emission affects the whole planet (GHG accumulation in the atmosphere).

3   Last, but certainly not least, modern economies use debt to create favourable terms of trade: importing oil without fully paying for it they push the strength of the exosomatic hypercycle (SEH) of their energy sector well beyond its biophysical limits. As the energy bill generally accounts for only a small share of the GDP of a developed country, a moderate increase in the national deficit can provide a large share of the net supply of energy carriers 'free of charge' in biophysical terms.

These three reasons explain the strategy of massive imports of energy carriers adopted by developed countries. Contrary to what is implicitly assumed by many superficial statements about our energetic predicament, so far, a high level of import of fossil energy has been very good for the economy of developed countries. An internalization of the biophysical costs of production of energy carriers would imply a sensible reduction of SEH.

11.3 The degree of openness of the metabolic pattern: the key role of imports and the details where the devil thrives…

11.3.1 The possible strategies for dealing with the impasse

If we want to account for the biophysical footprint associated with the consumption of an imported barrel of oil we have three options:

1   We can attribute to this flow an average requirement of physical gradients (tons of oil, cubic metres of natural gas, etc.), according to the conversion factors found within the country.

2   We can trace the various energy conversions that led to the generation of this imported flow across borders (life cycle assessment). For this task we have to look for the special combination of events (tracking indirect flows across the globe) that took place in that particular year and in different specific locations to generate the particular amount of imported energy carriers.

3   We can use flat values of physical requirement for typologies of production by adopting a protocol – to be decided case by case – in relation to the system (e.g. country, economic sector, city) under analysis and the purpose of the study.

Assuming that one would go for the accurate method – method number 2 – would it be possible to get a crisp and reliable number? For example, can we answer questions like these: What is the depletion of oil stocks (at the world level) that is associated with the consumption of a barrel of oil in USA? How much power capacity has to be invested in the loop of energy for energy for 1kWh of electricity consumed in Beijing? How much GHG emission can be associated with the delivery of 42GJ of gasoline (EC) to Italy?

According to what has been said so far in this book, it is not possible to answer these questions with a single crisp number. First of all, there are different types of primary energy sources, coming from different types of reserves (of different characteristics), which are exploited using different technologies. For example, even if we focus on fossil energy carriers (which can be of higher or lower quality), we will always find that they are extracted from different types of stocks (easier or more difficult to exploit) in different locations of the world (implying longer or shorter transportation costs depending on the location of the user) using different types of technologies in different countries.

For example, when considering the analysis of energy flows associated with the supply of a 'barrel of oil' to society we need specific pieces of information to determine the gross/net energy ratio. In fact, there is a series of steps through which the energy of this barrel moves when going from below the ground to the final end use.

- The first consumption of energy carriers is required to extract oil from the ground and to find new reserves. Depending on the quality of the oil field the fraction of energy loss for this step could go from 5 per cent (output/input 20/1) to 10 per cent (output/input 10/1). These losses may be higher when exploiting old and marginal reserves.
- Then according to Smil (2008c) about 10 per cent of the energy of a barrel of oil is used for non-energetic purposes (asphalt, plastic materials and other uses).
- There is another significant amount of energy carriers consumed in the refinery: an approximate 10 per cent of its original energy content (Smil, 2008c).

• Finally there are additional losses for transportation – which when using either large oil tankers or pipelines, are quite low – less than 2 per cent – compared with the others (Smil, 2008c).

All together we can assume as average a reduction to 71 per cent of the original quantity of energy content of the barrel of oil, that is, a ratio gross/net of about 1.4/1.

Then there is an additional complication related to the issue of the multiple scales at which energy analysis can be carried out. For example: How to calculate the energy lost for transportation of a barrel of oil to the USA? Can we assess the transportation cost to move the barrel from Saudi Arabia to the USA? The category of 'national state' is too generic to make possible an accurate assessment, especially when the national states have a large geographic size. For example, remaining within the example of the USA there are important differences if we deliver a barrel of oil to New York or San Francisco coming from Saudi Arabia or from Venezuela. What is the right scale to be used to get an acceptable level of accuracy?

This discussion drives us back to the existence of deep epistemological issues (identified in Part I) making it impossible to define a simple protocol for the quantitative description of complex networks of energy transformations. Non-equivalent flows are generated by conversions of different forms of energy taking place at different scales in different places. Therefore they can (or better they have to) be perceived as occurring at different levels of analysis. In this situation, it is impossible to properly handle all the required quantitative information in a substantive way by adopting just a narrative or a scale. It is simply not possible to develop the 'ultimate protocol' of energy accounting generating the magic number – the golden quality index indicating what is 'better' and what is 'worse'. There are always several relevant criteria and several relevant scales to be considered.

When facing this predicament, the best we can do is to develop an integrated set of 'ad hoc' grammars, which, depending on the different issues to be dealt with, can generate useful assessments. Needless to say, that these 'ad hoc' grammars will generate quantitative assessments which are only valid in relation to the specific issue definition, which in turn depends on the goal of the analysis.

That is, an assessment of the environmental impact useful for dealing with imported oil can be related to the entire planet (using average values of mix of oil types and average estimates of types of reserves or average technologies used in the various steps). Such a generic assessment will not refer to any specific national metabolic pattern. As an alternative, we can describe the special situation of a single country (e.g. Spain). In that case, one may even try to make an effort to track the mix of resource quality, the location of reserves. That is, we may try to individuate a specific type of oil (e.g. Arab Light) extracted in a particular place (e.g. Ghawar Field in Saudi Arabia) for which we can track the characteristics of both the PES and the technology used to exploit it. However, also when dealing with the specific analysis of a given country we should always be aware that the goal of the analysis will define the set of relevant attributes (criteria of performance) we are interested in. That is, how should we assess the energy spent in drilling in Saudi Arabia in relation to the metabolic pattern of Spain? Would it be a relevant piece of information (in relation to which criteria)? What if the oil used by Spain has been extracted in different countries and then refined in different refineries across the world at different levels of efficiencies (using different technological processes)? In this case, should we specify for each year the various sources of imported oil and the characteristics of each one of the refineries where it was processed? Would this be a sensitive choice when generating scenarios (what if in the next decade Spain will import its oil from different sources)? To whom should we allocate the energy cost of exploration and development of the oil fields? Should we account these energy expenditures as referring to the metabolic pattern of the exporting country, the importing country, or the country to which the oil company that did the discovery and makes the profit belongs?

11.3.2 'Doping' of the dynamic equilibrium between BEP and SEH with debts

Finally, we want to provide a few additional comments on the economic aspect of energy imports briefly mentioned above. This topic is important, since in the globalized economy, the vast majority of the fossil energy used by developed countries is in the form of imports. Therefore, a biophysical analysis of the metabolic pattern of a developed society carried out looking only at the energy flows taking place within their geographical borders – the energy balance found in energy statistics and the analysis of the metabolic pattern given in Chapter 10 – tends to provide an assessment of the value of BEP (assessed top-down with average data), which is above the value that would be feasible when considering all the biophysical factors determining the value of SEH (assessed bottom-up with local analysis of technical coefficients). That is, a much larger fraction of the production factors (power capacity, human labour and energy carriers) should be invested in the PS sector if modern societies were forced to be self-sufficient (generating their own supply of energy carriers using alternative energy sources). With the solution of massive imports, the investments of production factors embodied in the imported energy carriers can be externalized to the energy sector of other countries. By importing fossil energy modern countries can boost their biophysical net supply or the strength of its exosomatic hypercycle.

This biophysical boost can be additionally increased by adopting another type of boost, an economic boost – a favourable term of trade and a financial boost – an increase in the level of debt (credit leverage) in an economy can be used to get a large fraction of the input of energy carriers for free. In fact, when considering the functioning of the market we can define an 'output/input of energy carriers in a different way, using a quantitative analysis no longer related to biophysical quantities, but related to prices. That is, we can define: (i) that the output of energy carriers is proportional to the ratio $ of GDP/MJ of TET – e.g. how many US$ of GDP are generated by the country per MJ of energy getting into the economy; and (ii) the input as determined by the price "$/MJ of TET" – e.g. how many

US$ have to be paid to import one MJ of energy. As long as the amount of power capacity and labour needed to generate the added value for purchasing energy carriers is lower than the amount of power capacity and labour that would be required to directly produce (in biophysical terms) them, it is more convenient for the society to import energy carriers than produce them. Therefore, a favourable term of trade, determined by the relative value of these two ratios, gives the opportunity to get a supply of energy carriers from trade larger than the supply that would be obtained by investing energy carriers in the exploitation of PES. Robert Kaufmann and Charlie Hall (1981) have investigated this phenomenon for the USA showing that, depending on the terms of trade, energy carriers invested in the production of added value may provide a larger output/input, when buying energy carriers through the market, than the actual biophysical output/input associated with the direct exploitation of PES.

To make the life of developed countries easier, there is also the possibility of using debt (credit leverage) to stimulate economic growth. This option makes it possible for a developed society to get an additional bonus, by making available imported energy carriers on credit.

In general we can say that whenever a country is investing only a negligible part of its GDP in getting its energy inputs, it is almost unavoidable that its economic definition of BEP will be no longer determined by the biophysical factors determining the strength of the exosomatic hypercycle. Put in another way, cheap energy allows countries to ignore (at least for a while) the biophysical constraints associated with the dynamic budget of the metabolic pattern. In this situation the strategy of growth will be aimed at exploiting available stocks and filling available sinks as much as possible. Cheap energy means that a society is capable of externalizing a part of the 'biophysical costs' of its metabolic pattern outside its own borders. This fact makes it possible to lose the severity of: (i) its internal constraints – by moving the investment of production factors such as power capacity and labour that would be required in the energy sector to the dissipative compartments; and (ii) external constraints – by ignoring the negative effect of stock depletion and sink filling.

To confirm this hypothesis, we can mention here the historical analysis provided by Murphy and Hall (2011b) in relation to the effects that changes in the relative economic cost of energy had on the performance of the US economy. They provide a historic series showing the percentage of the GDP spent for energy, from 1970 to the crisis of 2008. According to their analysis the US economy got into a recession every time the expenditure on oil was higher than 6 per cent of the GDP. When explaining this economic reading using the concept of the metabolic pattern, we can say that the requirement of investment of a large fraction of GDP into the energy sector implies a negative effect on the possibility of investing the remaining GDP in the other compartments of the economy (this point has been demonstrated in Figure 7.1, page 164). Put in another way an excessive investment of the available GDP into just 'the purchase of energy carriers' (which still require additional investments in order to be able to express the other functions associated with a growing economy) had a negative effect on the emergent property of the whole metabolic pattern of the USA.

11.3.3 The temporary emancipation from land

The lesson to be learned from this example is clear. Stock-flow energy resources such as fossil energy represent an exceptional gift of favourable boundary conditions which can even be purchased by making debt. Import of energy makes it possible to externalize the actual biophysical costs of production to economic agents operating outside the physical border of national economies and pass on the economic cost of the imports to future generations (leaving them the burden of repaying the debt). The solution of making debt is temporary, but modern economies have proved that they can use this leverage very well for decades now!

However, if modern societies have to move to renewable primary energy sources belonging to the group of fund-flow energy sources, we will experience a situation in which, on the contrary, the huge requirement of biophysical gradients outside human control should mainly be available within the borders of each country. This would create a very high probability of severe external constraints. In order to milk a cow (fund-flow) you have to feed the cow. Promising the cow a massive amount of hay in the distant future will not do. If the cow does not eat, she cannot produce milk. Moreover, the exploitation of these renewable PES will require a large investment of energy carriers (an important internal loop of 'energy for energy'), when compared with the investment required right now to handle fossil energy based energy carriers. In turn, this larger internal loop of 'energy for energy' will translate into a large requirement of production factors (power capacity, labour, net energy carriers) to be invested in the energy sector of each economy. This reduction of SEH will imply a reduction in the availability of these production factors for final consumption (HH) or transaction activities (SG) – leading to a lower value of BEP.

On the positive side, when dealing with fund-flow PES it becomes much easier to individuate their relation with local biophysical constraints. Perhaps this will be a sobering experience for economists that will be forced to realize that the emancipation from land (land is no longer included among the production factors in modern economic theory) achieved by modern economies is temporary and it is due to the heavy reliance on stock-flow resources (Mayumi, 1991). That is, after assuming a massive movement of the metabolic pattern of modern societies to fund-flow PES it becomes much easier to make quantitative characterization of future scenarios. In relation to this point, especially relevant is the example of the low quality of agro-biofuels as alternative PES discussed in Chapter 7 (Figure 7.4, page 174). In relation to this point, when preparing the example of the impact matrix of the energy sector of Spain reported in Figure 11.2, we had to characterize the production of biodiesel in two different ways.

The first assessment reflects the conventional assessment found in literature: the actual technology of production of agro-biofuels carried out in developed countries based on massive injections of fossil energy inputs. Since the input of fossil energy is about 80 per cent of the output the process has an overall output/input EC ratio of 1.2/1, we refer to this assessment as 'biofuel fossil'. According to this analysis of the impact matrix, when a lot of oil is used to produce biodiesel, it does not make any sense to include this type of biodiesel production in the category of alternative PES. In fact, if it is true that this PES provides at the moment 0.01EJ to Spain, it is also true that it requires the consumption of 0.008EJ of fossil energy. This amount of fossil energy would not have been consumed, had this production of biodiesel not taken place.

The second assessment is obtained by taking seriously the zero-emission claim strived for in a low-carbon economy. This achievement would imply a massive internal loop of energy for energy: 5.8J of biodiesel should be produced in the agricultural sector and processed in the energy sector to get the net supply of 1J to society. In the second case, a 'fossil energy free' production would imply a dramatic increase in the requirement of gross production of EC fuels per unit of net supply of EC fuel, making this option clearly unpractical (the reader can recall the discussion on agro-biofuel production of ethanol in the USA, page 174). For example, if we wanted to cover the 1,600PJ of EC that Spain consumes in the form of fuels, with a PES such as biodiesel 'zero-emissions' – having a gross/net ratio $y_3 = 5.8/1$ – we should produce more than 9EJ of biodiesel to maintain self-sufficient and zero-growth the process. This would imply multiplying by 900 times some of the indicators of biophysical footprint (e.g. land requirement, water requirement, pesticides emissions) associated with this PES (the row labelled 'Biodiesel no fossil' in Figure 11.2, page 265).

12 Using MuSIASEM for studying scenarios based on alternatives to fossil energy

In this chapter we wrap up the material presented in Part II illustrating the potentiality of the MuSIASEM approach for practical applications. In particular, we provide an overview of how to combine the various quantitative protocols presented thus far in order to examine scenarios of metabolic patterns based on alternative energy sources.

In section 12.1 we show the peculiar characteristics of our proposed approach based on the use of grammar (semantic definitions of expected relations) which can be implemented using various non-equivalent methods of formalization. In section 12.2 we illustrate the use of this grammar for the analysis of the quality of alternative energy technologies. In section 12.3 we examine scenarios of metabolic patterns based on alternative energy sources and flag the dangerous underestimation of the present addiction of modern society to fossil energy.

12.1 Putting the pieces together

In Chapter 7 we illustrated the need for an integrated analysis of the metabolic pattern of society and argued that such analysis requires the use of non-equivalent perceptions and representations referring to different scales. In Chapter 8 we introduced the basic rationale of societal metabolism – associated with useful theoretical concepts – on which we built the multi-scale analysis of the metabolic pattern of modern society. In Chapter 9 we illustrated how to handle some of the epistemological troubles typical of energy analysis within this frame, namely the distinction between gross energy requirement and net energy carriers, the distinction between energy forms of different quality, and the impredicative nature of metabolic systems based on autocatalytic loops of energy. In Chapter 10 we showed that by mapping flows of energy carriers against a multi-level matrix of human activity we can study the viability and desirability of the metabolic pattern with regard to internal constraints (view from inside the system). In Chapter 11 we illustrated a similar approach based on multi-level matrices, which can be used to study the viability and desirability of the metabolic pattern in relation to external constraints (the external view). In this last chapter, we show how to combine all the conceptual tools presented so far into a coherent methodological approach useful to discuss future energy scenarios.

12.1.1 Pre-analytical considerations

Having accepted the existence of an epistemological challenge associated with the quantitative analysis of autopoietic systems operating across different levels of organization, we must realize that it is possible to assess the feasibility or desirability of a given metabolic pattern of society only after having addressed the following questions.

1   What is the set of functions to be expressed by the society and what organized structures does this require? This question forces us to describe the characteristics of structural-functional compartments generating the metabolic pattern at the local scale (see, for example, Figure 8.8, page 207).
2   What are the relations between specialized compartments in charge of expressing these functions over different hierarchical levels? (see, for example, Figure 4.5, page 88 and Figure 7.2, page 165).
3   What are the relative priorities that must be given to these various functions in case shortage of resources should require a re-adjustment of the metabolic pattern? In particular, what is the minimum value of BEP that must be guaranteed to avoid the collapse of the social fabric?

The feasibility and desirability of the metabolic pattern of society, when seen from 'within the black box', relates to the ability to stabilize in time a given pattern of conversion of energy carriers into end uses (the set of functions expressed by society). Therefore, feasibility and desirability in relation to internal constraints can only be defined in relation to the perception from within of 'how desirable the metabolic pattern is for those living in society'. Put another way, the integrated set of functions should guarantee a material standard of living that is considered acceptable by those living in the society. If this is not guaranteed, the social contract holding together the society is at risk and the transaction and transformation costs of the economic process will become huge (in the form of emigration, corruption, crime).

At the same time, it is essential to also assess the feasibility and desirability of the metabolic pattern, when seen from the 'outside the black box', in relation to the so-called external constraints: Is the metabolic pattern compatible with boundary conditions? To answer this question we must examine the ability to stabilize in time a given pattern of conversion of primary energy sources (determining a requirement of biophysical gradients outside human control) into a defined supply of energy carriers (both in quantity and types) needed to sustain the metabolic pattern. The requirement of input and the generation of waste associated with the metabolic pattern of society must be compatible with the metabolic pattern of the ecosystems embedding societal activity. That is, they must be compatible with the natural ecological processes making possible the reproduction of the ecological fund elements guaranteeing the stability of boundary conditions.

Thus, in order to be effective, a quantitative analysis of the metabolic pattern of society has to address first of all the issue of how to characterize 'what the metabolic system is and what it does' in relation to both the view from within and the view from outside. In relation to this point we can define the metabolic pattern in generic semantic terms by using terms such as requirement of energy inputs or exosomatic throughput (ET_i) which refer to the need for metabolizing energy. In the same way we can use other generic semantic terms referring to the use of production factors such as the profile of power levels – the exosomatic metabolic rate (EMR_i) – which together determine the requirement of production factors (power capacity and human labour), across the compartments of society defined at different hierarchical levels. However, at the moment of generating a quantitative assessment of flows and requirement we must be able to use protocols of quantifications that are different in relation to the view of the metabolic pattern that we want to adopt. The generic semantic terms ET_i or EMR_i have to be made less generic by choosing just a semantic energy form of reference (e.g. either gross energy requirement or net energy carrier) and then this characterization has to be quantified by using a formal category for the accounting (e.g. tons of oil equivalent or joules of energy carriers). As discussed before, it is impractical to reduce non-equivalent protocols of energy accounting into one single formal system serving all possible applications. Rather we have to learn how to formalize and integrate sets of semantic relations according to the narrative most suitable for the goal of the analysis.

12.1.2 Integrating the various protocols of accounting

When generating energy scenarios we are interested in studying both the internal and external constraints. In relation to this double task the MuSIASEM approach can be tailored to analyze the viability and desirability of the metabolic pattern of society in relation to *both* constraints, by establishing a bridge across the two non-equivalent representations (the view from within and from outside).

A stable metabolic pattern requires congruence between the characteristics of the various compartments determining the strength of the exosomatic hypercycle (SEH) and the characteristics of the various compartments determining the bio-economic pressure (BEP). The strength of the exosomatic hypercycle determines the ability to provide the required net supply of (i) energy carriers and material inputs (by the energy and mining sector), (ii) power capacity and other infrastructures (by the building and manufacturing sector), and (iii) food (by the agricultural sector) to the rest of society per hour of work in the hypercyclic compartment (PS). The bio-economic pressure represents the demand of society as a whole for (i) energy carriers and material inputs; (ii) power capacity and other infrastructures; (iii) food; (iv) transaction activities, (v) activities carried out in the household sector, per hour of work in the hypercyclic compartment.

This dynamic equilibrium between BEP and SEH can be described as an expected set of relations over quantities of energy defined on the basis of an appropriate category of accounting over the various compartments within the metabolic pattern. If we adopt a generic semantic definition of energy – total exosomatic throughput without specifying the formalization we can say that both BEP and SEH refer to the same ratio:

$$\text{BEP (requirement side)} = \text{TET/HA}_{PS} = \text{SEH (supply side)} = \text{TET/HA}_{PS}$$

However, as explained in Chapter 9 and Chapter 10 using the MuSIASEM approach we can express the constraints associated with this ratio using non-equivalent formalizations. That is, we can calculate this ratio by using quantitative assessments referring to non-equivalent external referents. This result can be obtained by adopting a characterization of the metabolic pattern based on multi-level matrices of data arrays.

In particular, writing the basic definition of bio-economic pressure in generic semantic terms:

$$\text{BEP} = \text{TET/HA}_{PS} = \text{EMR}_{SA} \times [\text{THA/HA}_{PW} \times \text{HA}_{PW}/(\text{HA}_{PW} - \text{HA}_{SG})]$$

we see that apart from the overall metabolic rate of society, several other factors determine the value of BEP. These other factors all relate to the allocation of human activity across the different compartments of society.

- THA/HA$_{PW}$ is the ratio between the total hours of human activity and the hours of human activity allocated to paid work. It is related to demographic (dependency ratio) and socio-economic factors (employment, retirement age, education, workload per year in the different sectors of the economy) (see Figures 8.3 and 8.4, pages 198 and 199);
- [HA$_{PW}$/(HA$_{PW}$ − HA$_{SG}$)] = HA$_{PW}$/HA$_{PS}$ is the ratio between the total hours in paid work and the labour hours allocated to the productive sectors (hyper-cyclic compartment). This ratio is related to the structure of the economy. It depends on the share of the employed population engaged in the service and government sector. In wealthy post-industrialized countries that share may well be greater than 70 per cent.

In the same way, writing down the set of relations between the factors determining the supply side of the total exosomatic throughput in generic semantic terms, we obtain the following equation:

$$\text{SEH} = \text{TET/HA}_{PS} = \text{EMR}_{PS} \times \text{ET}_{EM}/\text{ET}_{PS} \times [\text{output/input}]_{EC}$$

The formalization of these three semantic terms is more challenging. Suppose we want to characterize the three factors written on the right of the relation in terms of quantities of energy carriers:

- EMR$_{PS}$ in semantic terms (EMR$_{ECPS}$ using the notation given in Chapter 9) is the exosomatic metabolic rate in the primary and secondary production sectors (hypercyclic compartment) expressed in energy carriers. This ratio is directly related to the power capacity and labour hours allocated to this sector;

- ET_{EM}/ET_{PS} in semantic terms (EC_{EM}/EC_{PS} using the notation given in Chapter 9) is the ratio between the energy directly invested in energy acquisition (energy going into the energy sector) and the energy invested in producing power capacity and infrastructures (energy going into the hypercyclic compartment as a whole, including the energy sector). This ratio depends on the technology used in the energy and mining sector as well as on the quality of primary energy sources;
- $[output/input]_{EC}$ is the output/input ratio expressed in net energy carriers that refers to the process of exploitation of primary energy sources. This term refers to the output/input of energy for energy within the energy and mining sector. We saw in section 7.2.2 (Figure 7.5, page 177) that this value can be written GSEC/(GSEC-NSEC).

As discussed earlier we cannot express these factors (e.g. calculate the ratios) using scalar quantities. For example, when considering the ratio output/input of energy carriers in the energy sector – in our interpretation this should be the equivalent to the concept of EROI proposed by the school of Hall – we have to face the well-known fact that the energy carriers considered in the input and output flows are of different kinds. That is, we can write this ratio in semantic terms as the overall value of the gross supply of energy carriers divided by the overall value of the input of net energy carriers going into the exploitation process. But it is impossible to provide a direct quantitative assessment of the value of $[output/input]_{EC}$ for the whole energy sector. This is the reason why we suggest using a multi-level matrix of data arrays in order to preserve the original information about the mix of net energy carriers used in the energy sector (as an input) and the mix of energy carriers supplied by the energy sector to the rest of society (as the output).

The second obstacle is that it is difficult to calculate an actual biophysical value for the output/input ratio from a dataset of national energy statistics (by looking at energy flows within the EM sector) because of the heavy reliance on imports by the vast majority of developed countries. As discussed in Chapter 11 not all the energy inputs required to establish the autocatalytic loop energy for energy are invested in the EM sector of the country that is using the flow of energy carriers. In this respect, this value should rather be assessed by studying the characteristics of the technological processes used to generate each one of the imported inputs (a daunting task in modern economies) or apply standard energetic costs of energy carriers. In both cases the definition of borders in relation to national accounting would be lost.

In spite of the difficulties faced when selecting the particular protocol of accounting for the factors determining the value of BEP and SEH we can say that this approach defines an expected set of relations over quantities of energy flows and the compartments metabolizing these flows. We can decide to calculate these flows in different ways – choosing different protocols generating different

The semantic side of the grammar

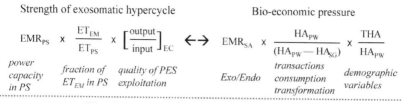

The formal side of the grammar

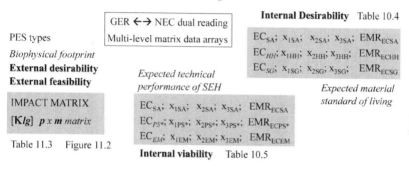

Figure 12.1 The implementation of the MuSIASEM for scenarios analysis: the expected set of relations between semantic and formal categories

numbers – but still we will find forced relations over the characteristics of the different compartments within the metabolic pattern.

For this reason we can use the semantic set of expected relations over the factors determining the two non-equivalent definitions of BEP and SEH (the supply and requirement side of the dynamic equilibrium) to integrate different views and protocols into a common narrative about the sustainability of the metabolic pattern. An overview of this integration is given in Figure 12.1:

The top of Figure 12.1 illustrates the semantic side of the grammar (discussed earlier), whereas the bottom part illustrates the formal side of the grammar. The semantic categories used to indicate the expected relations (upper part) can be transformed into quantitative assessments using the approach presented in Chapters 9–11.

12.2 Using the MuSIASEM approach to analyze the quality of alternative primary energy sources in terms of feasibility and desirability of scenarios

12.2.1 The semantic framework used to assess the quality of primary energy sources

Building on Chapters 6 and 7 we can say that:

1   When carrying out an analysis of the exploitation of primary energy sources it is essential to make the distinction between the gross output of energy carriers produced by the energy sector and the net supply delivered to the rest of society. For this reason the output/input of energy carriers used in the exploitation is a key piece of information. In our interpretation this would be the EROI index proposed by the school of Hall.

2   The concept of net energy analysis cannot be applied to the analysis of the whole autopoietic process of society. An analyst trying to generate one single quantitative assessment – a simple output/input ratio – over the entire process of self-organization of society will face an infinite recursive loop: every energy conversion expressing a function that is useful for the autopoietic process should be considered among the inputs. At the level of the whole society: output = input.

3   The assessment of the compatibility of the metabolic pattern with internal constraints requires us to consider not just an index, but several relevant characteristics of society. In particular, the exploitation of primary energy sources must demand only moderate investments of the production factors power capacity and human labour in the energy sector. This is a required condition to allow for a 'decent' standard of living so as to hold together the social fabric (reproduce the required institutions).

4   The compatibility of the metabolic pattern with external constraints affects the biophysical footprint of the mix of primary energy sources utilized by the energy sector to generate the required supply of energy carriers. This analysis entails an unavoidable degree of uncertainty, since out of a virtually infinite set of potentially relevant indicators of impact (in relation to both supply and sink capacity) we have to select a finite set of indicators in order to be able to handle the relative information in a quantitative analysis.

Given these considerations, we claim that it is impossible to assess the quality of a primary energy source if we do not first establish three sets of characteristics:

- the characteristics of the metabolic pattern that will use it;
- the characteristics of the biophysical gradients needed by the energy sector to generate the required net supply of energy carriers and the technical coefficients describing the process of exploitation;
- the characteristics of natural resources available and the characteristics of the ecosystems embedding the society.

Put another way, the quality of energy sources cannot be defined by using a 'one size fits all' index independent from the specific situation considered. In relation to this point, we claim that the rationale proposed with the MuSIASEM approach makes it possible to study the relations between the three sets of characteristics listed above. In fact, the MuSIASEM approach provides logical criteria that can be used to study the congruence among the factors determining the desirability and viability of the dynamic energy budget, associated with a given metabolic pattern, by calibrating the quantitative analysis on the specificity of the situation considered – Figure 12.1, page 279.

An overview of how to use the rationale of the MuSIASEM approach to analyze the quality of primary energy sources is given in Figure 12.2, page 281.

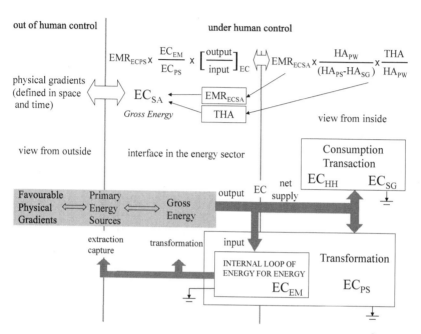

Figure 12.2 The characteristics of the energy sector: as expected by society and as determined by the quality of primary energy sources

On the left, we have the characterization of external constraints – which can be quantified by defining the biophysical footprint of the energy sector and can be related to the gross requirement of energy carriers – EC_{SA} to be used for: (i) the internal loop energy for energy – EC_{EM}; (ii) the operation of the hypercyclic compartment PS – EC_{PS}; (iii) the operation of the dissipative compartment made up by HH and SG – ($EC_{HH} + EC_{SG}$). It should be noted that the consumption of energy carriers for the internal loop within the EM sector (EC_{EM}) are included in the overall consumption of the hypercyclic sector (EC_{PS}). In quantitative terms, after having determined how the internal bio-economic pressure is translated into a requirement of external resources per hour of human activity, we can apply a quantitative factor determined by the population size (determining the size of THA) to assess the overall requirement of physical gradients that a specific metabolic pattern would require. In this way, we can look for an extensive variable (the scale of the metabolic pattern) and carry out the analysis of environmental impact using data handled within a geographic information system.

On the right, upper part, we have an overall description of the characteristics of the metabolic pattern useful for determining the material standard of living in the society, that is, the desirability of the set of end uses (the functions expressed by the various compartments of the society) in terms of BEP as illustrated in Chapter 10.

After framing the boundary conditions of the energy sector in this way, we can focus on the set of characteristics of the energy sector which are 'expected' by the society. In qualitative terms the characteristics of the EM sector must be integrated in the characteristics of the PS sector in order to generate a value of SEH compatible with the demand associated with the value of BEP. Therefore, we can use this set of expected relations to discuss in qualitative terms the relation between the characteristics of the EM sector (heavily dependent on the quality of the primary energy sources and the technology used to exploit them) and the overall characteristics of the metabolic pattern.

Given the average metabolic power of society (EMR_{ECSA}) we can see that an increase in material standard of living and a larger value of BEP translates into the ability of moving an increasing fraction of human activity to final consumption (HA_{HH}) and transaction activities (HA_{SG}). We saw in Chapter 10 how to analyze this type of phenomenon. In the middle of Figure 12.2 we have the interface between external and internal constraints. The viability of the metabolic pattern depends on the compatibility of the factors determining the strength of the exosomatic hypercycle (SEH) with both external constraints and internal constraints. As illustrated in the previous section if we express SEH in terms of gross supply of energy carriers then we can generate quantitative information useful for the analysis of the external constraints (Chapter 11). What we want to discuss here is the analysis of the factors determining the value of SEH and therefore the special role that the exploitation of primary energy sources plays in the generation of a desirable and viable metabolic pattern.

The amount of exosomatic energy under human control must be made available to the whole society by the energy invested in the energy sector (EC_{EM}). Therefore, the ratio EC_{SA}/EC_{EM} may be interpreted in very loose terms as the energy return on the investment calculated at a very large scale, where EC_{SA} is the return and EC_{EM} is the investment. However, as discussed in Chapter 6 and Chapter 7 the actual consumption of EC_{SA} depends on several factors, in particular the availability of production factors (human activity and power capacity). This explains why a more elaborate analysis is required. In relation to external constraints (the left side of the relation) the metabolic pattern of the energy sector, and more generally the hypercyclic compartment, must be compatible with the metabolic pattern of the ecosystems with which they interact. As a matter of fact, the very definition of the hypercyclic part of society individuates those functional compartments interacting directly with the context in terms of material and energy flows both on the supply and sink side (Figure 7.6, page 183). Beside the flows of energy and material inputs needed for the exosomatic metabolism, made available by the energy and mining (EM) sector, society needs food, made available by the agricultural sector (AG), and power capacity and infrastructure, made available by the building and manufacturing sector (BM).

When looking at the view from the inside (the definition of BEP) we use a set of variables:

$$EMR_{ECSA} \times \frac{HA_{PW}}{(HA_{PW} - HA_{SG})} \times \frac{THA}{HA_{PW}}$$

based on perceptions and representations of energy flows and demographic variables referring to the level of the whole society (level n – EMR_{SA}). However, the overall value of these variables can be defined on the basis of characteristics of certain sectors only: the household sector (HH) defined at level (n-1), and the service and government sector (SG) defined at level (n-2). But please note that the variables included in this relation do not include HA_{HH}, but HA_{PW} and HA_{SG}. The representation of the characteristics of society at level n allows us to establish a bridge with the larger scale, level (n+1) or the context in which the black box is operating. It is at this large scale level that we can check the availability of physical gradients outside human control.

The expression used to calculate the value of SEH:

$$EMR_{ECPS} \times \frac{EC_{EM}}{EC_{PS}} \times \frac{EC_{SA}}{EC_{EM}}$$

is obtained using factors defined across three hierarchical levels: the whole society (level n – EC_{SA}), the productive sectors (level n-2 – hypercyclic sector PS EMR_{PS} and EC_{PS}) and the energy and mining sector (level n-3 – EC_{EM}).

12.2.2 Relevant factors in the evaluation of the quality of energy sources

As noted earlier at the moment of examining the specific characteristics of an energy sector operating in a developed country (or any other country relying on import of energy) it is impossible to establish a direct relation between the description of the process of exploitation of primary energy sources (described in the bottom part of Figure 12.2) and the forced relation between SEH and BEP. On the other hand, we can imagine a relation between the amount of energy supplied to the society by an energy sector which is operating without import. In this situation we could imagine that the total output of the exploitation process should be equal to EC_{SA}. In this case we could write that:

$$EC_{EM} \times [output/input]_{EC} = \text{gross output} = EC_{SA}$$

By replacing the term EC_{EM} with the term ($EMR_{EM} \times HA_{EM}$) and dividing by the term HA_{PS}, we can write a definition of SEH based on the characteristics of this hypothetical fully self-sufficient energy sector using yet another expression:

$$\text{SEH} = \text{EC}_{SA}/\text{HA}_{PS} = EMR_{ECEM} \times \left[\frac{output}{input}\right]_{EC} \times \frac{HA_{EM}}{HA_{PS}}$$

At this point we can establish a direct relation between the characteristics determining the value of SEH described before and a hypothetical energy sector, fully self-sufficient in the generation of a net supply of energy carriers for society:

$$EMR_{ECPS} \times \frac{EC_{EM}}{EC_{PS}} \times \frac{EC_{SA}}{EC_{EM}} \longleftrightarrow EMR_{ECEM} \times \left[\frac{output}{input}\right]_{EC} \times \frac{HA_{EM}}{HA_{PS}}$$

We can interpret these two definitions as a definition based on a top-down representation (starting from the values found in a given country) on the left side, and a definition based on a bottom-up representation (starting from the values found when considering technical coefficients of the process of exploitation) on the right side. That is, the ratio $[output/input]_{EC}$ indicates the output obtained from the exploitation (the return) whereas the input of energy carriers indicates the requirement of power capacity and human activity required for the investment.

According to these relations, we can say that the lower the amount of energy carriers invested in the energy sector (EC_{EM}), the better for the metabolic pattern, in relation to both external and internal constraints. In fact any increase in EC_{EM} will be reflected in an increase in EC_{SA} and hence, because of its direct and indirect effect on the hypercyclic compartment, also in the biophysical footprint. An increase in EC_{EM} entails the requirement of more power capacity in the entire hypercyclic (productive) compartment (to avoid an increase in the requirement of labour that would reduce the value of BEP) and therefore a larger EMR_{ECPS} leading to an increase in EC_{PS}. In this regard, the $[output/input]_{EC}$ relative to the exploitation of primary energy sources is crucial. We believe that this is the point that Hall and his school want to make using the concept of the EROI index. When the value of this ratio drops below 2/1, a dramatic increase in the loop of energy for energy entails a colossal increase in EC_{EM} that will be reflected in an increase in EC_{PS} and in the overall requirement of HA_{PS}. This dramatic increase of investment of production factors in the hypercyclic compartment is likely to push the metabolic pattern outside the viability domain either because of an excessive requirement of power level in the productive sectors (a high EMR_{PS} requires a high investment power capacity level) or because of an increased labour demand in the energy sector (HA_{EM}).

In fact, there is little room to increase the labour hours engaged in the energy sector, as the ratio HA_{EM}/HA_{PS} does not tolerate much change. As discussed earlier, the total amount of labour (a valuable production factor) in the productive sectors is determined by the relation $HA_{PS} = HA_{EM} + HA_{AG} + HA_{BM}$, and hence should cover the requirement of human activity for producing the required energy carriers and minerals (EM), food and fibres (AG), and power capacity and infrastructures (BM). For this reason, a large increase in the internal requirement of labour in the loop of 'energy for energy' is likely to result incompatible with the viability of the metabolic pattern (see the dendrograms of human activity shown in Figure 8.3, page 198, Figure 8.4, page 199, Figure 10.1, page 236 and the discussion over the sudoku effect in Chapter 10, page 233). The profile of allocation of power capacity and human activity determining the value of BEP (desirability in relation to the material standard of living) must be compatible with the profile of allocation of power capacity and human activity in the sectors determining SEH. At the moment, the metabolic pattern of a developed country with a high material standard of living and large dependency ratio, requires that the amount of human labour invested in the energy sector (HA_{EM}) has to be extremely low (in the order of 1/1000 of THA!). The same is true for the amount of human labour invested in agriculture. For this reason, developed countries require the existence of large levels of power capacity in the productive sectors to compensate for the low input of labour.

The high dependency ratio associated with the ageing of the population of highly developed societies entails a double challenge for the stability of the metabolic pattern. Not only does it force these societies to operate with a small fraction of the total human activity in the productive sectors (a large value of THA/HA_{PS}), but also to allocate a large fraction of working activity (HA_{PW}) to the service and government sector to take care of the dependent population. Perhaps this process of demographic adjustment is at the basis of the formation of homogeneous profiles of allocation of human activity in developed societies (Giampietro *et al.*, 2011).

The socio-economic factors aggravating the shortage of hours of human activity in the paid work sector in post-industrial societies are:

- increase in life expectancy, entailing a reduction in the fraction of human activity available for the paid work sector (a larger value for THA/HA_{PW}) and also a larger requirement of labour in the service sector for taking care of the larger dependent population – an increase in the ratio $HA_{PW}/(HA_{PW} - HA_{SG})$; contraction of the average yearly working hours of the employed population (now consistently below 2,000 hours per year);
- a growing higher education sector (enrolment of young adults often above 50 per cent);
- high percentage of unemployment (double digits not uncommon), partly due to the increased importance given to preferences and choices of potential workers and to mismatches in specialization between offer and demand.

Paradoxically the analysis of the metabolic pattern of modern societies makes it possible to establish a clear relation between the quality of primary energy sources and the demographic structure of a society. This explains why the evaluation of the quality of an alternative energy technology can only be carried out within such a holistic multi-level analysis of the metabolic pattern. It requires us to establish a set of meaningful relations over what is required from society in terms of characteristics of net energy carriers and what can be delivered by the exploitation of a given primary energy source. This requires also checking the compatibility of the profile of allocation of production factors (labour and power capacity) with what is feasible and desirable in the given metabolic pattern according to the view from within.

The quality of alternative energy sources can be associated with the possibility of keeping low the difference between gross and net supply of energy carriers in the process of exploitation (Figure 6.4, page 142 and Figure 12.2, page 281) – the ratio $EC_{SA}/(EC_{SA} - EC_{EM})$. This characteristic becomes crucial when dealing with fund-flow primary energy sources, which typically have a low $[output/input]_{EC}$ ratio (when measured at the local scale) and therefore can be considered as having a 'low quality' when compared with fossil energy. However, when looking at the characteristics of a hypothetical self-sufficient energy sector which is generating the total amount of energy carriers consumed by society exploiting primary energy sources:

$$SEH = EC_{SA}/HA_{PS} = EMR_{ECEM} \times \left[\frac{output}{input} \right]_{EC} \times \frac{HA_{EM}}{HA_{PS}}$$

we can notice that the output/input energy ratio (the number that in our interpretation refers to the concept of EROI index) is only one of the relevant factors.

In relation to internal constraints

There is another crucial factor to be considered: the power level (EMR_{ECEM}). The pace of the flow at which the investment of energy carrier is made determines the requirement of production factors, that is it requires a compatible mix of power capacity and human labour in the energy sector. This information is related to the size of the $input_{EC}$;

In relation to external constraints

There is another crucial factor to be considered: the biophysical footprint – the requirement of physical gradients outside human control. This factor can only be assessed after gathering information about the quantity of PES available for sustaining the overall consumption of energy carriers EC_{SA}.

Why it is important to consider all these factors? Because when dealing with fund-flow energy sources (renewable resources) it is very likely that the information associated with the simple $[output/input]_{EC}$ ratio is not sufficient to assess the viability and desirability of alternative primary energy sources. We described in Figure 7.3, page 167 the systemic problems associated with the exploitation of the two most popular forms of agro-biofuels produced right now, ethanol from corn (USA) and ethanol from sugarcane (Brazil), and the importance of considering the non-linear effect of the value of the output/input in determining the ratio gross/net supply of energy carriers. The problem we want to address at this point is: can we use the MuSIASEM approach to analyze and compare the quality of the second generation of biofuels – e.g. cellulosic ethanol – in relation to the first generation? We do not have direct data for carrying out such an analysis, so we cannot provide an answer. However, we can comment on systemic features found when analyzing and comparing the production of ethanol in USA and Brazil. We compare in Table 12.1, page 287, the characteristics of these two systems (corn-ethanol and sugarcane-ethanol) with the characteristics of fossil energy (oil). What is important to observe here is that if we would rely only on the information given by the energy [output/input]$_{EC}$ ratio for assessing the second generation of biofuels we might get misleading indications. For example, the production of ethanol from sugarcane is characterized by a relatively high output/input energy ratio (7/1) (the classic EROI). This positive result is obtained because of the large input of human labour hours (a trade-off in favour of labour in the use of production factors). However, we saw earlier that too high an input of labour makes the exploitation process incompatible with the metabolic pattern of a developed society, where THA/HA$_{PS}$ must be very high. When looking at the net supply of energy carriers to society per hour of labour in the energy sector (EC$_{net\ supply}$/HA$_{EM}$) in Table 12.1, the mechanism generating the trade-off among production factors is evident. The production of ethanol from corn has a high value of EMR$_{ECEM}$ but (because of this) a low energy [output/input]$_{EC}$ ratio, whereas the production of ethanol from sugarcane has the reverse performance. Neither of these two systems is even close to matching the benchmark values of the exploitation of fossil energy. This information suggests that for the assessment of the potentiality of an alternative energy source (the second generation of biofuels or photovoltaic, or the fourth generation of nuclear energy) it would be wise to provide an integrated characterization of all these factors to assess the performance against the standard established by fossil energy.

Table 12.1 Comparing the characteristics of the exploitation process of various primary energy sources to generate a net supply of liquid fuels, measured in terms of energy carriers

Source: data from Giampietro and Mayumi, 2009

	EMR$_{ECEM}$ (MJ/h)	[output/input]$_{EC}$ (EROI index)	ECnet supply/HA$_{EM}$ (MJ/h)
Ethanol-corn	1,400	1.1/1	230
Ethanol-sugarcane	65	7.0/1	150–380
Fossil energy	> 2,000	10/1–20/1	20,000–50,000

12.3 The underestimation of our addiction to fossil energy

12.3.1 Fossil energy and the temporary emancipation from land

Fossil energy is a stock-flow primary energy source consisting of large reservoirs of potential chemical energy concentrated below ground. Stock-flow energy is associated with a favorable set of characteristics in relation to its exploitation, and for this reason it should be considered as a high-quality primary energy source. Indeed, stocks of fossil energy are concentrated in space and, therefore, using only a limited amount of land it is possible to generate a large net flow of energy carriers to support the energy consumption of society.

Vaclav Smil (2003) compared the density of different typologies of primary energy sources and the energy throughput density of different typologies of land use associated with the metabolism of developed societies (Figure 12.3, page 288). Thus, on the right side of this figure, we have the energy throughput density at which developed societies are using energy (energy consumption per hectare of land use typology); while on the left, we have the energy throughput density of the supply of energy carriers corresponding to various primary energy sources. We thus see that the spatial expression of the current metabolic pattern of modern society is possible because of the large difference (the graph has a logarithmic scale) in energy throughput density between the supply obtained from fossil energy ($10^3 - 10^4$ W/m^2) and the demand related to modern land uses ($10^2 - 10^3$ W/m^2). The energy throughput densities of consumption (the requirement of energy input per hectare) would not be possible if the supply were to be derived from biomass or biofuels with an energy throughput density that is three to four orders of magnitude smaller than that of fossil energy. As discussed before, external and internal constraints would make the dynamic energy budget infeasible. Thus, we can say that fossil energy, a stock-flow primary energy source, has provided us with a temporary emancipation from land, the traditional fund-flow primary energy source of humankind (Mayumi, 1991).

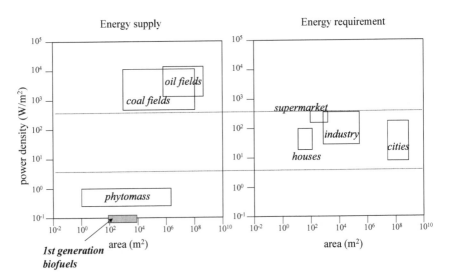

Figure 12.3 Power density gap: the density of supply and requirement of energy carriers for various land uses

Source: data from Smil, 2003, pp. 242–243

Another positive aspect of stock-flow resources is related to economies of scale. The high concentration of fossil energy stocks makes it possible to use a huge power capacity in their exploitation, which can be operated close to full capacity during the entire year. The resulting low cost of power generation in the exploitation allows exploiters to reach economies of scale (see the cost of power generation and the utilization factor in Chapter 5). For instance, the Bagger 288 shown in Figure 12.4 is used for extracting coal in an open mine in Germany. This machine extracts 240,000 tons of brown coal per day, and is operated by only seven persons. There are many similar examples of the adoption of large machine power capacity controlling huge amounts of energy flows while using only a limited amount of human labour, such as oil tankers crossing the seas and oil pipelines moving huge amounts of crude oil per day, or power plants generating electricity at a pace of hundreds of megawatts.

Figure 12.4 The Bagger 288, an example of large power capacity used in the exploitation of fossil energy
Source: courtesy of RWE Power AG

The situation is completely different if we have to rely on primary energy sources that are not based on stocks of potential chemical energy but on mechanical energy. Some of the so-called alternative energy sources belong to this second category – wind power, hydroelectric power, ocean waves. In this situation, depending on the specific concentration and characteristics of the exploitable energy source we are likely to experience low values for the output/input energy ratio. In general, diluted flows, in order to be exploited, have to be gathered and concentrated from large areas. Nature can provide hot spots for exploitation, such as the Niagara Falls, where humans do not have to invest for generating these favourable gradients. In this case, the quality depends on the level of concentration of the available gradient to be exploited. Indeed, when humans had to exploit low density gradients (e.g. the exploitation of the energy chain solar energy → biomass) the low density of biomass produced per year led to a serious combination of external and internal constraints on the expression of the metabolic pattern (Giampietro et al., 1997).

As explained in detail in Giampietro and Pimentel (1991) and Giampietro et al. (1997), the amount of applied power required for the exploitation of a land area increases in a non-linear way with the size of the area (see Figure 12.5). This is due to the increasing share of energy absorbed by the construction and operation of power capacity for travelling and transportation (in addition to the activities of exploitation). This problem is often intensified by strong seasonality in the activities to be performed. For this reason, many preindustrial communities living in ecosystems providing exploitable biomass at low density (e.g. pastoralists) adopted the solution of nomadism. In this situation the exploiters periodically or cyclically move, following available biomass, thus reducing the need for the costly practice of commuting.

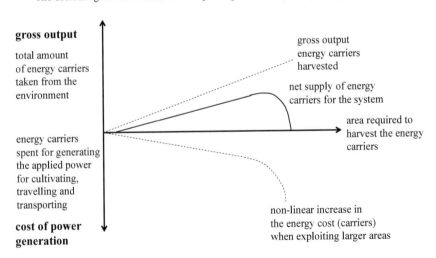

Figure 12.5 Schematic representation of the energetics of the exploitation of fund-flow energy
Sources: adaptation of Giampietro et al., 1997

12.3.2 Concentration of exploited gradients and the quality of alternative energy sources

As regards the evaluation of the systemic properties of the exploitation process for potential primary energy sources the concentration of the physical gradients to be exploited is a key factor. In relation to this point, Nobuo Kawamiya (1983) put forward an interesting narrative about the quality of different types of primary energy sources, based on the volumetric density of the flow of energy associated with the primary energy source. As illustrated in Figure 12.6, his definition is ambiguous since it refers to both stock-flow primary energy sources (fossil energy and nuclear energy) and fund-flow primary energy sources (solar radiation). Nevertheless, the chosen method of quantification, that is the energy density per kg of material input (mass) associated with the exploitation of a given primary energy source, can be easily associated with a corresponding requirement of production factors used in the process (power capacity and labour).

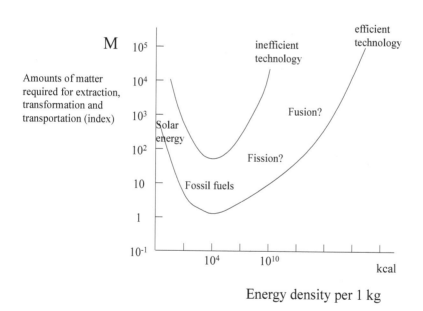

Figure 12.6 Material requirement and energy density for different PES
Source: Kawamiya, 1983, p. 62, used with permission from Kaimei

Kawamiya's idea of the quality of primary energy sources can be related to the issue of scale and the density of the energy form per unit of mass. For instance, the set of physical transformations carried out in the exploitation of fossil fuels refer to energy forms (chemical compounds, heat and mechanical energy) that are defined in a space–time scale that is similar to that of endosomatic conversions. On the contrary, solar radiation arrives to us in an extremely diluted form and its exploitation requires a large investment (of power capacity and labour) for its collection and transformation into a more concentrated form. When this operation is performed gratuitously by natural processes, as happened with the formation of fossil energy, we certainly can get a high return. But when dealing with the exploitation of fund-flow types of energy we have to deal with the mismatch of scales between the low density of the production process and the high density of the utilization process. This mismatch implies that chemical energy has to be gradually accumulated over very long periods of time before its utilization can take place, or that very large quantities of land are required to get a large flow of energy input. The opposite is true for the exploitation of nuclear energy. In this case, the density of the energy form exploited in the process is too high. Indeed, its exploitation is aimed at diluting, slowing down, and containing the set of energy transformations taking place in the fissile material. Also this mismatch of scale between the high density of the production process and the relatively low density of the utilization process of energy (the Rankine cycle generating electricity in a nuclear power plant) entails that huge investments are required to build nuclear reactors and in relation to the material flow associated with it, stocks of radioactive waste material (beside the heat waste) have to be accumulated after the utilization of energy has taken place.

Kawamiya's idea comes from Georgescu-Roegen's concern with material requirement:

> It [the necessary amount of matter for a technology] is high for weak-intensity energy (as is the solar radiation at the ground level) because such energy must be concentrated into a much higher intensity if it is to support the intensive industrial processes as those now supported by fossil fuels...
>
> (Georgescu-Roegen, 1979, p. 1050)

He also argues that the necessary amount of matter is high for high-intensity energy such as thermonuclear energy because high-intensity energy must be contained and controlled within a stable boundary. The conclusion that fossil fuels are superior is sometimes called Georgescu-Roegen's Fundamental Proposition (Kawamiya, 1983).

We see a certain similarity between the narrative proposed by Nobuo Kawamiya and the narrative proposed by Vaclav Smil based on the concept of energy throughput density (the density of energy form per unit of area). In relation to the current addiction to fossil energy of modern societies, Smil has made two interesting observations. First, it will be very difficult to move in a short period of time from predominantly fossil fuel exploitation to a different mix of energy carriers. In fact, the basic set of energy converters used by modern society is quite limited (e.g. the typologies of prime movers used for power generation and transportation are not many) and this set of converters has not changed dramatically in technological quality terms (e.g. beside the addition of electronic controls, the most common types of engine have remained the same in the last decades) – Smil, 2007. And second, Smil observes that a shift to alternative, fund-flow primary energy sources (no longer based on stock depletion) will require an extraordinary amount of economic (and biophysical) investments in infrastructures. These huge investments are needed at the very same moment in which the disposable investments are rapidly shrinking because of the progressive exhaustion of high-quality natural resources (Smil, 2008a, b). In conclusion, Smil (2003, 2006, 2009) has provided solid evidence against the chance of making a quick and easy exit out of our current dependence on fossil energy.

Thus far humankind has been good at making a change for the better, achieving quick and painless transitions from low-quality to better-quality primary energy sources (wood → coal → oil → natural gas). But will a transition in the opposite direction, from high-quality to low-quality primary energy sources, be equally fast and smooth?

In this context, we must flag a systemic flaw plaguing the discussion about and the assessments of the feasibility and desirability of alternative primary energy sources. As observed earlier, it is impossible to define 'the quality' of an energy source (the characteristics of the pattern of supply of energy carriers) if we do not first define the characteristics of the related pattern of demand. Nonetheless, the vast majority of existing discussions about and assessments of the quality of alternative energy sources are based on the hidden and uncontested assumption that alternative primary energy sources can easily substitute oil, natural gas and coal without causing serious problems while maintaining the same metabolic pattern that we enjoy now. These alternatives are assumed to be able to preserve the same profile of investments of energy inputs, power capacity, and human activity across the different compartments of society (the same value of BEP) by replacing the role of oil in the generation of the required SEH in the energy sector. Thus, the discussion about alternative primary energy sources has implicitly adopted the pre-analytical narrative assuming that:

- the supply side in the energy sector can be easily transformed from fossil energy dependence, given the proposed switch to alternative primary energy sources; and that
- the demand side of the metabolic pattern (the quantity and quality of consumption of energy, food, materials, goods, power capacity and infrastructures of the rest of the society) will remain the same.

Given this implicit assumption, in our view, no drastic shift to fund-flow energy type of alternative primary energy source to oil will take place in a feasible way (let alone desirable way) soon. Fund-flow energy type cannot generate values of SEH (bottom-up technical characteristics) that would be required to support the BEP observable in modern developed societies now (top-down statistical characteristics). In relation to this point, we want to stigmatize the systemic misunderstanding of the role that oil plays in modern economies. In fact, it seems that all the governments of the world are united in the campaign for a swift reduction of imports of oil. This goal assumes that continuous import of oil is bad for the economy and that if the economy would produce the same amount of energy carriers required for the current activities without resorting to importing oil, by using alternative energy sources, the economy would be better off. Since very few seem to object to this idea, very few seem to realize that modern economies generate added value by using energy, and not by producing energy. Probably because of the two hundred years of fossil fuels bonanza many forgot the fact that primary energy sources, oil in particular, are required at every stage of economic activities: production of energy carriers, production of other raw materials and the final products, distribution of materials and the final products through the transportation network, and consumption activities for reproducing population. So energy is the primary form of 'raw material': the indispensable primary resource input for doing anything. In our modern economy the ubiquitous input of fossil energy is taken for granted and often misunderstood. For example, the policy supporting corn-ethanol production in the USA has the effect of converting oil – the most valuable energy resource input we have at the moment –into ethanol – a less valuable energy resource input (moreover this conversion requires the destruction of food). Producing ethanol, which is a mere 'parasite' energy source (not a primary one), is just a waste of resources.

This is why we believe that the narratives used right now for solving our energy crisis are wrong. We do not have to find alternative primary energy sources to perpetuate our present metabolic pattern; this is a mission impossible. But rather we must change our metabolic pattern (the way we produce and consume energy carriers to fulfill a defined set of end uses under a given set of external constraints) in order to be able to use alternative primary energy sources. Of course we do understand that there is an incredible inertia (institutional lock-in) towards preserving the status quo, but the idea of using alternative primary energy sources in order to keep the existing pattern of consumption is simply a non-starter. We are living in a fossil energy civilization and this civilization does not work without fossil energy. If we want to propose scenarios without or with less fossil energy, we should start thinking about changing our existing metabolic pattern to accommodate the use of alternative energy sources.

For instance, we should reconsider the following characteristic of the supply side of the metabolic pattern of the fossil energy era. Our centralized system of production and distribution of energy carriers based on huge grids and long-distance transfers, based on huge power plants producing energy carriers in distant places, thousands of miles from the place of consumption. When using fossil energy we had the option of taking advantage of economies of scales but this option is not necessarily there when dealing with alternative energies. In the same way, in developed countries, the supply of all energy carriers is guaranteed according to quite high standards of performance (e.g. no interruptions, constant quality). Very often these high standards of quality are not really needed in relation to all possible uses. By modulating the quality of the supply – guaranteeing a high performance when it is really required and lowering the standard whenever this is possible – it would be possible to have a cheaper network of distributions and a larger use of local alternative sources.

In our view discussions about future energy scenarios should seriously take into consideration that the current set of characteristics of the metabolic pattern on the demand side can no longer be maintained. We will have to look for alternative metabolic patterns, based on both alternative primary energy sources and alternative patterns of consumption. In this alternative scenario, we envision a diversity of patterns of production and consumption of energy carriers, which will have to be more location-specific and more adaptable to the different identities of different socio-economic systems.

Conclusions

Where do we go from here?

A fish is the last to acknowledge the importance of water.

(Ewe proverb)

The present impasse

History has witnessed an impressive series of discoveries and technological breakthroughs that have benefited humankind immensely and that, at times, gave rise to powerful empires. But none of these 'sparks' comes even close to equaling the explosive human development from pre-industrial to post-industrial society in recent history. What is often overlooked though is that modern civilization as we now know it is not only the result of human ingenuity and centuries of struggle to accumulate knowledge and improve living conditions, but also of a very fortunate combination of events.

Indeed, laymen, politicians, and most scholars alike, seem to be unaware that the big discontinuity in the development of human society in the modern era, the time span running from pre-industrial to post-industrial times, has been made possible by: (i) the availability of an abundant and cheap supply of fossil energy; (ii) the development of technologies able to use this fossil energy to generate useful work at a low cost; and (iii) the development of social institutions capable of coordinating the resulting diversity of activities expressed in modern economies and of processing the relative flow of information. Without the combination of these three events, recent history would not have witnessed the dramatic metamorphosis from pre-industrial society into the present globalized post-industrial economy. Indeed, the discovery of fossil energy, notably oil, and the concomitant ability of effectively using it has been a critical ingredient for the exponential growth of the economic process. Instead of taking the ocean of *burning water* – the name given to petroleum in Japan in the seventh century (Encyclopedia Britannica, 1911) – in which we swim for granted, we should ponder the consequences of the crucial role it plays in guaranteeing our present material standard of living.

We cannot emphasize enough the importance of understanding the existing dependence on fossil energy because things will be, and in fact already are, rapidly changing. We are facing a progressive depletion of fossil energy stocks and the directly-related progressive decrease in the quality of fossil energy as primary energy source. Indeed, the best reservoirs of oil have been used first (Hall *et al.*, 1986) and we are witnessing a gradual but steady reduction of the output/input ratio of energy carriers in its exploitation (Murphy and Hall, 2011; Hall and Klitgaard, 2012). The implications of this fact on the characteristics of the metabolic pattern are that the strength of the exosomatic hypercycle (SEH) is bound to dramatically decrease due to the expansion in size of the internal loop of 'energy consumption for energy'. In turn, a higher consumption of energy for energy accelerates the rate of depletion of fossil energy stocks (given the widening of the gap between gross energy use and net energy carrier supply) and raises the cost of extraction (more power capacity and labour are required to exploit stocks of lower quality). This scenario relates to the phenomenon called 'peak oil'. After reaching peak oil it is no longer possible to continue increasing the rate of oil extraction worldwide. Then we can expect that it will become difficult to maintain even existing rates of extraction. This implies that, as economists would say, the era of cheap oil (and cheap energy) is over.

The end of cheap energy implies that the viability domain of the metabolic pattern of modern society is gradually contracting as both external and internal constraints tighten. As regards external constraints, fossil energy consumption can no longer be increased at will and the temporary solution of making debts to pay for it (externalization), is rapidly losing viability. Other critical material flows for the economy, such as water and certain metals, are also getting increasingly scarce, and besides peak oil we may well be experiencing 'peak everything else', an appropriate expression suggested by Richard Heinberg (2005). To make things worse, many other environmental services taken for granted in the past are now jeopardized by the dramatic expansion of human activity on a finite planet. In relation to internal constraints, the immense population size, the still growing dependency ratio in developed countries (due to longer life expectancy), and the high expectations for a quick improvement in the material standard of living in developing countries are generating a major stress on the social fabric worldwide.

The recent development of modern society can be neatly summarized as a takeover of our planet by the human species.

• The size of the human population literally exploded, following a clear exponential trend. In the last 35 years only, the population size doubled from 3 billion to more than 6 billion. This means that in the last three decades the population grew more (by over three billions) than in all the previous millennia together.
• The availability of ecological processes per capita at the global level has continuously diminished since the industrial revolution.
• In spite of the exponential population growth and resulting reduction in available ecological services per capita, for two hundred years now (from the year 1800 to 2000) humankind has been able to continually increase the amount of energy input consumed per capita.

The combination of these trends truly represents a remarkable success story for human ingenuity, but at the same time it is also reason for serious concern. The classic tale of the doubling of rice over the chessboard or of the growth of lily pads over the fresh water pond, reminds us of the incredible power of exponential growth (Bartlett, 2004). For this reason, we must contemplate the consequences of the obvious fact that, sooner or later (or perhaps already now), existing fossil energy reserves will no longer constitute an unlimited supply of cheap energy. As a matter of fact, today's high energy prices and growing concern about peak oil seem to confirm the wisdom of M. King Hubbert, who, as early as 1949, expressed his reserves about the unique and peculiar situation experienced by modern societies that rely on a huge supply of cheap fossil energy:

> The release of this energy is a unidirectional and irreversible process. It can only happen once, and the historical events associated with this release are necessarily without precedent, and are intrinsically incapable of repetition. It is clear, therefore, that our present position on the nearly vertical front slopes of these curves is a precarious one, and that the events which we are witnessing and experiencing, far from being 'normal,' are among the most abnormal and anomalous in the history of the world. Yet we cannot turn back; neither can we consolidate our gains and remain where we are. In fact, we have no choice but to proceed into a future, which we may be assured will differ markedly from anything we have experienced thus far.
>
> (Hubbert, 1949, pp. 103–109)

On granfalloons and ostrich policies

The need for rearranging the profile of allocation of power capacity over the functions expressed by the various compartments of society – interpreting the word 'power' in relation to energy flows – will bring about the need of also rearranging the existing profile of political power allocation among social activists (changing the status quo of the political power structure). This is probably the reason why the need to change our metabolic pattern is not considered relevant or urgent by the existing political establishment. Innovative ideas with the potential of bringing about real change are hard to accept by the establishment. As observed by Upton Sinclair: 'It is difficult to get a man to understand something, when his salary depends upon his not understanding it!' (http://en.wikiquote.org/wiki/Upton_Sinclair). This attitude encourages politically-correct scientific discussions about the predicament of 'energy, society and environment' and has led to the generation of a series of 'granfalloons' (a term suggested to us by Vaclav Smil, personal communication).

The term 'granfalloon' was originally introduced by Kurt Vonnegut (1963) to indicate a proud and meaningless association of human beings. Wikipedia provides the following definition (among others): 'a group of people who believe that they have a special connection and who believe they are helping to bring about a greater plan, but are actually not'. Granfalloons can be seen as social crusaders set on saving the world based on wishful thinking rather than on solid analysis.

Granfalloons in the field of sustainability are easy to spot: their chosen narrative is always focused on 'solutions' aimed at fixing the external world, which is invariably perceived as harbouring the problem. The granfalloon blissfully ignores that the problem may reside with ourselves, let alone that we might have to change ourselves in order to adjust to new boundary conditions. The typical definition of sustainability problems adopted by the granfalloon excludes by default the role of the story-teller (the power structure choosing the narrative) from the analysis. It is never considered among the things that might be changed within the chosen narrative and model. Are we running out of fossil energy but we need liquid fuels? Then the solution is to make agro-biofuels, it costs what it costs, and keep consuming liquid fuels as before (or more). Are we generating too much CO_2 in the atmosphere? Then the solution is to sequestrate CO_2 under the sea and keep emitting. Are we altering too much the habitat of wildlife and thus causing mass extinctions of species? Then the solution is to clone those species and continue destroying habitats. And the list could go on...

In this book we have looked at things in a different (most probably politically incorrect) way. We have presented an original method of energy analysis based on a representation of the metabolic pattern of society. With this approach we can frame the discussion of sustainability along either of the following two lines: (i) sustainability seen as fixing the external world according to the needs and the narrative chosen by a given story-teller (considering only the inside view); (ii) sustainability seen as an adaptation of the identity of the story-teller and of the narrative used to define the problem to 'inconvenient' perceptions of the external world (considering also the outside view). We strongly believe that simultaneously following both lines is the more suitable approach when addressing sustainability issues.

But it certainly is not the most popular one. This is neatly exemplified by an episode of *The Daily Show* of June 16, 2010 (http://www.thedailyshow.com/watch/wed-june-16-2010/an-energy-independent-future), showing a hilarious but at the same time scary set of videos starring the last eight presidents of the USA (all presidencies since the first energy crisis of the 1970s) talking to the nation about the energy crisis. It shows that over these four decades, when coming to the 'energy issue' the essence of their speech has not changed one little bit: 'very soon, the USA will move beyond the petroleum dependence and dependence on imports'. Beside the fact that this never happened and that the US dependence on both fossil energy and imports has been increasing in these four decades, all the presidential talks shown in the videos share the assumptions that: (i) it would be better for the US economy to produce energy carriers using alternative energy sources different from oil; and (ii) it is possible to do so in a decade or two (they all define very close deadlines for achieving the promised results).

Decision-making under uncertainty

Unfortunately, granfalloons and ostrich policies are not the only reasons for concern. Also the large dose of uncertainty (genuine ignorance) affecting any discussion of our energy future is worrisome. We have clearly expressed our concern about the energy future but it may well be possible that some of the innovative technologies that are presently in a premature stage of development (e.g. generation of hydrocarbon from genetically modified organisms, photovoltaic of the nth generation, and/or the mythical fusion) will eventually provide the badly needed 'plan B', a desirable and viable alternative to oil.

What is certain though is that we have to resort to a strategy of trial and error to deal with the present energetic predicament. The question is how expensive will these trials and errors be. Can we or can't we afford to invest in any crazy idea that may or may not result useful in the distant future? In the field of energy these questions are daunting. Long-term energy planning requires us to make important decisions entailing expensive investments without having in hand any reliable information on the possibility of success. In this situation one can only adopt a belief-based style of decision-making. Chi-Jen Yang comments on this uncomfortable situation:

> One cannot rationally choose between one unknown and another unknown... It is hard to say whether a belief-based decision is rational or irrational... decision makers have to make a choice without sufficient information that could fully justify any of the possible options... in such contexts, in other words, it is rational to be irrational.
>
> (Chi-Jen Yang, 2009, p. 8)

Still, beliefs have to be backed up by some informed reasoning. We have argued in this book that it is extremely important to have a basic understanding of the general features determining the existing energetic predicament and of the characteristics that are relevant to assess the quality of energy technologies. We claim that at present, apart from a tiny group of scholars dedicated to the study of the biophysical roots of the economic process, such understanding is lacking as witnessed by ongoing discussions over energy and sustainability and recent embarrassing blunders in energy policies, including heavy investments in agro bio-fuels and the big hopes for a nuclear renaissance. There are errors that can be avoided without the need for trials. Modern civilization is based on the human ability of using oil for making food (it saves land and labour). The idea of investing labour and land to make oil using food is bizarre, to say the least. Instead of investing money into the generation and maintenance of expensive white elephants, it certainly would help if the institutions in charge of designing and implementing energy policies would invest money in scientific research aimed at:

• clarifying the present terms of the energetic predicament;

- characterizing typologies of feasible metabolic patterns, by analyzing countries at different levels of technological progress;
- generating scenarios of viable metabolic patterns (viability domain) that allow for the informed elimination of nonsense policies and energy technologies (those predictably leading to unfeasible paths of development) from the list of options under consideration.

This would leave more resources for investment in the more promising technological innovations.

Unfortunately, after their victory over the prophets-of-doom in the bitter confrontation of the 1970s, Cornucopians have shaped the evolution of the debate on sustainability in the academic universe. Their conviction in perpetual economic growth on a finite planet seeped into all scientific endeavour. The study of energetics, which boomed in the 1970s, was simply abandoned in almost all academic programs. Great scholars, like Georgescu-Roegen, the father of bioeconomics, Odum, the father of system ecology, were marginalized. Scientific research on the biophysical roots of the economic process was, and still is, no longer fashionable. University programs on energy and development are now run by economists who base their accounting on the category of 'energy commodities' and study possible structural changes in the socio-economic system using prices. Given the crucial importance of the issue of scale in the analysis of the metabolic pattern of society, using prices to study structural changes of the economy is like using a microscope to study the ecology of elephants. Hall *et al.* nicely frame the present situation of the research on energy analysis as follows:

> There are not even targeted programs in NSF or the Department of Energy where one might apply if one wishes to undertake good objective, peer reviewed EROI analyses. Consequently much of what is written about energy is woefully misinformed or simply advocacy by various groups that hope to profit from various perceived alternatives.
>
> (Hall *et al.*, 2008, p. 121)

In this book, we have shown that it is possible to generate relevant information through energy analysis. We are well aware that no model can predict the future, and this applies also to the quantitative analysis developed with the MuSIASEM grammar. Still we claim that by combining semantic and formal analyses it is possible to generate a reliable body of knowledge that can help in selecting useful narratives in the discussion and making of energy policy. If we also apply some system thinking and innovative concepts (e.g. multi-scale analysis, impredicative loop analysis, sudoku effect) we can even generate robust scenarios and filter out impractical options. Unfortunately, as observed by Hall *et al.* (2008) in the previous quote, those carrying out theoretical studies of energy analysis do not even have the option of applying for research funds. Funds are only invested in solving the problem; in implementing a cure without bothering to learn first about the nature of the disease.

Appendix 1

The historical roots of the ambiguity of the quantification of energy

A.1 The beginnings of the field of energetics

At the time of Galileo and Newton, when the objectives of scientific investigation were still relatively simple, the description of events in classical mechanics was and could be based on: (i) a very small set of relevant attributes (e.g. position, speed, acceleration); and (ii) the adoption of a single scale at a time. In this situation a simple equation (e.g. $F = m \times a$) can be used to describe and predict the movements of both billiard balls and planets. The analysis of these energy exchanges could be handled with simple analytical tools, but only one scale at a time (by introducing the concept of force). For this reason a complex set of energy transformations cannot be described in a deterministic way according to the dictates of reductionism (one scale and a hierarchical level of organization at the time). This fact explains why the field of energetics – a systemic study of transformations among different energy forms – represented the first revolution in the classic universe of science: thermodynamics was developed outside the domain of traditional physics.

Much of the epistemological problems encountered in the field of energetics can be better understood in a historic light. The science of energetics was not developed within an established academic setting. On the contrary it started as an economic/engineering enterprise, in which theoretical discussions were following practical applications. For this reason, energetics started as a confused claim on the possibility of developing a science aimed at describing, measuring, studying, controlling and exploiting energy transformations – all types of energy transformations – as stated by Rankine in his introductory lectures.

Following the first experiments of the pioneers in this field, such as Carnot (1824) and Clapeyron (1834), it soon became clear that it was indeed possible to establish certain general relations in the process of conversions of heat energy into mechanical work (Joule, 1845). Based on this expected relation the 'science of energy' quickly experienced an extraordinary development. However, the academic interest was inspired by three distinct groups of pioneers, motivated by different interests and operating against different cultural backgrounds (Smith, 1998).

Of these groups, the most active one was based in Scotland and included no less than William Thomson (Lord Kelvin), James Joule, William Rankine, and James Maxwell. These brilliant men were not only scientists but above all engineers involved with the building and selling of engines and technology. They considered the theoretical development of this field, which Rankine baptized 'energetics', essential to gain credibility among potential buyers. To them, academic recognition meant a commercial edge on the competition, at that time populated by practitioners without a solid theoretical background.

A second group, with Wilhelm Ostwald and Georg Helm as leaders, was based in Germany. These scientists were looking for a new science of energy, capable of providing an alternative to the leading mechanical view of the external world (Ostwald, 1907; 1911). Ostwald, a professor of physical chemistry, after winning the Nobel Prize in Chemistry in 1909, became obsessed with the idea of establishing a new scientific discipline of energetics ('der energetische imperativ' or the energetic imperative) applicable to many domains of analysis, including the study of the functioning of human society.

A third group of scientists with heterogeneous backgrounds was concerned mainly with 'eliminating thermodynamics from its energetistic embellishments ... and the taking of some bold steps in the direction of axiomatization' (Smith, 1998, p. 68). This group includes names such as Ludwig Boltzmann, Max Plank and J. Willard Gibbs, who were key actors in strengthening the quantitative rigour of the formulation of thermodynamic laws.

The problem of how to use the abundant supply of coal to power prime movers to be used within the economy was a key driver of this scientific field. As a matter of fact, Fermi (1956, p. ix) was extremely clear when expressing his opinion about thermodynamics: 'Thermodynamics is mainly concerned with the transformation of heat into mechanical work, and the opposite transformation of mechanical work into heat'.

What is relevant to our discussion on energy analysis is the methodological approach used by the pioneers of this field to axiomatize and bring rigour to the analysis of energy transformations. In relation to this point Bridgman says: 'the energy concept has no meaning apart from a corresponding process. One cannot speak of the equivalence of the energy of mass and radiation unless there is some process (not necessarily reversible) by which one can get from mass to radiation' (Bridgman, 1961).

The quantitative analysis of the expected relations in a set of energy transformations was based on the definition of standard 'typologies' (definition of equivalence classes) of both energy forms and energy transformations. That is, typologies of energy forms and transformations (enthalpy transfer, adiabatic expansions, etc.) were imagined to take place in controlled settings: thermodynamic cycles. An example of this type of analysis is the Rankine cycle illustrated in Figure 1.2, page 20.

The result of this work was an axiomatization and rigorous analysis of the expected relations over investigated cycles. However, this extraordinary result was possible only because of the heroic simplifications adopted in describing the 'external world'.

The definitions of energy forms and the possible set of transformations were expressed in a predicative way. The external world of classic thermodynamics in which the thermodynamic cycles can take place – the associative context in which the thermodynamic variables make sense – is a world made of pipes, pistons, containers under pressure, and steam generators, whose performance is associated with ideal realizations.

As illustrated in Figure. 1.2, page 20, the set of energy forms and the set of energy conversions associated with the Rankine cycle (the predicative description of the energy transformation on the right of the figure) require the existence of a set of organized structures (on the left of the figure) capable of guaranteeing the validity of the ideal types used in the representation. These structures, by default, map onto the generic representation of energy transformations given in the cycle.

In the world of classic thermodynamics, the pipes should not leak, the containers should not explode, the pistons should have negligible frictions, but above all the transformations should be reversible for the ideal cycles. Ideal cycles are needed in order to have a standard against which to measure the efficiency of real cycles. The assumptions required to operate thermodynamic equations entail that the transformations can be measured and controlled within the required accuracy: the energy forms are well-defined and the system attributes do not change over the duration of the analysis. There are no other energy forms outside the closed set considered in the quantitative analysis.

A.2 The historical cause of the neglect of the issue of time scale in energetics

If we look for a historical explanation for the neglect of the issue of time scale in energetics we find the existence of a strong ideological bias associated with the love of western science for reductionism. As observed earlier, the pioneers of energetics had to deal with the existence of two forms of energy of different natures which could not be reduced into a substantive formal representation: (i) potential energy; and (ii) kinetic/mechanical energy. After the industrial revolution, the energy form of reference for potential energy became 'thermal energy', which later on was confused all together (in the practical accounting) with the calorific value associated with chemical bonds found in fossil energy. On the contrary, when dealing with kinetic energy it was always difficult to find a way to formalize it in substantive way, to the point that in the past kinetic energy was called *vis viva* – an expression that in Latin means 'living force'. The problem was generated by the fact that the quantification of the concepts of 'energy' and 'work' (quantities of energy without a time dimension) were not easily reducible to the quantification of concepts of 'force' (quantities of energy over a time dimension), without addressing the issue of scale. In fact, the definition of force has to do with the definition of a given power level: the coexistence of a flow element (the flow of energy input to be converted) and a fund element (the converter capable of realizing the conversion). Therefore, the presence of a time dimension in the quantitative assessment of energy transformation forces the analysts to deal with the issue of scale. As explained by Georgescu-Roegen (1971), in order to be able to define what is a flow and what is a fund element we must first of all define: (i) a time differential (the grain) used to describe changes in the flows; and (ii) a time duration (the extent) through which the fund elements are assumed to retain their original identity in the representation chosen by the analyst. For example, when considering a temporal scale, having an hour as time differential (the grain) and a year as time duration (the extent), a tractor is a fund element which is consuming fuel – a flow element. However, when considering a temporal scale having a year as time differential (the grain) and a century as time duration (the extent), the tractor becomes a flow element. That is, the number of tractors (the flow of power capacity) can be used to assess the technological input getting from the industrial sector – a fund element to the agricultural sector – another fund element in modern societies. That is, when dealing with the issue of multiple scales, any quantification is not 'substantive' but it depends on the pre-analytical definition of a relevant scale for the analysis. This source of impredicativity for quantitative analysis is a clear nuisance for reductionism. The rhetoric of an anonymous reviewer of Joule's Scientific Papers in the *Philosophical Magazine* (1884) describing Joule's achievement is very instructive:

> Not Copernicus and Galilei [sic], when they abolished the Ptolemaic system; not Newton, when he annihilated the Cartesian vortices; not Young and Fresnel, when they exploded the 'Corpuscular Theory'; not Faraday and Clerk-Maxwell, in their splendid victory over 'Actio in distans' – more thoroughly shattered a malignant and dangerous heresy, than did Joule when he overthrew the baleful giant FORCE, and firmly established, by lawful means, the beneficient rule of the rightful monarchy, ENERGY!
>
> (quoted in Smith, 1998, p.1)

It is clear from the series of emphatic statements given by this zealot reviewer that eliminating from the quantitative analysis the special attributes which must be associated with the concept of 'force' (requiring impredicativity in the choice of a relevant scale for its perception and pertinent representation – Giampietro *et al.* 2006) represented a big achievement for those working in energetics. Expelling the epistemological conundrum associated with the issue of scale (linked to the concept of force) paved the way for the application of reductionism to the science of energy. In fact, the need to reference a given power level – which entails the unavoidable existence of different typologies of converters and conversions to be carried out at different scales – entails acknowledging the fact that any chosen quantitative representation is only valid for the specific scale chosen and its pertinent descriptive domain. Thus, it is only when eliminating the reference to power levels that 'energy' and 'work' can finally be formalized in general terms using 'standard typologies of transformations' valid across different scales and descriptive domains.

> ... thermodynamic theory assumes that any motion can be reversible, if its speed is infinitesimally slow. Such a speed does eliminate friction from the

picture, but it introduces an even more essential obstacle. With an infinitesimally slow speed a piston would take an infinite time to move over any finite
distance.

(Georgescu-Roegen, 1979, pp. 1032–1033)

It should be noted that with the introduction of ideal thermodynamic cycles based
on assumptions of speed infinitesimally slow, the 'issue of power' and the issue
of scale were only apparently eliminated. We all know that the efficiency of a
given engine depends on the power level at which the engine is operated. For
example, the mileage of a car depends on the average speed at which it travels.

The relation between these two variables – the mileage (efficiency) and speed
(power) – is well known through experience by anyone driving a car. Therefore,
it should be possible to study such a relation using thermodynamic principles,
within the universe of classic thermodynamics, since physical laws and relative
equations should have a universal validity. However, if we try to study the relation between 'efficiency' and 'power' using thermodynamic cycles we would
discover that when dealing with different ranges of power levels we have to use
different types of thermodynamic cycles.

Put another way, we can obtain a quantification of the relation between efficiency and power level by studying expected relations between thermodynamic
variables within the Otto cycle to describe the performance of a car engine
running on gasoline. However, the identity of this cycle comes with a 'scale tag'
which is associated with the class of organized structure carrying out the transformations indicated in the chosen cycle (endothermic engines used in cars).

If we need to generate enough power to fly a Jumbo jet, then we should use a
different characterization of thermodynamic cycles – e.g. the Brayton cycle for
gas turbines used in an aeroplane engine. Again we find that the impredicative
definitions of the two concepts of 'efficiency level' and 'power level' in the
chosen thermodynamic cycle generate a quantitative representation which is scale
dependent. Depending on the range of power levels (a few HP or thousands of
HP), we will have to use different structural devices for conversions (different
typologies of power capacity) and therefore we will have to make reference to
different thermodynamic cycles for the resulting quantitative analysis. Those
willing to study the relation between efficiency and power level can only do so
after having individuated a specific range of power level, which in turn is associated with the need for using a specific thermodynamic cycle for the analysis.
'Certainly we cannot launch a rocket by heating the propelling gas with one
match flame after another.' (Georgescu-Roegen, 1977, p. 268.) At this point we
can go back to the discussion of the 'type' of information which is lost when
getting rid of the concept of force. Even students know that the representation of
a force requires the use of a vector, whereas the assessments of energy and work
are scalar quantities. In fact, the representation of a force entails two qualitative
aspects that clearly distinguish it from a scalar assessment. First, in a vector the
'quantitative information' (the length of the vector) must be combined to a spatial
reference: the direction and the sense of direction. Second, the very concept of

force is associated with a perception and representation of a change in time (so a time differential must be adopted in the analysis). In classical mechanics a force is what generates acceleration and acceleration is what is determined by a force. Hence, both the perception and the representation of force and acceleration are defined in an impredicative way (Rosen, 1985). That is the concept of force makes it possible to define the identity of a given state space (the method used to generate a quantitative representation) in relation to the pre-analytical choice of a given time–space differential. Therefore the concept of force requires a pre-analytical definition of the scale in order to be able to operate a measurement scheme and generate a quantitative analysis.

Using the same equation of motion we can define the motion of both planets and billiard balls. However, after having implemented this impredicative definition, if we want to generate a quantitative analysis, at the moment of using a measurement scheme, we are forced to select the scale – the 'grain' and the 'extent' used to measure and represent the movements of either billiard balls or planets. The issue of scale entails that the measurement scheme used to quantify the position and the speed of planets is not compatible with the measurement scheme used to quantify the position and speed of billiard balls (recall the discussion related to the joke of the Funtavesaurus in Figure 1.2, page 20). For these reasons, any quantification and representation of a 'force' requires a pre-analytical definition of a space–time scale for the domain used to describe changes in speed that defines: (i) the space–time differential (grain) in relation to (ii) the space–time domain of the analysis (extent). This is where the issue of scale enters into play when considering the physical 'size' of the energy converter required to express the required power capacity.

Concluding this section we can say that the issue of scale may be neglected in the ideal universe of mechanics, since mechanics refers to the analysis of expected relations over types, which are by definition out of scale (Allen and Starr, 1982; Giampietro *et al.*, 2006). In this ideal world, the issue of scale becomes relevant only in relation to the step of measurement, which is outside of the universe of quantitative analysis. The issue of scale can also be neglected, to a certain extent (after having selected a pertinent representation of the process to be modelled), in the ideal world of classic thermodynamics, made up of pipes, frictionless cylinders and isolated containers, where the structural setting is made by design, does not change in time and it is assumed to be pertinent by default. But the issue of scale cannot be neglected when dealing with the complexity of life in which humans operate: energy is about actual changes taking place in a finite time over physical realizations of types. Physical realizations of types are necessarily space–time scaled, they are path-dependent and therefore they have a metabolic identity which makes them all 'special'.

A.3 The second revolution of non-equilibrium thermodynamics

The first big epistemological revolution in science started in the first half of the nineteenth century in the field of classic (equilibrium) thermodynamics, with the introduction of the arrow of time. Equilibrium thermodynamics represented a first departure from mechanistic epistemology by introducing new concepts such as irreversibility and symmetry breaking: when describing real world processes nothing can be the same when it happens for the second time. The world of classic mechanics was shattered by the concept of indeterminacy when attempting to bridge the non-equivalent representation referring to the micro and the macro level.

The second revolution of non-equilibrium thermodynamics was initiated by the ideas of surplus entropy disposal by Schrödinger (1967, in an added note to Chapter VI of *What is Life*, 1945) and then by the work of the Prigogine school (Prigogine, 1961; Glansdorff and Prigogine, 1971; Nicolis and Prigogine, 1977; Prigogine, 1978; Prigogine and Stengers, 1984), with the introduction of the class of dissipative systems.

This change in narrative about energy conversions can only be handled after having abandoned one of the main ideological assumptions of reductionism: the possibility of defining a substantive representation of an event which is 'the same' for different observers and agents operating in different dimensions and scales. The revolution introduced by non-equilibrium thermodynamics was that entropy can be perceived as either good or bad depending on the perspective (or pre-analytical narrative) adopted for the analysis. Since dissipative systems are open systems feeding on 'negative entropy' (the expression coined by Schrödinger), they must take from their context what is good for them (producing a lot of entropy to be exported to the environment), which can have a negative result for the context. Clearly, the perspective from the inside (the more energy is dissipated, the more power is expressed, the better is the situation) has to be compatible with the existing boundary conditions (the context must make this discharge of entropy possible). In any case, with the introduction of the new non-equilibrium paradigm, quantitative science was confronted with the fact that, when dealing with complex dissipative systems, scientists can only work with system-dependent and context-dependent definitions of entities, which, to make things more difficult, change their identity in time.

As a consequence of this fact, in biology and ecology it was soon recognized that when dealing with living systems it is necessary to always adopt an impredicative definition of energy forms. Dissipative systems, especially those capable of expressing a clear activity of self-organization on a large scale, such as living systems, ecological systems or socio-economic systems, rapidly gained interest as a new relevant class of autopoietic systems associated with the ability of metabolizing energy. The epistemological revolution introduced by the concept of life is that it is impossible to develop in general terms an effective and useful accounting scheme which would provide useful information if we want to consider at the same time the point of view of a living system together with the point of view of its context. The non-equilibrium thermodynamic of living systems entails the existence of a Yin-Yang tension in the relative analysis. Living systems, and more generally autopoietic systems, (systems making themselves) can only be described by adopting two non-equivalent views: (i) the view from inside the system – useful to describe the energy transformations of the parts operating within the black box (the ability to express power and generate entropy to be exported to the context); and (ii) the view from outside the system – to describe the energy transformations associated with the interaction of the black box (seen as a whole) and its environment (the ability to maintain favourable boundary conditions for the dissipative system, in spite of its activity). These two views are not reducible to each other. Therefore, the epistemological challenges posed by the analysis of living systems bring us back to the problem generated by the need to simultaneously handle multiple scales and non-equivalent descriptive domains.

Unfortunately, this dramatic change of narratives in thermodynamics, in the scientific perception of the role of energy transformations in the process of self-organization of complex autopoietic systems, was pretty much ignored by the practictioners of energy accounting. In fact, the most important field of application of energy accounting, so far, has been engineering, in which the optimization of energy transformations take place in human made plants. When dealing with the energetic of industrial plants these innovative concepts referring to life and self-organization are neither needed nor applicable. An industrial plant is made by design and it does not self-organize in time. Therefore, because of this reason, it is possible to define for industrial plants clear goals, costs and operating conditions. These characteristics make it possible to apply to them concepts derived from classic thermodynamics with success (e.g. exergy analysis). When dealing with the performance of industrial plants, reductionism can represent an invaluable tool to generate useful quantitative analysis.

We list below four theoretical concepts associated with the class of complex self-organizing systems which have been studied under different names: 'complex adaptive systems' (Holland, 2006; Gell-Mann 1994); 'autopoietic systems' (Maturana and Varela, 1980, 1998; Kampis, 1991); 'metabolic systems' (Odum, H.T., 1971; 1996; Ulanowicz, 1986; Fischer-Kowalski and Haberl, 2007; Giampietro *et al.*, 2011):

1: Autopoiesis

These self-organising systems define for themselves which energy forms are relevant for analyzing their energetics (metabolic pattern). Autopoietic indicates 'the circular organization' of living systems and the dynamics of the autonomy proper to them as a whole. For this reason, it is impossible to apply the standard characterization useful in classical thermodynamics to these systems. For example, Schneider and Kay (1994, p. 26) introduced 'the restated second law' as: 'ecosystems will develop structures and functions selected to most effectively dissipate the gradients imposed on them while allowing for the continued existence of the ecosystem'. However, Schneider and Kay were forced to admit the difficulty in formalizing entropy and entropy production in general terms for non-equilibrium systems, a difficulty which is reflected in an unavoidable ambiguity in the meaning of the expression 'gradients'.

As a matter of fact, the very definition of 'life' has been associated with this peculiarity. Schrödinger (1967) addressed the special status of living systems in his short book carrying the provocative title: *What is life?* His main point is that living systems have an identity which imposes a given perspective on the external world. To make this point, Schrödinger introduces a controversial narrative: that of living systems feeding on 'negative entropy' (negentropy). This entails that the definition of negentropy must be specified for different typologies of living systems.

The concept of negentropy was reformulated later on in a more conventional way as 'the existence of a "system-specific" set of favourable boundary conditions determining the possibility for the living system to discharge entropy'. However, in our interpretation the main point of Schrödinger remains valid: an operational definition of what should be considered as 'a resource' or what should be considered as 'waste' for a living system is not substantive, but it depends on the identity (in particular the specific characteristics) of the metabolic system under study. For example, human excrements are waste for modern humans but at the same time a valuable resource for soil insects.

This impredicative definition of energetic concepts – in particular that the specific definition of potential energy depends on the identity of the converter – entails a loss of relevance of the general principles developed in classic thermodynamics:

> No one is claiming that the first law of thermodynamics is in error. It is only that its utility is nowhere as universally great as most think it to be. In ecology, as in all other disciplines that treat dissipative systems, the first law is not violated, but it simply does not tell us very much that is interesting about how a system is behaving...
>
> (Ulanowicz, 1997, p. 24)

According to another pioneer of teheoretical ecology, H.T. Odum, ecosystems are self-organizing through 'informed autocatalytic loops' (Odum, 1971). This implies that they use recipes (recorded information) to guide their process of self-organization and this translates into a definition of a metabolic identity 'frozen' in time (their path dependent definition of negative entropy).

2: Multi-scale analysis must use non-equivalent representations

The second condition concerns the fact that these systems operate on multiple scales and hence they require the simultaneous adoption of non-equivalent representations. The example of the failure to develop one single assessment for the energetic equivalent of one hour of human labour may illustrate this point (see Table 2.1, page 40). Every time we choose a particular hierarchical level of analysis for assessing an energy flow (e.g. an individual worker over a day) we also have to select a space-time scale at which we will describe the relative set of energy conversions. When dealing with general concepts – such as the energetics of human labour – depending on the purpose of the analysis the resulting set of relevant energy flows may be assessed either over the time span of an hour, a day, a month, a year, the entire life-span of the worker, or even in relation to the community to which the worker belongs. Depending on the narrative we choose, we have to adopt a non-equivalent definition of the worker's context (environment) and as a consequence of this choice we will generate an assessment not reducible to the others. If workers are seen as individuals operating over a one-hour time period, then muscles are our energy converters, operating within the human body. If workers are seen as members of a community, then individual human beings are the basic functional units operating within the community. According to the goal of the analysis, the definition of the identity of the basic converters using energy input must result compatible with the identity of the energy carriers: individual human beings eat food while developed countries eat fossil energy. This implies that, whatever we choose as a quantitative model to carry out energy analysis, the various identities involved: the energy carriers, parts, whole and environment, have to make sense in their reciprocal constraining. Obviously, distinct choices of focal level also require the adoption of distinct systems of accounting for inputs and outputs.

3: Becoming systems

Systems far away from thermodynamic equilibrium are becoming in time because of their metabolic nature. Therefore social and ecological systems are always qualitatively as well as quantitatively evolving or co-evolving with their environment. According to the vivid image proposed by Prigogine in his book *From being to becoming* (1978) the predicament of modeling those systems is that dissipative systems are always 'becoming' something else in time. This characteristic makes a substantive formal representation of their energetic interactions with their context virtually impossible. Given this unavoidable evolutionary nature, a predicative representation – the standard tool of hard science – is far from satisfactory for simulating their evolution (Giampietro et al, 2011).

The phenomenon of emergence, typical of living and social systems, points at the obvious but often neglected fact that a metabolic system requires a continuous update of the selection of approaches used for their quantitative analysis.

4: The strength of their identity depends on their power level

Their ability to metabolize energy flows in time (power level or metabolic rate) is essential for expressing functions and reproducing themselves. As a matter of fact, the drive toward an increased metabolic rate can be related directly to the second law of thermodynamics. In their interpretation of the second law Schneider and Kay state that '...ecosystems develop in a way which systematically increases their ability to degrade the incoming solar energy...' (Schneider and Kay, 1994, p. 38). A similar view had already been presented under a different guise, by the energetic analysis of living systems by A.J. Lotka: '...in the struggle for existence, the advantage must go to those organisms whose energy capturing devices are most efficient in directing available energies into channels favorable to the preservation of the species...' (Lotka, 1922, p. 147).

Building on Lotka's maximum energy flux principle H.T. Odum proposed a general principle for the development of ecological systems: the maximum power principle (Odum and Pinkerton, 1955, elaborated further in Odum, 1996; see also Hall, 1995):

> Under the appropriate conditions, maximum power output is the criterion for the survival of many kinds of systems, both living and non-living. In other words, we are taking 'survival of the fittest' to mean persistence of those forms which can command the greatest useful energy per unit time (power output)...
>
> (Odum and Pinkerton, 1955, p. 332)

Similar ideas were adopted in the social sciences. For instance, Leslie White stated that 'the primary function of culture' determining the level of progress is its ability to 'harness and control energy' (White, 1943).

A.4 The implications of these four theoretical concepts

To wrap up our discussion about the challenges to be faced when developing an energy accounting for socio-economic systems, we can look at the experience had in the energetic analysis of ecosystems in theoretical ecology. Using the words of Robert Ulanowicz (1986; 1997), a pioneer of the energetic analysis of ecosystems, who focuses in particular on the pattern of growth and development of natural communities: '...a knowledge of the flow structure within a natural community is assumed to be sufficient to describe the behavior of far-from-equilibrium, self-organizing systems' (Ulanowicz, 1986).

The lesson of theoretical ecology is that an energetic analysis of complex networks of energy transformations is possible. However, such analysis has to be tailored on the specific characteristics of the complex system under study. It has to be based on the knowable characteristics of individual elements of the system – e.g. the species belonging to a given ecosystem – and the overall configuration of the resulting network – e.g. the set of community interactions. In scientific jargon, we say that such analysis requires a pre-analytical definition of a grammar – see Box A.1.

The definition of a grammar refers to the following set of pre-analytical choices (for a more detailed discussion see Chapter 6 in Giampietro *et al.*, 2011):

- taxonomy (the categories of categories) associated with the chosen narratives – the set of semantic and formal categories which are used in the analysis;
- relative vocabularies or the lists of both semantic and formal categories used in the representation;
- list of expected relations over the various categories determined by either logical connections (over the semantic categories) or a set of production rules

---

Box A.1 On the concept of grammar

A grammar is a set of expected relations between a given set of semantic categories and a given set of formal categories. With the expression 'semantic category' we refer to a definition of an equivalence class based on the common meaning assigned to a label. Examples of semantic categories are: 'primary energy sources' (which can include fossil energy, nuclear energy, solar energy, hydropower); 'exosomatic throughput'; 'energy carriers' (electricity, fuels, heat) or 'end uses' (illumination, transportation, refrigeration). With the expression 'formal category' we refer to a definition of an equivalence class that can be quantified using a numerical assessment based on a defined protocol and a related measurement scheme. Examples of formal categories are: 'Joules of thermal energy' and 'Watt' (Joule/sec), measuring a given form of power. In order to generate an effective quantitative energy analysis we need to handle simultaneously semantic and formal categories. More on this concept in Giampietro *et al.* (2011).

(over the formal categories) determining a given representation of these relations;

* availability of required data.

In practical terms, we can study the energetics of ecosystems in terms of indices and expected relations over components, but, in order to do so, we have first of all to adopt a representation of 'what the ecosystem is' and 'what the ecosystem does' which must be specific (in terms of the grammar adopted) for each typology of ecosystem considered. The grammar useful to describe the energetics of a marine ecosystem is different from the grammar useful to describe a terrestrial ecosystem. In the same way, the graphical representation useful for studying the energetics of a tropical forest is different from the graphical representation useful for representing a prairie.

A.5 The attempts to apply thermodynamic analysis to human societies

According to the material presented both in this appendix and in the main text of this book we can say that it is impossible to develop a substantive formalization – a universally valid protocol – to assess the energetics of complex autopoietic systems operating across scales and evolving in time.

Therefore, the theoretical umbrella of classical thermodynamics cannot be used to provide substantive quantitative indices of 'quality' in the accounting of generic 'energy flows' metabolized by generic 'socio-economic systems'. The attempts to define in substantive terms – 'once and for all' and 'one size fits all' – the quality of energy input are bound to fail when applied to complex metabolic systems operating across multiple scales far from thermodynamic equilibrium. In fact, for these systems none of the conditions required to operate thermodynamic equilibrium grammars is even close to being fulfilled.

Three main attempts in this direction are described in Box A.2.

Box A.2 Three attempts to deal in quantitative terms with the quality of energy in substantive terms

Entropy

Entropy has been often proposed as an index of quality of 'energy' (Georgescu-Roegen, 1971). However, the concept of entropy has always been used in a metaphorical way in relation to large-scale sustainability problems. In fact, it is almost impossible to find an operational application of the concept of entropy in the analysis of complex systems operating across multiple-scales. The only exception we found is the work of Murota and Tsuchida 1985 assessing the entropy balance of the whole planet Earth (see Mayumi and Giampietro, 2004).

Exergy

Exergy has been proposed (Rant, 1956; Szargut *et al.*, 1988, 1998) as a substantive index of quality for 'energy' – a label used with an unspecified categorization of the term energy. However, the very definition of exergy implies serious doubt about the possibility of achieving this goal. In fact, when adopting a very strict (ideal) thermodynamic definition of it, we should consider 'exergy' as a state variable of a thermodynamic system. This would require assuming that the environment with which the system is interacting is perfectly known and that it is not affected by the ongoing energy transformations. When adopting a more realistic definition of exergy, as proposed by Sven Jørgensen, who has been exploring for decades the applicability of the concept of exergy to the analysis of complex metabolic systems, exergy should be rather considered as: 'the maximum entropy-free energy a system is able to transfer to the environment. As seen from this definition, exergy (Ex) is not a state variable because it is dependent on the environment' (Jørgensen, 1982, p. 61).

A similar take can be found in the work of Gaudreau *et al.* (2009): 'Exergy is a context sensitive thermodynamic concept because it is always measured with respect to a reference environment'. But if we accept this point, when dealing with large-scale processes, e.g. time durations of several years and large space domains, it becomes impossible to define a meaningful reference environment. During a year the average temperature of the environment changes with the seasons and over the planet the boundary conditions are different in different places (night/day, north/south).

Moreover, as discussed earlier, the special internal characteristics of the metabolic systems do entail that it is impossible to define 'a priori' what should be considered as an input of energy (or exergy) and what as an output of work for the system (see Figure 1.3, page 24). In conclusion we can say that the movement from a quantitative analysis based on 'energy' to a quantitative analysis based on 'exergy' does not avoid the epistemological predicament implied by autopoietic systems. When dealing with the analysis of these systems it is their special identity that determines what should be considered an 'energy input'.

Calorific value equivalent

Incredible but true, using the calorific value to account and aggregate different energy forms is still a common practice. As noted by Cleveland: 'there is still a widespread use of aggregating different energy forms by their heat units' a practice that 'embodies a serious flaw: it ignores qualitative differences among energy vectors' (Cleveland, 2010). As we pointed out in Part I of this book, different energy forms can be aggregated only after adopting a clearly defined grammar and after having defined a set of criteria determining equivalence classes. The calorific value is just one of many possible criteria of equivalence. This means that different energy forms can certainly be aggregated using their calorimetric equivalence, but if and only if: (i) they are all used as fuels, within a specified integrated set of energy conversions; and (ii) their calorific value is the only relevant attribute of performance.

An example of this misuse of energy aggregation in the accounting of energy flows to characterize the metabolic pattern of complex societies can be found in the MEFA protocol (Haberl *et al.*, 2006). In this approach 'calorific equivalence' is used to sum together all different types of energy forms, including the energy of gasoline, of orange juice, and of manure (see Giampietro, 2006).

The new field of non-equilibrium thermodynamics proved to be very fruitful in terms of a semantic enrichment of our understanding of both life and evolution. However, it did not generate, so far, any useful quantitative method to represent in a systemic and substantive way relevant characteristics of the metabolic pattern of complex dissipative systems across scales. As discussed in the main text of this book, in order to carry out an energy analysis of complex metabolic systems we have to learn how to sum 'apples' and 'oranges' and how to deal with the issue of multiple scales. In relation to this goal, the analysts have to develop 'task-dependent grammars', which are specific for different types of quantitative analysis, and that have to be tailored on the specificity of the metabolic systems under study. In this book we tried to open a path in this direction.

Appendix 2

The tautology used to generate the quantitative assessments in the flow chart illustrated in Figure 4.2

In this section we examine the quantitative assessment of energy flows in the Sankey diagram illustrated in Figure 4.2, page 80, in relation to the inconsistency in the definition of different semantic categories all handled using a single system of quantitative representation. Looking at the graph, we see that on the extreme left of the graph there are incoming energy flows such as natural gas, coal, and oil – the energy input associated with the exploitation of primary energy sources (PES). They are all quantified using the unit 'quad'. Therefore, these 'quantities of energy' can safely be assigned to the semantic category 'gross energy equivalent assigned to primary energy sources'. However, within this overall assessment expressed in 'gross energy requirement' (GER) we still have to deal with the presence of two non-reducible semantic categories 'thermal energy' (fossil energy) and 'mechanical energy' (non-thermal electricity). This problem has been solved by adopting the partial substitution method for calculating non-thermal electricity (expressing mechanical energy inputs in their thermal equivalent), therefore the quantitative assessment of GER is using the thermal energy form of reference measured in 'quads'.

Because of this choice, at the top left of Figure 4.2, enclosed in the box labeled 'non-fossil PES for electricity', we have a series of virtual values of 'primary energy source consumption equivalent' that account for the electricity generated from non-fossil primary energy sources, such as solar, nuclear, hydro, wind and geothermal. These virtual values correspond to the calculation of the 'gross customer bill equivalent' for the donations (the electricity generated from non-fossil energy sources) in the example of the restaurant, page 63. To this purpose, the quads of *vis electrica* generated by non-thermal power plants are multiplied by a common factor of equivalence to generate an overall gross energy requirement (thermal) of electricity: 39.98 quads.

In the middle of the graph, the energy flows coming out of the energy sector, still measured in quads of GER-thermal, are divided into six compartments obtained by sub-dividing the traditional three sectors: (1) residential and commercial sector; (2) industrial sector; and (3) the transportation sector. The resulting six subsectors are: (1a) residential, (1b) commercial, (2) industrial (no change), (3a) auto, (3b) freight, and (3c) aviation sector.

For each one of these six compartments the 'quantities of energy' are respectively: (1a) **11.02 quads**, (1b) **8.37 quads**, (2) **23.49 quads**, (3a) **17.16 quads**; (3b) **7.77 quads**, and (3c) **3.39 quads**. These quantities, summing into a total of **71.2 quads**, are qualitatively different from the original amount of primary energy sources entering into the system (**97.1 quads** of GER-thermal). Using the terminology adopted by early energy analysts, we could say that the energy on the left is a sort of 'gross' energy used by the entire system (the whole economy in order to make energy carriers) while that in the middle we have flows of 'net' energy (the net supply of energy carriers) used by the various sectors of the economy. That is, using our terminology, the 'quantities of quads' in the middle of the graph cannot but refer to energy carriers having a well-defined identity. In fact, it is hard to imagine that the 3.39 quads of energy going into the aviation sector would consist of coal or electricity. But if this is true, then, due to the specificity of the activities carried out within different compartments, it is obvious that the quantitative assessments of these energy flows are referring to specific mixes of energy carriers of different kinds. For example, we can see from the graph that the residential sector consumes a mix made up of 4.62 quads of electricity, 4.47 quads of natural gas, and 1.44 quads of oil. Therefore, the numbers written in the middle of the graph must be referring to net quantities of energy carriers, difficult to aggregate in single number, and not to gross quantities of primary energy.

Let's now consider the structure of the flows in this graph. We can clearly see the existence of two types of losses: one refers to the loss of primary energy sources to make energy carriers, the other refers to the loss of energy carriers (of different kinds) to generate end uses. The existence of two different typologies of losses implies the need to make a logical distinction between semantic categories to be used in energy accounting.

First the logical difference between the semantic categories: (i) gross energy requirement-thermal; and (ii) net energy carriers in a mix of different kinds. This distinction entails the existence of an unavoidable amount of energy losses due to the conversion GER–NEC.

Conversion #1 from GER to NEC (losses for the generation of energy carriers)

97.1 quads (GER) minus 25.9 quads (losses#1 for electricity) → 71.2 quads of EC

Note: these figures are measured in quads of GER-thermal.

These 25.9 quads of losses are required by the laws of thermodynamics – see the Rankine cycle described in Chapter 1, page 12 in order to make possible the transformation of energy forms accounted as GER (thermal energy) into energy forms accounted as EC (a mix of thermal energy and *vis electrica*).

But after accepting this point, then we must conclude that the numbers written in the middle of the flow chart (after the losses) refer to energy quantities (expressed in 'quads') that have a different quality and therefore refer to the semantic category of 'energy carriers'. Whereas the numbers on the left of the flow chart (before the losses) refer to energy quantities (expressed in 'quads') belonging to the semantic category of 'gross energy requirement'.

Continuing our journey towards the right of the graph of Figure 4.2 we find a second set of conversions which implies an additional typology of energy loss. This second type of energy loss is associated with the transformation of quantities of energy carriers into quantities of power output (energy services) required for generating end uses.

Conversion #2 moving from EC to EU (for the generation of power output)

71.2 quads of EC minus 28.7 quads (losses#2) → 42.5 quads (EU)

What is the semantic category used to measure the losses#2?

It should be noted that when measuring this second conversion, the assessment of the losses from conversion of energy carriers into power output can only be referred to as quads of EC and no longer as quads of GER-thermal. The amount of *vis electrica* entering into an air conditioning is definitely made up of electricy power' measured in volt-amperes. In the same way, it is a net amount of joules of gasoline which is entering into the engine of a car. But if this is true, then the sum of these losses – 28.7 quads – is a number obtained by summing quads of *vis electrica* to quads of fuels and to quads of heat. This sum refers to quantities of energy referring to energy carriers of different kinds. Are these quantitative assessments – referring to different semantic categories of energy forms – summed without using any conversion factor?

In spite of this question, when looking at the overall balance given in Figure 4.2, we find that all numbers are expressed using the semantic category GER-thermal and the formal category 'quads'. These numbers provide a perfect balance: the total input (measured in joules of GER-thermal) on the left is matched by the sum of the three terms (measured in what?) on the right.

97.1 quads (GER) ←→ 42.5 quads (EU) + 25.9 quads (loss#1) + 28.7 quads (loss#2)

However, since 'apples' cannot be summed to 'oranges', such an overall balance of the energy flows expressed in a unique numeraire has to be based on some heroic as well as dubious assumptions made by the analysts. Let's consider these quantitative 'assessments' given on the right one at the time.

End uses

The 42.5 quads of 'End uses' are still expressed in quads of GER-thermal, whereas they clearly should not be. As noted earlier, it is impossible to quantify EU in quantitative terms using energy units, let alone when using quads of GER-thermal. This means that these numbers have been generated using standard factors of efficiency applied to generic conversions of energy carriers into generic typologies of end uses. That is, they have been obtained by reducing the amount of energy carriers used by power capacity by a certain fraction determined by the efficiency of the conversion process. Examples of these generic assessments of conversion include: 'the average efficiency of engines in transportation' or 'the average efficiency of air conditioners in cooling a room'. As a matter of fact, this is exactly the approach that has been used for making this flow chart. We can even identify the various conversion factors adopted by the analysts to generate the numbers found in Figure 4.2. For the residential, the commercial and the industrial sectors the quads of energy carriers (measured in GER) have been reduced by 20 per cent (quads of EC → 'quads' of EU), thus assuming an efficiency of power generation of 80 per cent. For the transportation sector we find a set of different conversion factors. For the auto sector a reduction of 75 per cent is applied (only 25% of the quads of energy carrier are accounted into end use), for the freight sector we see a reduction of 60 per cent, and for the aviation sector a reduction of 75 per cent is applied (efficiency of power generation of 25 per cent). As argued earlier, estimates of conversions of energy input into flows of applied power do not provide any reliable assessment of the actual usefulness of the work done in real situations (quads or joules of end uses cannot be defined). However, even if we would accept this method of quantification of end uses based on the application of a standard conversion factor (percentage of efficiency) in the transformation of energy carriers into useful energy – we should start the accounting using quantities of energy belonging to the category of 'energy carriers' – quantities of net energy and not gross energy requirement-thermal. If we want to express the losses associated with end uses in quantities of energy referring to GER-thermal, then we should first consider the overall effect of the series of two losses (GER → EC → EU). These in turn depend on the first conversion (the mix of primary energy sources used to make electricity and technical coefficients of the different power plants involved) and the second conversion (the mix of carriers used in the various compartments and the technical coefficients of the energy converters). Applying a standard flat 80 per cent of conversion efficiency to the different mixes of energy carriers (especially electricity) and different typologies of power capacity used in the residential, commercial and industrial sectors makes little sense.

Losses in the first conversion

The 25.9 quads of losses refer to the quantity of gross energy requirement lost in the generation of energy carriers. The problem with this specific representation is that these losses are considered and calculated only in relation to the production of electricity. But there are other losses associated with the making of energy carriers, such as the energy spent in oil fields and coal mines for extracting raw materials or in the refineries for the production of fuels. These additional losses are not considered in the assessment of this first conversion. Unless we specify the mix of primary energy sources used to generate electricity (energy carriers) and the mix of energy carriers used in the six sub-economic sectors represented in Figure 4.2, it is impossible to assess any systemic feature of these losses in relation to the efficiency of the whole economy.

Losses in the second conversion

As mentioned in the previous discussion of end uses, the assessment of 28.7 quads of losses in the second conversion refer to theoretical losses calculated on the basis of standard 'typical' efficiencies. This assessment refers to the fraction of energy carriers (e.g. the gasoline used by car or electric power used in illumination) lost in the conversion into end uses. Therefore, these numbers should be expressed in quads of energy carrier (quantities of energy mapping onto quantities of gasoline or *vis electrica*) and not in quads of GER-thermal (mapping onto tons of oil equivalent), given that the converters for which we calculate a typical efficiency can only consume their specific energy carriers.

An effective system of accounting of energy flows through the economy should keep track of the various conversions taking place across different energy forms (semantic categories) to avoid losing valuable information. It is essential to map: (i) the relation between the mix of primary energy sources and the gross energy requirement they generate; then (ii) the relation between gross energy requirement and the mix of energy carriers (first loss); and finally (iii) the relation between energy carriers (divided by type) and the end uses they power across different functional compartments of society (second loss).

However, if we sum together the two types of loss referring to different types of conversion (across different semantic categories of energy forms) we end up muddling the accounting of the efficiency of the individual conversions (that refer to an unspecified mix of different typologies of energy carriers used in an unspecified mix of different typologies of end uses). Because of this confusion it becomes difficult to use the quantitative information to study the characteristics of the metabolic pattern of modern societies and to make future scenarios.

Wrapping up this discussion, we can say that in the representation of Figure 4.2:

1   The numbers on the left of the graph report quantities of energy referring to gross energy requirement-thermal equivalent (the required number of restaurant customers, relevant for checking external constraints) – some of which are 'virtual'.
2   the numbers in the middle tell us about the energy carriers used in the society (the disposable cash for the charitable project).

3   The numbers on the right claim to tell us, using dubious protocols, about the final achievement (the services provided to retired musicians).

If we accept this narrative, then we must acknowledge the elephant in the room: the quantitative representation of 'overall energy losses' (54.6 quads) is located on the extreme right of the graph together with the 'achievements' (42.5 quads of end uses). It is easy to understand that this location is required to balance the accounting in syntactic terms (the two items on the right must sum up to the 97.1 quads entering and flowing through the society) but this location represents a logical incongruence in the representation.

This logical incongruence is highlighted by the fact that the theoretical assessments of quads of 'useful energy' in end uses – an energy form that cannot be quantified – are the basis for the quantitative balancing of such accounting. That is, the quantitative balancing of EC $\leftrightarrow$ EU is based on a tautology. Starting from theoretical estimates of typologies of conversions EC $\rightarrow$ EU the flat 80 per cent factor applied to the residential, commercial and industrial, and the other three flat conversion factors applied to the three sub-sectors of the transportation sector – they calculate the second type of losses. Then by subtracting these estimated losses from the amount of energy carriers in the middle, they finally fix the balance. Clearly, this tautological definition of quantitative assessments makes useless the quantitative information given on the right side of the flow chart.

This example backs up our claim that it is impossible to use a single system of quantification (e.g. joules of gross energy requirement thermal equivalent) to provide useful information in relation to both external constraints (what is needed by society) and internal constraints (the performance of individual sub-sectors of society).

References

Ahl, V. and Allen, T. F. H. 1996. *Hierarchy Theory*. Columbia University Press.

Al-Ghandoor A., Jaber J. O. and Al-Hinti I. 2009. Assessment of energy and exergy efficiencies of power generation sub-sector in Jordan. *Jordan Journal of Mechanical and Industrial Engineering* 3(1): 1–8.

Allen, T. F. H. and Hoekstra, T. W. 1992. *Toward a Unified Ecology*. New York, Columbia University Press.

Allen, T. F. H. and Starr, T. 1982. *Hierarchy: Perspectives for Ecological Complexity*. Chicago, University of Chicago Press.

Amendola, G. M. 2005. *Dall' energetica all'exergetica*. Rome, Aracne Editrice.

Ayres, R. U., Ayres, L. W. and Masini, A. 2005. An application of exergy analysis for five basic metals industries. In R. U. Ayres, A. Von Gleich and S. Gössling (eds) *Sustainable Metals Management*. Dordrecht, Kluwer Academic Publishers.

Ayres, R. U., van den Bergh, J. C. J. M. and Gowdy, J.M. 2001. Strong versus weak sustainability: economics, natural sciences and 'consilience'. *Environmental Ethics* 23 (1): 155–168.

Barker, J. 2011. How many 'energy slaves' do we employ? Altenergymag.com http://www.earthtoys.com/emagazine.php?issue_number=06.08.01&article=slaves

Batty, J. C., Hamad, S. N. and Keller, J. 1975. Energy inputs to irrigation. *Journal of Irrigation and Drainage* 101(4): 293–307.

Biennial International Workshop Advances in Energy Studies (BIWAES) 2010. http://www.societalmetabolism.org/aes2010.html

Board on Energy and Environmental Systems, National Research Council with Curt Suplee – The National Academies (BEES) 2008. *What You Need to Know About Energy Board on Energy and Environmental Systems*. http://www.nap.edu/catalog/12204.html

Brekke, K. A. 1997. *Economic Growth and the Environment: on the measurement of income and welfare*. Cheltenham, Edward Elgar.

Bridgman, P. 1961. *The Nature of Thermodynamics*. New York, Harper.

Brody, S. 1945. *Bioenergetics and Growth*. New York, Reinhold Publishing Co., p. 1023.

Bullard, C. W. III and Herendeen R. A. 1975. The energy cost of goods and services. *Energy Policy* (December 1975): 268–278.

Carnot, S. 1824. *Reflexions Sur la Puissance Motrice du Feu sur les Machines Propres a Developper cette Puissance*. Paris, Bachelier libraire.

Chapman, P. F. 1974. Energy costs: a review of methods. *Energy Policy* 2(2): 91–103.

Cipolla, C. 1965. *Guns, Sails and Empires: technological innovation and the early phases of European expansion, 1400–1700*. New York, Pantheon Books.

Clapeyron, E. (1834) 1960. Memoir on the motive power of heat. In E. Mendoza (ed.)

Reflections on the Motive Power of Fire and Other Papers on the SecondLaw of Thermodynamics. New York, Dover, pp.71–105.

Cleveland, C. 2010. Net energy analysis. *The Encyclopedia of Earth*. http://www.eoearth.org/article/Net_energy_analysis

Cleveland, C. J. and O'Connor, P. A. 2011. Energy return on investment (EROI) of oil shale. *Sustainability* 3: 2307–2322.

Cleveland, C. J., Costanza R., Hall, C. A. S. and Kaufmann, R. 1984. Energy and the U.S. Economy: a biophysical perspective. *Science* (August 31): 890–897.

Common, M. and Perrings, C. 1992. Towards an ecological economics of sustainability. *Ecological Economics* 6: 7–34.

Conrad, M. 1983. *Adaptability: the significance of variability from molecule to ecosystem.* New York, Plenum.

Cottrell, W. F. 1955. *Energy and Society: the relation between energy, social change, and economic development.* New York, McGraw-Hill.

Crane, D. 2003. Energy analysis: a primer. In R. Douthwaite (ed.) *Before the Wells Run Dry: Ireland's transition to renewable energy.* Green Books. http://ww.feaste.org/documents/wells/three/panel1.html

Daly, H. E. 1971. Toward a stationary-state economy. In J. Harte and R. Socolow (eds) *Patient Earth.* New York, Holt, Rinehart and Winston, pp. 226–244.

Daly, H. E. 1994. Operationalizing sustainable development by investing in natural capital., in A. M. Jansson, M. Hammer, C. Folke and R. Costanza (eds) *Investing in Natural Capital.* Washington, DC, Island Press, pp. 22–37.

Dekkers, W. A. Lange, J. M. and de Wit, C.T. 1978. Energy production and use in Dutch agriculture. *Netherlands Journal of Agricultural Sciences* 22: 107–118.

Dinçer, I. and Rosen, A. 2007. *Exergy: energy, environment and sustainable development.* Amsterdam, Elsevier.

Durnin, J. V. G. A. and Passmore, R. 1967. *Energy, Work and Leisure.* London, Heinemann.

Ehrlich, P. R. 1968. *The Population Bomb.* New York, Ballantine Books.

Eigen, M. 1971. Self organization of matter and the evolution of biological macro molecules. *Naturwissenschaften* 58(10): 465–523.

Energy Information Administration (EIA). 2011. *What is energy?* http://www.eia.gov/energyexplained/index.cfm?page=about_home

EPRI, 2011. US Water Consumption for Power Production. *The Next Half Century, Topical Report March 2002.* http://www.epriweb.com/public/000000000001006786.pdf

Ertsvag, I. 2001. Society exergy analysis: a comparison of different societies *Energy* 26: 253–270.

European Communities. 2004. Facing the challenge: the Lisbon strategy for growth and employment. Report from the high level group chaired by Wim Kok. Luxembourg, p. 10.

Eurostat 2007. http://ec.europa.eu/energy/energy_policy/doc/factsheets/mix/ mix_es_en.pdf

Fargione, J., Hill, J., Tilman, D., Polasky, S. and Hawthorne, P. 2008. Land clearing and the biofuel carbon debt. *Science* 319(5867): 1235–1238.

Farrell, A. E., Plevin, R. J., Turner, B. T., Jones, A. D., O'Hare, M. O. and Kammen D. M. 2006. 'Ethanol can contribute to energy and environmental goals', *Science* 311: 506–508.

Fermi, E. 1956. *Thermodynamics* New York, Dover.

Feynman, R., Leighton, B. and Sands, M. 1963. *The Feynman Lectures on Physics: mainly mechanics, radiation, and heat, volume I.* California, Addison-Wesley Publishing Company.

Fischer-Kowalski, M. and Haberl, H. 2007. *Socioecological Transitions and Global Change*. London, Edward Elgar.

Fluck, R. C. 1981. Net energy sequestered in agricultural labor. *Transactions of the American Society of Agricultural Engineers* 24: 1449–1455.

Fluck, R. C. 1992. Energy of human labor. In R. C. Fluck (ed.) *Energy in Farm Production* (Vol. 6 of *Energy in World Agriculture*). Amsterdam, Elsevier pp. 31–37.

Fraley, D. W. and McDonald, C. L. 1978. Issues in net energy analysis. In F. Roberts (ed.) *Symposium Papers: energy modelling and net energy analysis, Colorado Springs, August 21–25*. Chicago, Institute of Gas Technology pp. 161–181.

Fraser, R. A. and Kay, J. J. 2002. Exergy analysis of ecosystems: establishing a role for the thermal remote sensing. In D. Quattrocchi and J. Luvall J, (eds). *Thermal Remote Sensing in Land Surface Processes*. London, Taylor and Francis.

Funtowicz, S. O. and Ravetz, J. R. 1990. *Uncertainty and Quality in Science Policy*. Dordrecht, Kluwer Academic.

Gaudreau, K., Gibson, R. B., and Fraser, R. A. 2009. *Integrated Sustainability and Systems Assessment Applied to Small-Scale Biodiesel in Barbados*. http://www.scribd.com/doc/38563557/Gaudreau-Et-Al-Sustainability-Assessment-and-energetics

Gell-Mann, M. 1994. *The Quark and the Jaguar*. New York, W. H. Freeman and Company.

General Accounting Office (GAO) 1982. *DOE funds New Energy Technologies without Estimating Potential Net Energy Yields*. Washington DC, US General Accounting Office. http://www.legistorm.com/showFile/L2xzX3Njb3JlL2dhby9wZGYvMTk4Mi83/full113 19.pdf

Georgescu-Roegen, N. 1971. *The Entropy Law and the Economic Process*. Cambridge, Mass., Harvard University Press.

Georgescu-Roegen, N. 1975. Energy and economic myths. *Southern Economic Journal* 41: 347–381.

Georgescu-Roegen, N. 1979. Energy analysis and economic valuation. *Southern Economic Journal* 45: 1023–1058.

Gever, J., Kaufmann, R., Skole, D. and Vörösmarty, C. 1991. *Beyond Oil: the threat to food and fuel in the coming decades*. Niwot, University Press of Colorado.

Giampietro, M. 1997. Socioeconomic constraints to farming with biodiversity. *Agriculture, Ecosystems and Environment* 62: 145–167.

Giampietro, M. 2002. Energy use in agriculture. *Encyclopedia of Life Sciences*. Nature Publishing Group. http://www.els.net/

Giampietro, M. 2003. *Multi-Scale Integrated Analysis of Agro-ecosystems*. Boca Raton, CRC Press, p. 472.

Giampietro, M. 2006. Comments on 'The Energetic Metabolism of the European Union and the United States' by Haberl and Colleagues: theoretical and practical considerations on the meaning and usefulness of traditional energy analysis. *Journal of Industrial Ecology* 10(4): 173–185.

Giampietro, M. 2008. The future of agriculture: GMOs and the agonizing paradigm of industrial agriculture. In A. Guimaraes Pereira and S. Funtowicz, (eds) *Science for Policy: challenges and opportunities*. New Delhi, Oxford University Press.

Giampietro, M., Allen, T. F. H. and Mayumi, K. 2006. The epistemological predicament associated with purposive quantitative analysis. *Ecological Complexity* 3: 307–327.

Giampietro, M., Bukkens, S. G. F. and Pimentel, D. 1993. Labor productivity: a biophysical definition and assessment. *Human Ecology* 21(3): 229–260.

Giampietro, M., Bukkens, S. G. F. and Pimentel, D. 1997. The link between resources, technology and standard of living: examples and applications. In L. Freese (ed.) *Advances in Human Ecology, Volume 6.* Greenwich, CT, JAI Press, pp. 129–199.

Giampietro, M. and Mayumi, K. 1997. A dynamic model of socioeconomic systems based on hierarchy theory and its application to sustainability. *Structural Change and Economic Dynamics* 8(4): 453–470.

Giampietro, M. and Mayumi, K. 2000. Multiple-scale integrated assessment of societal metabolism: introducing the approach. *Population and Environment* 22(2): 109–154.

Giampietro, M and Mayumi, K. 2004. Complex systems and energy. In C. Cleveland (ed.) *Encyclopedia of energy* vol. 1. San Diego, CA, Elsevier, pp. 617–631.

Giampietro, M. and Mayumi, K. 2008. Complex systems thinking and renewable energy systems. In D. Pimentel (ed.) *Biofuels, Solar and Wind and Renewable Energy Systems: Benefits and Risks.* Ithaca, NY, Springer.

Giampietro, M. and Mayumi, K. 2009. *The Biofuel Delusion: the fallacy of large scale agro-biofuels production.* London, Earthscan.

Giampietro, M., Mayumi, K. and Munda, G. 2006. Integrated assessment and energy analysis: quality assurance in multi-criteria analysis of sustainability. *Energy* 31(1): 59–86.

Giampietro, M., Mayumi, K. and Sorman, A. H. 2011. *The Metabolic Pattern of Societies: where economists fall short.* London, Routledge.

Giampietro, M. and Pimentel, D. 1990. Assessment of the energetics of human labor. *Agriculture, Ecosystems and Environment* 32: 257–272.

Giampietro, M. and Pimentel, D. 1991. Energy efficiency: assessing the interaction between humans and their environment. *Ecological Economics* 4: 117–144.

Giampietro, M. and Pimentel, D. 1992. Energy efficiency and nutrition in societies based on human labor. *Ecology of Food and Nutrition* 28: 11–32.

Gilliland, M. W. 1975. Energy analysis and public policy: the energy unit measures environmental consequences, economic costs, material needs, and resource availability. *Science* 189: 1051–1056.

Glansdorff, P. and Prigogine, I. 1971. *Thermodynamics Theory of Structure, Stability and Fluctuations.* New York, Wiley.

Grinevald, J. 2007. La biosphère de l'anthropocène: climat et pétrole, la double menace. Repères transdicsiplinaires (1824–2007). *Stratégies énergétiques, Biosphère et Société* Geneva, Georg.

Grinevald, J. 1976. La révolution carnotiene: thermodynamique, économie et idéologie. *Revue européenne des sciences socials* 36: 39–79.

Haberl, H., Weisz, H., Amann, C., Bondeau, A., Eisenmenger, N., Erb, K.-H., Fischer-Kowalski, M. and Krausmann, F. 2006. The energetic metabolism of the EU-15 and the USA: decadal energy input time-series with an emphasis on biomass. *Journal of Industrial Ecology* 10(4): 151–171.

Hall, C. A. S 1995. *Maximum Power: the ideas and applications of H.T.Odum.* Boulder, CO, Colorado University Press.

Hall, C. A. S, Balogh, S. and Murphy, D. J. R. 2009. What is the minimum EROI that a sustainable society must have? *Energies* 2: 25–47. www.mdpi.com/journal/energies

Hall, C. A. S., Cleveland, C. J. and Berger, M. 1981. Energy return on investment for United States petroleum, coal and uranium. In W. J. Mitsch, R. W. Bosserman and J. M. Klopatek (eds) *Energy and Economic Modelling..* Amsterdam, Elsevier Scientific, pp. 715–724.

Hall, C. A. S., Cleveland, C. J. and Kaufmann, R. 1986. *Energy and Resource Quality: the Ecology of the Economic Process.* New York, Wiley-Interscience.

Hall, C. A. S. and Klitgaard, K. A. 2012. *Energy and the Wealth of Nations: understanding the biophysical economy.* Springer, p. 407.

Hall, C. A. S., Powers, R. and Schoenberg, W. 2008. Peak oil, EROI, investments and the economy in an uncertain future. In D. Pimentel (ed.) *Biofuels, Solar and Wind as Renewable Energy Systems.* Springer, pp. 109–132.

Hannon, B. 1973. The Structure of ecosystems. *Journal of Theoretical Biology* 41: 535–546.

Hardin, G. 1972. *Exploring New Ethics for Survival: the voyage of the spaceship Beagle.* New York, Viking Press.

Hardin, G. 1968. The Tragedy of the Commons. *Science* 162(3859): 1243–1248.

Hartwick, J. M. 1977. Intergenerational equity and the investing of rents from exhaustible resources. *American Economic Review* 67: 972–974.

Heinberg, R. 2005. *The Party's Over: oil, war and the fate of industrial societies*, 2nd edn. New Society Publishers.

Herendeen, R. A. 1978. Energy analysis of two technologies: gasohol and solar satellite power station. In F. Roberts (ed.) *Symposium Papers: energy modelling and net energy analysis, Colorado Springs, August 21–25, 1978.* Chicago, Institute of Gas Technology, pp. 145–159.

Herendeen, R. A. 1998. *Ecological numeracy: quantitative analysis of environmental issues.* New York, John Wiley & Sons.

Herendeen, R. A. 1998. Embodied energy, embodied everything ... now what? In S. Ulgiati, (ed.) *Advances in Energy Analysis: energy flows in ecology and economy.* Proceedings of the 1st Workshop, Advances in Energy Analysis, Porto Venere, Italy, 26–30 May 1998. Museo della Scienza e dell' Informazione Scientifica a Roma, Rome, pp. 13–48.

Herendeen, R. A. 2004. Goods and services: energy costs *Encyclopedia of Energy* 3: 33–41.

Herendeen, R. A., Kary, T. and Rebitzer, J. 1979. Energy analysis of the solar power satellite. *Science* 205(4405): 451–454.

Herold, A. 2003. Comparison of CO2 emission factors for fuels used in greenhouse gas inventories and consequences for monitoring and reporting under the EC emissions trading scheme., ETC/ACC Technical paper 2003/10, European Topic Centre on Air and Climate Change.

Heun, M. K. and de Wit, M. 2011. Energy return on (energy) invested (EROI), oil prices, and energy transitions. *Energy Policy* 1185(1): 102–118.

Holland, J. H. 2006. Studying complex adaptive systems *Journal of Systems Science and Complexity* 19: 1–8.

Holling, C. S. 1995. Biodiversity in the functioning of ecosystems: an ecological synthesis. In C. Perring (ed) *Biodiversity Loss.* Cambridge, Cambridge University Press, pp. 44–83.

Holling, C. S. 1973. Resilience and stability of ecological systems. *Annual Review of Ecological Systems*, 4: 1–24.

Hubbert, M. K. 1949. Energy from fossil fuels. *Science* 109: 103–109.

Hudson, J. C. 1975. Sugarcane: its energy relationship with fossil fuel. *Span* 18: 12–14.

Huettner, D. A. 1978. Energy analysis and ultimate limits. In F. Roberts (ed.) *Symposium Papers: energy modelling and net energy analysis, Colorado Springs, August 21–25, 1978.* Chicago, Institute of Gas Technology, pp. 279–288.

Huettner, D. A. 1976. Net energy analysis: an economic assessment. *Science* 192(4235): 101–104.

Institut d'Estadística de Catalunya (IDESCAT) 2011 http://www.idescat.cat/

Institute of Gas Technology (IGT) 1978. *Energy Modeling and Net Energy Analysis Symposium Papers August 21–25.* Colorado Springs, CO, Institute of Gas Technology.

International Energy Agency (IEA) 1975. Report of the NSF-Stanford Workshop on Net Energy Analysis: August 25–28, 1975. California, Institute of Energy Studies, Stanford University.

International Federation of Institutes for Advanced Study (IFIAS) 1974. Energy analysis: International Federation of Institutes for Advanced Study, Workshop on Methodology and Conventions – Report no. 6. Stockholm, IFIAS, p. 89.

International Federation of Institutes for Advanced Study (IFIAS) 1978. Workshop report:energy analysis and economics IFIAS, Lidingö, Sweden, June 1975. *Resources and Energy* 1: 151–204.

James, W. P. T. and Schofield, E. C. 1990. *Human energy requirement.* Oxford, Oxford University Press.

Jevons, W. S. (1865) 1906. *The Coal Question: an inquiry concerning the progress of the nation, and the probable exhaustion of our coal mines,* 3rd edn. New York, Augustus M. Kelley.

Joint Committee for Guides in Metrology Working Group 2 (JCGM/WG2) 2008. http://www.nist.gov/pml/div688/grp40/upload/International-Vocabulary-of-Metrology.pdf

Jones, M. R. 1989. Analysis of the use of energy in agriculture –approaches and problems. *Agricultural Systems* 29: 339–355.

Jørgensen, S. E. 1982. Exergy and buffering capacity in ecological systems. In W. J. Mitsch, R. K. Ragade, R. W. Bosserman and J. A. Dillon (eds) *Energetics and Systems.* Ann Arbor, Ann Arbor Science Publishers, pp. 61–72.

Joule, J. P. 1845. On the Mechanical Equivalent of Heat. *Brit. Assoc. Rep., trans. Chemical Sect.* Read at the British Association in Cambridge, p.31.

Kampis, G. 1991. *Self-Modifying Systems in Biology and Cognitive Science: a new framework for dynamics, information, and complexity.* Oxford, Pergamon Press, p. 543.

Kaufmann, R. and Hall, C. A. S. 1981. Energy return on investment for imported petroleum fuels. In W. J. Mitsch, R. W. Bosserman, and J. M. Klopatek (eds.) *Energy and Economic Modelling..* Amsterdam, Elsevier Scientific, pp. 697–701.

Kawamiya, N. 1983. *Entropii to Kougyoushakai no Sentaku* (English translation *Entropy and Future Choices for the Industrial Society*). Tokyo, Kaimei.

Kay, J. J. 2000. Ecosystems as self-organizing holarchic open systems: narratives and the second law of thermodynamics. In S. E. Jørgensen and F. Muller (eds) *Handbook of ecosystems theories and management.* London, Lewis Publishers, pp. 135–60.

Koestler, A. 1969. Beyond atomism and holism – the concept of the Holon. In A. Koestler A. 1968. *The Ghost in the Machine.* New York, MacMillan.

Koestler, A. 1978. *Janus: a summing up.* London, Hutchinson.

Koestler, A. and Smythies, J. R. (eds) *Beyond reductionism.* London, Hutchinson, 192–232.

Kubiszewski, I., Cleveland, C. J. and Endres, P. K. 2010. Meta-analysis of net energy return for wind power systems. *Renewable Energy* 35: 218–225.

Leach, G. 1975. Net energy analysis – is it any use? *Energy Policy* (December 1975): 332–344.

Lenzen, M. 2008. Life cycle energy and greenhouse gas emissions of nuclear energy: a review. *Energy Conversion & Management* 49: 2178–2199.

Leontief, W. W. 1986. *Input-Output Economics,* 2nd edn. New York, Oxford University Press.

Lawrence Livermore National Laboratory (LLNL) 2011. US Energy Flow Charts https://flowcharts.llnl.gov/

Long, T.V. II 1978. Comparing methods of energy analysis in an economic framework. In F. Roberts (ed.) *Symposium Papers: energy modelling and net energy analysis, Colorado Springs, August 21–25, 1978.* Chicago, Institute of Gas Technology, pp. 263–278.

Lotka, A. J. 1956. *Elements of Mathematical Biology.* New York, Dover.

Lotka, A. J. 1922. Contribution to the energetics of evolution. *Proceedings of the National Academy of Sciences* 8: 147–151.

Maddox, K. P. 1978. Energy analysis and resource substitution. In F. Roberts (ed.) *Symposium Papers: energy Modelling and Net Energy Analysis, Colorado Springs, August 21–25, 1978.* Chicago, Institute of Gas Technology, pp. 133–144.

Mansure, A. J. and Blankenship, D. A. 2010. Energy return on energy investment, an important figure-of-merit for assessing energy alternatives. *Proceedings Thirty-Fifth Workshop on Geothermal Reservoir Engineering*, Stanford University, (February 1–3) SGP-TR-188. http://pangea.stanford.edu/ERE/pdf/IGAstandard/SGW/2010/mansure.pdf

Margalef, R. 1968. *Perspectives in Ecological Theory.* Chicago, Univeristy of Chicago Press.

Martinez-Alier, J. 2011. The EROI of agriculture and its use by the Via Campesina. *The Journal of Peasant Studies* 38(1): 145–160.

Martinez-Alier, J. 1995. Political ecology, distributional conflicts and economic incom-mensurability. *New Left Review* 211: 70–88.

Martinez-Alier, J. 1987 *Ecological Economics.* Oxford, Basil Blackwell.

Maturana, H. R. and Varela, F. J. 1998. *The Tree of Knowledge: the biological roots of human understanding.* Boston, Shambhala Publications.

Maturana, H. R. and Varela, F. J. 1980. *Autopoiesis and Cognition: the realization of the living.* Hingham, MA, D. Reidel Publishing Company.

Maxwell, J. C. 1877. Hermann Ludwig Ferdinand Helmohotlz 1876–1877. *Nature* 15(March 8): 389–391.

Mayumi, K. 1991. Temporary emancipation from land: from the industrial revolution to the present time. *Ecological Economics* 4: 35–56.

Mayumi, K. and Giampietro, M. 2004. Entropy in ecological economics. In P. Safanov and J. Proops (eds) *Modelling in Ecological Economics.* Northhampton, MA, Edward Elgar, pp. 80–101.

Meadows, D. H., Randers J., Meadows D. L. and Behrens W. W. 1972. *The Limits to Growth: a report for the club of Rome's Project on the Predicament of Mankind.* Potomac Associates.

Mendelssohn, K. 1974. *The Riddle of the Pyramids.* London, Thames & Hudson.

Mitchell, C. and Cleveland, C. J. 1993. Resource scarcity, energy use and environmental impact: a case study of the New Bedford, Massachusetts, USA, Fisheries. *Environmental Management* 17(3): 305–317.

Mortimer, N.D. 1991. Energy analysis of renewable energy sources. *Energy Policy* (May): 374–385.

Murota, T. and Tsuchida, A. 1985. Fundamentals in the entropy theory of watercycle, ecocycle, and human economy. In *The Conference on Man's Coevolution with the Biosphere in the Age of Advanced Technology.* Toronto, York University, January 21–25.

Murphy, D. J. and Hall, C. A. S. 2011a. Energy return on investment, peak oil, and the end of economic growth. In R. Costanza, K. Limburg and I. Kubiszewski (eds) *Ecological Economics Reviews. Annals of the New York Academy of Sciences* 1219: 52–72.

Murphy, D. J. and Hall, C. A. S. 2011b. Adjusting the economy to the new energy realities of the second half of the age of oil. *Ecological Modelling* 223: 67–71.

Murphy, D. J., Hall, C. A. S., Dale, M. and Cleveland, C. 2011. Order from chaos: a preliminary protocol for determining the EROI of fuels. *Sustainability* 3: 1888–1907.

Nicolis, G. and Prigogine, I. 1977. *Self-Organization in Non-Equilibrium Systems*. New York, Wiley.

Nikiforuk, A. 2011. You and your slaves. *The Tyee 5 May 2011*. http://thetyee.ca/Opinion/2011/05/05/EnergySlaves/

Nilsson, S. and Kristofersen, L. 1976. Energy analysis and economics: report from an IFIAS workshop. *Ambio* 5(1): 27–29.

Norman, M. J. T. 1978. Energy inputs and outputs of subsistence cropping systems in the tropics. *Agro-Ecosystems* 4: 355–366.

North, D. C. 1990. *Institutions, Institutional Change and Economic Performance*. Cambridge University Press.

Nuclear Energy Institute 2011. http://www.nei.org/resourcesandstats/nuclear_statistics/ nuclearwasteamountsandonsitestorage/ visited 30th June 2011

Odum, E. P. 1971. *Fundamentals of Ecology*, third edition. Philadelphia, W. B. Saunders.

Odum, H. T. 1971. *Environment, Power, and Society*. New York, Wiley-Interscience.

Odum, H. T. 1973. Energy, ecology and economics. *AMBIO* 2(6): 220–227.

Odum, H. T. 1977. Letter to *Science* on energy analysis. *Science* (April 15): 261.Downloaded from www.sciencemag.org on April 14, 2010.

Odum, H. T. 1983. *Systems Ecology*. New York, John Wiley.

Odum, H. T. 1996. *Environmental Accounting: emergy and environmental decision making*. New York, John Wiley.

Odum, H. T. and Arding J. E. 1991. EMergy analysis of shrimp mariculture in Ecuador. *Department of Environmental Engineering Sciences, University of Florida, Working Paper prepared for Coastal Resources Center*. Narragansett, RI, University of Rhode Island. http://www.cep.ees.ufl.edu/pubs/OdumArding.1991.ShrimpEcuador.Working Paper.pdf

Odum, H. T. and Pinkerton, R. C. 1955. Time's speed regulator: the optimum efficiency for maximum power output in physical and biological systems. *American Scientist*, 43: 321–43.

O'Neill, R. V. 1989. Perspectives in hierarchy and scale. In J. Roughgarden, R. M. May and S. Levin (eds) *Perspectives in Ecological Theory*. Princeton, NJ, Princeton University Press.

O'Neill, R. V., DeAngelis, D. L., Waide, J. B. and Allen, T. F. H. 1986. *A Hierarchical Concept of Ecosystems*. Princeton, NJ, Princeton University Press.

Organisation for Economic Co-operation and Development/International Energy Agency (OECD/IEA) 2004. *Energy Statistics Manual*. http://www.iea.org/textbase/nppdf/free/ 2004/statistics_manual.pdf

Ostwald, W. 1911. Efficiency. *The Independent* 71: 867–871.

Ostwald, W. 1907. The modern theory of energetics. *The Monist* 17: 511.

Parolini, G. 1984. *Energetica – from the notes of the course (1976)*, Edizioni Sistema, Roma.

Pastore, G., Giampietro, M. and Mayumi, K. 2000. Societal metabolism and multiple-scale integrated assessment: empirical validation and examples of application. *Population and Environment* 22,(2): 211–254.

Pattee, H. H. (ed.) 1973. *Hierarchy Theory*. New York, George Braziller, Inc.

Pearce, D. W., Barbier, E. and Markandya, A. 1990. *Sustainable Development: economics and environment in the third world*. London, Edward Elgar and London, Earthscan.

Pimentel, D. and Pimentel, M. 1979. *Food Energy and Society*. London, Edward Arnold Ltd.

Poincaré, H. 1913. *The Foundations of Science* (Translated by G. B. Halsted). New York, The Science Press.

Prigogine, I. 1978. *From Being to Becoming*. San Francisco, W.H. Freeman.

Prigogine, I. 1961. *Introduction to Thermodynamics of Irreversible Processes*, 2nd edn. New York, Wiley.

Prigogine, I. and Stengers, I. 1984. *Order Out of Chaos*. New York, Bantam Books.

Proops, J. L. R. 1987. "Entropy, Information, and Confusion in the social sciences" *The Journal of Interdiscipinary Economics* 1: 225–242

Raadal, H. L., Gagnon, L., Modahl, I. S. and Hanssen, O. J. 2011. Life cycle greenhouse gas (GHG) emissions from the generation of wind and hydro power. *Renewable and Sustainable Energy Reviews* 15: 3417–3422.

Ramos-Martin, J., Cañella-Bolta, S., Giampietro, M. and Gamboa, G. 2009. Catalonia's energy metabolism: using the MuSIASEM approach at different scales. *Energy Policy* 37: 4658–4671.

Rankine, W. J. M. 1855. Outline of the science of energetics. *Proceedings of the Royal Philosophical Society of Glasgow* 3: 121–141. http://en.wikisource.org/wiki/Outlines_of_the_Science_of_Energetics

Rankine, W. J. M. 1853. On the general law of the transformation of energy *London, Edinburgh and Dublin Philosophical Magazine and Journal of Science*. Series 4, 5(30): 106–117.

Rant, Z. 1956. Exergy, a new word for technical available work (in German). *Forschungenim Ingenieurwesen*. 22(1): 36–37.

Rappaport, R. A. 1971. The flow of energy in an agricultural society. *Scientific American* 224: 117–133.

Revelle, R. 1976. Energy use in rural India. *Science* 192: 969–975.

Rosen, R. 2000. *Essays on Life Itself*. New York, Columbia University Press.

Rosen, R. 1985. *Anticipatory Systems: philosophical, mathematical and methodological foundations*. New York, Pergamon Press.

Salthe, S. N. 1985. *Evolving Hierarchical Systems*. New York, Columbia University Press.

Schneider, E. D. and Kay, J. J. 1994. Life as a manifestation of the second law of thermodynamics. *Mathematical and Computer Modelling* 19(6–8): 25–48.

Schrödinger, E. 1967. *What is Life & Mind and Matter*. Cambridge University Press.

Searchinger, T., Heimlich, R., Houghton, R.A., Dong, F., Elobeid, A., Fabiosa, J., Tokgoz, S., Hayes, D. and Yu, T.-H. 2008. Use of US croplands for biofuels increases greenhouse gases through emissions from land-use change. *Science* 319: 1238–1240.

Sedlik, B. R. 1978. Some theoretical considerations of net energy analysis. In F. Roberts (ed.) *Symposium Papers: energy Modelling and Net Energy Analysis, Colorado Springs, August 21–25, 1978*. Chicago, Institute of Gas Technology, pp. 245–261.

Simon, H. A. 1962. The architecture of complexity. *Proceedings American Philosophical Society* 106: 467–482.

Simon, J. 1981. *The Ultimate Resource*. Princeton, NJ, Princeton University Press.

Slesser, M. 1975. Accounting for energy. *Nature* 254 (March 20): 170–172.

Slesser, M. 1977. Letter to *Science* on energy analysis. *Science* (April 15): 259–261. www.sciencemag.org accessed April 14, 2010

Slesser, M. 1987. Net energy as an energy planning tool. *Energy Policy* (June): 228–238.

Slesser, M. 2003. Using the net energy concept to model the future. In R. Douthwaite (ed.)

Before the wells run dry: Ireland's transition to renewable energy. Green Books. http://ww.feaste.org/documents/wells/two/slesser.html

Slesser, M., and King, J. 2003. *Not by money alone: Economics as Nature Intended* Jon Carpenter Publishing.

Smil, V. 1991. *General Energetics*, New York, Wiley.

Smil, V. 2000. Horse Power. *Nature* 405: 125.

Smil, V. 2001. *Enriching the Earth*. Cambridge, MA, The MIT Press.

Smil, V. 2003. *Energy at the Crossroads: global perspectives and uncertainties.* Cambridge, MA, The MIT Press.

Smil, V. 2006. 21st century energy: some sobering thoughts. *OECD Observer* 258–59 (December). http://www.oecdobserver.org/news/fullstory.php/aid/2083/21st_century_energy:_Some_sobering_thoughts.html

Smil, V. 2007. The two prime movers of globalization: history and impact of diesel engines and gas turbines. *Journal of Global History* 2: 373–394.

Smil, V. 2008a. *Energy in Nature and Society: eneral energetics of complex systems.* Cambridge, MA, The MIT Press.

Smil, V. 2008b. A reality check on the Pickens energy plan. *Environment 360.* http://e360.yale.edu/feature/a_reality_check_on_the_pickens_energy_plan_/2058/

Smil, V. 2008c. *Oil: a beginner's guide.* Oxford, Oneworld.

Smil, V. 2009. US energy policy the need for radical departures. *Issues in Science and Technology* (summer): 47–50.

Smith, C. 1998. *The Science of Energy: a cultural history of energy physics in Victorian Britain.* Chicago, The University of Chicago Press.

Soddy, F. 1926. *Wealth, Virtual Wealth and Debt.* London, George Allen & Unwin.

Solow, R. M. 1974. The economics of resources or the resources of economics. Richard T. Ely Lecture, *American Economic Review* (May): 1–14.

Solow, R. M. 1986. On the intergenerational allocation of natural resources. *Scandinavian Journal of Economics* 88: 141–149.

Sorman, A. H. 2011. The energetic metabolism of societies (Ph.D. dissertation Institute of Environmental Science and Technology). Bellaterra, Spain, Universitat Autònoma Barcelona.

Sovacool, B. K. 2008. Valuing the greenhouse emissions from nuclear power: a critical survey. *Energy Policy* 36: 2950–2963.

Stout, B. A. 1991. *Handbook of Energy for World Agriculture.* New York, Elsevier.

Stout, B. A. (ed.) 1992. *Energy in World Agriculture* (6 volumes). Amsterdam, Elsevier.

Szargut, J., Morris, D. and Steward, F. 1998. *Exergy Analysis of Thermal, Chemical, and Metallurgical Processes.* New York, Hemisphere Publishing Corporation.

Szargut, J., Morris, D. R. and Steward, F. R. 1988. *Exergy Analysis of Thermal, Chemical, and Metallurgical Processes*, Springer-Verlag.

Tyedmers, P. 2004. Fisheries and energy use. In C. J Cleveland (ed.) *Encyclopedia of Energy* 2: 683—693.

Ubbelohde, A. R. 1955. *Man and Energy.* New York, George Braziller, Inc.

Ulanowicz, R. E. 1986. *Growth and Development: ecosystem phenomenology.* New York, Springer-Verlag.

Ulanowicz, R. E. 1997. *Ecology, the Ascendent Perspective.* New York, Columbia University Press.

Ulgiati, S. 2001. A comprehensive energy and economic assessment of biofuels: when 'green' is not enough. *Critical Reviews in Plant Sciences* 20: 71– 106.

Ulgiati, S., Brown, M. T., Giampietro, M., Herendeen, R. A. and Mayumi, K. (eds) 1998.

Advances in Energy Studies: energy flows in ecology and economy. Rome, Museum of Science and Scientific Information.

UNESA 2011 – http://www.unesa.es/

United Nation Department of International Economic and Social Affairs. Statistical Office (UNSD) 1982. *Concepts and methods in energy statistics, with special reference to energy accounts and balances: a technical report*, Series F.29.
http://og.ssb.no/ogwebpage/oldmanuals/SeriesF_29E.pdf
http://unstats.un.org/unsd/publication/SeriesF/SeriesF_29e.pdf

Vernadsky, V. (1926) 1986. *The Biosphere* (first published in Russian in 1926). English translation, Oracle, AZ, Synergetic Press.

Vernadsky, V. (1924) 2007. *Essays on Geochemistry & the Biosphere* (translated by Olga Barash). Santa Fe, NM, Synergetic Press.

Vonnegut, K. 1963. *Cat's Cradle*. Austin, TX, Holt, Rinehar and Winston.

Wall, G. 2003. Exergy tools proceedings of the institution of mechanical engineers. *Part A: Journal of Power and Energy* 217: 125–136. http://pia.sagepub.com/content/217/2/125

Wattenberg, B. 2012. The First Measured Century – Chapter 14 Business – PBS available at: http://www.pbs.org/fmc/book/14business8.htm (accessed 17 June 2012).

Webb, M. and Pearce, D. 1975. The economics of energy analysis. *Energy Policy* (December): 318–331.

Westerterp, K. R. 2004. Diet induced thermogenesis. *Nutrition and Metabolism* 1: 5. http://www.nutritionandmetabolism.com/content/1/1/5

White, L. A. 1943. Energy and evolution of culture. *American Anthropologist* 14: 335–356.

Whyte, L. L., Wilson, A. G. and Wilson, D. (eds) 1969. *Hierarchical Structures*, New York, Elsevier.

Williams, D. W., McCarty, T. R., Gunkel, W. W., Price, D. R. and Jewell, W. J. 1975. Energy utilization on beef feed lots and dairy farms. In W. J. Jewell (ed.) *Energy, Agriculture and Waste Management*. Ann Arbor, Ann Arbor Science Publishers, pp. 29–47.

World forum 98 (2012) http://worldforum98.percepticon.com/sustainability/article_durr.html

Yan, Q., Wang, A., Wang, G., Yu, W., Chen, Q. 2011. Nuclear power development in China and uranium demand forecast: based on analysis of global current situation, *Progress in Nuclear Energy* 53(6): 742–747.

Yang, C.-J. 2009. *Belief-Based Energy Technology Development in the United States*. Amherst, NY, Cambria Press.

Zipf, G. K. 1941. *National Unity and Disunity: the nation as a bio-social organism*. Bloomington, IN, The Principia Press.

Index